Social Security versus Private Saving

List of Contributors

David Barros, University College of North Wales

Willem H. Buiter, Princeton University

Rudolf Dennerlein, International Institute for Empirical Social Economics (INIFES), Augsburg

Michael Denny, University of Toronto

N. Bulent Gultekin, The Amos Tuck School of Business Administration, Dartmouth College

Peter Hurler, INIFES, Augsburg

Charles Lieberman, University of Maryland

Dennis E. Logue, The Amos Tuck School of Business Administration, Dartmouth College

Aleksander Markowski, Central Bank of Sweden

Bruno A. Oudet, University of Grenoble

Edward E. Palmer, National Institute of Economic Research, Stockholm

Martin Pfaff, University of Augsburg and INIFES, Augsburg

Samuel A. Rea, Jr., University of Toronto

Jack R.S. Revell, University College of North Wales

Robert J. Schmitz, Indiana University

James Tobin, Yale University

Paul Wachtel, New York University

Social Security versus Private Saving

Edited by
George M. von Furstenberg

Volume I in the Series on Capital Investment and Saving
Sponsored by the American Council of Life Insurance

Ballinger Publishing Company • Cambridge, Massachusetts
A Subsidiary of Harper & Row, Publishers, Inc.

This book is printed on recycled paper.

International Standard Book Number: 0-88410-675-6

Library of Congress Catalog Card Number: 79-16389

Printed in the United States of America

Library of Congress Cataloging in Publication Data

Main entry under title:

Social Security versus private saving.

(Series on capital investment and saving; v. 1)
"Sponsored by the American Council of Life Insurance."
Includes index.
1. Saving and investment. 2. Social security. 3. Debts, Public. I. Von Furstenberg, George M., 1941- II. American Council of Life Insurance. III. Series.
HC79.S3S6 332′.0415 79-16389
ISBN 0-88410-675-6

Contents

List of Tables

List of Figures

Foreword

In 1976, the American Council of Life Insurance through its Subcommittee on Economic Research explored the possibility of a study of capital investment and saving requirements focused on the prospects for continuing economic growth. The subcommittee prepared and discussed drafts for such a project, which in many ways was considered to be a renewal of a similar study in the 1950s, sponsored by the life insurance business, under the direction of Professor Simon Kuznets.

To guide in the planning and development of the project, an Advisory Committee was established which consisted of the following: Professor James S. Duesenberry (Harvard), Dr. Solomon Fabricant (National Bureau of Economic Research), Professor Paul W. McCracken (University of Michigan), Dr. Robert A. Rennie (Nationwide), Dr. Francis H. Schott (The Equitable Life Assurance Society), Professor Ezra Solomon (Stanford), Mr. Albert T. Sommers (The Conference Board), Professor Murray L. Weidenbaum (Washington University), and Dr. Kenneth M. Wright (American Council of Life Insurance). In the summer of 1976, Dr. George M. von Furstenberg, then Professor of Economics at Indiana University, agreed to serve as Project Director to organize the research for this study.

To carry out this project, Dr. von Furstenberg assembled a distinguished group of scholars both in the United States and abroad. In the tradition of Simon Kuznets' study, the present project probes the underlying causes and determinants of saving, investment, and economic growth and examines the ways in which government and other institutions affect capital formation.

Under Dr. von Furstenberg, this work has been carried out with thoroughness and insight. The council is indeed pleased to see the completion and publication of the three volumes that comprise this study.

Kenneth M. Wright
American Council of Life Insurance
Washington, D.C.

Preface

Because of the sharp decline in productivity growth and the deterioration of economic performance during recent years, capital formation has moved to the forefront of national economic concerns. The diagnosis of the current malaise involves many facets, not all of which are limited to the United States.

Volume I, *Social Security versus Private Saving*, examines how the rapid growth of social insurance wealth and of other government debt may have reduced the supply of private saving available for capital formation. This investigation analyzes the experience of several postindustrial democracies and advances the theoretical work with life cycle and macroeconomic models of saving across generations.

Volume II, *The Government and Capital Formation*, places fiscal and monetary policy impacts on saving into a broader context to examine their ultimate effect on potential output and capital intensity. The government's own infrastructure investments are considered also, as are capital imports from abroad. Specific studies of inflation effects on saving and of tax incentives and regulatory disincentives to investment conclude this volume.

Volume III, *Capital, Efficiency and Growth*, joins the issues at the highest level by documenting the importance of capital and technological progress to economic growth through detailed analyses, sector by sector. It also shows how and why the decline in some of the traditional sources of growth makes capital all the more important to what growth there is. The implication is that increased investment in tangible capital and in research and development, as well as an improved allocation of investment resources, are indispensable to restoring some of the buoyancy of living standards and opportunity characteristic of earlier decades.

The purpose of all three volumes is to improve and broaden the analytical base for addressing current policy issues in the area of saving and capital and to bring new evidence and policy alternatives before the public. To meet these objectives in both a coherent and unbiased fashion, outlines of each of the interlocking studies were agreed upon with the editor. Subsequently, however, editorial comments and the comments of outside readers were designed only to improve the technical quality and stylistic appearance of the work submitted. All contributors cooperated by making extensive revisions with alacrity and a quest for perfection. Much of the retyping was supervised by Mrs. Linda Steinwachs of Indiana University, who also provided valuable editorial assistance throughout the three-year work phase of the project.

George M. von Furstenberg
Indiana University
Bloomington

Chapter 1

Introduction

The breakdown of mutual private support in the context of three-generational families has increased the demand for government provision for old age in the course of the present century. Central government has taken over the function of ensuring at least a minimum standard of living for the aged regardless of their ability or willingness to save prior to retirement. Furthermore, guided by a social insurance rather than a mere antipoverty rationale, earnings-related pensions have increasingly been provided for all workers regardless of their nonlabor incomes or accumulated private savings. Although the U.S. government has been a latecomer to the field, the replacement rates of preretirement earnings afforded under social security are now about as high as in other highly developed democracies.[1] Correspondingly, there has been mounting concern about the long-term consequences of shifting provision for income maintenance during retirement from the private to the public sector.

While society's obligation to alleviate indigence among the aged, regardless of "fault," has not been seriously questioned, the necessity of socializing earnings-related pensions and the wisdom of providing them on a pay-as-you-go basis have both been challenged.[2] In countries as diverse as the United States, Canada, Sweden, the United Kingdom, France, and West Germany, which are represented in the first two, empirical parts of this volume, voluntary private saving still matters greatly to aggregate capital formation. However, the substitution of government-created social insurance wealth for private savings may have adverse consequences for long-term output and living standards because capital inputs and perhaps even some labor inputs are discouraged. Both the conceptual basis of these current concerns and the actual magnitude of any reduction in the supply of factor services induced by social security are analyzed in this volume. Experts from a number of countries wrestle with the size, design, and funding of their programs and analyze the macroeconomic consequences of social security's impact on household behavior over the life cycle from a common perspective. A theme underlying many of these applied studies as well as the somewhat more abstract demonstrations in the third part of this volume, particularly that by Willem Buiter, is that government actions are generally not neutralized by private countermeasures. Hence, for good or evil, government matters, and it shares responsibility for economic outcomes.

In the area of social security, the government's influence derives, in part, from the uniqueness of its debts. Governments with unbridled taxing and borrowing power can be expected to honor their deferred liabilities even without current set-asides. Free from the requirement to fund their pension liabilities actuarially through the accumulation of budgetary reserves, governments are in a position to create individual private wealth by fiat. If a person close to retirement is promised increased retirement benefits, he rightly considers his wealth to have risen and he may increase his spending accordingly. In so doing, however, he makes plain to younger members of the work-force and to future generations that the increased retirement wealth, while real enough for him, is fictitious for society as a whole. Indeed, to the extent national saving falls, national wealth is reduced if such wealth is defined as the discounted present value of the future gross product of human capital, object capital, and land.

Mindful of such negative consequences for their heirs, some of those whom growing social security wealth has enabled to increase their lifetime consumption may refuse to take advantage of this opportunity to benefit themselves at the expense of later generations. Rather, as Martin Feldstein, characterizing a position taken by Robert Barro, has recently put it [2, 1978, p. 39], they may provide an extra bequest. "[That bequest] will in effect endow an annuity to compensate all future generations for the difference between the retirement income they would receive from private saving and the retirement income they obtain from social security for the same sacrifice of preretirement income in the form of taxes." However, Feldstein argues persuasively that such solicitude is likely to be rare.

Parents in the middle or lower middle of the U.S. income distribution, who receive the bulk of their income in the form of earnings covered by social security taxes, make large gifts to their children by rearing them and having them educated with far less government support than is customary in other advanced countries. As Allan Drazen [11, 1978] and Feldstein have explained, such parents may not be inclined to heap tangible bequests on their offspring as well nor may they care to hold their issue harmless for government-imposed transfers from young to old.[3] Benevolence toward one's offspring does not have to be so extreme as to make the marginal utility to parents of additional consumption by descendants exceed that of the parents' own consumption. Particularly if the descendants can be expected to support themselves at a permanent income level at least as high as that of their parents, many parents may feel they have done more than enough even without leaving tangible bequests (in forms other than human capital). Consequently such parents would be quite content to accept gifts from the young to the old arranged via the government's social security programs without wanting to return them.

In the second chapter of this volume, Willem Buiter and James Tobin demonstrate that, under the above and several other conditions, government financial and tax policies need not be powerless to affect the equilibrium of the economy because of offsetting private actions. The supposition that households consider themselves taxed just as surely by government debt as by outright taxes comes under direct attack. If the equivalence between taxes and debt fails, then government-created social insurance wealth encourages present consumption at the expense of future consumption. The resulting reduction in saving and capital formation, which is bound to occur in the absence of a long-run analogue to the Keynesian paradox of thrift, may also reduce national welfare since capital intensities are not allocatively excessive to start with. For this reason, the massive amount of fictional wealth created by the largely unfunded or pay-as-you-go social security systems of the postindustrial countries represented in this volume has come to be viewed as a burden depressing aggregate supply rather than as a blessing for stimulating aggregate demand.

I. THE ECONOMIC MEANING OF FUNDING

As explained by Bulent Gultekin and Dennis Logue in the third chapter in this volume, social insurance wealth is the difference between the value of the future benefits to be derived from a particular retirement income program and the value of the stream of personal contributions yet to be made to that program, both discounted to the present at some realistic rate of interest. Since private pension wealth would be measured precisely in the same fashion, the very existence of social security wealth does not make it fictional unless the government chooses to leave such wealth unfunded. Under a pay-as-you-go system, such as that prevailing in the United States, there is no funding. In that case any increase in social security benefits and contributions does not change the government surplus or deficit, so that there is no change in government saving as its deferred liabilities rise. Private saving is, however, depressed by the pay-as-you-go increase in social security because it adds to a form of retirement wealth which is a close substitute for life insurance, private pensions, and other forms of providing for old age and survivors while at the same time leaving current disposable income unchanged for the group of contributors and beneficiaries combined. Since life insurance companies and private pension funds, unlike the government, do not dissave or consume the contributions or premiums currently received, but use them to fund the increase in future pension liabilities on an actuarially sound basis, they do not dissipate personal saving in the form of insurance contributions or premium payments, while the government may. It is this act of dissipation that would make government-created insurance wealth fictional.

Unfortunately, it is not always easy to recognize when social insurance wealth is funded since the existence of a segregated fund is immaterial in theory, though not in terms of political budget linkages and revealed intentions, to deciding whether or not the government has in fact funded its obligations. Funding provisions may be educational in that they prevent the future costs of current programs from being hidden from the public. Still, the application of simple accounting concepts to separate funds and programs ignores the manifold offsets that may occur in the government's budget as a whole.

In accounting, unlike in economics, the degree to which future obligations are funded can be determined simply by the application of established rules. Thus, any deferred liability is fully funded if it is matched by a reserve or a charge against profits equal to the present value of the deferred liability. However, in a business organization, unless the reserve assets are segregated and held externally or in escrow, the mere existence of a reserve account does not imply that the deferred liability can or will in fact be paid when due since the business may become insolvent in the interim. In the case of large governments with sufficient taxing and borrowing power, the risk of insolvency does not arise and the insurance reserves need not be segregated from other financial assets, nor need insurance obligations be segregated from other current or deferred liabilities to assure full funding. Though the maintenance of a segregated fund and the emphasis on funding future obligations in budget planning may promote fiscal discipline and economic funding politically, such a fund is neither necessary nor sufficient to achieve such an outcome.

To determine whether funding has occurred in government, a rather more complex and conjectural measurement task must be accomplished than to set the reserve fund balances against the present value of insurance obligations net of the future contributions of those currently covered. Were it not for debt limitations, any unit of government could achieve full funding in the accounting sense almost by a stroke of the pen. All that would be required is for the general fund to increase its debt to the social-insurance fund until the latter is actuarially "sound." Obviously, however, any increase in the reserves of the insurance funds that is achieved by merely increasing the debt of the general funds does not achieve any funding in the economic sense. From the economic point of view, such a bookkeeping transaction would be immaterial since it does not change the sum total of government sector saving or dissaving.

Similarly, increasing social security taxes and reducing other taxes, or, more topically, vice versa (see [10, Congressional Budget Office, 1978]), does not change the degree to which social insurance obligations are funded in an economic sense. Earmarking of taxes to pay for social insurance benefits may be worthwhile pedagogically to keep the link between social insurance tax costs and government benefits clearly in the public eye. Furthermore, it is indispensable if the substitution of private for part of the public pension plans, discussed later in this introduction, is to be attractive for employers. However, apart from the effect on reform options, it makes no difference which taxes are used to pay for social insurance benefits and whether taxes are credited to a "fund" or not. Social security benefits could be handled just like welfare benefits in the budget, and this fact alone would not logically reflect on the degree to which they are funded, though it may do so in terms of political probabilities.

The economic meaning of full funding is therefore far removed from the accounting trappings or modalities of government insurance funds. Full funding occurs when the increase in government taxes discourages private spending by the same amount as the rise in promissory social insurance wealth and benefit payments provided by the government, net of any induced changes in other government spending, increases it. If such a match were achieved, at least on average, every year, the time path of national saving and total investment would be unaffected by the institution or expansion of social-insurance programs. More pertinently, one can dismiss ancient history as bygone and determine the conditions under which full funding might be achieved at the margin currently. To this must be added that government investment should be included in national saving for this purpose, as it is in the accounting conventions of Canada and most other countries. In economic theory, at least, and in the reality of states such as Singapore, an increase in government investment can be used to fund social insurance obligations just as surely as an increase in the budget surplus that permits additional private investment to occur in a full-employment economy.

To make any headway in this compensatory setting, where funding can only be determined hypothetically or relative to the unobserved alternative level of national saving without social insurance, this alternative must be prespecified. To provide a framework for orderly discussion, it may, for instance, be assumed that all government expenditures and taxes other than those referring specifically to social insurance would have been (1) the same as they actually were in the absence of that program and (2) exactly equal to what policymakers desired for stabilization and growth purposes. In practice the second assumption implies that Keynesian aggregate demand effects from an increase in social security benefits, taxes, or wealth are ignored but that the neoclassical effects from a reduction in saving to an induced lowering of capital intensiveness and potential output are allowed full sway since they represent deviations from the assumed optimum.

The first assumption is clearly inapplicable in countries such as England and France, where annual contributions from the general budget have always accounted for about 20 percent of trust fund receipts. It is also not strictly applicable to the United States since the number of families entitled to supplemental security income and other government help would obviously be greater in the absence of government pension and retirement programs. The second assumption is also unrealistic since the balance between social insurance benefits and contributions has often been changed for short-run stabilization purposes. The advantage of these assumptions, then, does not lie in their realism or consistency, but in their enabling the discussion of full funding to be restricted to the relation between social insurance taxes and benefits so that a zero net effect on aggregate demand at the margin can be identified as full economic funding. Such a fixed reference point is necessary to measure the degree to which actual social insurance programs have in fact stimulated personal consumption expenditures and reduced personal, total private, and national saving.

The point of reference implicitly chosen in the empirical studies represented in this volume is similar to that just described. In countries in which pay-as-you-go financing, with or without some transfers from the general fund, is the rule, the effects of social insurance wealth and of the associated taxes and benefits are investigated only in personal consumption or saving functions. Government saving is thus assumed to be the same without social insurance as it actually was, and national saving is changed by as much as personal saving. If national saving falls, the resulting reduction in private investment is assumed to have led to a decline in potential output without further depressing the national saving rate, as would have been expected with a Keynesian or nonproportional saving function. In countries such as the United States, Great Britain, and France, personal or total private saving is assumed to tell the whole story.

On the other hand, in countries in which substantial funds were accumulated, as, for instance, in Sweden and Canada, the government's social insurance saving is treated as net additional saving attributable to the institution of government pension programs. In these countries, therefore, the increase in government saving must be considered as a partial offset to the reduction in personal saving before the net effect on the national saving rate can be determined. Thus, in each instance, the economic effects of social insurance receipts and expenditures and of the social insurance wealth created are analyzed as if there were no compensatory adjustments in other government programs or in other parts of the budget.

Pay-as-you-go finance, by definition, does not affect disposable income in the short run. Still, any tax-transfer can affect saving if the consumption propensities of beneficiaries and contributors differ at the margin, as the studies for the United States, Sweden, and Germany point out. Furthermore, Paul Wachtel shows in this volume that the marginal propensities to consume differ greatly from the average propensities of different age groups, so that the former cannot be approximated by the latter. Rather, the aged may save much more at the margin than their low average propensity to save or a simple life cycle model would suggest. Still, any direct effects on saving from redistributing current income among different age groups are likely to be small compared with the wealth effects associated with the pay-as-you-go system.

These effects may be explored by adding social insurance wealth (SIW) to the aggregate consumption function. However, if social security coverage is universal and replacement rates are fixed, significant differences in social insurance wealth can be observed only among workers in different age groups. The youngest workers have the lowest SIW and those at the threshold of retirement have the highest. However, since the young worker knows that he will inevitably experience a rise in SIW as he continues working to old age, there is no reason to think that his saving decisions are influenced any less than those of older workers to the extent that his saving is intended for the protection of living standards in old age. Life cycle theory assumes that people look ahead to their retirement years and deduces that the ratio of net worth to income they desire rises with age, normally until (shortly before) retirement. Thus, unexpected disturbances of this ratio—not, however, its rise over the life cycle per se—cause saving to change. Only because the probability of reaching retirement is lower for a young worker than for an older worker on actuarial grounds and only to the extent younger workers place greater emphasis on saving for reasons other than old-age protection, a point emphasized in the study for West Germany, may the existence of social security programs have less effect on the current private saving of the young.

Any firm estimate of the degree to which social security wealth substitutes for privately accumulated wealth can therefore be obtained only if the saving behavior of covered and noncovered workers of the same age could be compared. Time-series studies of aggregate saving behavior attempt to make up for the lack of such data by analyzing the effect of differences in contribution and benefit levels and, hence, social security wealth, between succeeding generations.[4] Little attention is generally paid to the fact that these generations are not comparable in the initial stages of the program since aggregate social insurance wealth rises over time because of the aging of the first generation of covered workers even if the benefit formula is unchanged. In the study by Aleksander Markowski and Edward Palmer for Sweden in this volume, age-adjusted changes in social insurance wealth are, therefore, approximated simply by (a fixed multiple of) changes in the average social security benefits received by retirees in constant dollars (kronas).

II. THE COST OF SOCIAL SECURITY IN DIFFERENT COUNTRIES

In developed countries the ratio of man-made fixed capital (including residential capital) to GNP is generally estimated to range from 2 to 4.[5] In several of these same countries the magnitude of government-made fictional wealth approaches a similar level. Social insurance wealth appears to be around twice as large as GNP in both the United States and France. Although it is still considerably lower in Canada and Great Britain, both of these countries have recently enacted programs that will accelerate the growth of social insurance wealth in relation to GNP. If national saving is reduced annually even by a small fraction of that insurance wealth, say 2 percent, a decline in national saving equal to 4 percent of GNP can easily reduce the amount of national saving by 20 to 30 percent annually. The gross national saving rate is between 12 to 20 percent of GNP in most developed countries included in this volume and significantly higher only in Japan. It is therefore most important for gauging the growth prospects of postindustrial societies to determine exactly how large the reduction of national saving may be that stems from past and prospective levels of social insurance wealth.

Empirically, this determination is fraught with difficulties, in part because social security may have encouraged earlier retirement [7, Campbell and Campbell, 1976; 22, Quinn, 1977; 21, Pellechio, 1978]. Such a prospect would cause people to save more and, possibly, to work longer hours (see [4, Burkhauser and Turner, 1978]) while they are still working since they must sustain themselves for a longer period in retirement. In the study for Canada by Michael Denny and Samuel Rea in this volume, this saving-increasing effect of earlier retirement is found to be so strong as to turn what would otherwise have been a 3.1 percentage point decline in the personal saving rate into a 5.5 percentage point increase. Such an increase is nothing to cheer about, however, since it is bought at the cost of reduced labor force participation once earlier retirements have begun to set in. People can rationally prefer lower object consumption with more leisure to greater consumption with less leisure when they lower their retirement age. However, it is shown later in this introduction that they may not reduce their lifetime object consumption by as much as the labor incomes no longer earned and the marginal product lost to society as a result of their earlier exit from the labor force. Particularly in view of the thesis that leisure and object consumption are complementary, which is advanced by Robert Schmitz in this volume, bequests may be lowered instead. The long-term as opposed to the short-term adjustment to the prospect of earlier retirement may therefore be not nearly as favorable to capital formation as is frequently supposed.

For the United States, the study by Gultekin and Logue has identified a more direct avenue than wealth through which personal saving may be depressed in both the short and the long run. Neoclassical theory and a considerable body of evidence suggest that total labor compensation, including both employer and employee contributions for social insurance, determines the demand for labor. As a result, real compensation per hour does not rise when social insurance contributions are raised except in the short run, before wage and salary scales are renegotiated. In countries like Sweden this lag may be shortened because employer contributions for public and private pension plans combined are specified as part of the basic contract. This means that workers eventually pay for all of the social security contributions connected with their employ through a reduction in take-home pay.

If they view these contributions as saving that, although technically forced upon them, will ultimately be repaid in the form of retirement benefits, they would rationally reduce their voluntary saving by about as much as the amount of these contributions. The main difference between forced and voluntary retirement saving would be that the explicit or implicit interest on the latter is included in the national income accounts concept of disposable income, while the implicit interest on social insurance contributions is not. Eliminating this asymmetry, the true economic income of those who have made social insurance contributions in the past is therefore higher than reported in the national income accounts. Their consumption in relation to NIA income will therefore be higher also. As a result, private personal saving may be reduced by even more than the amount of annual contributions for social insurance. This may explain why an increase in CSI that is not accompanied by a cut in other taxes, so that the government surplus increases and disposable income declines, was found to reduce personal saving by more than the amount of the CSI increase in the study for the United States. However, if the government surplus and disposable income are held constant conceptually (or through a matching cut in other taxes), the effect was less than one-to-one. Because there are considerable doubts about whether the social security wealth variable has been added correctly in past studies, the change in focus from social security wealth to contributions for social insurance in studies of the savings substitution question appears most promising.

International Comparisons

Precise comparisons of the ratios of public retirement benefits or contributions to personal disposable income or GNP are difficult because of differences in the types of programs included by each country, because the earnings-related part of public pensions may be integrated with private pensions, and because social security may be provided by several levels of government.[6] Furthermore, old-age benefits are taxable in some countries but not in others, and this may affect their relative size. However, it seems quite clear that, among the countries included in this volume, Sweden, France, and West Germany provide the highest levels of old-age, disability, and survivors benefits, accounting for over 20 percent of personal disposable income in the mid-1970s, compared to less than 10 percent in the United States and Canada and little more than 10 percent in the United Kingdom if expenditures by the National Health Service are excluded. Correspondingly, the U.K. state pension replaced only about 35 percent of preretirement earnings, compared with over 60 percent in Sweden, France, and West Germany.

As pointed out in the study by David Barros in this volume, the offset between public and private provision for social insurance is striking in cross-country comparisons. While complementary private pension schemes replaced about 30 percent of average wages in the United Kingdom, where the replacement rates under the public programs are low, they replaced only 12 percent in West Germany, where the public replacement rates are high.

Direct evidence of the offset between organized private saving and increased levels of public pension benefits and contributions has also been provided for several countries represented in this volume, though West Germany may be an exception to this trend. The degree of offset within any country depends critically not only on the average replacement rate under social security but also on the tax incentives for private pension plans which have changed frequently in all the countries concerned.

In the United States there is as yet little evidence that social security has decimated private industrial pension plans, but there are growing signs that substitution may be increasing in the future [20, Munnell, 1978; 17, Logue, 1979]. Gultekin and Logue also report in this volume that life insurance is becoming relatively less important in household portfolios as time goes on. Since life insurance now has less to do with insuring people's lives than with providing annuities or lump-sum settlements upon retirement, a direct effect of social security on this type of saving is quite probable. Several of the studies thus emphasize that even if social security had little effect on the aggregate amount of personal saving, it would undoubtedly influence the composition of private portfolios, or the form in which these savings are held.

III. THE EFFECT OF DEMOGRAPHIC FACTORS ON SAVING

Apart from growing social security wealth, declining population growth, increasing labor force participation by women, and the growing weight of retirees in the population pyramid are experiences common to most of the countries included in this study. In fully articulated life cycle models, decisions about education, work, and saving and about such matters as having children and leaving bequests are all made together and interdependently in view of the objective opportunities (wage rates, interest rates, taxes, life expectancies) available. Even if demographic changes could be treated as exogenous, the effect of such changes on aggregate saving is difficult to isolate because induced changes in economic data may offset much of the effect that might be deduced, *ceteris paribus*, from a given cause.

Paul Wachtel's contribution to this volume provides several examples of such offsets. He finds that if the relative income of the household heads in each age group were fixed, the redistribution of the population toward low savers and away from the high-saving thirty-five to sixty-four age group would, by itself, tend to lower personal saving by 3 percent per decade or by a cumulative total of 9 percent over the period 1954–85. However, since the relative incomes of the prime-age households have risen as their relative size has declined, the percent of total income in each age group has hardly changed at all, leaving total saving almost unaffected by demographic change. Looking into the future, Robert Schmitz is less optimistic as he identifies slackening borrowing constraints on the young and smaller planned families as factors reducing saving.

On theoretical grounds, Wachtel also points to another endogenous change that may offset some of the reduction in current saving that may result from the growth in the share of retirees in the population. If such growth reduces saving, it will drive up the interest rate and hence make younger workers redistribute some of their planned saving from later to earlier years of their expected working life remaining. Since the rise in the interest rate raises the difference between that rate and the subjective time preference rate if the latter is fixed, workers will find it advantageous to save more early rather than late in their work-life, because the market rewards for deferring consumption have risen. The net result may be a far smaller reduction in aggregate saving than the aging of the population, by itself, would suggest. As previously noted in the discussion of the economic meaning of funding, the effects of any change, considered in isolation from behaviorally, politically, or macroeconomically related changes, may be quite different from the final net effects that result from interactive adjustments.

Robert Schmitz derives other interesting conclusions from an expanded life cycle model in which the allocation of time between work and leisure depends on the size of earnings available at various stages of the life cycle with or without dependents and the participation of secondary workers in the household. He finds that increased earnings may very well all be saved, and that consumption may even fall temporarily if members of the household work more to take advantage of unusual opportunities that may present themselves during their life cycle. Such behavior may suggest that the extent to which households provide for retirement or bequests is highly elastic with respect to their income. This may explain why some studies, including the studies by Martin Pfaff et al. and Bruno Oudet for Germany and France in this volume, find it difficult to document any substitution effect from social security wealth on private contractual saving for those who have recently become comparatively wealthy. Furthermore, new opportunities may change tastes endogenously leading to unstable subjective time preference rates or accumulation plans whose size and timing are seemingly inconsistent with simple models of household behavior over the life cycle.[7]

IV. ALTERNATIVES FOR POLICY

Given all the cautions about the difference between partial and "general equilibrium" effects and the need for policymakers to look at the "total picture" represented by the latter, can anything still be said about the weight of the evidence and where it may point? Except for France, and Germany, where the evidence is, as yet, sketchy, there is some agreement that social security wealth or the associated taxes will reduce private saving in the future. Whether this will lead to a parallel reduction in national saving and hence private capital formation depends on the degree of economic funding, or on the extent to which government-sector saving is increased to offset the decline in private sector saving.

In contrast to the United States, both Sweden and Canada have achieved a considerable degree of funding in that sense. It appears, however, that such funding is, in part, used for increased capital formation by various levels of government. One may surmise that the political incentives to fund social insurance obligations are far less if no such investments are made. Since stimulating government investment has not been one of the objectives of the advocates of greater funding in the United States, one may also hypothesize that pay-as-you-go financing is the best that can be hoped for. This is particularly likely in view of the large payroll tax increases which are already required under current legislation merely to maintain rough pay-as-you-go balance in the next one or two decades before financing problems become even more serious [6, Campbell, 1978; 23, Robertson, 1978].

With funding of public pensions politically unattainable, there are a few alternative reforms that could mitigate the resulting reductions in national saving, output, and living standards from the trend that would otherwise prevail. One of these, the elimination of the social security retirement earnings test and the removal of other impediments to later retirement, would undoubtedly raise potential output, but it may not increase saving. The other, integration of the earnings-related portion of social security with government-insured private pensions, promises to raise both. An examination of how both types of measures might work follows.

Later Retirement

Though a start to relax the social security retirement income test and to lift mandatory retirement before age seventy has already been made in the United States through the 1977 Amendments to the Social Security Act and the 1978 Amendments to the Age Discrimination in Employment Act (see [24, Sheppard and Rix, 1977; 9, Colberg, 1978; 18, Macdonald, 1978]), financial disincentives still weigh on those who consider working past the age of sixty-five. If the United States would follow Canada, Britain, Sweden,[8] and other countries in eliminating retirement earnings tests entirely and succeed in raising the average age at which people would choose to retire, potential output would undoubtedly be increased. However, simple life cycle models of saving behavior suggest strongly that personal saving would be reduced by later retirement.

Even ignoring the fact that a rise in the labor-capital ratio raises the return on capital and, hence, corporate saving—so that total private saving need not change in the same direction as personal saving—this section attempts to show that the models used to deduce adverse effects on saving from later retirement are often excessively simple. With appropriate modifications they would not necessarily show that personal saving declines. Once uncertainty and the residual or involuntary nature of many bequests are recognized, later retirement may even increase personal saving, though it would be foolhardy to advocate later retirement primarily for that end.

The naive model on which economists frequently base their conclusion that earlier retirement reduces personal saving is represented by illustrations A and B in Table 1–1. There the representative individual works for either four or five periods (decades) and lives in retirement for either two decades or one. In each case the individual

Table 1–1. Illustrations of the Effect of Retirement Age on the Accumulated Stock of Savings

	Working				*Working or Retired*	*Retired*	*Stable Population Totals*
Period	*(1)*	*(2)*	*(3)*	*(4)*	*(5)*	*(6)*	
			Illustration A: Early Retirement				
Earnings	100.0	100.0	100.0	100.0	0	0	400.0
Interest Income[a]	0	5.0	11.2	19.0	28.8	16.0	80.0
Consumption	80.0	80.0	80.0	80.0	80.0	80.0	480.0
Accumulated Savings	20.0	45.0	76.2	115.2	64.0	0	320.4
			Illustration B: Late Retirement				
Earnings	100.0	100.0	100.0	100.0	100.0	0	500.0
Interest Income[a]	0	2.2	5.0	8.4	12.8	18.2	46.6
Consumption	91.1	91.1	91.1	91.1	91.1	91.1	546.6
Accumulated Savings	8.9	20.0	33.9	51.2	72.9	0	186.9
			Illustration C: Option of Late Retirement Exercised by Half				
Earnings	100.0	100.0	100.0	100.0	0 or 100.0	0	450.0
Interest Income[a]	0	4.5	10.1	17.1	25.9	14.4 or 25.5	77.6
Consumption	82.0	82.0	82.0	82.0	72.0 or 127.6[b]	72.0 or 127.5[b]	527.6
Accumulated Savings	18.0	40.5	68.6	103.7	57.6 or 102.0	0	310.6

[a]Interest income is calculated at the rate of 25 percent on the accumulated savings of the preceding period throughout although a change in capital intensities indicated by the sum total of accumulated savings held by each cohort would, of course, affect the equilibrium level of the interest rate as explained in the text.

[b]The slight discrepancy is due to the need to round 127.55 once up and once down to leave no bequests.

knows at the beginning of his working life exactly how much he (or she) will be earning (a constant stream of 100 units of real labor income per period is used in the illustrations for simplicity), what the period-to-period interest rate will be (assumed to be 25 percent per decade or around 2 percent per annum in real terms), when he will retire, and when he will die. Armed with this perfect foreknowledge, he then sets out to maximize lifetime utility by planning his saving so that he can consume the same amount each period, assuming his subjective time preference rate is equal to the market rate of interest. In illustration A the individual thus saves 20 plus the interest on past accumulations of savings during each of the four work periods and consumes 80 in each of the six periods of life so as to leave nothing behind. In illustration B, the individual has planned on retiring later and saves only 8.9 plus interest in each work period. His consumption is 91.1 per period throughout, and he again manages to consume all his income just before he dies.

To obtain the steady-state capital stock in the two illustrations when the population is stationary and everybody dies at the same age, one can simply assume that there is one individual (or any equal number of individuals) alive in each of the six periods. By summing the accumulated savings shown in each, total savings and capital outstanding are then equal to 320.4 in A but to only 186.9 in B at any one time. The certain prospect of later retirement thus reduces the stock of capital by 41.7 percent while increasing the supply of labor by 25 percent. Because of the 53.4 percent reduction in the capital-labor ratio, output would be only 7.5 percent higher in illustration B than in A if technology is represented by a stationary Cobb-Douglas production function with a net capital coefficient (income share) of 20 percent. If one redid illustration B to take account of the fact that the period-to-period interest rate should also be 84 percent higher than the 25 percent assumed before, the stock of savings and capital in B could be either higher or lower than 186.9,[9] but it would certainly remain far below the 320.4 associated with the earlier retirement solution in A. Thus, regardless of interest rate effects, the naive life cycle model suggests that later retirement reduces saving dramatically for single-minded individuals with perfect foresight.

Considering, however, that nobody can know for sure that his health, strength, and future tastes, as well as labor market conditions are such as to make him continue at work during the fifth period (age sixty-five to seventy-five) distinguished in Table 1–1, such an outcome is far from certain. Assume, for instance, that 50 percent retire at age sixty-five and the other 50 percent work on till age seventy-five, but that individuals know only at age sixty-five to which group they belong. Each individual must therefore prepare for the contingency that he will have no earnings past age sixty-five. If he planned his consumption as in illustration B as if he could be certain of retiring only at seventy-five and nature or the employer proves him wrong, he would suffer a drastic reduction in living standards during his unexpectedly long retirement years.

Aware of this risk, individuals who are risk averse will not increase consumption per period by nearly as much as the difference between 91.1 in B and 80.0 in A, nor will they be content simply to split the difference. Rather, assume they increase their consumption to only 82.0 per period, so that the prospect of some reduction in living standards, should they retire early, is just compensated by a large increase in living standards (or bequests), should they retire late. Such trade-offs are natural for risk-averse individuals who suffer more loss of utility from a given dollar reduction in retirement income, cutting into habitual necessities, than they gain from the same dollar increase, permitting some unaccustomed luxuries.

Upon reaching the age of sixty-five, 50 percent of all individuals acquire the certain knowledge that they will work to age seventy-five. They will consume 127.5 in each of the two periods remaining, while the other half, who retire at sixty-five, reduce consumption from 82 to 72 per period remaining. Weighting each of these groups by one-half during the last two periods of their lives and adding accumulated savings, as before, yields a total stock of savings of 310.6, which is close to the 320.4 obtained in illustration A where the prospect of early retirement is certain for all.

If one now adds the consideration of uncertain lifetimes and assumes that one-half the population dies at the end of the fifth period and the remaining half at the end of the sixth period, but that individuals again cannot know beforehand to which group they belong, the first group would end up leaving bequests of 40 in illustration A, raising the stock of savings to 360.4, but 49.8 in illustration C, raising the stock of saving from 310.6 to 360.4 as well.[10] Thus with a few steps in the direction of greater realism one can easily generate the result that later retirement need not reduce personal saving. If individuals evaluated the option of later retirement, which they may or may not be able or willing to use when they reach the age of sixty-five, in such a way as to increase consumption during each of the first four periods from 80 to 81 rather than to 82, the stock of savings would actually be higher with this option than without, even if the time of death remained certain. Thus the question of how changing the retirement age affects personal saving cannot be resolved by a priori judgments derived from overly simple models. Only slightly more subtle models such as those underlying illustration C already suggest that the direction of the effect is indeterminate in theory.

The Integration of Public and Private Pension Plans

Integration of public and private pension plans is little known in the United States, although private plans may take credit for specified portions of social security benefits to meet the nondiscrimination test among employees that is imposed on qualified plans by the Internal Revenue Code. In Sweden pensions are funded with a monopoly, so that establishment of a single pension account per person is greatly facilitated, even if workers are covered by many different private plans during their lifetime. Furthermore, labor contracts tend to specify the total pension contributions employers must make to private and public pension programs combined, and both types of programs are financed by employers almost exclusively. As a result, an increase in contributions to the public plan leads to an automatic decline in contributions to private plans, at least in the short run. Thus, the introduction of the Supplementary Pension Scheme providing earnings-related pensions from 1960 on had a very pronounced effect on private pensions, whose premiums dropped in 1961 to less than 20 percent of the value they had in 1959. It took almost ten years thereafter for the nominal volume of private pension contributions to regain its 1959 level in Sweden.

Britain has used the split of the pension system into a basic portion, providing a fixed amount of minimum benefits to all retired, and an earnings-related portion to permit integration by means of contracting out of the earnings-related part. That part provides retirement benefits equal to 25 percent of the excess of earnings over the basic minimum up to seven times that minimum, where this excess is averaged over the twenty years of highest earnings. Since 1961, employers may, however, contract their employees out of the earnings-related part of the state pension scheme provided the benefits under their plans are no less generous than those afforded by the second tier of the state scheme. With many businesses exercising this option, which lowers employer contributions to public plans from 12.25 percent to 7.75 percent of covered earnings, private plan membership almost doubled, from 4.3 million in 1956 to 8.1 million in 1967, out of a total labor force of 23 million in Britain.

Canada also has a split system of public retirement insurance, with the Old Age Security program providing a demogrant for all elderly, while the Canada Pension Plan (CPP) adds an earnings-related portion. Contracting out is not allowed in Canada. However, most of the large company pension plans are integrated with the government pensions in such a way that a rise in CPP benefits automatically produces a decline in private plan benefits.[11]

It seems, therefore, that the question of pension fund integration and of the increased scope of private insurance within a system of assured retirement benefits deserves much further study than it has hitherto received in the United States. The discussion should not be limited to integrating just the public plans with each other. Integration also bears on the choice of general revenue versus payroll tax financing of old-age and survivors' insurance. Contributions for social security cannot be reduced for those employers providing for at least equal benefits under private plans once general revenue financing has been adopted. The destruction of financial incentives would thus foreclose consideration of integration in the future. Without integration, however, the government must raise benefit and contribution levels for all in an attempt to provide an adequate retirement program for some. Those who have no other sources of retirement income thus drive up the benefit and contributions structure for all.

Once a contributory or noncontributory government program providing for basic benefits is in effect, there is no reason whatever to disallow reduced contributions to public programs as increased contributions to government-supervised private programs are undertaken by the private sector. If security in retirement rather than an increased government role per se is the goal, the government should be indifferent to the source of the benefits provided they are equally secure. In the United States, the Employee Retirement Income Security Act of 1974 (ERISA) has gone a long way to make company and union pension programs a closer substitute for public pensions in this regard. Although there are no provisions for portability and immediate vesting of pension rights in ERISA, paternalistic arguments against integration are now far less convincing. Among the countries represented in this volume, Britain, at least, has designed integration in such a way that private plans may "crowd out" the earnings-related portion of public pension schemes so as to make increased private provision financially attractive. This example is surely worth studying and perhaps worth emulating in the United States.

If, as a practical matter, public pension and social security programs will never be funded actuarially in the United States and several other countries, then allowing government-supervised substitution of private for public retirement plans is the only way to achieve at least partial funding.[12] Such a substitution would reduce payroll taxes and social security wealth simultaneously so as to reduce the adverse impact on capital formation documented in the first parts of this volume. Since integration has as yet been little discussed in the United States and the mechanics of how integration may work are unfamiliar, the appendix to this editorial introduction outlines the contrasting methods of integration applied in Sweden and Canada on the one hand and in Britain on the other.

Appendix

ALTERNATIVE FORMS OF INTEGRATION OF PUBLIC AND PRIVATE PENSION PLANS

Based on information, materials, and drafts provided by Edward E. Palmer and Aleksander Markowski, Samuel A. Rea, and Jack R.S. Revell, all of whom also contributed to other portions of this volume, two divergent forms of integration appear to be used which are potentially of great interest to the choices confronting the United States. In Sweden and Canada integration means that the growth of public pensions may permit employers to reduce contributions to private pensions. In Britain, however, increased contributions to private plans may enable employers to reduce their contributions to the public scheme. Since private plans are funded actuarially while the public schemes are not fully funded, only the latter form of integration is likely to add to national saving and private capital formation.

A–I. SWEDEN (Edward E. Palmer and Aleksander Markowski)

The Swedish public and private group insurance system is rather complicated; knowledge of its institutions is not very common even in Sweden. The rate of employer contributions as well as the future pension benefits are prescribed by law in the case of *Allmänna tilläggspensionsförsäkringen* (ATP) and by union contracts in the case of private group insurance. (There are four main central union contracts which contain the guidelines for local union contracts: one for blue-collar workers, one for white-collar workers, one for local government employees, and one for central government employees.) Hence, every employer knows exactly the amount of insurance contributions he has to pay. Employer contributions depend on the employee's current income and are not affected by the employee's past income.

The offset between employer contributions for ATP and private group insurance can occur only when a new union contract is written. Such offset occurred in 1960 upon introduction of ATP. The future private group insurance benefits were then reduced approximately by the amount of the future ATP benefits. Benefit payments are administered centrally, each form of insurance separately. The appropriate company (in the case of private group insurance) or authority (in the case of ATP and public employees) has also the records of all future benefit recipients. Thus the employer has nothing to do with benefit payments.

Old-age pensions are comprised of basic old-age social security and ATP, which are public schemes, and private pension schemes. The public schemes are financed through employer contributions; basic old-age social security is unfunded and ATP is partly funded. Private schemes are either group schemes, financed by employers, or insurance arranged and financed by the individual. This latter form will not be discussed here. The public and employer-financed pension schemes follow well-defined rules which are outlined below.

Benefits

Basic old-age social security benefits are paid out to *all* Swedish citizens (and Scandinavian residents) who have reached sixty-five—regardless of whether they have spent time in the labor force. All other old-age pension forms require participation in the labor force.

(1) Basic old-age social security pensions are paid to *all* Swedish citizens (and Scandinavian residents of five years) beginning at age sixty-five. For a single individual, an old-age social security pension amounts to 95 percent of the so-called basic amount (the base). (For married couples with both partners receiving old-age social security, pensions benefits are 77.5 percent of the base for each spouse.) The basic amount was a little under $2,400 in January 1976. The basic amount is adjusted whenever the consumer price index has changed by at least 3 percent since the previous setting. A recipient need not retire to receive benefits, and benefits constitute taxable income.

(2) ATP benefits accrue to *all resident participants in the labor force*, provided they have worked a minimum of three years. ATP participation is compulsory for all but the self-employed, who can affiliate themselves voluntarily. Generally, recipients must have reached sixty-five years of age though earlier retire-

ment with partial benefits is also possible. The recipient need not retire to receive full benefits. Benefits constitute taxable income. The ATP pension is calculated as follows:

$$\text{ATP} = 0.60 \times \frac{n}{30} \times \bar{P} \times B$$

where ATP = amount of pension;

n = number of years of gainful activity (with a minimum of three years and a maximum of thirty years);

$\bar{P}$ = average of pension points for fifteen best earning years;

B = the basic amount for the current pension year.

Pension points for an earning year are calculated as

$$P = \frac{\text{annual income} - \text{basic amount}}{\text{basic amount}}$$

with a maximum of 6.5 points allowable each year. The following table illustrates the calculation of pension points using the 1976 base of approximately $2,400.

Annual Income	*Pension Points*
$10,000	3.17
$15,000	5.25
$18,000	6.50
$25,000	9.42 gives 6.50 due to the maximum limit

(3) Public employees' pensions amount to 65 percent of the employee's salary during his last five years, with the grade's salary level being calculated at its level during his final year of employment. Thirty years of service are generally required to obtain a full pension. The pension is reduced by 1/120 for each quarter lacking. Since government employees are covered by basic old-age social security and ATP, in practice public employee pensions provide only a *supplement*. The public pension supplement changes with time at the same rate as the basic amount.

(4) ITP, the private pension scheme for white-collar workers, provides a *supplement* to basic old-age social security and ATP. ITP is a private group scheme that arose as a result of central union-management negotiations that took place when the public ATP program was introduced. At the outset, it included all white-collar workers covered by private employer group pension schemes prior to the introduction of ATP in 1960 as well as white-collar employees who previously had not been covered. (The introduction of ATP meant that those already covered by private group schemes had already contributed "too much" to their pension funds, given the complete restructuring of private group insurance necessitated by the introduction of ATP. Obligations of this nature were paid off with special salary increases.) Individuals cannot directly choose to belong to ITP. Instead, ITP comes automatically with union affiliation.

ITP benefits are also calculated with pension points, defined above. Since the purpose of ITP is to supplement ATP, the number of permissible pension points surpasses the maximum of 6.5 allowable by ATP. In 1977 a retired person of sixty-five or over covered by ITP would receive the following supplements to his two public pensions:

Pension Points	*Percent of Basic Amount Paid Out as Benefits for Each Pension Point within the Given Bracket*
0–7.5	10.0 %
7.5–10.0	65.0 %
10.0–12.5	58.5 %
12.5–15.0	39.0 %
15.0–20.0	32.5 %
20.0–30.0	6.5 %

where thirty years are required to obtain full benefits. The recipient's income during his last five years of employment provides the basis for the calculation. (During the last five prepension years of employment, salary used as the base for ITP can only grow as fast as the consumer price index, to prevent manipulation of the benefit base.)

The pension of a white-collar worker who is covered by ITP and has an average income of $30,000 per year can be illustrated with the following hypothetical example (assuming the 1976 base of about $2,400 and full benefits):

Benefit Type	*Calculation*	*Benefits*
A. Basic old-age social security (for a person who is single or whose spouse has not reached age 65)	0.95 × 2,400	$ 2,280
B. ATP (maximum possible)	0.60 × 6.5 × 2,400	9,360
C. ITP		
1. for income in 0–7.5 bracket	0.10 × 7.5 × 2,400	1,800
2. for income in 7.5–10.0 bracket	0.65 × 2.5 × 2,400	3,900
3. for income in 10.0–12.5 bracket	0.585 × 2.5 × 2,400	3,510
Sum		9,210
D. Total Benefits	A + B + C	$20,850

Since the 1976 base is used in this example, the pension sum is in 1976 prices. The base is adjusted for changes in the consumer price index, which means that a 10 percent rise in consumer prices in 1977 would cause the base and, hence, the pension paid out, to increase by 10 percent. This protects the pensioner against inflation.

(5) STP, the private pension scheme introduced in 1973 for blue-collar workers, provides a supplement to ATP of an amount which, in practice, equals 10 percent of the wage earner's final wage, with a maximum set at 7.5 times the $2,400 base. In 1976, 7.5 × base was $18,000, which would thus give a maximum (full-benefit) supplement of $1,800. Had the person in our example above been covered by STP instead of ITP his pension benefits would not have included points C.2 and C.3.

Financing of Public Old-Age Pensions

In principle, basic old-age social security is financed with employer contributions and is not funded. ATP is financed through employer contributions and is funded, though it is, strictly speaking, not an actuarial system since the employer-contribution rates are determined by Parliament. Detailed actuarial calculations constitute, however, the main decision material for Parliament's deliberations.

Financing of Private Old-Age Pensions Provided by Employers

Pension funds can be retained within businesses, though, since 1960, these funds must be insured with a private organization called PRI. PRI also maintains a register of all its members and performs the necessary actuarial calculations. The alternative to belonging to the PRI system is to belong to SPP. In addition to maintaining member registers and performing actuarial calculations, SPP invests business pension funds. This private organization existed long before 1960. From the point of view of the insurance beneficiary there is no difference between PRI and SPP, since they are strictly administrative and investment organizations.

Since 1960, all private benefits have been determined in *central* labor-management negotiations. That is, private pension (and other insurance) and wage changes are bargained for at the same time. In principle, this means that the trade-off between different forms of work remuneration is an explicit negotiation topic and that negotiated benefits are for very broad employment categories.

In sum, what is important for the private pension beneficiary today is whether he belongs to ITP or STP, which is determined by union contract. Employers, whose employees are covered by either ITP or STP, can then choose between retaining their own pension funds and, thus, belonging to PRI or joining SPP. There is no third choice. Both PRI and SPP perform the administrative tasks involved and, in addition, vest the pension rights of all members. Thus, going from one employer to another in the private sector does not affect benefits. Finally, it can be pointed out that individuals can make additional arrangements on a private, individual basis with established insurance companies. This is also fairly common.

A–II. CANADA (Samuel A. Rea)

During 1970, only one in three private pension plans was integrated with Canada or Quebec Pension Plans, but almost 75 percent of the total members of all plans participated in integrated plans. There are two basic methods of integration, ranging from partial to full offset of private against government pension benefits.

Under "formula integration" a lower level of benefits and contributions applies on annual earnings up to some income limit, usually the year's maximum pensionable earnings (YMPE) under the Canada Pension Plan. Thus a dual rate or step rate is used under which private pensions are reduced up to the coverage limit of public pensions but not above. Alternatively, a bottom slice of earnings may be declared ineligible for private pensions entirely so that integration with government benefits is achieved by ignoring a slice of earnings (usually less than the YMPE) for both contributions and pension purposes.

Under the second approach, "full integration" or "direct offset" is achieved by making the calculated pension inclusive of all or part of the government pension. Since under some of these plans an increase in government pensions due to cost of living increases all goes to reduce the private pension costs of employers, restrictions on the degree of offset have recently been enacted in several provinces. To maintain the real purchasing power of the total pension income after retirement, no further offsetting can now be done in these provinces once a person has begun receiving payments of a pension. In addition, several provinces have prohibited any offset against private pension claims accrued up to 1966 or 1967.

The amount of a pension that an employer may offset against the benefits to which an employee is entitled under Old Age Security and the Canada or Quebec Pension Plans depends upon the employee's number of years of service with that particular employer. For instance, if an employee retires with total government pension benefits of B in the first year after working for his last employer for ten years, then that employer may reduce his private pension by a maximum of 30 percent of B in Manitoba. However, since previous employers may act likewise if their pension plans so provide, the offset may be 100 percent in the first year of retirement if the employee has worked for a minimum of thirty-three and one-third years during his lifetime.

Though integration is frequently only partial and there are statutory limitations on integration in several provinces, a rise in public pension has the potential of diminishing private pensions to a substantial degree. The degree of nationalization induced in the market for pensions will continue to grow in future years since the YMPE, which was $8,300 in 1976, is scheduled to grow by 12.5 percent per year until it catches up with average earnings. The retirement test and the implied tax on retirement earnings were eliminated under the Canada Pension Plan in 1975 and under the Quebec Pension Plan in 1977.

A–III. GREAT BRITAIN (Jack R.S. Revell)

In Britain, contracting out of a portion of social security was first permitted in 1961 when a graduated public pension scheme providing for earnings-related contributions and benefits was introduced. Part III of the Social Security Pensions Act of 1975 contains the provisions that govern the use of the contracting-out option past April 6, 1978. If that option is used, each employer is responsible only for the period that an employee is working for him. When an employee moves from one contracted-out scheme to another, his preserved pension benefits are transferred in a lump sum. If the employee moves to an employer who is not contracted out, the scheme that he is leaving has to make a lump-sum payment to the state scheme. If the employee moves from employment that is not contracted out to a contracted-out scheme, the accrued benefits in the state scheme are preserved.

Contracted-out schemes may have early retirement rules. Early retirement may be permitted on any grounds and the member may be offered a reduced rate of pension to take account of the years before normal pension age during which it is paid. Similarly, schemes may provide for pension payments to be postponed if that member continues in employment after attaining pensionable age, but only with the member's consent. If such consent is given, pension payments must be increased by 1/8 percent for each complete week of the whole period of postponement. Since the member has the option of receiving full benefits upon reaching his pensionable age regardless of continued employment, if he deems the implied "interest" on postponements insufficient, late retirement is not discouraged financially. In Britain, the normal pension age is sixty-five for men and sixty for women, unless special factors, such as ill health, entitle them to pensions at a younger age.

In a pamphlet entitled "Notes on Pensions, Number 3: Social Security Pensions Act 1975," published by the (British) National Association of Pension Funds (NAPF) in January 1978, the contracting-out option is described and factors affecting the decision to contract out are discussed. Because of the special interest that the British model may hold, particularly for readers in the United States, two sections of that publication are reproduced verbatim below, with permission.

The Contracting-Out Option

Occupational pension schemes, which provide the benefits outlined below, will be allowed to contract-out of the state earnings related pension scheme. The terms are as follows:

(a) The occupational scheme must provide a pension of at least 1 1/4 percent (1/80th) of "pensionable pay" for each year of membership up to a pension of half pensionable pay. Pensionable pay may be based on final salary or on average annual salary revalued each year in line with the movement of earnings generally. Certain emoluments can be excluded from this definition of salary and there are special arrangements for schemes that are benefit or salary integrated with the State Flat Rate Benefit Scheme. The Occupational Pensions Board has published Memorandum No. 29 which sets out in detail the alternatives.

(b) In addition to the general requirement set out above the scheme will also have to guarantee a minimum pension. For members who are within 20 years of State scheme retirement age when the new State scheme starts, the guaranteed minimum pension will be 1 1/4 percent of up-rated "upper band earnings" for each year of contracted-out service. For all other members the guaranteed minimum pension will be 25 percent of up-rated "upper band earnings" divided by the number of years from the start of the new scheme until State scheme pension age for each year of contracted-out service. In assessing the up-rated "upper band earnings" the 20 best years rule will not apply for the guaranteed minimum pension. ["Upper band earnings" are earnings approximately between the basic pension and a ceiling of 7 × the basic pension (£120.00 a week in April 1978).]

(c) The occupational scheme must provide a widow with a pension not less than 5/8 percent of "pensionable pay" for each year of the member's contracted-out service. The scheme widow's pension must not be less than a minimum equal to half the guaranteed minimum retirement pension, described in (b) above, secured at date of death.

(d) The State earnings-related pension will increase in line with the movement of prices. Contracted-out schemes will not be required to increase pensions after award, but members of occupational pension schemes that are contracted-out will not suffer as a result as they will receive increases on their State pension as if they had not been contracted-out. The method to be used is that when an employee reaches State retirement age a total notional State pension will be calculated as if he had never been contracted-out, and from this notional State pension will be deducted the guaranteed minimum pension(s) to be paid by the occupational schemes in respect of contracted-out service. When State pensions are increased the increase will apply to the notional State pension and there will then be deducted from this new increased notional State pension the original guaranteed minimum pension(s), in order to determine the new actual State pension.

(e) If an employee leaves service the following main provisions apply:

(i) If he has less than 5 years contracted-out service and does not qualify for a preserved pension under the Social Security Act 1973, the scheme may either preserve the accrued guaranteed minimum pension, or alternatively this may be cancelled by payment back into the State scheme of the total accumulated contributions (without interest) that would have been paid to the State scheme had the employee not been contracted-out. This payment is known as the "contributions equivalent premium." It is permissible to recover from any contribution refund due to the employee that part of the "contribution equivalent premium" representing accumulated employees' contributions.

(ii) Where a "contributions equivalent premium" is not payable, or is not paid, the guaranteed minimum pension has to be preserved by the scheme, but there is a choice: — the guaranteed minimum pension has to be increased during the period up to State pension age in line with the movement in general levels of earnings, or the accrued guaranteed minimum pension can be increased by a maximum of 5 percent per annum, but in this case a special payment known as the "limited revaluation premium" has to be paid to the State scheme since the State scheme will be bearing the cost of any increase in excess of 5 percent per annum, or — the guaranteed minimum pension has to be increased during the period up to State pension age at a fixed rate of 8 1/2 percent each year.

Whichever choice is made it has to apply to all leavers. The "limited revaluation premium" is not based on an accumulation of contributions but will be an age and sex related premium applied to the amount of guaranteed minimum pension at date of termination of service. Following representations made by the Association and others, the Government agreed that premiums would be determined in such a way as to limit the risk to an employer that might arise due to changes in investment conditions, etc. Full details have been published by the DHSS in leaflet NP24. [DHSS is the Department of Health and Social Security.]

(f) The provisions concerning the arrangements should a scheme cease to contract-out are extremely complex. This complexity has arisen in the main because the Government has accepted to a certain extent representations made by the Association and others to limit the open-ended risk to employers. In essence, where a scheme ceases to be contracted-out, the employer has a choice, subject to the approval of the Occupational Pensions Board, between

(i) preserving guaranteed minimum pensions in the scheme (with or without limiting the liability to revalue by paying limited revaluation premiums);

(ii) transferring the member's pension to another contracted-out scheme; or

(iii) buying back the scheme members fully into the State scheme by means of an "accrued rights premium" (for members who are not yet entitled to a guaranteed minimum pension) or by means of a "pensioner's rights premium" (for members who are already entitled to a guaranteed minimum pension). In calculating the amount of a limited revaluation premium, an accrued rights premium or a pensioner's rights premium when a scheme has ceased to be contracted-out, the amount of the guaranteed minimum pension (which will determine the amount of the premium) will be calculated—unless the employer elects otherwise—as if the general level of earnings had increased by 12 percent per annum in the previous 5 years. (The amount of accrued rights to guaranteed minimum pension remaining in the scheme or transferred to another scheme is not affected by this 12 percent option.) The accrued rights premium and the pensioner's rights premium will vary according to investment conditions etc.

(g) It will be necessary to accord some priority in winding-up to benefits arising in respect of contracted-out service. These provisions have to be looked at together with any existing priority rule and no general guidance can be given.

(h) The Occupational Pensions Board will have to be satisfied that the financial resources of the scheme are adequate. OPB Memorandum No. 31 sets out their requirements.

(i) If a scheme is used for contracting-out then for those members contracted-out there will be a reduction of employee and employer contributions to the State scheme. The contribution reduction is meant to reflect the cost of providing through the occupational scheme the benefits foregone under the State earnings-related pension scheme. The initial reduction will be 2 1/2 percent for employees and 4 1/2 percent for employers on the slice of earnings between the base level and the ceiling. The contribution reduction for contracted-out employees will be decreased at five yearly intervals. The reason for this is that the amount of pension foregone in the State scheme will vary according to the age of the employee at the start of the scheme and the average cost of providing the pension foregone will, therefore, fall over the years due to the 20 year maturity period.

(j) In order to obtain a contracting-out certificate it will be necessary, besides meeting the other contracting-out requirements, to satisfy the Occupational Pensions Board that all employees have been informed and that consultation has taken place with the appropriate recognized Trades Union(s). Details are contained in OPB Memorandum No. 31.

Factors Affecting Decision to Contract-Out

Many employers will have had experience of the factors which went into making a decision on contracting-out under the old graduated scheme or seeking recognition under the Social Security Act 1973. The factors on this occasion are perhaps a little more complicated, some of which will be unique to each employer so that some employers might well decide that it would be best to contract-out and some might not for equally good reasons. The main factors, not necessarily of equal importance, to be considered are:

(a) *Current benefit levels*—are these sufficiently high to enable the occupational scheme to contract-out? If not, then the choice must rest among

  (i) improving these benefit levels in order to contract-out;

  (ii) making no change but not contracting-out; or

  (iii) adjusting the benefit levels downwards to limit total costs to current levels.

(b) *Age and Sex distribution*—is the contribution reduction consistent with the occupational scheme's actual age and sex distribution?

(c) *Investment Earnings*—will future investment earnings be sufficient to match members' earnings? In short would it make financial sense (or on the contrary not make sense) to contract-out of the State earnings related pension scheme?

(d) *Early Leavers—ceasing to contract-out*—what are the risks implied in the terms concerning early leavers, ceasing to contract-out, and termination of the scheme? Are these terms such as to modify or eliminate any investment risks under (c) above?

(e) *Changes in Contracting-out terms*—what is the risk that the contracting-out terms or the structure of the State scheme might change, possibly with retrospective effect?

(f) *Attitude of members*—are they likely to prefer to be contracted-out or not contracted-out? Apart from political and emotional reasons there is the material consideration in favor of contracting-out in that contributions to an occupational scheme will be tax deductible but the equivalent contributions to the State scheme will not.

(g) *Benefit structure of the scheme*—a few schemes will be able to make a decision not to contract-out without any major change to the benefit structure of the occupational scheme. For others a decision not to contract-out might require significant changes in the benefit structure leading to serious employee relations difficulties. Because of these employee relations difficulties or for other reasons a scheme might find that by not contracting-out the overall benefits (State and scheme combined) are higher than at present even after cutting back somewhat for the new earnings related State scheme. This would lead to increased costs and might more than counterbalance other financial factors tending to make the scheme participate.

(h) *Administration problems*—will the administration problems be more burdensome if it is decided to contract-out or will it be more difficult administratively not to contract-out?

A–IV. COMPARISON WITH THE UNITED STATES

In the United States, what integration there is resembles the Swedish rather than the British model. Increased social security benefits and contributions can crowd out private benefits, though they may also lower the incremental costs of providing additional pension benefits to high-salaried employees on a nondiscriminatory basis. Under private company plans benefits generally bear a uniform relationship to compensation with some possible modifications for length of service.

In a plan that provides no integrated death or disability benefits, the maximum percentage of social security benefits that can be integrated is 37.5 percent of the appropriate covered compensation level (the average monthly wage on which social security benefits are computed). If the private plan provides benefits with respect to final average pay in excess of some amount that is higher than the appropriate covered compensation level, the maximum percentage must be reduced. For plans that integrate on the basis of contributions, the basic rate was 7 percent in 1978.

Regardless of which method of integration is chosen, base increases in the ceiling on wages subject to social security taxes and a rise in social security tax rates on employers can thus lower employer contributions to private plans. For further details see the 1978 edition of *Tax Facts on Life Insurance* and the overview provided in Joseph J. Melone and Everett T. Allen, Jr., *Pension Planning* (Homewood, Ill.: Irwin, 1972).

NOTES TO CHAPTER 1

1. Unlike democracies, dictatorships often seem to place little emphasis on the welfare of the aged. Thus, Bernice Madison, reporting in the *Wall Street Journal* of May 19, 1978, on her forthcoming work, estimated that while most Soviet pensioners have *only* their pension to live on, the average pension amounts appeared to range from a mere $33 a month for collective farmers to $55 for industrial workers and employees in a recent year (1975?). Even after noting that the relative price of certain necessities, such as housing and medical care, is much lower in the Soviet Union than in the United States, she concluded that "the overall situation is meager." For further details see [19, n.d.]. However, it should not be assumed that the correlation between democratic forms of government and political concern for the aged is perfectly positive. Thus, both old-age and survivors' insurance were introduced in imperial Germany already in 1889, while strictly democratic Switzerland had neither before 1948 [1, 1978, p. 22]. Thus, it is not clear that the social insurance budget is *inevitably* too large in democracies, as has sometimes been claimed.

2. In academic circles of the United States the challenge originated with Martin Feldstein, who has since extended his analysis to other countries [13, 1977]. It has also been taken up by many others (see [15, Institute for Contemporary Studies, 1978: 7, Campbell, 1979]). Outside such circles, the clearest recent definition of the reform issues is due to the former chief actuary of the Social Security Administration, Haeworth Robertson [23, 1978].

3. Though John Brittain [4, 1978, pp. 11–18] finds that wealthy people continue accumulating in old age, despite tax incentives to make inter vivos gifts to their children, almost 80 percent of heads of U.S. households aged sixty-five and over reported having received no inheritances during their lifetime in a 1962 survey.

4. Doubts about the ability of past and perhaps all conceivable time-series studies to isolate the effect of the social security program on private saving have been supported by Louis Esposito [12, 1978].

5. For broader definitions and measures of wealth by sector for the United States see Raymond Goldsmith [14, forthcoming].

6. After discussing problems of comparability, estimates for a number of countries are provided by the International Labor Association [16, 1976; also in 1, 1978].

7. In recent tests Betsy White [25, 1978] has found that the values of aggregate personal saving simulated with life cycle models are at best about 60 percent of the observed values.

8. Some of the retirement provisions prevailing in these countries are described in the appendix to this introduction.

9. Assuming a period-to-period interest rate of 46 percent rather than 25 percent in illustration B yields consumption of 94.7 per period. Accumulated savings, summed over all of the equal-sized cohorts assumed to populate each of the six periods, would then be only 148.4, compared with the 186.9 shown in Table 1–1. However, a flat consumption stream is optimal only if the subjective discount rate is assumed to rise with the market rate of interest. If it remains lower, then more will be saved early during the working life and less later. Thus, if a rising consumption path that starts out at 89.5 in period 1 and ends at 107.0 in period 6 while increasing by 3.5 each period in the interim should come close to the optimal path, the sum total of accumulated savings would be 195.0, assuming all lifetime income is consumed before death.

10. Though the time of death is correctly represented as a surprise that makes analyses based on the assumption of certainty blanch, the fact that the probability of death rises with advancing age would make retirees plan a consumption stream which declines with age if any bequests they may leave are involuntary. In the example given in the text, this additional reduction in the stock of accumulated savings during the fifth period was not considered. Even so, in a continuous model without financial intermediation, positive bequests would be left by all who cannot obtain gifts from their children or emergency relief from other sources. In the absence of public and private charity, no one, except the suicidal, would rationally risk consuming all his assets today not knowing that he will be dead (from causes other than starvation) tomorrow. Hence some bequests would be left by all who have not invested all of their assets in annuity contracts prior to death. For further discussion see [3, Barro and Friedman, 1977; 25, White, 1978, p. 559].

11. The fact that privately covered employees could, at least until recently, stand to lose some of the benefits from past contributions to company plans whenever CPP benefits were raised has not stanched political demands for increases in the latter. Samuel Rea has speculated about the reasons for this amazing fact. In correspondence with the editor he suggested that the loss of private pension benefits through integration may result from the usual preoccupation among noneconomists with the replacement rate rather than with the rate of return on pension contributions.

12. In 1978, Switzerland considered adding a "second column" of earnings-related pensions to the basic system to raise the replacement rate over 60 percent. The program, though compulsory, is to be administered by private financial institutions (banks) in an actuarially sound manner.

REFERENCES

1. ASSOCIATION INTERNATIONALE POUR L'ETUDE DE L'ECONOMIE DE L'ASSURANCE. *Staat—Sicherheit—Versicherung, Teil I—Ein Internationaler Vergleich.* A study conducted by W. ACKERMANN under the direction of M. HALLER. Geneva: The Association's Etudes et Dossiers No. 19, 1978.

2. BARRO, ROBERT J. *The Impact of Social Security on Private Saving, Evidence from U.S. Time Series.* With a Reply by MARTIN FELDSTEIN. Washington, D.C.: American Enterprise Institute, Studies in Social Security and Retirement Policies, 1978.

3. ____ , and FRIEDMAN, JAMES W. "On Uncertain Lifetimes," *Journal of Political Economy*, Aug. 1977, *85*(4), pp. 843–50.

4. BRITTAIN, JOHN A. *Inheritance and the Inequality of Material Wealth.* Washington, D.C.: Brookings Institution, 1978.

5. BURKHAUSER, RICHARD V. and TURNER, JOHN A. "A Time-Series Analysis of Social Security and Its Effect on the Market Work of Men at Younger Ages," *Journal of Political Economy*, Aug. 1978, *86*(4), pp. 701–16.

6. CAMPBELL, COLIN D. *The 1977 Amendments to the Social Security Act.* Washington, D.C.: American Enterprise Institute, Special Analysis No. 78–2, 1978.

7. ____ , ed. *Financing Social Security.* Washington, D.C.: American Enterprise Institute, 1979.

8. ____ , and CAMPBELL, ROSEMARY G. "Conflicting Views on the Effect of Old-Age and Survivors Insurance on Retirement," *Economic Inquiry*, Sept. 1976, *14*(3), pp. 369–88.

9. COLBERG, MARSHALL R. *The Social Security Retirement Test, Right or Wrong?* Washington, D.C.: American Enterprise Institute, Studies in Social Security and Retirement Policy, 1978.

10. CONGRESSIONAL BUDGET OFFICE. *Aggregate Economic Effects of Changes in Social Security Taxes.* Technical Analysis Paper. Washington, D.C.: U.S.G.P.O., 1978.

11. DRAZEN, ALLAN. "Government Debt, Human Capital, and Bequests in a Life-Cycle Model," *Journal of Political Economy*, June 1978, *86*(3), pp. 505–16.

12. ESPOSITO, LOUIS. "Effect of Social Security on Saving: Review of Studies Using U.S. Time-Series Data," *Social Security Bulletin*, May 1978, *41*(5), pp. 9–17.

13. FELDSTEIN, MARTIN S. "Social Security and Private Savings: International Evidence in an Extended Life-cycle Model," in *The Economics of Public Services.* Edited by MARTIN S. FELDSTEIN and ROBERT P. INMAN. London: The Macmillan Press, Ltd., 1977.

14. GOLDSMITH, RAYMOND W. *The National Balance Sheet of the United States, 1953–1975.* New York: National Bureau of Economic Research, forthcoming.

15. INSTITUTE FOR CONTEMPORARY STUDIES. *The Crisis in Social Security: Problems and Prospects.* San Francisco: Institute for Contemporary Studies, rev. ed. 1978.

16. INTERNATIONAL LABOUR OFFICE. *The Cost of Social Security.* Eighth International Inquiry, 1967–1971. Geneva: International Labour Organisation, 1976.

17. LOGUE, DENNIS E. "How Social Security May Undermine the Private Industrial Pension System," in *Financing Social Security.* Edited by COLIN D. CAMPBELL. Washington, D.C.: American Enterprise Institute, 1979.

18. MACDONALD, ROBERT M. *Mandatory Retirement and the Law.* Washington, D.C.: American Enterprise Institute, Studies in Social Security and Retirement Policy, 1978.

19. MADISON, BERNICE. "Soviet Income Maintenance Programs in the Struggle against Poverty." Paper prepared for a colloquium held at the Kennan Institute for Advanced Russian Studies, Woodrow Wilson International Center for Scholars, Washington, D.C., n.d.

20. MUNNELL, ALICIA H. "Are Private Pensions Doomed?" *New England Economic Review*, March/April 1978, pp. 5–20.

21. PELLECHIO, ANTHONY. Social Security and Retirement Behavior. Unpublished doctoral dissertation. Harvard University, 1978.

22. QUINN, JOSEPH F. *The Early Retirement Decision: Evidence from the 1969 Retirement History Study.* U.S. Social Security Administration, Office of Research and Statistics staff paper No. 29. Washington, D.C.: U.S.G.P.O., 1977.

23. ROBERTSON, A. HAEWORTH. *Social Security, Prospect for Change.* New York: William M. Mercer, Inc., 1978.

24. SHEPPARD, HAROLD L., and RIX, SARA E. *The Graying of Working America: The Coming Crisis in Retirement-Age Policy.* New York: Free Press, 1977.

25. WHITE, BETSY B. "Empirical Tests of the Life Cycle Hypothesis," *American Economic Review*, Sept. 1978, *68*(4), pp. 547–60.

Part I

Empirical Studies: United States

Chapter 2

Debt Neutrality: A Brief Review of Doctrine and Evidence

Willem H. Buiter and James Tobin

The macroeconomic theory of public debt has become increasingly controversial in recent years. The debate concerns not only the explicit interest-bearing financial obligations of the government but also its implicit deferred liabilities for social insurance benefits. This chapter provides some historical background for the current theoretical debate. It also reviews some empirical tests of the proposition that government debt is neutral in real macroeconomic effects, and offers some additional tests. The conclusions are generally against the neutrality thesis. The evidence is that tax and debt finance of government expenditure are not equivalent in their effects on private saving and consumption. Debt issue does absorb private saving. That is why it is more of a stimulus to the economy in the short run than tax finance, and why it may diminish private capital formation in the long run. A number of studies in this volume express concern over the effects of unfunded social security programs on capital formation, and this chapter indicates that the concern is well founded.

I. HISTORICAL PERSPECTIVES

The influence on the consumption-investment mix of alternative methods of financing a given volume of government spending has been a subject of debate since Adam Smith [63, 1776; 16, Cannan, (1776) 1937] and David Ricardo [56, 1817; 57, 1820]. In recent years, under the rubrics of "debt neutrality" and "ultrarationality," the issues are restated as "Are government bonds net wealth?" and "Are future taxes anticipated by consumers?" [19, David and Scadding, 1974; 33, Kochin, 1974; 17, Carlson and Spencer, 1975; 3, Barro, 1974; 4, 1974; 5, 1977; 11, Buchanan, 1976; 23, Feldstein, 1976; 13, Buiter, 1977].

The "new classical macroeconomics" gives some dramatic answers to these questions. The effect of government, it says, is fully measured by the size and content of real government spending, regardless of how this spending is financed. Thus the Modigliani-Miller theorem for corporate finance [45, Modigliani and Miller, 1958; 65, Stiglitz, 1969; 66, 1974] is extended from the household sector vis-à-vis the corporate sector to the private sector as a whole vis-à-vis the public sector. An important recent statement of this theorem for public sector financing has been made by Barro [31, 1974]. Less formal statements can be found in the popular writings of Milton Friedman [26, 1978, p. 59]. "The total tax burden on the American people is what the government spends, not those receipts called taxes. Any deficit is borne by the public in the form of hidden taxes—either inflation or the even more effectively hidden tax corresponding to borrowing from the public." Buchanan [11, 1976] has referred to the alleged neutrality of public sector financing as the "Ricardian Equivalence Theorem."

It is true that Ricardo stated the argument with characteristic clarity. He also added important qualifications, however, and concluded, almost passionately, that deferment of taxes by internal borrowing is bad fiscal policy. Ricardo, like Adam Smith before him, argued that given the volume and composition of what would today be called "exhaustive" public spending (government purchases), taxes reduce mainly current consumption while internal borrowing results in reduced saving and private capital formation. He thus refuted rather than upheld the notion that the form of financing is irrelevant.[1] In fact, after giving a clear statement in his *Principles* of the "Ricardian equivalence theorem," Ricardo proceeds to deny emphatically its validity. His grounds were partly what is now called "public debt illusion" [72, Vickrey, 1961], and partly his fear that expectations of future taxes would induce evasive behavior, even including emigration. Here are the master's own words [39, McCulloch, (1817) 1871, pp. 146–47], first stating the equivalence theorem:

> When, for the expenses of a year's war, twenty millions are raised by means of a loan, it is the twenty millions which are withdrawn from the

productive capital of the nation. The million per annum which is raised by taxes to pay the interest of this loan, is merely transferred from those who pay it to those who receive it, from the contributor to the tax, to the national creditor. The real expense is the twenty millions, and not the interest which must be paid for it. Whether the interest be or not be paid, the country will be neither richer nor poorer. Government might at once have required the twenty millions in shape of taxes, in which case it would not have been necessary to raise annual taxes to the amount of a million.

In *Funding System*, Ricardo [64, Sraffa, (1820) 1951, p. 187] also makes the point, since reformulated by Barro [3, 1974], that the intergenerational redistribution of income associated with a switch from tax financing to borrowing could be neutralized by offsetting changes in voluntary intergenerational gifts and bequests (italics added):

It would be difficult to convince a man possessed of 20,000 £ or any other sum, that a perpetual payment of 50 £ per annum was equally burdensome with a single tax of 1,000 £. He would have some vague notion that the 50 £ per annum would be paid by posterity, and would not be paid by him; *but if he leaves his fortune to his son, and leaves it charged with this perpetual tax, where is the difference whether he leaves him 20,000 £, with the tax, or 19,000 £ without it?*"

Having thus stated the equivalence theorem, Ricardo [64, Sraffa, (1820) 1951, p. 187] quickly proceeds to deny its validity: "That an annual tax of 50 £ is not deemed the same in amount as 1,000 £ ready money, must have been observed by everybody." One of the reasons given is public debt illusion [39, McCulloch, (1817), 1871, p. 148]:

. . . it must not be inferred that I consider the system of borrowing as the best calculated to defray the extraordinary expenses of the state. It is a system which tends to make us less thrifty—to blind us to our real situation. If the expenses of a war be 40 millions per annum, and the share which a man would have to contribute towards that annual expense were 100 pounds, he would endeavor, on being at once called upon for this portion, to save speedily the 100 pounds from his income. By the system of loans, he is called upon to pay only the interest of this 100 pounds, or 5 pounds per annum, and considers that he does enough by saving this 5 pounds from his expenditure, and then deludes himself with the belief that he is as rich as before. The whole nation, by reasoning and acting in this manner, save only the interest of 40 millions, or two millions.

Evasive behavior, to the point of emigrating in order to avoid the continuing stream of taxes is given as another argument against borrowing in the same place [p. 148]:

> . . . it becomes the interest of every contributor to withdraw his shoulder from the burthen and to shift this payment from himself to another; and the temptation to remove himself and his capital to another country, where he will exempted from such burthens, becomes at last irresistible, and overcomes the natural reluctance which every man feels to quit the place of his birth, and the scene of his early associations.

Finally, to leave no room for any doubt about his feelings on the subject, he concludes:

> It must, however, be admitted, that during peace, our unceasing efforts should be directed towards paying off that part of the debt which has been contracted during war; and that no temptation of relief, no desire of escape from present, and I hope temporary distresses, should induce us to relax in our attention to that great object.

This excursion into the early history of economic thought leads us to conclude that the "Neo-Ricardian Equivalence Theorem" should be relabeled the "Non-Ricardian Equivalence Theorem" and Ricardo's doctrine relabeled the "Ricardian Nonequivalence Theorem."

In the last thirty years, the issue of the differential incidence of tax financing and borrowing has resurfaced a number of times. Until the burden-of-the-debt controversy which followed the publication of James Buchanan's *Public Principles of Public Debt* [9, 1958], post-World War II economists generally agreed with the "equivalence theorem." At least they agreed to it as applied to fully employed economies. A country fights and pays for a war with current resources. This burden cannot be postponed by borrowing internally. This went along with a clear distinction between internal debt—"we owe it to ourselves"—and external debt.

There never has been any serious argument about the burden of the external debt in an economy with full employment. In the short run, the ability to borrow abroad, that is, to run a current account deficit, enables a country to absorb more resources than it currently produces. Such borrowed real resources can be used to boost current consumption, public or private, or can be devoted to public or private capital formation. In the case of a consumption loan a real burden is placed on the future, when current account surpluses will have to be generated in order to service and repay the overseas debt. If the current account deficit is devoted to domestic capital formation, future generations will be better off if the social rate of return on the additional domestic investment exceeds the marginal cost of foreign borrowing, and worse off if the opposite holds. To the extent that, in long-run equilibrium, rates of return are equalized between countries joined by well-functioning financial markets, foreign borrowing cannot enhance future consumption possibilities.

But, as regards internally held debt, popular concern about the debt burden on future generations was considered a naive fallacy. This classical doctrine was conveniently married to Keynesianism. The "functional finance" doctrine associated with Abba Lerner [37, 1943; 38, 1946] downgraded the debt burden. The only purpose of taxation—and one which it was deemed capable of achieving—was to control private spending, mainly consumption spending, so as to achieve the right amount of aggregate demand and to avoid inflation at full employment. The marriage produced somewhat inconsistent views of the long-run and the short-run effects of borrowing. Lerner et al. seemed to say that the debt stock did not substitute for the capital stock in the long run, but that saving was absorbed in the short run by public sector deficits financed by bond issue.

Also during the 1940s a debate began about the proper base for the real balance effect proposed by Gottfried Haberler [28, 1941] and Arthur Pigou [54, 1943; 55, 1947] and elaborated upon by James Tobin [69, 1947; 70, 1952], Don Patinkin [48, 1948; 49, 1956], and John Gurley and Edward Shaw [27, 1960]. Exactly the same issue was involved as in the debt neutrality debate: Does the base for the wealth effect include only base money? all nominal public debt? any nominal debt? nothing? Don Patinkin [48, 1948, pp. 550–51] argued that the base " . . . clearly consists of the net obligation of the government to the private sector of the economy. That is, it consists primarily of the total interest- and non-interest-bearing government debt held outside the treasury and central bank."[2] Shortly afterwards, in a discussion of the wealth effect in private consumption, Tobin [70, 1952, p. 117] questioned the full inclusion of interest-bearing public debt in net private wealth.

> How is it possible that society merely by the device of incurring a debt to itself can deceive itself into believing that it is wealthier? Do not the additional taxes which are necessary to carry the interest charges reduce the value of other components of private wealth? There certainly must be effects in this direction.

Reasons mentioned for the incompleteness of the offset included the government's option of paying the interest on its debt not by taxes but by incurring further debt and the effect of the creation of public debt on the *distribution* and *composition* of private wealth, especially with regard to liquidity.

The "burden of the debt" controversy of the late 1950s and 1960s concerned the long-run effects of substitution of borrowing for tax financing, the same issue that Ricardo had addressed: Does public debt diminish private demand for private financial claims and for stocks of real reproducible capital? Can the burden of current exhaustive government spending be shifted to future generations? The major protagonists were Buchanan [9, 1958; 10, 1964], James Meade [40, 1958], William Bowen, Richard Davis, and David Kopf [8, 1960], Vickrey [72, 1961], Modigliani [44, 1961], Ezra Mishan [42, 1963], James Ferguson [25, 1964] and Earl Thompson [68, 1967]. In this debate Buchanan and some others objected both to classical neutrality doctrine and to functional finance in any form. But they seemed to define burden as compulsory payment—debt purchases are voluntary, tax payments are not—and thus their claim that the burden was postponable was almost tautological. The main area of controversy was clarified by the "neoclassical synthesis" (see Paul Samuelson [58, 1951; 59, 1955]), applied to the debt controversy most notably by Modigliani [44, 1961]. It focused attention on the central issue, whether and how public debt absorbs saving permanently and thus reduces the long-run capital stock.

In 1965 Peter Diamond [21, 1965] first applied the overlapping generations model developed by Samuelson [60, 1958] to the analysis of the longer-run effects of public debt on capital formation. He also considered the consequences of overseas borrowing by the public sector. His model did not permit private domestic agents access to international capital markets. This part of this analysis therefore has limited applicability to developed market economies integrated into an international financial system. Less developed countries where the government is the sole agent with international credit-worthiness are more closely approximated by the open economy Diamond model. This is an area that deserves further research.

A considerable amount of further theoretical work has built on the closed overlapping generations growth model (e.g., David Cass and Menahem Yaari [18, 1967], Feldstein [22, 1974; 23, 1976; 24, 1976], Barro [3, 1974; 4, 1976], Buiter [14, this volume], Tobin and Buiter [71, 1980]).

Empirical work on debt neutrality has been scant; some recent contributions are reviewed in the next section. One area that has long attracted interest and continues to be investigated in depth is the effect of social security on private and national saving [22, Feldstein, 1974; 46, Munnell, 1974; 47, 1976; 5, Barro, 1977]. An unfunded, "pay-as-you-go" social security scheme is a tax-transfer scheme that redistributes income between working and retired people. Its effect on saving and the long-run capital stock is governed by the same considerations as the effect of a change in the government's borrowing-taxation mix. On these issues the new classical macroeconomics, as exemplified by Barro [3, 1974] and by Merton Miller and Charles Upton [41, 1974], has a striking and extreme view: Voluntary private intergenerational transfers can and will offset the involuntary public intergenerational transfers associated with public borrowing and social security. The private transfers negate any effects of public debt and social security on aggregate saving and the long-run capital stock. The most vocal opponent of this view is again James Buchanan [12, Buchanan and Wagner, 1977]. Unfortunately their sweeping condemnation of deficit finance—which they represent as the major source of most our current economic ills—is not complemented by a tightly reasoned economic analysis of the sources of nonequivalence.

Elsewhere in these volumes [14, 71] we seek to make clear again what seemed obvious to Ricardo 150 years ago. Here we turn to empirical findings adduced by proponents of "Ricardian" equivalence. We find that empirical evidence better supports Ricardo's final judgment.

II. EMPIRICAL FINDINGS RELEVANT TO THE DEBT-NEUTRALITY ISSUE

Very little empirical research has been addressed directly to the debt-neutrality issue. In a paper by Kochin [33, 1974] some simple consumption functions are estimated that include the federal budget deficit as one of the explanatory variables. A paper by David and Scadding [19, 1974] analyzes "Denison's Law" [20, 1958], the proposition that the gross private savings ratio (GPSR) has been very stable in the United States. While this phenomenon is different from debt-neutrality, the authors' interpretation of GPSR stability as reflecting "ultra-rational" behavior is germane to the debt-neutrality issue.

Finally, a fairly sizable volume of research, while not addressed directly to the debt-neutrality issue, nevertheless has important implications for it. Recent work by Feldstein [22, 1974; 24, 1976], Munnell [46, 1974], and Barro [5, 1977] on the relation between social security and private saving extends earlier research in this area by George Katona [31, 1960; 32, 1965]. Phillip Cagan [15, 1965], Lester Taylor [67, 1971], and Thomas Juster and Paul Wachtel [30, 1972]. These three bodies of empirical research will be discussed in turn.

Are Government Deficits Equivalent to Current Taxes?

To test the hypothesis that government deficits are equivalent to explicit current taxes, Kochin [33, 1974, p. 391] estimated the equations given below:

$$CND = \underset{(1.81)}{5.56} + \underset{(3.79)}{0.283}\, YD - \underset{(2.56)}{0.224}\, FDEF + \underset{(5.12)}{0.643}\, CND_{-1} \tag{1}$$

$R^2 = 0.9989$; $SE = 2.23$; $DW = 0.680$; annual data 1952–71.

$$\Delta CND = \underset{(3.44)}{2.88} + \underset{(7.86)}{0.392}\, \Delta YD - \underset{(2.95)}{0.109}\, \Delta FDEF + \underset{(2.42)}{0.218}\, \Delta CND_{-1} \tag{2}$$

$R^2 = 0.892$; $SE = 1.26$; $DW = 1.79$; annual data 1952–71.

CND denotes consumer expenditures on nondurables and services. *YD* is personal disposable income and *FDEF* the federal deficit. Each variable is deflated by the implicit price index for consumption expenditures.

Kochin finds that the negative significant coefficient on *FDEF* supports the debt-neutrality thesis. However, it does not support its strict and strong form, because it is smaller in absolute value than the coefficient of *YD* (markedly so in the second equation). In any case, a number of econometric and economic objections can be made to Kochin's regressions.

1. First, there are familiar problems of simultaneity and identification. In cyclical fluctuations, consumer spending, disposable income, and the federal surplus all move together. History seldom performs the critical experiment of raising disposable income and reducing the federal surplus by equal amounts. So it is difficult to estimate the separate *YD* and *FDEF* effects. Moreover, a high propensity to spend means a buoyant economy and a low deficit, reverse causation which Kochin's regressions do not screen out. Kochin attempts to solve this problem by using the full-employment deficit, in equations not reported here. But this is for other reasons quite inappropriate. Except at full employment, the full employment deficit does not provide a measure of the present value of the future taxes required to service the debt issued.

2. Why is only the *federal* deficit considered equivalent to current taxes? The claim that households internalize public debts is surely more credible for state and local governments. They are subject to legal and economic debt limits; they cannot print money; there are

fairly direct links between their outlays, including debt service, and their tax levies.

3. If the household sector subsumes the public sector under its own behavior, we can surely expect it to do the same for the corporate sector. *Private* disposable income, inclusive of corporate retained earnings, rather than *personal* disposable income, should be entered as an argument in (1) and (2).

4. Kochin apparently views spending on consumer durables as a form of saving; this accounts for his choice of *CND* rather than personal consumption expenditures as the dependent variables in his regressions. Conceptually the proper dependent variable is consumption, including imputed services from durables. The excess of the value of these services over depreciation of the stock should be imputed as income and added to the National Income Accounts calculation of disposable income.

5. It is probably better to specify the consumption function in per capita terms.

6. The two regressions differ in economic substance as well as in their assumptions about the serial dependence of errors. The second implies a time trend in *CND*, absent in the first.

Kochin's investigation was motivated by his observation that unusually high saving rates occurred in the late 1960s and early 1970s when the federal deficit was high. His results, whatever their econometric merits, are dramatically altered when the years 1972–76 are added to the sample. Personal saving definitely did not adjust to offset the federal budget deficits run in 1975 and 1976.

Probably owing to data revisions for his sample period, we were unable to duplicate exactly the results obtained by Kochin. Our equations (1a) and (2a) are Kochin's specifications[3] using the data provided in the 1978 *Economic Report of the President.*

$$\underset{}{CND} = \underset{(1.26)}{4.504} + \underset{(3.45)}{0.2498}\, YD - \underset{(2.43)}{0.1781}\, FDEF + \underset{(6.94)}{0.6981}\, CND_{-1} \tag{1a}$$

$\bar{R}^2 = 0.999$; $SE = 2.66$; $DW = 1.21$; annual data 1952–71.

$$\Delta CND = \underset{(2.55)}{4.069} + \underset{(5.20)}{0.355}\, \Delta YD - \underset{(1.85)}{0.086}\, \Delta FDEF + \underset{(2.10)}{0.268}\, \Delta CND_{-1} \tag{2a}$$

$\bar{R}^2 = 0.790$; $SE = 2.28$; $DW = 2.17$; annual data 1952–71.

Adding the years 1972–1976 to the sample has the result, hardly surprising in the light of the high spending propensities and deficits of recent years, of depriving the federal deficit of all explanatory power, as shown in equations (1b) and (2b).[4]

$$CND = 7.503 + 0.381\,YD + 0.018\,FDEF + 0.516\,CND_{-1} \quad (1b)$$
$$(1.97) \quad (5.41) \quad (0.26) \quad (5.25)$$

$\bar{R}^2 = 0.999$; $SE = 3.97$; $DW = 1.41$; annual data 1949–76.

$$\Delta CND = 4.639 + 0.406\,\Delta YD - 0.035\,\Delta FDEF + 0.195\,\Delta CND_{-1} \quad (2b)$$
$$(2.13) \quad (5.98) \quad (0.60) \quad (1.54)$$

$\bar{R}^2 = 0.657$; $SE = 4.18$; $DW = 1.83$; annual data 1950–76.

To correct the specifications and statistical procedures, we modified Kochin's original equation in three ways. First, the equation was specified in per capita terms.[5] Second, the total public sector deficit rather than just the federal deficit was used. Third, the business sector was subsumed under the household sector. Let y denote per capita real national income, g per capita purchases of goods and services by governments (federal, state, and local), $gdef$ the real per capita public sector deficit, and t real per capita taxes net of transfers ($gdef \equiv g - t$). The appropriate per capita real income concept is $y - t - gdef = y - g$, if, from the point of view of the private sector, public sector deficits are equivalent to current taxes. We test the hypothesis that y, t, and $gdef$ have the same coefficients. Both real per capita consumption spending on nondurables and services, cnd, and total real per capita consumer expenditures, c, are used as dependent variables. The results are presented in equations (3) through (8), using annual data for 1949 through 1976.

$$cnd = -133.139 + 0.224\,y - 0.337\,t - 0.254\,gdef + 0.798\,cnd_{-1} \quad (3)$$
$$(1.57) \quad (4.43) \quad (1.30) \quad (1.04) \quad (13.46)$$

$\bar{R}^2 = 0.998$; $SE = 19.34$; $SSR = 8{,}604$; $DW = 1.73$.

$$cnd = -114.730 + 0.192\,y - 0.239\,g + 0.821\,cnd_{-1} \quad (4)$$
$$(1.38) \quad (4.64) \quad (0.98) \quad (14.81)$$

$\bar{R}^2 = 0.998$; $SE = 19.42$; $SSR = 9{,}050$; $DW = 1.78$.

$$cnd = -97.002 + 0.186\,(y-g) + 0.813\,cnd_{-1} \quad (5)$$
$$(4.48) \quad (6.11) \quad (20.68)$$

$\bar{R}^2 = 0.998$; $SE = 19.05$; $SSR = 9{,}068$; $DW = 1.75$.

$$c = -218.806 + 0.424\,y - 0.682\,t - 0.496\,gdef + 0.652\,c_{-1} \qquad (6)$$
$$\quad (1.26) \quad (4.05) \quad (1.26) \quad (0.99) \quad (6.24)$$
$$\bar{R}^2 = 0.994;\; SE = 40.23;\; SSR = 37{,}218;\; DW = 1.44.$$

$$c = -156.242 + 0.352\,y - 0.408\,g + 0.682\,c_{-1} \qquad (7)$$
$$\quad (0.932) \quad (4.03) \quad (0.82) \quad (6.63)$$
$$\bar{R}^2 = 0.994;\; SE = 40.63;\; SSR = 39{,}621;\; DW = 1.51.$$

$$c = -135.697 + 0.345\,(y-g) + 0.673\,c_{-1} \qquad (8)$$
$$\quad (2.97) \quad (5.08) \quad (9.04)$$
$$\bar{R}^2 = 0.994;\; SE = 39.82;\; SSR = 39{,}648;\; DW = 1.50.$$

Equations (3) through (8) indicate that the debt-neutrality hypothesis is not supported for either consumption spending on nondurables and services or for total consumer spending. In equations (4) and (7), the coefficient on *g* has the "right" sign but is insignificantly different from zero. In equations (3) and (6) both *t* and *gdef* have the right signs but are statistically insignificant. Accurate estimation of the coefficients on *y*, *t*, *gdef*, and *g* is complicated by considerable collinearity among these variables in annual data for 1948–76 as shown by the *matrix of zero-order correlation coefficients* below:

	y	*t*	*gdef*
t	0.91		
gdef	0.38	−0.03	
g	0.99	0.88	0.44

The lack of statistical significance of the variables that should reflect the presence or absence of debt neutrality [*g* and *gdef*] is reflected in our inability to reject the hypothesis that the coefficients on *y*, −*t*, and −*gdef* are the same, at the 5 percent level of significance. This holds both when *cnd* is the dependent variable [equation (3) vs. (5)] and when *c* is the dependent variable [equation (6) vs. (8)]. The hypotheses that *t* and *gdef* have the same coefficients [equation (3) vs. (4) or equation (6) vs. (7)] and that *y* and *g* have the same coefficients [equation (4) vs. (5) or equation (7) vs. (8)] similarly cannot be rejected. This gives scant comfort to proponents of debt neutrality, however; the coefficients of *g* and *gdef* are statistically insignificantly different from zero, and therefore also differ insignificantly from values close to zero.

Success, as measured by high $\bar{R}^2$, significant *t*-statistics, and an acceptable Durbin-Watson statistic, is cheap in aggregate time series analysis. This should be kept in mind when evaluating the significance of the "successful" equations (5) and (8). The simplest Keynesian consumption function is estimated in (9), in which *yd* denotes real per capita personal disposable income.

$$c = \underset{(4.53)}{123.431} + \underset{(100.44)}{0.875}\, yd \qquad (9)$$

$\bar{R}^2 = 0.997$; $SE = 27.01$; $SSR = 18{,}970$; $DW = 1.47$;[6] annual data 1949–76.

In terms of conventional statistical criteria, (9) (and its first-order autocorrelation-corrected version) is preferable to (8). For nondurables and services, permanent disposable income[7] in equation (10) also performs as well as the corresponding debt-neutral specification (5).

$$cnd = \underset{(1.28)}{31.747} + \underset{(6.39)}{0.369}\, yd + \underset{(6.46)}{0.528}\, cnd_{-1} \qquad (10)$$

$\bar{R}^2 = 0.998$; $SE = 18.52$; $SSR = 8{,}577$; $DW = 1.51$; annual data 1949–76.

The Stability of the Private Saving Rate

David and Scadding [19, 1974] draw attention to the historical stability in the United States of the ratio, GPSR, of gross private saving to GNP. The explanation, they say, is what they call "ultrarationality." However, their "ultrarationality" is by no means the same rationality invoked by proponents of public debt neutrality. The debt-neutrality proposition relates to the stability of *social saving* (private + public) as a function of social wealth or permanent social real income. A stable private saving ratio, in conjunction with significant variation in the public saving ratio, is inconsistent with the debt-neutrality proposition. David and Scadding [19, 1974, p. 236] impute to private savers quite a different interpretation of the meaning of shifts between taxes and debt in the financing of public expenditure:

> [The] regularity in the GPSR . . . is not the result of constant sectoral savings propensities, of a stable distribution of output between the public and the private sectors, and, within the latter, of a stable division of income between the corporate and household sectors. . . . First there has been a shift in the composition of private saving away from personal saving to corporate saving and expenditure on consumer durables. Second, the

> total of private saving has been almost totally insensitive to the share of output absorbed by the public sector, given the level of output. . . . [The second point] implies a high degree of substitutability . . . between private consumption and taxes and between private investment and government dissaving.

This reasoning is an exercise in arithmetic dressed up as theory. Assume, for the sake of argument, that personal saving, corporate saving, and the accumulation of consumer durables are perfect substitutes. Let S denote gross private saving, C private consumption, T taxes net of transfers, Y gross national product, I gross domestic capital formation, G government spending on goods and services, and X the international current account surplus. From the national income accounting identities we have

$$\frac{S}{Y} \equiv \frac{Y-(C+T)}{Y} \equiv \frac{I+X+G-T}{Y} \quad . \tag{11}$$

Constancy of S/Y means that, for given Y, C and T are perfect substitutes and also that $I + X$ and $G - T$ are perfect substitutes. Going straight from these *ex post* accounting identities to *ex ante* structural behavioral relationships, David and Scadding [19, 1974, p. 243] come up with a startling proposition: " . . . An extra dollar of government deficit will displace a dollar of private investment expenditure because households autonomously treat deficits as public investment and regard the public and private sector's investment projects as interchangeable." Applied literally to year-to-year variations in budget outcomes, this would impute to private savers belief that the public sector increased its investment between 1974 and 1975 by $60 billion and cut it the next year by $30 billion! This could only be described as ultrairrationality. Some of the evidence presented by David and Scadding [19, 1974, pp. 236–38] can be interpreted as suggesting that their proposition does not apply to short-run cyclical variations of public sector deficits and surpluses, which result from fluctuations in the tax base and from discretionary countercyclical fiscal policies; instead they intend it, like the "Denison's Law" which inspired their article, to apply only to longer-run variations as reflected in deficits averaged across business cycles. This restriction would deprive their "ultrarationality" of its most striking policy implications; their proposition could not be used to argue that deficit spending is ineffective for short-run stabilization because it displaces private investment. The policy conclusions drawn by David and Scadding [19, 1974, p. 245], however, are that "fiscal policy would be useless for stabilization purposes." This requires their form of ultrarationality to be operative in the short run and not merely "on average" over the cycle. While this interpretation of David and Scadding's findings is in agreement with their emphasis on the smallness of the *year-to-year variability* in the GPSR (in addition to the absence of a trend in this ratio), it requires the rather unusual view of public sector deficits and public sector investment referred to earlier.

The GPSR is quite stable, as shown in Table 2–1, which presents summary statistics for it and eight other saving ratios. The most important features of Table 2–1 are the following: First, the gross private saving ratio is much more stable (as measured by range, standard deviation, or coefficient of variation) than either the personal saving ratio (PSR) or the gross national saving ratio (GSSR).[8] Second, the net saving ratios, whether private or public, are much less stable than the gross saving ratios. The reasons for this disquieting result are not clear.[9] In principle, rational or ultrarational behavior should lead to greater stability in net saving ratios.[10]

Further investigating the phenomena reported in Table 2–1, we estimated a large number of simple saving functions with alternative dependent and independent variables. The measure of saving used as dependent variable included all combinations of net and gross, private and social, and saving with and without purchases of consumer durables. Explanatory variables were appropriately matched to the

Table 2–1. Stability of Saving Rates, 1948–76

	Mean	*Range*	*Standard Deviation*	*Coefficient of Variation*
GPSR	0.167	0.147–0.179	0.006	0.036
GPSR′	0.256	0.238–0.274	0.009	0.035
NPSR	0.084	0.064–0.100	0.010	0.119
NPSR′	0.182	0.160–0.208	0.012	0.066
GSSR	0.163	0.137–0.202	0.015	0.092
GSSR′	0.252	0.224–0.302	0.018	0.071
NSSR	0.080	0.034–0.134	0.021	0.263
NSSR′	0.178	0.132–0.239	0.024	0.135
PSR	0.082	0.048–0.102	0.012	0.146

Annual data 1948–76; source: *Economic Report of the President 1978*. GPSR = Gross private saving ratio; GPSR′ = (gross private saving + gross purchases of consumer durables)/GNP; NPSR = net private saving ratio; NPSR′ = (net private saving + gross purchases of consumer durables)/NNP; GSSR = gross national saving (private + public)/GNP; NSSR = net national saving/NNP; NSSR′ = (net national saving + gross purchases of consumer durables)/NNP; PSR = personal saving/personal disposable income.

saving concept. They included GNP, NNP, GNP or NNP minus public sector purchases of goods and services, and personal income. Some regressions also included lagged dependent variables. None of these equations performed as well as the simple traditional consumption functions given in (9) and (10), or as the restricted debt-neutrality equations (5) and (8). The saving functions that incorporated the debt-neutrality assumption, that is, those with national saving as the dependent variable, were dominated by those that had private saving as the dependent variable.[11]

The stability of the GPSR is an interesting phenomenon deserving a credible explanation. Perhaps the answer should be sought on the right-hand side of equation (11) as well as on the left-hand side, in the offsets to private saving as well as in private saving behavior. In cyclical fluctuations, I/Y tends to be positively correlated with Y, while endogenous components of X/Y and $(G-T)/Y$ are negatively correlated. If fluctuations in Y are driven by autonomous variations of I, X, and $G-T$, including those engineered by deliberate compensatory policy, the sum of the ratios could be fairly stable. In the longer run, the explanation of Denison's Law may be different before and after the Great Depression and Second World War. In the earlier period, there were strong economic and political constraints holding X/Y and $(G-T)/Y$ constant and close to zero. As Simon Kuznets [34, 1952; 35, 1961; 36, 1961] observed, gross domestic private investment was a fairly constant share of national product over the decades since the Civil War. This stylized fact of economic growth can be attributed to technology and to the long-term stability of the real interest rate. Since World War II the constraints on X/Y and $(G-T)/Y$ have been relaxed. But the national commitment to full employment and the "fiscal revolution" have meant that, secularly as well as cyclically, $(G-T)/Y$ bends to adapt in compensation for variation in I/Y and X/Y.

None of these suggestions is inconsistent with one of the implications of David-Scadding "ultrarationality." This is that, in the long run, anyway, households pay attention to the increments of wealth they acquire via equity appreciation reflecting the retention and reinvestment of corporate profits. Nonhuman wealth, in one form or another, is a significant variable in most modern empirical consumption functions (e.g., [1, Arena, 1964; 2, 1965; 7, Bosworth, 1975; 43, Mishkin, 1977]). These equations generally imply that retained earnings fully reflected in stock values will eventually increase consumption and displace other forms of wealth accumulation. They also imply that the effects of retained earnings on consumption and personal saving are much slower than those of dividend distributions.

But for the long run this component of "ultrarationality" is much more credible, and much more consistent with evidence, than the second component, the notion that private savers regard a public deficit as the counterpart of public investment and as equivalent to private capital formation.

Saving Out of Different Types of Income

Social insurance and other public and private programs compelling saving for retirement and other contingencies have grown spectacularly since World War II. What effect has their growth had on other, discretionary private saving? What is the net effect on funds available for capital formation?

Recently a number of observers have sounded the alarm that social insurance (OASI) and other government pension plans are significantly diminishing national saving and investment. Feldstein [22, 1974] estimates that social security depresses personal saving by as much as 30 to 50 percent. Munnell [47, 1976] concludes that personal saving has been reduced by private pension plans. The negative effects alleged by these critics arise from the unfunded "pay-as-you-go" nature of some of these programs. For example, the social security taxes or contributions paid by or for workers are not invested to provide for the benefits to which these workers will be entitled on retirement. They do not suffice for that. They are used to pay contemporary beneficiaries. In effect the government is engaging in deficit finance. The debt is not explicitly evidenced by bills, notes, or bonds; it is the implicit commitment to pay benefits to current participants when they later become eligible. In other words, the taxes (or contributions) to pay these commitments have been postponed; they will be levied on the generation at work when the currently contributing participants have retired. In the view of Feldstein and other critics, participants reduce their discretionary saving because their compulsory saving and the associated prospect of benefits fulfill the same purpose.

Clearly those who worry about unfunded retirement plans are not believers in the neo- (or non-) Ricardian equivalence theorem.[12] They do not regard the net debt to future beneficiaries as innocuous. If they are analytically and empirically correct, then the protagonists of debt neutrality are wrong. Barro [3, 1974; 4, 1976; 5, 1977] says that Feldstein et al. forgot that the public, knowing full well that future social security taxes will have to be higher to pay for benefits already committed, will save enough to pay the extra future taxes. This additional saving may be done by the future beneficiaries themselves, to make up by gifts or bequests the taxes the younger generation will have to pay. Or it may be done by the future taxpayers themselves. The critics of unfunded pension plans tend to use the life cycle model of saving behavior, or at any rate a model that imputes finite horizons to savers. The advocates of debt neutrality assume infinite horizons, or the equivalent obtained via endless linkage of generations through operative bequest or gift motives.

From this perspective we can review some of the evidence on the substitutability between compulsory or contractual saving and discretionary saving.

Taylor [67, 1971] concludes from his time series analysis of personal saving that households consider contributions to social insurance a form of saving. He finds a very large (−2) negative marginal propensity to save in other forms with respect to social security. This estimate is consistent with one form of "ultrarationality": worker-consumers appear to take into account their employers' contributions as well as their own. His basic equation is [67, 1971, p. 391]:

$$\underset{(43.79)}{S_t = 0.955\, S_{t-1}} + \underset{(4.21)}{0.449\, \Delta L} - \underset{(0.86)}{0.277\, \Delta p} + \underset{(2.86)}{0.893\, \Delta TR} - \underset{(3.30)}{2.16\, \Delta SI} \qquad (12)$$

$$-\underset{(4.87)}{0.901\, \Delta T} + \underset{(2.08)}{3.65\, \Delta r}$$

$\bar{R}^2 = 0.899$; $SE = 2.01$; DW: missing; data: 1953 I–1969 IV.

S denotes saving, ΔL the change in labor income, Δp the change in income from property, ΔTR the change in transfer income, ΔSI the change in personal contributions to social security, ΔT the change in personal tax payments, and Δr the change in the nominal yield on Baa bonds. All variables except the interest rate are in billions of current dollars.

The interpretation of these coefficients is not straightforward. The several income components differ in their positions in the transitory-permanent spectrum: household distributions by total income, wealth, or age differ for the various income components. Furthermore they are imperfect substitutes because of differences in the liquidity and marketability of the assets that yield the income or taxes. The high marginal propensity to save out of transfer payments is undoubtedly due partly to the liquidity and wealth positions of the recipients and partly to the transitory, cyclical nature of some transfer increases and reductions. On the whole, the Taylor study provides strong though indirect evidence against the behavioral hypotheses underlying the debt neutrality thesis, and provides moderate support for the worries of the critics of unfunded pensions and retirement insurance, by concluding that the various components, positive and negative, of personal disposable income are not perfect dollar-for-dollar substitutes for each other.

A similar conclusion was reached by Juster and Wachtel [30, 1972]. When they reestimated equation (12) for the period 1954 I–1972 III, the only significant change was a reduction in the numerical value of the coefficient on the change in personal social security contributions (ΔSI) from −2.16 to −1.55. (From the debt neutrality point of view this would indicate a decline in the "degree of ultrarationality" of worker-consumers with respect to employers' contributions to only 50 percent.)

Earlier studies by Cagan [15, 1965] and Katona [31, 1960; 32, 1965] found that households do not curtail discretionary saving when they are covered by compulsory retirement plans. The studies of Taylor, Katona, and Cagan unfortunately are not comparable. Taylor uses aggregate time series data, Katona a cross-section sample of households, and Cagan both types of data.[13] Cagan [15, 1965. p. 43], like Taylor, found an almost dollar-for-dollar offset of discretionary saving for contractual saving when he analyzed aggregate time series. In the decade and a half before 1963, the "aggregate personal saving-income ratio declines slightly while group pension funds (including government plans but excluding social security) have increased dramatically, indicating a full offset to pension growth by reductions in other forms of saving."

A closer look by Cagan at household saving behavior after a household has come under a pension plan, however, yields results that are the opposite of those suggested by the aggregate saving ratio: the net addition to aggregate personal saving apparently equals the full amount of employees' and employers' contributions. Katona, in his analyses of sample survey data, found that discretionary saving, if anything, increases. In another contribution he argues [31, 1960, p. 98] that the reason for the complementarity observed, in cross-section data, between discretionary private saving and "collective security plans" could be a major shift in the ways financial provision is made for old age. ". . . In former generations financial protection for old age was not generally achieved by individual saving efforts. In many socioeconomic groups this type of aid was provided by relatives, particularly grown children. Also, at the present time and probably for years to come, there is a considerable gap between the standard of living to which an employed family is accustomed and the standard of living provided by social security benefits and private pension plans. It is conceivable, therefore, that the minimal protection afforded by collective insurance plans may even stimulate people to save in order to achieve more adequate protection. Without these plans, economic insecurity would be inescapable for many lower- and middle-income families. With these plans people may be feeling closer to their goal and highly motivated to attain it."

While the attitude toward risk attributed, in this quotation, to a representative household may be somewhat perplexing, the point about the major shift in the ways financial provision is made for old age is important. It is consistent with the view that in Western society a combination of factors—affluence, mobility and independence, lengthened life—has weakened the lineal and extended family and the responsibility felt by and expected of children for taking care of aged parents. Social security and the proliferation of private pension plans are a collective response to this phenomenon. During the transition to the new system, these institutions brought financial independence in old age within reach for the first time for many people, and consequently did not lead them to reduce other provisions but perhaps even encouraged them. After the transition, however, substitution—though not necessarily perfect substitution—between one form of saving and the other would become the likely pattern.

The only conclusive evidence on the extent to which voluntary intrafamily intergenerational transfers offset the effects of social security would be panel data on intrafamily transfers combined with accurate measures of the social security wealth "owned" by each family member. Unfortunately it seems unlikely that some of the required data on intrafamily transfers, especially the in-kind ones, will ever be available. A recent attempt by Barro [5, 1978] to evaluate the effect of social security on private saving therefore resorted to estimating the net response of aggregate private saving to social security using time series data. The specifications he considered were very similar to those adopted by Feldstein [22, 1974]. A social security wealth variable is added as an argument to a (rather unconventional) permanent-income type consumption function which has as its arguments current and lagged personal disposable income, net corporate retained earnings, the total public sector surplus, the unemployment rate, a measure of nonhuman wealth, and the stock of consumer durables. The social security wealth variable is supposed to measure the perceived net increase in permanent income—given current disposable income and the other arguments—that is implied by the expected future benefit payments and the expected future social security taxes. The calculation of such a measure is a heroic task. In spite of the considerable care Feldstein [22, 1974, pt. III] devoted to coverage, life expectancy and age structure, benefit and tax rates, growth of real per capita income, and the discount rate, the final product retains many arbitrary features. Feldstein assumed, for example, that the anticipated ratio of benefits to disposable income since the beginnings of the social security system was constant at its average value over the period the program has been in existence. Barro retained this assumption in some of his regressions. In others he made the equally arbitrary assumption that anticipated future benefits and anticipated future coverage (both relative to disposable income) correspond to their current values. This is an area where the use of more sophisticated expectations mechanisms (including rational expectations) cna be expected to yield interesting results. Feldstein's [22, 1974] findings that social security depresses private saving are confirmed in two[14] of Barro's regressions. In both of these the unemployment rate is omitted as an argument. The remaining regressions yield insignificant or even perverse coefficients for the social security wealth variable. In view of the shortcomings of the social security wealth variable and the rather ad hoc selection of other arguments for his consumption functions, Barro's results cannot be regarded as conclusive evidence either in favor or against the existence of a depressing effect of social security on private saving.

III. CONCLUSION

The debt-neutrality issue is important for a number of reasons. To the historian of economic thought it is of interest as one of the most ancient areas of professional inquiry and argument, spanning the two centuries since *The Wealth of Nations.*

To the economic theorist debt neutrality raises fundamental issues about the interrelationship of private and public economic activity. The subjects of public finance, macroeconomics, monetary theory, corporate finance, and international finance each contribute their varied perspectives to our understanding of the issues involved.

To the applied economist and the economic policymaker the debt neutrality debate is of the utmost importance. From a long-run perspective it concerns the consequences of alternative public sector financing rules for the growth of the domestic capital stock. From a short- and medium-term point of view the usefulness of deficit financing as a stabilization instrument is at stake.

On the basis of currently available theoretical models and empirical evidence our provisional conclusion is that the case for debt neutrality is not well established. Further empirical work is urgently required, however, before any conclusion can be more than tentative.

NOTES TO CHAPTER 2

1. Both Smith and Ricardo were, of course, assuming a fully employed economy.

2. Patinkin's later views on this subject were less sanguine. A compromise solution adopted by him was to define $M_O/p + k\ V_O/rp$ as the proper base for the operation of the real balance effect. (M_O is the initial stock of government money, V_O the number of government bonds, where each bond is a perpetuity with a coupon of \$1, r is the nominal rate of interest, and p the price level.) The constant k is between zero and one, measuring the degree to which individuals do not discount the future tax liabilities connected with government bonds [50, Patinkin, 1965, p. 289]. The debate about the proper base for the real balance effect has been continued in the inside money-outside money controversy [3, Boris Pesek and Thomas Saving, 1967; 61, Saving, 1970; 62, 1971; 51, Patinkin, 1969; 52, 1971; 29, Harry Johnson, 1969] about the role of private bank money as a component of net (private) wealth.

3. As it was not clear from Kochin's paper whether data points had been lost because of the lagged dependent variable in (1) and the difference operator in (2), we also estimated (1a) for the period 1953–71 and (2a) for the period 1954–71. The discrepancies were greater in each case.

4. We start our sample in 1948, but the results for the period 1952–76 are not significantly different from those reported here.

5. The population series is from the *Economic Report of the President*, 1978, Table B.22.

6. Correcting for first order autocorrelation yielded the following equation:

$$c = \underset{(4.04)}{122.91} + \underset{(89.99)}{0.876}\ yd$$

$\bar{R}^2 = 0.997$; $SE = 26.90$; $SSR = 18{,}809$; $DW = 1.59$; $\rho = 0.121$.

7. Permanent disposable income is defined here as the infinite sum of current and past values of disposable income, with declining geometric weights.

8. GPSR′, NPSR′, GSSR′, and NSSR′ include gross purchases of consumer durables in the numerator but do not include the imputed rental income from the ownership of durables in the denominator. No guess was ventured as to the magnitude of depreciation of consumer durables.

9. The unreliability of the capital consumption data may be part of the explanation.

10. Some of the same points are made by Boskin [6, 1978].

11. These results can be obtained from the authors on request.

12. Since the way in which the social security benefit formula is designed penalizes late retirement, individuals may choose to shorten their working life. This distortionary effect of social security would be a source of concern even to those who accept all other propositions required for debt-neutrality.

13. Katona's definition of saving is very narrow and amounts to the change in net liquid assets, disregarding nonliquid assets (such as houses, equity in life insurance and pension funds) and liabilities.

14. If we are willing to accept a t-statistic of 1.8, one more equation shows a positive significant effect of one of the social security wealth variables on consumption.

REFERENCES

1. ARENA, JOHN J. "Capital Gains and the 'Life Cycle' Hypothesis of Saving," *American Economic Review*, March 1964, *54* (2), pp. 107–11.

2. ____. "Postwar Stock Market Changes and Consumer Spending," *Review of Economics and Statistics*, Nov. 1965, *47* (4), pp, 375–91.

3. BARRO, ROBERT J. "Are Government Bonds Net Wealth?" *Journal of Political Economy*, Nov./Dec. 1974, *82*(6), pp. 1095–1117.

4. ____. "Reply to Feldstein and Buchanan," *Journal of Political Economy*, April 1976, *84*(2), pp. 343–49.

5. ____. *The Impact of Social Security on Private Saving, Evidence from U.S. Time Series.* With a Reply by MARTIN S. FELDSTEIN. Washington, D.C.: American Enterprise Institute, Studies in Social Security and Retirement Policies, 1978.

6. BOSKIN, MICHAEL J. "Taxation, Saving and the Rate of Interest," *Journal of Political Economy*, April 1978, *86*(2), Part II, pp. S3–S27.

7. BOSWORTH, BARRY. "The Stock Market and the Economy," *Brookings Papers on Economic Activity*, 1975, (2), pp. 257–90.

8. BOWEN, WILLIAM G., DAVIS, RICHARD G., and KOPF, DAVID H. "The Public Debt: A Burden on Future Generations," *American Economic Review*, Sept. 1960, *50*(4), pp. 701–706.

9. BUCHANAN, JAMES M. *Public Principles of Public Debt.* Homewood, Ill.: Irwin, 1958.

10. ____. "Public Debt, Cost Theory and the Fiscal Illusion," in *Public Debt and Future Generations.* Edited by JAMES E. FERGUSON. Chapel Hill: University of North Carolina Press, 1964.

11. ____. "Barro on the Ricardian Equivalence Theorem," *Journal of Political Economy*, April 1976, *84*(2), pp. 337–42.

12. ____, and WAGNER, RICHARE E. *Democracy in Deficit: The Political Legacy of Lord Keynes.* New York: Academic Press, 1977.

13. BUITER, WILLEM H. "Crowding Out and the Effectiveness of Fiscal Policy," *Journal of Public Economics*, June 1977, *7*(3), pp. 309–28.

14. ____. "Government Finance in an Overlapping Generations Model with Gifts and Bequests," this volume.

15. CAGAN, PHILLIP. "The Effect of Pension Plans on Aggregate Saving," *NBER Occasional Paper*, No. 95, 1965.

16. CANNAN, EDWIN, ed. *An Inquiry into the Nature and Causes of the Wealth of Nations, by ADAM SMITH.* New York: The Modern Library, 1937.

17. CARLSON, KEITH M., and SPENCER, ROGER W. "Crowding Out and Its Critics," *Federal Reserve Bank of St. Louis Review*, Dec. 1975, *57*(12), pp. 2–17.

18. CASS, DAVID, and YAARI, MENAHEM E. "Individual Saving, Aggregate Capital Accumulation and Efficient Growth," in *Essays on the Theory of*

Optimal Economic Growth. Edited by KARL SHELL. New York: Maple Press, 1967.

19. DAVID, PAUL A., and SCADDING, JOHN L. "Private Savings: 'Ultra-rationality,' Aggregation and Denison's Law," *Journal of Political Economy*, March/April 1974, *82*(1), pp. 225–49.

20. DENISON, EDWARD F. "A Note on Private Saving," *Review of Economics and Statistics*, August 1958, *40*(3), pp. 261–67.

21. DIAMOND, PETER A. "National Debt in a Neo-classical Growth Model," *American Economic Review*, Dec. 1965, *55*(5), pp. 1126–50.

22. FELDSTEIN, MARTIN S. "Social Security, Induced Retirement and Aggregate Capital Accumulation," *Journal of Political Economy*, Sept./Oct. 1974, *82*(5), pp. 905–26.

23. ____. "Perceived Wealth in Bonds and Social Security: A Comment," *Journal of Political Economy*, April 1976, *84*(2), pp. 331–36.

24. ____. "Social Security and Saving: The Extended Life Cycle Theory," *American Economic Review*, May 1976, *66*(2), pp. 77–86.

25. FERGUSON, JAMES M., ed. *Public Debt and Future Generations.* Chapel Hill, N.C.: University of North Carolina Press, 1964.

26. FRIEDMAN, MILTON. "The Kemp-Roth Free Lunch," *Newsweek*, Aug. 7, 1978, p. 59.

27. GURLEY, JOHN G., and SHAW, EDWARD S. *Money in a Theory of Finance.* Washington, D.C.: Brookings Institution, 1960.

28. HABERLER, GOTTFRIED. *Prosperity and Depression.* Third edition. Geneva: League of Nations, 1941.

29. JOHNSON, HARRY G. "Inside Money, Outside Money, Income, Wealth and Welfare in Monetary Theory," *Journal of Money, Credit and Banking*, Feb. 1969, *1*(1), pp. 30–45.

30. JUSTER, THOMAS F., and WACHTEL, PAUL. "A Note on Inflation and the Saving Rate," *Brookings Papers on Economic Activity*, 1972, (3), pp. 765–78.

31. KATONA, GEORGE. *The Powerful Consumer.* New York: McGraw-Hill, 1960.

32. ____. *Private Pensions and Individual Saving.* University of Michigan Survey Research Center, Monograph 40, 1965.

33. KOCHIN, LEWIS A. "Are Future Taxes Anticipated by Consumers?" *Journal of Money, Credit and Banking*, August 1974, *6*(3), pp. 385–94.

34. KUZNETS, SIMON. "Long-Term Changes in the National Product of the United States of America since 1870," in *Income and Wealth in the United States: Trends and Structure.* International Association for Research in Income and Wealth. Cambridge, England: Bowes and Bowes, 1952.

35. ____. *Capital in the American Economy: Its Formation and Financing.* New York: National Bureau of Economic Research, 1961.

36. ____. "Quantitative Aspects of the Economic Growth of Nations, IV: Long Term Trends in Capital Formation Proportions," *Economic Development and Cultural Change*, July 1961, *9*(4), Part II (entire issue).

37. LERNER, ABBA P. "Functional Finance and the Federal Debt," *Social Research*, Feb. 1943, *10*(1), pp. 38–51.

38. ____. *The Economics of Control.* New York: Macmillan, 1946.

39. MCCULLOCH, J.R., ed. *The Works of David Ricardo.* London: John Murray, 1871.

40. MEADE, JAMES A. "Is the National Debt a Burden?" *Oxford Economic Papers*, June 1958, *10*(2), pp. 163–83.

41. MILLER, MERTON H., and UPTON, CHARLES W. *Macroeconomics, A Neoclassical Introduction.* Homewood, Ill.: Irwin, 1974.

42. MISHAN, EZRA J. "How to Make a Burden of the Public Debt," *Journal of Political Economy*, Dec. 1963, *71* (6), pp. 529–42.

43. MISHKIN, FREDERIC S. "What Depressed the Consumer? The Household Balance Sheet and the 1973–75 Recession," *Brooking Papers on Economic Activity*, 1977, (1), pp. 123–64.

44. MODIGLIANI, FRANCO. "Long-Run Implications of Alternative Fiscal Policies and the Burden of the National Debt," *Economic Journal*, Dec. 1961, *71* (284), pp. 730–55.

45. ____, and MILLER, MERTON H. "The Cost of Capital, Corporation Finance, and the Theory of Investment," *American Economic Review*, June 1958, *48*(3), pp. 261–97.

46. MUNNELL, ALICIA H. *The Effect of Social Security on Personal Saving.* Cambridge, Mass.: Ballinger Publishing Company, 1974.

47. ____. "Private Pensions and Saving: New Evidence," *Journal of Political Economy*, Oct. 1976, *84*(5), pp. 1013–32.

48. PATINKIN, DON. "Price Flexibility and Full Employment," *American Economic Review*, Sept. 1948, *38*(4), pp. 543–64.

49. ____. *Money, Interest and Prices.* Evanston, Ill.: Row, Peterson, 1956.

50. ____. *Money, Interest and Prices*, 2nd edition. New York: Harper and Row, 1965.

51. ____. "Money and Wealth: A Review Article," *Journal of Economic Literature*, Dec. 1969, *7*(4), pp. 1140–60.

52. ____. "Inside Money, Monopoly Bank Profits and the Real Balance Effect," *Journal of Money, Credit, and Banking*, May 1971, *3*(2), Part I, pp. 271–75.

53. PESEK, BORIS, and SAVING, THOMAS R. *Money, Wealth and Economic Theory.* New York: Macmillan, 1967.

54. PIGOU, ARTHUR C. "The Classical Stationary State," *Economic Journal*, Dec. 1943, *53*(212), pp. 343–51.

55. ____. "Economic Progress in a Stable Environment," *Economica*, Aug. 1947, *14*(55), pp. 180–88.

56. RICARDO, DAVID. "On the Principles of Political Economy and Taxation." in *The Works of David Ricardo.* Edited by J.R. MCCULLOCH. London: John Murray, 1871.

57. ____. "Funding System," in *The Works and Correspondence of David Ricardo*, Vol. IV. Edited by PIERO SRAFFA. Cambridge, England: Cambridge University Press, 1951.

58. SAMUELSON, PAUL A. "Principles and Rules in Modern Fiscal Policy: A Neo-Classical Reformulation," in *Money, Trade and Economic Growth: Essays in Honor of Henry Williams.* New York: Macmillan, 1951.

59. ____. "The New Look in Tax and Fiscal Policy," Joint Committee on the Economic Report, 84th Congress, 1st Session, Federal Tax Policy for Economic Growth and Stability, Nov. 9, 1955. Washington, D.C.: U.S.G.P.O., 1956, pp. 229–34.

60. ____. "An Exact Consumption Loan Model of Interest with or without the Social Contrivance of Money," *Journal of Political Economy*, Dec. 1953, *66*(6), pp. 467–82.

61. SAVING, THOMAS R. "Outside Money, Inside Money and the Real Balance Effect," *Journal of Money, Credit and Banking*, Feb. 1970, *2*(1), pp. 83–99.

62. ____. "Inside Money, Short-Run Rents and the Real-Balance Effect," *Journal of Money, Credit and Banking*, May 1971, *3*(2), Part I, pp. 276–80.

63. SMITH, ADAM. "An Inquiry into the Nature and Causes of the Wealth of Nations," in *An Inquiry into the Nature and Causes of the Wealth of Nations.* Edited by EDWIN CANNAN. New York: The Modern Library, 1937.

64. SRAFFA, PIERO. *The Works and Correspondence of David Ricardo*, Vol. IV. Cambridge, England: Cambridge University Press, 1951.

65. STIGLITZ, JOSEPH E. "A Re-Examination of the Modigliani-Miller Theorem," *American Economic Review*, Dec. 1969, *59*(5), pp. 784–93.

66. ____. "On the Irrelevance of Corporate Financial Policy," *American Economic Review*, Dec. 1974, *64*(5), pp. 851–66.

67. TAYLOR, LESTER D. "Saving Out of Different Types of Income," *Brookings Papers on Economic Activity*, 1971, (2), pp. 383–407.

68. THOMPSON, EARL A. "Debt Instruments in Both Macroeconomic Theory and Capital Theory," *American Economic Review*, Dec. 1967, *57*(5), pp. 1196–1210.

69. TOBIN, JAMES. "Money Wage Rates and Employment," in *The New Economics.* Edited by SEYMOUR E. HARRIS. New York: Alfred A. Knopf, 1947. Reprinted in JAMES TOBIN, *Essays in Economics*, Vol. 1. Chicago: Markham, 1971.

70. ____. "Asset Holdings and Spending Decisions," *American Economic Review*, May 1952, *42*(3), pp. 109–23.

71. ____, and BUITER, WILLEM. "Fiscal and Monetary Policies, Capital Formation and Economic Activity," in *The Government and Capital Formation.* Edited by GEORGE M. VON FURSTENBERG. Cambridge, Mass.: Ballinger Publishing Co., 1980.

72. VICKREY, WILLIAM. "The Burden of the Public Debt: Comment," *American Economic Review*, March 1961, *51*(1), pp. 132–37.

Chapter 3

Social Security and Personal Saving: Survey and New Evidence

N. Bulent Gultekin and Dennis E. Logue

The massive amount of fictional wealth created by the unfunded, pay-as-you-go Social Security System and by partially funded private and government pension programs has alarmed public policymakers and business leaders. Their concern is about the effect which this type of wealth has upon the level of aggregate private saving and its composition. Essentially the main question is whether "sufficient" productive investment is being undertaken in the United States [16, Feldstein, 1977]. If individuals feel that adequate financing of their retirement years is available from fictional wealth, they may not save as much as they would otherwise. Alternatively, the taxes necessary to sustain payments to those already drawing upon fictional wealth may be so high as to prevent adequate saving by current wage earners. No productive real assets lie behind fictional wealth. The result of too much reliance on expected annuities from fictional wealth and too little reliance on private wealth will be a gross inadequacy of private saving and, ultimately, a reduction in productive investment. In consequence, the national economic growth rate may decline, and the tax burden on future generations necessary to maintain pay-as-you-go financing of these retirement income programs will become increasingly heavy.

The description of the problem generally stops here. But it is only here that the issue becomes interesting, for future generations may not accept this burden graciously. In fact, unfunded retirement income programs could be recontracted in their favor, leaving the generations of people who made decisions based upon fictional wealth worse off. In view of the uncertainty posed by the threat of recontracting, that is, of drastic reductions in the actual magnitude of benefits, a rational response by current generations is to ensure that the burden on future generations does not become large enough to prompt recontracting.

There are only two nearly foolproof ways of doing this. First, current generations can have more children so that future burdens are spread more thinly. Second, current generations can place less faith on present retirement income programs and save more on their own, perhaps entirely ignoring the existence of fictional wealth. Recent demographic trends suggest that the former is not happening, and this in part is responsible for the current problems with the Social Security System [27, Kaplan, 1976]. It is the purpose of this chapter to determine to what extent the latter may be occurring.

The Scope of Fictional Wealth

Fictional wealth is the difference between the lump-sum present value of the benefits to be derived from a particular retirement income program and the present value of the stream of personal contributions to that program discounted at some realistic rate of interest. In pension programs which are both economically and actuarily sound, there is no fictional wealth. Only in pension programs which promise payments in excess of realistic revenue expectations will fictional wealth exist. Social security is a good example of a fictional wealth generator. Pension and retirement programs for federal workers are partly funded, partly pay-as-you-go. Among state and local government programs, some are fully funded, others very nearly pay-as-you-go. Although, in principle, all should be very close to fully funded, the system taken as a whole is in a deficit position. Private corporate plans are mostly funded, though in absolute terms unfunded vested liabilities are large.

Estimates made for 1975 (prior to the social security legislation of 1977 which by raising taxes will tend to reduce the system's actuarial deficit) suggested that the Social Security System, which covers roughly 80 million workers, had an actuarial deficit of approximately $2 trillion [27, Kaplan, 1977, p. 7]. Other federal government pension programs, namely the civil service retirement program and the military retirement program, currently covering approximately 2.7 million and 2.2 million employees, respectively, had actuarial liabilities in excess of assets and prospective assets at current rates of accumulation (actuarial deficit) in 1975 of approximately $167 billion and $235 billion, respectively, compared with assets of $38 billion [40, Munnell and Connolly, 1976, pp. 76, 102].

State and local government pension programs, covering around 12 million employees, had an estimated $177 billion actuarial deficit in 1975, compared with assets of approximately $106 billion [40, Munnell and Connolly, 1976, pp. 76, 102]. Private sector pension plans covered roughly 30 million employees in 1975 and had assets of approximately $215 billion. No good external estimate of the magnitude of unfunded liabilities exists, but a tally of corporate reports by A.F. Ehrbar [13, 1977, p. 104] suggests they were approximately $50 billion in 1975. Total fictional wealth approximated $2.6 trillion in 1975. This amount is so large that one must pause to ask whether this could be paid even if there were no effects of this fictional wealth on private saving.

Recently enacted legislation, the Employee Retirement Income Security Act of 1974 (ERISA), was aimed in part at correcting the underfunding of pension plans in the private sector. One of its provisions requires that private plans must be fully funded within forty years. Another of its provisions limits the ability of an employer to recontract pension benefits by putting a fairly stringent limit on the number of years that an employee can remain unvested in the pension plan and requiring the adoption of comparatively liberal age and eligibility standards for participation in the plan. Similar legislation does not exist for government employee pension plans or for the Social Security System. Attempts to place the Social Security System on a firmer financial footing through increased taxation were recently passed (Public Law 95–216, December 20, 1977). However, there have been no serious attempts to reduce social security benefits; on the other hand, there have been recent attempts by Congress to reduce social security taxes from the levels set in the 1977 legislation. This would entail general revenue financing but completely skirts the question of the influence of high tax rates on personal saving.

Relative to the actuarial deficit in the Social Security System, the deficits in the other retirement income programs are quite small. It is thus easy to understand why social security has received the most attention in the dispute over private saving. Moreover, the social security deficit has grown continuously; large deficits in the other systems are more recent. The Social Security System covers more employees, 80 million, than any of the other retirement income programs. Private sector programs cover 30 million workers, but the private programs seem not to be in such grave difficulty. Other government programs—federal and state and local—are, however, also in severe actuarial deficit; they have created substantial fictional wealth in recent years, but even now cover at most 18 million employees.

Prior to the mid-1960s, unfunded liabilities of state and local governments were low absolutely because they had only half or fewer employees than they have now, wages were relatively low, and pension benefits were low even relative to wages. At the federal level, the story was much the same for civil service. For the military, the draft enabled the maintenance of sizable armed forces with high turnover at low wage rates, so future pension costs only had to be reckoned for career military personnel, and this comprised a small fraction of total military manpower. In short, fictional wealth creation by programs other than social security has been comparatively small until recently and, at any rate, does not affect nearly as many individuals.

While the principal focus of this chapter is thus the influence of social security wealth on saving, attention is also paid in our empirical work to private pension fund assets. These have often been cited as having a special influence on private saving [8, Cagan, 1965].

Fictional wealth created by government programs can be recontracted. Private pension plans are less amenable to recontracting because of ERISA. Federal civil service employees and the military and state and local government employees could be required to increase their contributions by sizable margins. Similarly, the payment of pension benefits to retired government employees who are currently holding nongovernment jobs could be curtailed. Also, federal employees and those state and local employees who are not now members of the Social Security System could be forced to join the system; then their regular pension benefits could be integrated with their social security benefits, thus effectively reducing regular benefits. These considerations argue for focusing mainly upon the Social Security System as the prime creator of fictional wealth.

Methods of Analysis

Two broad forms of analysis are used in our assessment of fictional wealth. The first is termed primitive. In effect, we examine the outcome of economic behavior to see if the creation of fictional wealth has any detectable effect. The literature is surveyed selectively, and we search out relationships without regard to causality. The implicit model accepts the fact that, if there is growing scarcity of capital, rates of return on existing capital should rise. Accordingly, a rise in fictional wealth should, if accompanied by a reduction in private saving, be associated with higher real rates of return on physical capital, other things equal. We find this not to be the case.

The second class of models explored is the life cycle model of saving and consumption developed by Albert Ando and Franco Modigliani [1, 1963]. This model has been used by other researchers to determine the effects of social security wealth on saving. After a careful review of the work of others with this model, we formulate our own version, which includes actual pension fund assets and some additional variables. This model is estimated using flow of funds measures of personal saving; these include investment in consumer durables. The results of our estimation using this conceptual basis suggest that social security wealth has some effect on personal saving. Moreover, we find that the magnitude of social security contributions has influenced personal saving. Both social security wealth and contributions have over the years moved quite closely together. It is thus unfortunate that empirically the results do not yield clear guidance as to which of these is the most direct channel of influence. However, a causal relationship between social security taxes and personal saving seems most consistent with neoclassical models of economic behavior.

Next, household portfolio behavior is examined. Our emphasis on household behavior intentionally ignores the potentially offsetting saving behavior of corporations. We seek to determine whether social security wealth and/or social security contributions have had any influence on the allocation of household assets among financial instruments. Social security wealth and taxes are found to play important roles in determining the composition of household savings.

The chapter ends with a brief evaluation of the wealth effects and possible effects on saving of the recent change in social security tax rates and wage bases, and how the move to put the system on a comparatively sound financial footing may affect personal saving. We also consider the possible influence on saving and the Social Security System that may arise from the prohibition of mandatory retirement at age sixty-five.

I. PRIMITIVE EVIDENCE

The social security program was started in the mid-1930s at the depth of the Great Depression. Its goals were to force individuals to "save" on a regular basis through their periodic social security contributions, to provide a retirement income floor, and to encourage older workers to leave the work-force, thus opening jobs for younger workers.

The present structure of benefits is generous relative to the level of benefits which prevailed earlier. Benefits have been raised on twelve occasions; on the last such occasion Congress indexed benefits to consumer prices so that constant real purchasing power could be achieved by beneficiaries. In 1939, the maximum individual monthly benefit was $80 per month; by 1975 it was $523.28. More tellingly, in 1950, the average annual benefit paid by social security was $816.82 in 1970 dollars, but by 1974 the average annual benefit has risen to $1,729.20 in 1970 dollars [33, Logue, 1979, Chapters 1, 6]. The social security tax rate or wage base has been raised twenty-two times since 1939, and large increases in both rates and base took effect in 1979. In the early days of the program, maximum contributions were comparatively small, $30.00 per year. In 1978, maximum social security taxes to be paid by employees stand at $1,071, and in 1979 the maximum rises to $1,404. On an aggregate basis, social security contributions as a percent of GNP were 0.1 percent in 1950, 2.1 percent in 1960, 3.9 percent in 1970, and 4.6 percent in 1977.

David and Scadding [11, 1974] examined the ratio of corporate saving to gross national product and personal saving to gross national product. A simple treatment of the personal saving rate shows a secular decline; however, when consumer durable purchases and the imputed return on durables are included, there is no secular trend in that saving rate. Together, the corporate and personal saving interact effectively. When the personal saving rate dips, the corporate saving rate seems to rise, and vice versa, so that corporate saving appears to be a good substitute for personal saving. The net effect is that the sum of the two, the gross private saving rate, does not vary much from year to year.

If social security wealth affected saving, the private saving rate should reflect this. Similarly, if other types of fictional pension wealth affected saving, there should be a noticeable downward trend in the private saving rate, particularly the personal saving rate; but this has not been the case. Regarding the funded portion of retirement income programs, pension funds offered by corporations, state and local governments, and the federal government—if these were not perceived by individuals as being real wealth, but rather were suspected of being fictional—an upward trend in the personal saving rate would have been expected. But this was not found, either. On the basis of this primitive evidence, there appears to have been no aggregate consequence of fictional wealth. Moreover, there seems to have been a substitution between pension saving and other savings, with the former expanding relative to the latter so as to keep the gross private saving rate approximately constant.

David and Scadding also note that, over the period studied, there was a significant shift in the gross composition of personal saving away from traditional modes and toward durable goods. Fictional wealth may have contributed to this shift; this issue will be taken up in some detail later.

Rates of Return

If fictional wealth creates disincentives to save, then one would expect a secular rise in the rate of return on real assets. Similarly, if saving in the form of consumer durable purchases was causing problems in the accumulation of capital for investment, rates of return on real capital should rise over time, coincident with increases in fictional wealth. Recently, studies by Daniel Holland and Stewart Myers [24, 1977] and Martin Feldstein and Lawrence Summers [18, 1977] have addressed this issue. Neither pair of researchers finds any evidence of rising rates of return.

Holland and Myers's work is more recent and complete. They examine the rate of return of all nonfinancial corporations and define rate of return as operating income, that is, aftertax profits with inventory valuation and capital consumption adjustments plus net interest paid divided by the replacement cost of nonfinancial corporations' depreciable net capital stock and inventories. Before-tax and after-tax rates of return are computed. For illustrative purposes the before-tax rates of return averaged 10.0 percent in the period 1936–40, 13.5 percent in the period 1951–55, 13.6 percent in the 1961–65 period, 12.8 percent over 1966–70, and 9.4 percent for the years 1971–76. After-tax rates of return followed much the same pattern, though they differed by more than a scale factor, owing to changes in effective corporate tax rates. If anything, returns on real capital seem to have declined recently, not risen.

This evidence is not conclusive because it refers to average rates of return, not returns on incremental investment. The returns on incremental investment over the period of greatest growth in fictional wealth, the late 1960s and early 1970s, could have been quite substantial; but this is hard to document, and, to us, unlikely.

At this stage, another type of explicit measure must be introduced—a real measure of net social security wealth. This wealth was first computed by Martin Feldstein [14, 1974] and used subsequently in work by Alicia Munnell [36, 1974], Michael Darby, [10, 1977], and Robert Barro [3, 1978]. The same data are used here, with updated estimates of Feldstein's original work.

At any given time the aggregate discounted expected social security benefits to be received by those currently working and those already retired are measured. Then they are netted against the aggregate discounted expected future social security taxes to be paid by those currently working. The result is fictional or social security wealth. It represents an economically meaningful estimate of the actuarial deficit of the Social Security System. Though one may quibble with the rates chosen for discounting, this measure seems fair. Having no obvious biases, it should at least be highly correlated with measures using other discount rates. For illustrative purposes, in 1972 dollars net social security wealth approximated $158 billion in 1940, $246.1 billion in 1950, $527 billion in 1960, $1.2 trillion in 1970, and $1.6 trillion in 1974, according to Feldstein's calculations.

With social security wealth growing, and rates of return on capital stable, statistical analysis designed to uncover any direct relationship between the two without regard to other factors is bound to fail. There seems to be no such simple connection. In fact, both types of primitive evidence—gross private saving rates and rates of return on real capital—suggest fictional wealth has no discernible effect on aggregate saving. Primitive evidence sheds little light, however, on the relationship between the composition of private saving and social security wealth. Moreover, because it does not explore all the determinants of saving, it permits no definitive conclusion.

Survey Evidence

Phillip Cagan [8, 1965] and George Katona [29. 1965] began their inquiries with some notion of the life cycle and substitutability between personal assets and assets accumulated through a type of forced saving. They did not explicitly address the social security issue, but did ask whether the existence of private pension plans had any effect on personal saving. Both found that personal saving was enhanced by the existence of private pension plans.

Cagan surveyed the saving behavior of 15,000 members of the Consumers Union. He observed what he called a "recognition effect." The existence of private pensions heightened awareness of retirement prospects and hence encouraged individual saving.

Katona interviewed roughly 2,000 consumers in 1962–63, and also found that personal saving is positively influenced by private pension plans. Katona argued that individuals with pension plans believe the goal of adequate retirement income to be quite feasible and hence save on their own so that this goal can be reached. Absence of a pension plan makes this goal seem so much more difficult that it becomes apparently unreachable. Accordingly, less private saving is done.

Neither researcher considered the fact that private pension benefits are often coupled with mandatory retirement provisions. These mandatory retirement provisions can result in a longer retirement period. Hence saving could be stimulated by that prospect, not by recognition and not by goal feasibility. Moreover, both researchers were dealing with comparatively elite samples which may be subject to self-selection bias. Therefore, the findings of their research should not be taken to imply anything about the behavior of the mass of individuals confronted with fictional retirement wealth.

II. LIFE CYCLE MODELS OF SAVING AND ACCUMULATION

This model of consumption/investment decisions begins with the explicit premises that the rationale for working and earning income is to consume and that a smooth consumption stream over time is to be preferred to a bumpy one.

An individual implicitly makes several estimates at the time work-life commences. These are first, the length of life; second, the retirement date; and third, the present value, using some satisfactory discount rate, of future income. With these estimates an individual can plan consumption over the life cycle [31, Lesnoy and Hambor, 1975].

Initially, annual income may be low relative to the size of the annuity that might be purchased if lifetime income were available in a lump sum at the start of a working career. Accordingly, since a higher level of consumption could be afforded with only modest changes in the time pattern of actual income, the individual may borrow against future income to improve current consumption opportunities. The amount borrowed to supplement current actual income will depend upon estimates of future income, interest rates, the size of the accumulation of wealth that the individual wants for retirement purposes, and the degree of certainty surrounding the expectation of future income. For those individuals whose forebears left inheritances or lump-sum wealth, the consumption pattern depends on current income and willingness to draw down wealth, in addition to borrowing opportunities and personal circumstances.

Later in life, the typical individual finds that his actual annual income exceeds the annuity that could have been purchased with a lump-sum payment at the beginning of his career. The excess funds are initially used to pay back past borrowings and are subsequently invested for retirement purposes. The magnitude of the funds set aside annually for retirement purposes is a function first of the estimated years between retirement and death; second, of the return that might be earned on those funds prior to and during retirement years; and third, of desired consumption during retirement years. Savings are drawn down to support consumption during retirement years, and, in the model's simplest form, wealth is exhausted at the time of death.

This life cycle model of consumption/investment decisions requires an array of complex calculations; nonetheless, empirical work done by Ando and Modigliani [1, 1963] and others appears to support it. It is a utility maximizing model and demands only that people act in what they perceive to be their self-interest. It is within this framework that the influence of social security wealth, or indeed any kind of fictional wealth may be analyzed.

Social security forces saving throughout the life cycle. In the early working years, rather than not saving at all a worker now is forced to save. If the returns on social security saving were the same as the returns on regular saving, or alternatively, comparable to borrowing rates, social security would have no influence on the lifetime pattern of consumption/investment decisions depicted by the model. In the early years of a working career, when borrowing would normally occur, the worker will borrow just a little more than otherwise, roughly enough to offset the consumption-reducing effects of forced social security saving. The qualification is used because differences in the rate of return on social security saving and the borrowing rate may prevent a complete offset. Behavior later in a worker's life cycle would be analogous. In short, the worker could just about fully offset the entire effect of forced social security saving through private action. This would be true if the Social Security System were actuarially fair, yielded only market rates of return, and had no other effects. These conditions may not hold.

The first violation occurs because of the age-dependent nature of the Social Security System. Heavy financial penalties are levied against any worker who continues working after the age of sixty-five. Social security payments are reduced by roughly 50 cents for every dollar of earned income. Thus, the Social Security System induces earlier retirement [5, Boskin, 1977; 9, Campbell and Campbell, 1976; 14, Feldstein, 1974; 36, Munnell, 1974].

When the Social Security System was first established, the age of sixty-five was chosen for beginning to collect retirement benefits. Remaining life expectancy at age sixty-five in the late 1930s was generally less than ten years, depending on sex and race. (Good data on mortality of blacks is not available.) So the financial penalties associated with failure to retire at sixty-five were not great. Currently, however, remaining life expectancy at age sixty-five ranges from 13.1 to 17.3 years, depending on race and sex, and the penalties are operative until one reaches the age of seventy-two.

The combined result of the social security and mandatory retirement provisions has been to encourage, in some cases force, workers to retire earlier than they otherwise might chose. In the life cycle model elaborated earlier, this encourages personal saving because it lengthens the retirement period and shortens working life. It reduces an individual's lifetime income expectation. This feature of the social security program could lead to higher rather than lower personal saving.

For many of those currently retired and receiving benefits, the real rate of return on their social security contributions has exceeded the rates of return that could have been achieved through market investments of similar risk. Over the past fifty years, the real realized return on Treasury bills has approximated 0.1 percent and the real realized return on Treasury bonds has approximated 1 percent [26, Ibbotson and Sinquefield, 1977]. The benefit structure is skewed, however, so that the rate of return achieved by low-income workers, those earning less than the annual social security wage base, is greater than those earning the social security wage base or more. To yield higher than market returns, the system cannot pay benefits out of an accumulated trust fund, past contributions plus investment returns. Rather it must sponsor intergenerational transfers from current workers to former workers. To the extent that current workers believe that the system may continue to pay higher than market returns, which it will unless major changes are made [28, Kaplan, 1978], personal saving may be reduced by more than the amount of any increase in social security benefits and contributions. In the context of the life cycle model, if a starting worker realizes that the return on forced social security saving can exceed market returns, he may borrow more earlier in life and save less later in life.

The model can be made more complex by asking whether there are any private actions that might be undertaken which nullify the negative influence on saving. The existence of private intergenerational transfers might provide just such an offset. Theoretical arguments on their behalf were developed by Barro [2, 1974] and Merton Miller and Charles Upton [34, 1974].

There are two plausible types of private intergenerational transfers. The first goes from parents to children in the form of bequests or inheritances. The second might go from children to parents in the form of gifts, by allowing retired parents to live with them or in some other way.

Consider the bequest motive. Parents' life cycle consumption/investment decisionmaking may be influenced by the consumption opportunities of their children. For example, if a child qualifies for a special tour of Europe, the parents may offer to pay for it. Alternatively, parents may derive utility themselves from making bequests, irrespective of how these might influence their children's consumption.

An increase in social security benefits depresses the after-tax earnings and consumption possibilities of the current generation who pay taxes to finance the increase. The equilibrium of those who are in dissaving or retirement phases of their life cycles is upset by an increase in social security benefits. To restore equilibrium, they will increase the magnitude of their bequest. The extra saving that goes into this bequest will, under ideal conditions, compensate for the increase in social security taxes that must be borne by their children.

Barro's argument is more complex; it requires either that every generation behave this way or that the first generation establish a bequest large enough to provide an annuity from which future social security taxes can be paid.

The argument can also work in reverse. Suppose a given generation expects support in their old age from their children, and children voluntarily support their parents in old age. In this situation, the Social Security System relieves the private burden of providing old-age support, but makes it a public burden. In the private framework, there is an intergenerational transfer just as in the public system. There may in fact be, under highly idealized conditions, a one-for-one substitution. In this case, social security would again leave private saving unaffected.

It may be helpful to summarize the theoretical influences which social security may have on personal saving. First, it induces earlier retirement, lengthening the retirement period and thus encouraging saving. Second, the returns on social security saving may exceed returns on personal saving, so social security may reduce personal saving. Third, if an operative bequest motive is at work and recognition of the impact of social security on future generations is considered, the detrimental effect of social security on saving can be offset either by private bequests or by a reduction in voluntary transfers from children to parents.

Empirical work is necessary to resolve these issues, but, before that, a number of other factors deserve mention.

First, demographic factors are at work which will influence the Social Security System in the United States. In 1974, the proportion of people aged sixty-five and over was approximately 10.3 percent. By 1985, this proportion will climb to 10.8 percent, to 11.0 percent in 2000, to 15.0 percent by 2025, and to 16.0 percent by 2050, and, assuming zero population growth will remain there [43, Schulz, 1976, pp. 5, 6]. The proportion of people to be assisted by social security benefits is rising. To maintain the present level of benefits in a pay-as-you-go system, the tax burden on working generations must rise, perhaps by as much as 50 percent in real terms. Even with an operative bequest motive, it is unclear whether sufficient increases in saving could be achieved to offset this influence. Additionally, with such potentially high tax rates, social security beneficiaries may run the risk of being recontracted, that is, they may experience a substantial, legislatively condoned reduction in real benefits.

The life cycle model above does not take account of this type of uncertainty, though it should. Even without a bequest motive, to the extent that future social security benefits are uncertain personal saving will decline less than otherwise.

Second, the presence of this type of uncertainty provides an additional reason for bequests and inheritances. To avoid recontracting, potential retirees may do what they can to insure that income opportunities are sufficient for future generations so that the social security benefits funded from future taxes are not burdensome. In the Barro [2, 1974] and Miller-Upton [35, 1974] formulations, bequests are private, and they represent transfers of fungible wealth. They are parents to children arrangements, but they need not be. Bequests could be made institutionally by building schools, investing heavily in research and development, and so forth. Similarly, bequests, even private bequests, can be aimed at building human capital in children. For example, funds, which would be classified as consumption in the National Income and Product Accounts, could be expended on a child's education which, in turn, would enable him or her to earn a higher income in later life.

Life Cycle Model Estimates

Numerous empirical attempts have been made to characterize the essence of the life cycle model of consumption and savings. At least four researchers, Martin Feldstein [14, 1974; 15, 1976], Alicia Munnell [36, 1974], Michael Darby [10, 1977], and Robert Barro [3, 1978], have addressed the issue of the influence of social security wealth on consumption/savings decisions, and their work will be reviewed here. Two other papers, one by Martin Feldstein and Anthony Pellechio [17, 1977] and one by Lawrence Kotlikoff [30, 1977], ask the more direct question of what has been the effect of social security on wealth accumulation. This work is also examined. All except Barro find that the Social Security System significantly depressed personal saving and wealth accumulation.

Feldstein [14, 1974] made the seminal contribution in this area. Moreover, he constructed a measure of social security wealth widely used by other researchers. For this measure, he computed the present value of future benefits which people working at various times expected to receive. This is gross social security wealth. By deducting the discounted value of expected future social security taxes, he obtained a time series measure of net social security wealth. He then used these in a regression analysis which was designed to determine the influence of social security on personal consumption expenditures. Using the net social security wealth concept and putting all dollar variables in real (1971) per capita dollars, he obtained the following representative results (*t*-values in parentheses):

For the period 1929–71, excluding 1941–46:

$$\begin{aligned}\text{Personal Consumption Expenditures} = {} & \underset{(8.1)}{218} + \underset{(11.7)}{0.528} \text{ Disposable Personel Income} \\ & + \underset{(4.0)}{0.137} \text{ Disposable Personal Income Lagged} \\ & + \underset{(5.1)}{0.376} \text{ Corporate Retained Earnings} \\ & + \underset{(3.2)}{0.013} \text{ Net Worth of Households Lagged} \\ & + \underset{(3.6)}{0.032} \text{ Social Security Wealth (net)}\end{aligned}$$

$SSR = 3{,}548$; Durbin-Watson Statistic 1.85 (no other summary statistics).

For the period 1947–71:

$$\begin{aligned}\text{Personal Consumption Expenditures} = {} & \underset{(2.2)}{232} + \underset{(6.4)}{0.535} \text{ Disposable Personal Income} \\ & + \underset{(1.4)}{0.119} \text{ Disposable Personal Income Lagged} \\ & + \underset{(2.6)}{0.349} \text{ Corporate Retained Earnings} \\ & + \underset{(2.0)}{0.014} \text{ Net Worth of Households Lagged} \\ & + \underset{(1.2)}{0.035} \text{ Social Security Wealth (net)}\end{aligned}$$

$SSR = 2{,}926$; Durbin-Watson Statistic = 1.78 (no other summary statisitcs)

Feldstein's elegant model says that personal consumption this period is a function of income, this period's and last's, corporate retained earnings, last period's regular wealth, and social security wealth. His results using other measures of social security wealth are qualitatively similar and show comparable effects on consumption.

Feldstein found that every one-dollar increase in net social security wealth would induce more than 3 cents of added consumption. This coefficient is comparatively stable between the two periods, but it is not statistically significant for the period 1947–71.

Though Feldstein's theoretical formulation clearly recognized the induced retirement effect of social security, there was no variable explicitly designed to account for it in his formulation. Munnell [36, 1974] did attempt to construct such a variable.

Munnell hypothesized that there would be both a saving and retirement effect of social security. Our concern is primarily with the saving effect. Formulating equations in real ($1958) per capita terms, representative results (Munnell, Table 3) are:

For the period 1929–69, excluding 1941–46:

$$
\begin{aligned}
\text{Personal Saving} = {} & \underset{(0.6)}{84.63} + \underset{(1.8)}{0.199}\ \text{Disposable Personal Income} \\
& \underset{(0.9)}{-0.012}\ \text{Household Net Worth Lagged} \\
& \underset{(1.1)}{-0.033}\ \text{Social Security Wealth (net)} \\
& \underset{(1.1)}{-0.144}\ \text{Disposable Personal Income} \times \text{Labor Force Participation for Men over 65} \\
& \underset{(2.7)}{-5.35}\ \text{Unemployment Rate}
\end{aligned}
$$

$R^2 = 0.91$ (no other summary statistics)

For the period 1946–69:

$$
\begin{aligned}
\text{Personal Saving} = {} & \underset{(1.2)}{-197.2} + \underset{(2.7)}{0.487}\ \text{Disposable Personal Income} \\
& \underset{(0.8)}{-0.017}\ \text{Household Net Worth Lagged} \\
& \underset{(2.3)}{-0.117}\ \text{Social Security Wealth (net)} \\
& \underset{(1.4)}{-0.198}\ \text{Disposable Personel Income} \times \text{Labor Force Participation for Men over 65} \\
& \underset{(1.6)}{-8.428}\ \text{Unemployment Rate}
\end{aligned}
$$

$R^2 = 0.70$ (no other summary statistics)

The induced retirement effect was intended to be captured by the labor-force participation variable, but it is certainly not clear that this is the best that could be done. Other equations designed to explain retirement saving were also formulated. These, too, show that social security has a negative influence on saving overall, but a positive influence on retirement saving owing to the induced retirement effect.

For Michael Darby [10, 1977] the basic concepts employed are similar, but different variables are used. Notable among these are the lagged stock of consumer durables in lieu of wealth. Also, the relative price of durables to nondurables, the nominal interest rate for long-term government bonds, and the money supply are included among the explanatory variables.

Darby, as others, measures in real ($1958) per capita terms. His dependent variable is consumer expenditures:

For the period 1929–74, 1941–46 excluded, representative results are:

Consumer Expenditures:	=	21.65 + 0.835 (1.25) (23.30)	Permanent Income
		+0.546 (13.77)	Transitory Income
		+0.039 (0.79)	Money Stock (M2)
		−0.148 (−2.57)	Stock of Consumers' Durable Goods Lagged
		−22.01 (−1.23)	Ratio of Durable Goods Prices to Nondurable Goods Prices
		+3.54 (2.89)	Nominal Yield on Long-term Government Bonds
		+0.025 (1.33)	Social Security Wealth (net)

$\bar{R}^2 = 0.9997$; $SEE = 2.58$; Durbin-Watson Statistic = 2.27

For the period 1947–74:

Consumer Expenditures:	=	−5.36 + 0.905 (−0.09) (13.36)	Permanent Income
		+0.539 (6.90)	Transitory Income
		+0.010 (1.15)	Money Stock (M2)

For the period 1947–74: *(continued)*	−0.178 (−2.25)	Stock of Consumers Durables Lagged
	−14.56 (−0.32)	Ratio of Durable Goods Prices to Nondurable Goods Prices
	+1.83 (0.90)	Nominal Interest Rate on Long-term Government Bonds
	+0.003 (0.09)	Social Security Wealth (net)

$\bar{R}^2 = 0.9995$; $SEE = 2.97$; Durbin-Watson Statistic = 2.33

For other definitions of the money stock and for other social security wealth measures, comparable results were obtained.

As in the other regression surveyed, the social security wealth variable again has the "correct" sign. The existence of social security wealth seems to reduce personal saving. However, no researcher has found the variable, any variable measuring social security wealth—gross wealth, net wealth, or simply annual social security contributions—to be significant in both the overall and the recent period.

When data drawn from the period of the Great Depression and prior to the inauguration of the Social Security System are used, social security appears to influence consumption. But it is unclear whether the result occurs because of a true social security effect or because of the uniqueness of the observations from the depression years.

Robert Barro [3, 1978] also makes life cycle estimates of the effect of social security wealth. Table 3–1 shows some representative results. Besides standard income and wealth variables, Barro includes the real nonresidential business capital stock, the lagged stock of consumer durables net of housing, a measure of the government surplus or deficit, corporate retained earnings, and the unemployment rate multiplied by personal disposable income in his specification. Two specifications of social security wealth are used. One is the Feldstein measure of gross social security wealth. The second is a measure of his own construction: social security benefits per recipient multiplied by the ratio of covered workers in a year to total labor force. We report findings only from the gross social security wealth measure.

Barro points out that social security wealth is only nearly significant when the unemployment rate is left out of the equation. He also finds that its importance is diminished substantially when no intercept is allowed in the regression equation.

Table 3–1. Representative Summary of Barro's Results on Consumer Expenditures *(t-values in parentheses)*[a]

	Constant	*Disposable Personal Income*	*Disposable Personal Income Lagged*	*Household Net Worth Lagged*	*Real per Capita Capital Stock*	*Stock of Household Durables Net of Housing Lagged*
Period 1929–1974	—	0.79 (19.75)	0.10 (2.50)		0.035 (1.59)	−0.153 (−2.19)
	146 (1.76)	0.71 (10.14)	0.08 (2.00)		0.005 (0.19)	−0.016 (−0.16)
	138 (1.86)	0.70 (11.67)	0.09 (2.25)	0.004 (0.57)		−0.019 (−0.30)
Period 1947–1974	—	0.75 (10.71)	0.16 (2.29)	0.008 (1.00)		−0.062 (−0.78)
	113 (0.53)	0.69 (4.93)	0.13 (1.44)	0.005 (0.50)		−0.050 (−0.60)

Table 3–1. continued

	Social Security Wealth Gross	*Personal Disposable Income × Unemployment Rate*	*Retained Earnings*	*Government Surplus*	R^2	*D.W.*
Period 1929–1974	0.005 (0.56)	0.38 (4.22)	0.17 (1.55)	0.21 (3.00)	0.99	2.11
	0.015 (1.50)	0.27 (2.45)	0.27 (2.25)	0.22 (3.50)	0.99	2.15
	0.014 (1.40)	0.27 (2.45)	0.25 (2.08)	0.20 (2.90)	0.99	2.13
Period 1947–1974	−0.005 (−0.50)	0.37 (2.47)	0.21 (1.17)	0.20 (2.50)	0.99	1.98
	0.014 (0.39)	0.36 (2.40)	0.24 (1.26)	0.20 (2.50)	0.99	1.98

[a] *t*-values from our calculations; not reported in original paper.

Barro's results show that the government surplus or deficit has an effect on consumption. A one-dollar government surplus leads, other things equal, to an approximately 20-cent rise in consumption expenditures. Correspondingly, a deficit leads to a reduction in consumption expenditures. The trade-off is not one-for-one.

When the government promises to pay a certain benefit, it is analogous to the government's issuing a bond. If the government funds the bond or backs the bond with a real asset, no fictional wealth is created. If there is no funding, fictional wealth is created so long as both future tax liabilities and bond returns are discounted at different rates.

With operative bequest motives, government budget surpluses and deficits should not have a statistically significant partial influence on consumption, particularly when income and employment are held constant. During government budget surplus periods, individuals should save less than otherwise by exactly the amount of the surplus. During deficits, savings should rise by the amount of the deficit, since deficits ultimately impact upon future taxes. Barro's finding of only a partial private offset to government saving suggests an imperfect bequest motive. Moreover, it suggests the possibility of "crowding out," that is, of government debt absorbing too great a portion of private saving. If a one-dollar deficit increases saving by only 20 cents, 80 percent of the deficit must be financed by funds that might otherwise be directed to private investment.

For illustrative purposes only, Table 3–2 shows the effect on personal saving which social security wealth would have had in 1974 if each of the estimated equations were correct.

Table 3–2. Estimated Effects of Social Security on Personal Saving in 1974

	Coefficient on Social Security Wealth	*Estimated Personal Saving without Social Security*	*Difference between Estimated and Actual Saving*
Feldstein	0.035 (net)	$135.4 billion	$63.68 billion
Munnell (pure saving effect)		$131.74 billion	$64.04 billion
[net saving effect (1969)] [a]		$41.8 billion	–$3.6 billion
Darby	0.025 (net)	$117.19 billion	$45.49 billion
Barro	0.014 (gross)	$114.51 billion	$42.81 billion

[a]Representative estimates across each author's set of regressions are reported here. Munnell's net 1969 results were obtained from [37, 1977, p. 117].

New Time-Series Estimates

As is evident, the time-series data useful for life cycle model testing have been used many times. It is questionable whether slightly respecified equations will yield results which are any more or less convincing than those which have already been reported. Nonetheless, there are some intriguing aspects that have not yet been explored.

The first is whether investment in human capital has any influence on personal saving. As noted, bequests may be left in at least two forms: first, actual wealth, and second, investment in human capital could be made on behalf of future generations. In the latter instance, the normal way in which personal saving is reported will not reflect this type of saving. Investment in human capital is generally accounted for as consumption expenditures. In our estimation, we use private expenditures on education and research as a proxy for human capital expenditures. This proxy is imperfect, but is very likely highly correlated with whatever a perfect measure might be. A negative sign is expected.

A second notable difference between our specification and others is that we attempt to represent fictional wealth coming from other government pension programs. This is done for federal civil service employees and for state and local government employees. Military is excluded because it is difficult, if not impossible, to get a reasonably satisfactory measure of the percentage of military who expect to collect pension benefits. The existence of the draft until the early 1970s makes proportional estimates highly questionable.

The proxy used for this type of fictional wealth was constructed as follows. Average pension benefits for state and local and federal civil service government employees were computed for each sample year. This average benefit was multiplied by the then current number of workers in each category. This yielded a crude proxy for one year's expected benefits, for each category of government employee. The actual size of the state and local pension fund was then deducted from the state and local annual benefit to current employees. If assets exceeded the annual benefit, the amount was noted as zero. Otherwise, the amount was a positive number. This was added to the federal civil service fictional wealth proxy. This measure essentially assumes that anticipated future benefits and anticipated contributions to pension funds roughly correspond to their current values. This measure is not an actuarial wealth variable such as Feldstein's social security measure. It does not consider possible future changes in benefit or contribution levels. It measures the amount which might be paid in any future year when all current workers have retired less the amount that is on hand. Construction of an actuarially sound time-series measure would not be possible without much more detail on local government finances and government employee demographics than is generally available. Nonetheless, this measure may have reasonable correlation with more satisfactory measures.

Another feature of our model is our distinction between real pension fund wealth, that is, actual pension fund assets, and net personal financial assets. Personal financial assets are safe in the sense that they can always be converted into consumption goods. The assets of private and state and local pension funds are not easily convertible. If an employee is fired prior to vesting, his share of pension fund assets is lost. Similarly, through a series of bad investments or if security market performance is poorer than expected, pension fund assets may be inadequate to meet expectations. In short, pension fund assets are riskier than personally held assets and hence should have a different influence on saving behavior.

As wealth, we measure only net financial wealth. The value of the stock of durable goods and residences is excluded. The rationale for this is that these types of assets are not liquid. They are not easily converted to other types of consumption goods. Accordingly, they may not "count" to the same extent as net financial assets. We obtain measures of net financial assets from the flow of funds accounts.

To measure net saving, personal saving as defined in the flow of funds accounts was used. From personal saving, contributions to private pension and state and local pension funds were deducted. The remainder can be viewed as discretionary saving. This measure of net saving includes purchases of consumer durables and residences and is net of the increase in all liabilities. This approach assumes that saving is initially unallocated between financial assets and durables and residences. People first decide to save and then decide upon the allocation of savings.

We estimate over the period 1947 through 1974 so that the period of the Great Depression is excluded. We also estimate on a per capita basis, as well as on a per household basis, on the premise that there may be some interesting differences in per capita and per household results. These may arise as a result of the fact that over the estimation period the average size of households declined and an increasing number of households included more than a single wage earner.

Feldstein's measure of net social security wealth was used. We also experimented with gross social security contributions. Our intent is the distinction between the competing hypotheses that the Social

Security System affects saving through its fictional wealth effect or through its tax requirements.

The other variables used in the regression are similar to those used in other investigations, hence they need no further elaboration. (Complete definitions and sources for all variables are given in the appendix to this chapter.)

Our model, estimated in real 1972 dollars on a per capita and per household basis, is:

Net Personal Saving (flow of funds basis) = Constant +

b_1 Personal Disposable Income + b_2 Personal Disposable Income Lagged

+ b_3 Corporate Retained Earnings + b_4 Federal Government Budget Surplus

+ b_5 Unemployment Rate

+ b_6 Private Expenditures on Education and Research

+ b_7 Real Rate of Return on Corporate Bonds

+ b_8 Social Security Wealth (net) or + b_8' Annual Social Security Contributions

+ b_9 Total Pension Fund Assets (private plus state and local)

+ b_{10} Net Personal Financial Assets Lagged and Net of Pension Fund Assets

+ b_{11} Fictional Federal and State and Local Government Pension Fund Wealth

The results, shown in Table 3–3, suggest that it makes little difference whether estimation is done on a per capita or on a per household basis; the sum of the income coefficients is consistently 0.2 to 0.25. The coefficient on the federal government budget surplus is always positive, though never significant. Contrary to Barro's findings, a positive coefficient implies that, the larger the government budget surplus, the higher will be personal saving. The coefficient on corporate retained earnings of around 0.5 is consistently significant and, surprisingly, positive. Results by Paul Wachtel [46, 1977] indicate that inflation positively influences real saving. Our observations contain a period of comparatively high inflation. The positive association between personal saving and retained earnings, therefore, may have been induced by the recent U.S. inflationary experience or by transitory components of personal income correlating positively with transitory components of retained earnings in the cyclical context.

As anticipated, the unemployment rate negatively influences personal saving. Our human capital proxy, expenditures on education and research, is positively related to personal saving. This is contrary

Table 3–3. New Time Series on the Influence of Social Security on Saving. Dependent Variable: Net Saving Less Pension Contributions on a Flow of Funds Basis *(t-values in parentheses)*

Independent Variables	*Per Capita Measures*				*Per Household Measures*			
Constant	−322.72 (−1.32)	−268.07 (−1.08)	−287.34 (−0.96)	−213.36 (−0.71)	−1554.50 (−1.75)	−1473.98 (−1.528)	−1736.01 (−1.60)	−1631.92 (−1.36)
Personal Disposable Income	0.3596 (3.533)	0.3703 (3.758)	0.3688 (3.002)	0.3743 (3.134)	0.3828 (3.296)	0.3754 (3.055)	0.4208 (2.964)	0.4102 (2.684)
Personal Disposable Income Lagged	−0.1366 (−1.55)	−0.1966 (−1.865)	−0.1377 (−1.36)	−0.2083 (−1.75)	−0.0927 (−1.125)	−0.1058 (−1.07)	−0.0786 (−0.86)	−0.0928 (−0.834)
Corporate Retained Earnings	0.5225 (2.64)	0.4785 (2.362)	0.5785 (2.76)	0.5173 (2.44)	0.4738 (2.301)	0.4851 (2.24)	0.5097 (2.416)	0.5212 (2.344)
Federal Government Budget Surplus	0.0874 (0.761)	0.0750 (0.626)	0.0498 (0.421)	0.0469 (0.38)	0.1163 (0.985)	0.1097 (0.885)	0.0912 (0.759)	0.0847 (0.669)
Unemployment Rate	−667.80 (−1.28)	−572.71 (−1.070)	−1054.74 (−2.078)	−888.46 (−1.68)	−2340.96 (−1.324)	−2239.43 (−1.203)	−3437.12 (−1.990)	−3306.42 (−1.778)
Private Expenditure on Education and Research	5.5424 (1.72)	5.9995 (1.84)	4.8650 (1.43)	5.6110 (1.64)	5.3225 (1.52)	5.5999 (1.49)	4.2942 (1.79)	4.6001 (1.171)
Real Rate of Return on Corporate Bonds	40.41 (0.477)	1.565 (0.016)	59.45 (0.66)	10.75 (0.108)	246.64 (0.89)	217.14 (0.71)	316.94 (1.113)	286.01 (0.892)

Social Security Wealth Net	—	—	−0.0580 (−1.37)	−0.0461 (−1.06)	—	—	−0.0581 (−1.638)	−0.0555 (−1.456)
Annual Social Security Contribution	−0.881 (−2.03)	−0.739 (−1.63)	—	—	−0.757 (−2.04)	−0.733 (−1.86)	—	—
Total Pension Fund Assets	−0.155 (−1.49)	−0.154 (−1.49)	−0.095 (−0.87)	−0.1012 (−0.94)	−0.1898 (−1.69)	−0.1886 (−1.64)	−0.1367 (−1.177)	−0.1375 (−1.15)
Net Personal Financial Assets Lagged and Net of Pension Fund Assets	−0.0062 (−1.44)	−0.0242 (−1.51)	−0.0068 (−1.48)	−0.0270 (−1.639)	−0.0290 (−2.08)	−0.0290 (−2.01)	−0.0315 (−2.06)	−0.0312 (−1.974)
Fictional Government Pension Fund Wealth	—	1.2770 (0.911)	—	1.4559 (0.992)	—	0.3679 (0.257)	—	0.3593 (0.238)
$\bar{R}^2$	0.889	0.889	0.876	0.879	0.837	0.841	0.838	0.829
F Statistic	22.60	20.60	20.07	18.79	14.82	13.98	15.02	12.90
$D.W.$ Statistic	1.87	1.98	1.80	1.98	1.57	1.78	1.82	1.85

to expectations and suggests that investment in human capital is not a substitute for investment in other assets. On the other hand, a much more complex mechanism may be at work. Expenditures on education, which often are not tax deductible, are rising much more rapidly than after-tax income; so is the cost. Our price deflator may not have accurately captured this difference. Further, knowing that the cost of educating the next generation to compete successfully for satisfactory employment is itself rising—if for no other reason than that more years of schooling are necessary—may encourage higher saving by the current generation (see, for example [12, Denison, 1974]).

The real rate of return on corporate bonds positively influences saving though it is insignificant statistically. This broad result is consistent with recent work by Michael Boskin [6, 1978].

Total pension fund assets negatively influence personal saving, net of pension fund contributions. Coefficients generally fall within the range of −0.1 to −0.19, suggesting that a dollar increase in pension fund assets reduces personal saving by 10 to 19 cents. The coefficients are generally not statistically significant. Pension benefits *are* uncertain from the point of view of the prospective recipient due to vesting provisions, fund solvency, and so forth, so one would not expect one-to-one substitution.

The coefficients on net social security wealth fall within a range of −0.046 to −0.058. For every dollar increase in net social security wealth, achievable by increasing benefits without a corresponding rise in taxes, personal saving declines by approximately 5 cents. This trade-off, compared to that for pension fund assets, could be taken to imply that net social security wealth is riskier. A second possibility is that a bequest motive may be operative. Recognizing that net social security wealth is "fictional" and that burdens will have to be borne by future generations, savers during our sample period may simply have offset this future burden privately. The numerical finding is consistent with Feldstein's. He observed a 3.5 cent increase in consumption for a dollar's rise in social security wealth.

Finally, the difference between the coefficients on private pension wealth and social security wealth could reflect the fact that almost all members of the work force belong to the Social Security System, yet only about one-third now belong to private pension systems. Suppose that it is the annuity which each pension purchases which enters life cycle consumption/investment calculations. Those covered by private pensions may be older and higher paid on average than are typical social security contributors. There are few limits on private pension wage bases, and, because of the integration of social security with private benefits that many employers use, private pension benefits are likely to be heavily skewed toward higher-paid employees. Then private pensions would have a higher annuity value than prospective social security benefits. In this instance, private pension wealth would merit a larger offset to personal saving than would social security wealth. However, private pension assets are not fictional. As a result, an imperfect substitution of pension assets for personal saving such as the one found leads to an expansion of aggregate saving and investment, rather than a decline. This finding is compatible with results obtained by Munnell [37, 1976].

The coefficients on social security contributions are negative, nearly always statistically significant, and fall within a range of −0.73 to −0.88. These coefficients are not, however, statistically different from unity. This suggests the possibility of an approximately dollar-for-dollar trade-off between social security contributions and personal saving. But the overall effect is not altogether clear, for it includes effects on personal disposable income and the government deficit, too.

Suppose social security taxes were increased by $1.00. Personal disposable income would be reduced by $1.00, if there were no corresponding reduction in other taxes and social security benefits were not increased to offset the higher level of collections. Suppose the funds were used to build the trust fund. Using some representative results from Table 3−3, a $1.00 reduction in disposable personal income would lead to a reduction in personal saving of $0.37. The government deficit would be reduced by $1.00, so personal saving would rise by $0.08. The $1.00 in higher social security taxes would itself reduce personal saving by $0.74. The net reduction in personal saving would, therefore, be $1.03 ($0.37−$0.08 + $0.74). Higher social security taxes without an increase in benefits would reduce net social security wealth. In effect, this would lower the rate of return expected on social security contributions.

An alternative experiment allows a rise in personal income to correspond with an increase in social security taxes. This is what has tended to happen in recent years. Increases in taxes have gone to support higher OASDI (Old Age, Survivors, Disability, and Health Insurance) benefit levels. In this case disposable personal income keeps pace with social security taxes. Increases in social security taxes raise net social security wealth so long as the expected rate of return on current contributions does not change. However, the recipients of these benefits very likely have a lower propensity to save than do current contributors. The life cycle model predicts no or very little saving done by the aged, except for bequests. Accordingly, the measured propensity to save out of income would decline. Thus the reduction in personal saving as a result of higher social security taxes would be greater than suggested by the regression coefficient on these taxes, even ignoring the net rise in social security wealth. This experiment recognizes that, so long as social security benefits rise with social security taxes, implying no increase in trust funds, aggregate demand should not decline in the face of higher taxes.

The results regarding social security pose a dilemma. On the one hand, if net social security wealth has a negative effect on personal saving, then any reduction in net social security wealth will lead to higher personal saving. A reduction can result from either a reduction in promised benefits or an increase in social security taxes. A reduction in promised benefits, unaccompanied by a reduction in current benefits, leaves disposable personal income unchanged, so the expected effect is an increase in personal saving. On the other hand, if social security contributions alone lead to a reduction in personal saving, a reduction in social security wealth through a tax increase unaccompanied by an increase in current benefits may lead to a decrease, not an increase, in personal saving. This would be the case if an actuarially sound trust fund were to be established.

Higher taxes of, say, $1.00, would reduce disposable personal income by $1.00 for a decline in personal saving of, roughly, $0.37. Higher taxes of $1.00 annually for an individual with twenty years to retirement and a discount rate of 6 percent would reduce social security wealth by $11.47, the present value of twenty future contributions. This reduction in social security wealth would increase personal saving by 0.058 × $11.47, or $0.66. A net increase in saving of $0.66−$0.37, or $0.29, results.

Additionally, if the government budget deficit were reduced, personal saving would rise by $0.08. Together, reducing social security wealth through higher taxes could lead to increased personal saving of $0.29 + $0.08, or $0.37 per dollar of social security taxes. But the immediate impact of an increase in these taxes is a reduction of personal saving by $0.74. The net result is a reduction of saving by $0.74−$0.37, or $0.37.

If one believes the "wealth" formulation, higher social security taxes unaccompanied by higher benefits could lead to an increase in personal saving. If the "contributions" formulation is correct, a reduction in personal saving could be a consequence of higher social security taxes.

Theory does not provide adequate insight into this issue, and our empirical work was not able to distinguish between the two competing hypotheses with sufficient rigor. We are, however, inclined to believe that the social security tax, not wealth, possesses the more operative depressing effect on personal saving. The logic of the operative bequest motive as elaborated by Barro and Miller and Upton is persuasive. Individuals are clever enough to pierce the veil of fictional wealth. Taxes, on the other hand, simply cannot be avoided and hence impinge on behavior. Either way, though, the social security program does reduce personal saving.

Finally, our proxy for fictional federal and state and local government pension wealth is, contrary to expectations, positive, but not statistically significant. Fictional government pension wealth does not seem to affect personal saving one way or the other. If anything, it suggests that government employees save more than others. This may be due to the fact that federal employees at least are not members of the Social Security System.

It could also be due to the fact that greater job security in government jobs encourages a different consumption pattern, namely, greater investment in homes and durable goods. It may simply suggest that these workers are more highly paid than comparably skilled civilian workers. Finally, it could be a result of the earlier retirement options available to government employees. Higher current saving would be natural for anyone contemplating a longer retirement period. This latter explanation would not hold if the number of government employees were constant over the sample period. That would mean a roughly constant portion in retirement, a dissaving period. But growth in government employment has been such that the proportion of those in retirement relative to those working has declined markedly over time. So the two groups would not be expected to "cancel" each other out in our estimates of personal saving.

Cross Section Estimates of the Effect of Social Security on Wealth Accumulation

Feldstein and Pellechio [17, 1977], Munnell [37, 1976], and Kotlikoff [30, 1977] have made use of cross-section data to determine the effect of social security on wealth accumulation. All have found an effect, though the nature of the effect differs.

Feldstein and Pellechio make use of the data provided in the Federal Reserve Board's *Survey of Financial Characteristics*, which gives detailed balance sheets and income statement data for a large sample of consumers. Their study uses data pertaining to employed males between the ages of fifty-five to sixty-four covered by social security. Households with unusual characteristics, outliers, were eliminated.

Feldstein and Pellechio relate household net worth to various income measures and each household's net social security wealth. Depending on sample weightings, marriage, and so on, coefficients on social security wealth vary, but fall within the range of −0.67 to −1.67. All coefficient estimates are statistically significant. All imply that social security wealth reduces household wealth accumulation. Most estimates are less than unity, implying that a dollar increase in social security wealth reduces net private household wealth by less than one dollar.

This model is simple and persuasive. However, a question might be raised concerning the amount of variance in the social security wealth variable among sample units. During the period over which these households contributed to social security, the social security wage base was comparatively low and stable. Household social security wealth would necessarily be a function of the wage base. Accordingly, there may not be substantial variation among sample households in the social security wealth variable. In short, this cross-section approach may be flawed.

In a study by Kotlikoff, data from the National Longitudinal Survey of men aged forty-five to fifty-nine were used. Data used were collected in 1965 and 1966.

In the first regression experiment, the dependent variable is household net worth. Independent variables include income measures and an array of demographic and sociological variables. Social security is represented by two different variables. One variable is the sum of the household's lifetime accumulated taxes based on the average of 1965 and 1966 labor income. The second variable measures the present value of the future benefits minus the present value of future taxes minus accumulated taxes.

The coefficient on the expected future benefits less taxes is positive, but not significant statistically. The coefficient on past taxes, however, is negative, −0.666, and statistically significant. This suggests that, for every dollar of social security taxes paid, accumulation is reduced by nearly $0.67; it implies that social security taxes are financed out of "saving."

Using the same basic data, Kotlikoff tests for an effect on annual saving. In lieu of the present value of past social security taxes, the present contribution to social security is used. It carries a coefficient of −2.419 but is not statistically significant. Moreover, the variable relating to future net benefits is positive and statistically significant; this is perverse.

Returning to Kotlikoff's accumulation equation, he tests what he terms a household budget constraint. The variables to capture this are simply the past tax and future net social security wealth variables multiplied by a dummy variable which has the value of unity when the household owns a home and zero otherwise. The coefficient on past social security taxes, given home ownership, is 1.173 and statistically significant. According to Kotlikoff [30, 1977, p. 32]: "These findings imply essentially a dollar for dollar replacement of savings by tax contributions for non-homeowners and a zero reduction in savings for homeowners. Since homeowners constitute a large proportion of this sample (70 percent) and of household heads in general, this finding greatly narrows the scope for an aggregate reduction in savings due to social security."

Kotlikoff's accumulation and saving equations also test for an effect of private and government pension funds. These are measured using dummy variables. In the accumulation of household net worth equation, membership in any pension plan reduces accumulation by $1,053.60, although this variable is not statistically significant. The dummy variable which measures whether the household contains someone covered by a government pension plan has a value of $141.27, suggesting accumulation rises when there is government pension. However, this coefficient is again not statistically significant. In his saving equation, annual saving is depressed by membership in a pension plan by $729.98 annually; the coefficient is not statistically significant. For government employees covered by pension plans, saving is positively and significantly raised by $1,682.20.

While these general results are suggestive, they may be somewhat unreliable. The principal reason for our reservation concerns the measurement of net worth and saving. Kotlikoff's saving variable, so far as we could discern, is unlike the National Income Account's saving measure in that his does not include employer or employee contributions to pension plans. If pension saving substitutes for personal saving, then pension plan membership ought to be negatively associated with personal saving almost by definition. Similarly, it is uncertain whether the equity value of investment in housing is included in his measure of net worth. If it is, then Kotlikoff's results showing a different association between social security taxes and net worth for homeowners and nonhomeowners may not be terribly revealing. Homeowners may simply accumulate more because of other tax savings associated with home ownership. It is not clear that there is any interaction between the combined effect of social security taxes and home ownership and asset accumulation.

Kotlikoff's study suffers because the sample chosen was compact in terms of age, past social security taxes, and future benefits net of social security taxes. When independent variables have low variance, they do not contain a great deal of information. Accordingly, inferences may be misleading.

Kotlikoff's study has some other problems as well. These were pointed out by George von Furstenberg [21, 1977]. Briefly they include (1) the fact that employer contributions are not accounted for in past social security taxes paid: (2) the estimation of taxes paid on labor income fails to take account of possibly higher marginal tax rates due to nonlabor income; the income tax bite is underestimated; (3) the specification of net worth is ambiguous; (4) nonlabor income is excluded; (5) use of constant discount rates over the life cycle. These are valid criticisms to be sure, but they may not destroy the principal conclusions.

Feldstein and Pellechio's contentions receive some marginal support from Kotlikoff's results. Both papers suggest a depressing effect of social security on personal saving. Mechanisms, however, differ. For Feldstein and Pellechio, households look to future benefits and adjust saving accordingly. For Kotlikoff, it is past taxes which depress household wealth accumulation and saving; tax payments are thus financial out of "saving."

We turn finally to work by Munnell. She used data from the National Longitudinal Survey collected over the period 1966–71. The survey included 5,000 men aged forty-five to fifty-nine in 1966. Again the life cycle model is used as the foundation for testing. Results suggest that, for the 1966–69 period, coverage by a private pension plan reduced annual savings by $671, and coverage by the Social Security System led to a reduction in private savings of $1,420 annually. For the 1969–71 period, private pension coverage led to a $2,431 reduction in annual saving, while social security led to a $1,815 reduction. With regard to private pensions, Munnell points out that pension fund contributions grew by more than the amount by which personal saving was reduced due to pension coverage. Overall capital accumulation was enhanced by private pensions. Munnell argues that employees will discount their employer's pension fund contributions because of uncertainty surrounding their vesting status, fund solvency, and so forth. In this interpretation, the amount by which personal saving is reduced equals the certainty equivalent of the amount contributed to pension plans.

Munnell's findings differ from Kotlikoff's. Kotlikoff observes that saving (or wealth accumulation) is affected by social security taxes. Munnell finds that annual saving is reduced by a multiple of annual social security taxes, which in, say, 1969–71 were $750. Munnell's findings suggest a very substantial impact on personal saving of expected future social security benefits.

The cross-sectional studies agree that social security reduces personal saving, but the reason is by no means clear. It is not obvious whether the impact on saving comes about as a result of social security taxation or whether it stems from expectations of future benefits. Which of these explanations is true is crucial to an understanding of the likely impact of policy changes on personal saving, as well as on national saving.

The nature of the influence of social security is ambiguous. On the one hand, it may stem from net social security wealth, which is discounted expected benefits less the present value of future taxes. On the other, it may stem merely from taxes. Growth in both measures is correlated enough to preclude confident disentanglement of the competing hypotheses. The theory of bequests, however, lends marginal support to the notion that it may be the tax effect which drives personal saving, rather than the expected wealth effect.

The Bottom Line on Life Cycle Models

The weight of evidence favors the view that the Social Security System depresses personal saving. Other forms of fictional wealth, primarily generated by unfunded federal and state and local government pension programs, seem to have little influence on personal saving.

The negative influence of net social security wealth on personal saving ranges according to all estimates from 1.5 cents to 5.5 cents per dollar. Social security contributions may reduce personal saving by roughly 80 cents per dollar. Cross-sectional studies reveal that past social security taxes have reduced household net worth accumulation. Some further insight into this question may, however, be provided by a different class of models.

III. THE ALLOCATION OF HOUSEHOLD ASSETS

In addition to the negative influence which the Social Security System apparently has on personal saving, there may also be portfolio allocation effects. For example, the Social Security System provides survivor benefits to spouses of covered workers and also provides disability benefits. Accordingly, the need for personal insurance may be reduced.

Table 3–4 shows the percentage of personal saving put in different forms during the postwar period; it also illustrates the percentage of personal income which becomes personal disposable income. Regarding the latter, it is obvious that tax burdens have increased.

Table 3–4. Allocation of Household Assets

Average Over	*Disposable Personal Income as % of Personal Income*	*Net Saving as % of Personal Income*[a]	*Net Acquisition of Financial Assets as % of Personal Income*[b]	*Increase in Liabilities as % of Personal Income*	*Changes in Life Insurance Reserves as % of Personal Income*
1946–1950	90.0	9.05	6.4	4.2	1.5
1951–1955	88.2	7.95	7.6	4.8	1.0
1956–1960	87.9	7.06	8.1	4.5	0.9
1961–1965	87.5	7.31	9.8	5.5	0.9
1966–1970	85.9	8.67	9.7	4.1	0.7
1971–1975	85.8	9.07	12.1	5.6	0.6
1976	85.8	9.90	12.8	7.0	0.5
1977 (est.)	85.2	8.90	13.9	9.5	0.5

Table 3–4. continued

Average Over	*Changes in Pension Fund Reserves as % of Personal Income*	*Changes in Equity and Investment Co. Share Holdings as % of Personal Income*	*Changes in Savings Accounts and Credit Market Instrument Holdings as % of Personal Income*	*Household Capital Expenditures as % of Personal Income*[c]
1946–1950	1.3	0.4	2.2	15.8
1951–1955	1.7	0.4	3.8	18.1
1956–1960	2.0	0.3	4.9	17.1
1961–1965	2.2	–0.3	6.5	16.2
1966–1970	2.3	–0.5	5.8	15.3
1971–1975	2.6	–0.3	8.6	15.5
1976	3.4	–0.3	9.6	16.4
1977 (est.)	3.6	–0.2	9.9	17.0

Source: Board of Governors of the Federal Reserve System, *Flow of Funds Accounts*, 1946–1975, and *Flow of Funds Accounts*, 2nd Quarter 1978.

[a] All variables are defined as in *Flow of Funds Accounts.* Net Saving (line 9) is defined as net saving NIA basis plus net consumer durables, credits from government insurance, and capital gains dividends.

[b] Net acquisition of financial assets (line 18) includes purchase of securities less sale of secondary market securities. It does not include household issuance of liabilities. Net financial investment equals net acquisition of financial assets minus net increase in liabilities (line 38).

[c] Household Capital Expenditures are net of sales to others but does not reflect an adjustment for capital consumption. The data were taken from line 13 of the *Flow of Funds Accounts.*

Net saving as a percent of personal income has remained roughly constant; this implies that, other things equal, personal saving as a percent of personal disposable income has tended to rise during the postwar period.

The chart also reveals that both net acquisition of financial assets and liabilities have risen. The difference between these has also increased over time.

Changes in life insurance reserves as a percent of personal income have declined. This is probably a direct effect of the structure of social security benefits. Private and government pension fund contributions have risen as a percent of personal income. Apart from other possible reasons for this growth, this has surely been prompted by the favorable tax treatment given pension fund contributions. Income placed in pension funds is not taxed at the time of its receipt. Rather taxation is deferred until pension benefits begin. Presumably the retired employee is in a lower tax bracket than he was prior to retirement. So, in addition to the tax deferral, undiscounted tax payments may be lower.

Gross household purchases of durable goods and newly constructed residences remained relatively constant during the postwar period; there is no apparent trend.

The percentage of personal income directed toward savings accounts and other credit market instruments has risen over time. There has been a sharp increase in the personal holdings of fixed income investments. At the same time, there has been a sharp decrease in the percentage of savings placed in equity investments.

These portfolio tendencies have been countered by the behavior of the pension funds to which employees and their employers have been contributing. Table 3–5 shows the average size of pension funds for selected years over the postwar period and the percent of funds invested in equities. For private pension funds the average proportion of total assets invested in equities has risen from 11.2 to 64.9 percent. For state and local government pension funds, the average percentage invested in equities has risen from 0.43 to 23.6 over the period.

As can be observed from Table 3–4, there are some changes in the allocation of saving among different asset categories since 1946. Since the Social Security System represents one of the most profound changes in the financial picture of the household sector, it seems plausible, at least initially, that social security has been partly responsible for the change in the allocation of saving. The most obvious impact of social security is in the area of life insurance. Here the

Table 3–5. Pension Fund Asset Allocation

	Corporate Pension Funds		*State and Local Government Pension Funds*	
	Average Amount Invested in Equities (millions)	*Percent of Total Funds Invested in Equities*	*Average Amount Invested in Equities (millions)*	*Percent of Total Funds Invested in Equities*
1946–1950	$ 558.4	11.2	16.0	0.43
1951–1955	2,966.4	23.9	94.2	1.7
1956–1960	11,437.0	39.1	400.0	2.5
1961–1965	29,374.0	51.3	1,580.0	5.7
1966–1970	56,108.0	58.5	5,980.0	12.3
1971–1975	89,251.0	64.9	20,280.0	23.6

Source: Board of Governors of the Federal Reserve System, *Flow of Funds Accounts*, 1946–1975, and *Flow of Funds Accounts Assets and Liabilities Outstanding*, December 1977.

direction of effect and the motivation are apparent. Growth in survivor benefits and growth in disability benefits have simply made life insurance less necessary. Less obvious is the impact which the Social Security System has had on the allocation of household savings between fixed income and equity investments. To see how social security may have influenced this split, a formal structure of household decisionmaking must be introduced.

Assume that households or individuals are risk-averse. For supporting evidence, see Marshall Blume and Irwin Friend [4, 1975]. Less risk is preferred to more, and only disproportionately higher expected returns can prompt the undertaking of additional risk. Further assume that individuals do in fact have a forecast of required annual income in retirement years, consistent, say, with a life cycle model and also some fixed bequest target. With these assumptions, the alteration in portfolio structure can be analyzed.

Social security benefits are now indexed for inflation, so real social security benefits are constant or rising owing to the now corrected double indexing "mistakes." Prior to 1975, they were not. However, they were adjusted with sufficient frequency to give the impression of nearly constant or generally increasing real benefits. Social security has proven to be a good inflation hedge.

Equities were traditionally viewed as playing the role of inflation hedge, at least until the last few years, when the equity markets have declined even in nominal terms. Social security now plays this role. By assumption, individuals have a fixed wealth goal for retirement and are risk averse. Social security has reduced the need for equity investment in individual portfolios. The wealth goal can be achieved through a combination of social security and less risky investments.

Though the data do not reveal this, it should be noted that social security may ultimately reduce the importance of pension funds. While Table 3–4 shows pension fund reserves getting an increasing share of savings, this trend may not continue. Recent work by Munnell [39, 1978] and Logue [33, 1979] suggests that private pension funds may be adversely affected by the growth of the Social Security System. Munnell uses a life cycle equation to estimate private pension fund growth and adds social security wealth as an independent variable. A negative influence is reported.

Logue begins from a different perspective. He views private pensions as incentive schemes which encourage worker loyalty and discourage turnover and shirking through vesting and eligibility provisions. Private pensions help keep employee monitoring and training costs low. Now assume once again a fixed retirement income goal. As real social security benefits expand, the net incentive effect of fixed expected real private pension benefits must decline. To maintain the same incentive effects, employers will have to expand private pension benefits, but the added costs may not be justified by the constant advantages. Ultimately, if real growth in social security benefits continues, private pension plans may contract. Whether personal or household saving behavior will offset this contraction remains unsettled.

A final point concerning pension funds and social security ought to be made. There is a possibility that higher social security taxes could lead to a rise in pension fund contributions. This arises as a result of the way in which social security taxes are levied against different categories of income. Suppose an employer can give an employee a direct salary increment or can increase nontaxable fringe benefits. Other things the same, many employees would prefer the latter. Now extend this example. An employer can either give an employee a salary increase which is subject to both federal income taxation and social security taxation, assuming the raise would leave the employee at or below the social security wage base, or could increase pension fund contributions on the employee's behalf. If the pension fund contribution is chosen, income taxes are deferred and social security taxes are completely avoided because social security taxes are not levied on pension fund benefits. In this view, rising social security taxes tend to encourage pension fund growth, or at least mitigate the adverse impact of social security benefits and taxes on pension funds. This argument cannot be pushed too far because so many individuals already earn the social security wage base or more, and because of capital markets constraints which prevent workers from borrowing too much against expected pension income; current income is required for survival.

A Stock Adjustment Model of Savings Allocation

Hendrik Houthakker and Lester Taylor [25, 1970] have developed a model for analyzing consumer demand. It does not require specification of a complete structure; thus it may provide the simplest approach to examining asset allocation. It is a reduced form of a dynamic model and has successfully been applied by Wachtel [46, 1977] in studying the influence of inflation and inflation uncertainty on personal saving and asset allocations. We adopt this model to explore the influence of social security on personal demand for different types of assets. It is:

Savings Allocated to Component i = Constant
+ b_1 Savings Allocated to Component i Last Period
+ b_2 Personal Disposable Income
+ b_3 Personal Disposable Income Lagged
+ b_4 Change in the Price Level
+ b_5 Price Level Lagged
+ b_6 Change in Net Social Security Wealth + b_7 Net Social Security Wealth Lagged
or + b'_6 Change in Social Security Contributions + b'_7 Change in Social Security Contributions Lagged

Savings data are taken from the quarterly Flow of Funds (FOF) accounts. Price level changes are measured using the Consumer Price Index: Wachtel showed that this measure is a reasonable surrogate for uncertainty concerning future inflation rates. Net social security wealth is as before. Social security contributions are employee plus employer contributions.

The model is estimated in constant 1972 dollars on a per capita basis for the period from the third quarter 1952 through the second quarter 1974 and for several subperiods. Structural coefficients can be derived from the reduced-form equation. Of particular interest are the structural coefficients on the social security variables. The structural coefficients relating the savings component to the social security variable can be written

$$\gamma = \frac{2(b_6 - 0.5b_7)}{b_1 + 1} \ .$$

Its derivation appears in Houthakker and Taylor.

The long-run effect of social security on the relevant saving variable, other things constant, can similarly be measured as

$$\phi = b_7/(1 - b_1) \ .$$

Its derivation is also in Houthakker and Taylor.

The above model is estimated for the following savings measures and components: (1) Personal saving derived from the National Income and Product Accounts: (2) net saving of households, personal trust, and nonprofit organizations on a Flow of Funds account basis (this includes net investment in consumer durables); (3) net increase in liabilities from the Flow of Funds accounts; (4) net financial investment from the Flow of Funds accounts; and (5) changes in private pension fund reserves. Of these, net financial investment may be of most interest since it represents the contribution of the household sector to the financing of both business and government. Results for various components of saving using the net social security wealth concept as one of the explanatory variables are shown in Table 3–6, panels A, B, and C. Results using social security contributions instead of wealth are reported in Table 3–7, panels A, B, and C.

Using the net social security wealth concept, the estimated regression coefficients for social security variables are typically negative for the entire period and each subperiod. Thus, an increase in social security wealth reduced the amount of saving allocated to most of the components distinguished in Table 3–6. Exceptions to this occur in the instance of private pension fund reserves and for the net increase in liabilities. The signs of other variables are about as one might expect in view of Wachtel's inflation results.

The structural coefficients on net social security wealth, γ, suggest a negative influence of social security on personal saving (NIPA), net financial investment, and life insurance reserves. Social security wealth has a positive influence on net saving (FOF basis), private pension fund reserves, increases in financial liabilities generally, and on home mortgage liabilities. The long-term coefficients, ϕ, indicate that both personal saving and net saving are negatively influenced by social security. Significantly, the magnitudes of the long-term coefficients are approximately equal to the magnitudes of the coefficients on net social security wealth estimates in the life cycle equations. Similarly, net liabilities and life insurance reserves are negatively influenced by social security. Net financial investment and pension fund reserves are, surprisingly, positively influenced in the long run by net social security wealth. Since pension fund reserves are part of net financial investment, this finding may result from the sort of income tax effect described above.

Results from the overall period contrast with results from the two subperiods. For the first subperiod, net social security wealth had a small positive effect on net saving; for the second, a large negative effect appeared. Moreover, a negative long-run coefficient for social security is estimated for pension funds in both subperiods. In the early subperiod there is a negative structural coefficient; however, a positive coefficient is computed for the latter period. In the latter period, the long-term coefficients of social security on each type of

Table 3–6. Estimates Using Net Social Security Wealth *(t-values in parentheses)*

Independent Variable \ *Dependent Variable*	*Panel A* Entire Period, 1952 III–1974 II					
	Personal Saving (NIPA)	*Net Saving (FOF)*	*Net Increase in Liabilities*	*Net Financial Investment*	*Life Insurance Reserves*	*Pension Fund Reserves*
Constant	−37.0066 (−0.764)	−121.0534 (−1.928)	−57.9088 (−0.742)	−78.1935 (−0.742)	6.3311 (1.146)	−27.8986 (−1.325)
Dependent Variable Lagged	0.7653 (10.138)	0.6812 (9.294)	0.7218 (10.382)	0.3627 (10.382)	0.6464 (7.614)	−0.1253 (−1.056)
Change in Disposable Personal Income	0.5221 (6.430)	0.8019 (12.176)	0.3882 (2.483)	0.2834 (2.483)	0.0257 (2.626)	0.0745 (1.867)
Disposable Personal Income Lagged	0.0698 (1.543)	0.1573 (2.606)	0.0081 (0.117)	0.0514 (0.117)	0.0041 (0.802)	0.0093 (0.505)
Change in Consumer Prices	13.3296 (2.048)	22.1223 (4.096)	−16.0007 (−1.314)	−35.2087 (−1.314)	−0.1375 (−0.160)	2.6431 (0.818)
Consumer Prices Lagged	−1.2801 (−1.813)	−2.6572 (−3.003)	2.0121 (−1.654)	−1.3209 (−1.654)	−0.0922 (−1.005)	0.6786 (2.092)

Change in Net Social Security Wealth[a]	−0.0299 (−2.938)	−0.0065 (−0.731)	0.0021 (0.116)	−0.0261 (−1.009)	0.0006 (−0.441)	0.0054 (1.067)
Net Social Security Wealth Lagged[a]	−0.0104 (−1.183)	−0.0176 (−1.918)	−0.0121 (−0.814)	−0.0187 (0.908)	−0.0004 (−0.421)	0.0065 (1.649)
$\bar{R}^2$	0.9050	0.9795	0.7909	0.7307	0.5383	0.8554
SEE	16.4114	13.5706	30.6977	42.9632	2.1687	8.1623
DW	1.8518	2.242	2.2684	2.1504	1.8736	1.9613
γ	−0.0280	0.0027	0.0095	−0.0520	−0.0001	0.0087
ϕ	−0.0443	−0.0552	−0.0434	0.0293	−0.0017	0.0048

[a]Interpolations from the annual Feldstein-Munnell estimates are used for each quarter.

(Table 3–6. continued overleaf)

Table 3–6. continued

Independent Variable \ Dependent Variable	*Panel B* — *First Subperiod, 1952 III–1963 II*					
	Personal Saving (NIPA)	*Net Saving (FOF)*	*Net Increase in Liabilities*	*Net Financial Investment*	*Life Insurance Reserves*	*Pension Fund Reserves*
Constant	6.8130 (0.031)	−191.4720 (−1.029)	76.4215 (−0.203)	−43.7666 (−0.078)	−3.2206 (−0.107)	−7.9604 (−0.092)
Dependent Variable Lagged	0.7320 (5.800)	0.6018 (4.940)	0.6735 (5.018)	0.3520 (2.270)	0.6838 (5.594)	−0.3391 (−2.087)
Change in Disposable Personal Income	0.4370 (2.850)	0.6568 (5.385)	0.5680 (2.173)	0.0525 (0.129)	0.0424 (2.082)	0.0360 (0.613)
Disposable Personal Income Lagged	0.0412 (0.314)	0.2640 (2.004)	0.0726 (0.317)	−0.0399 (−0.122)	0.0124 (0.644)	−0.0299 (−0.595)
Change in Consumer Prices	5.1275 (0.474)	18.3455 (2.218)	−11.5798 (−0.694)	51.828 (1.992)	0.1117 (0.083)	6.4060 (1.600)
Consumer Prices Lagged	−0.7084 (−0.387)	−6.6548 (−2.763)	−1.6332 (−0.479)	3.2475 (0.705)	−0.3989 (−1.330)	2.8070 (3.621)

Change in Net Social Security Wealth	−0.0158 (−0.832)	0.0022 (1.400)	0.0381 (1.296)	0.0065 (0.137)	0.0019 (0.791)	−0.0028 (−0.388)
Net Social Security Wealth Lagged	−0.0088 (−0.380)	−0.0035 (−0.190)	0.0074 (0.204)	−0.0014 (−0.024)	0.0008 (0.261)	−0.0027 (−0.297)
$\bar{R}^2$	0.5366	0.8388	0.6031	0.1625	0.6540	0.5401
SEE	14.8384	11.7656	23.4856	37.0578	1.9257	5.7182
DW	1.9392	2.3217	1.9791	2.0029	0.9653	1.8620
γ	−0.0132	0.0049	0.0411	0.0107	0.0018	−0.0044
ϕ	−0.0328	−0.0087	0.0227	−0.0022	0.0025	−0.0020

(Table 3–6. continued overleaf)

Table 3–6. continued

Independent Variable / Dependent Variable	*Panel C* *Second Subperiod, 1963 III–1974 II*					
	Personal Saving (NIPA)	*Net Saving (FOF)*	*Net Increase in Liabilities*	*Net Financial Investment*	*Life Insurance Reserves*	*Pension Fund Reserves*
Constant	−39.7262 (−0.478)	−149.8152 (−1.543)	−41.5744 (−0.287)	−174.2948 (−0.850)	14.0465 (1.522)	−37.2377 (−1.010)
Dependent Variable Lagged	0.8093 (7.574)	0.6221 (5.471)	0.6942 (6.623)	0.3544 (2.257)	0.3481 (2.251)	−0.1867 (−1.069)
Change in Disposable Personal Income	0.6329 (5.033)	0.8462 (8.419)	0.2787 (1.082)	0.5896 (1.855)	0.0300 (1.944)	0.1307 (2.048)
Disposable Personal Income Lagged	0.0947 (0.950)	0.1695 (1.632)	−0.0383 (−0.208)	0.3624 (1.455)	0.0171 (1.495)	0.0877 (1.879)
Change in Consumer Prices	20.1577 (2.089)	20.6440 (2.557)	−26.2158 (−1.337)	31.8619 (1.266)	−1.5037 (−1.270)	3.1325 (0.634)
Consumer Prices Lagged	−2.1385 (−1.419)	−2.5716 (−1.741)	3.4424 (1.172)	−5.9744 (−1.536)	−0.1925 (−1.071)	−0.4595 (−0.621)

Change in Net Social Security Wealth	−0.0400 (−2.174)	−0.0101 (−0.646)	−0.0036 (−0.097)	−0.1014 (−2.124)	−0.0033 (−1.488)	−0.0063 (−0.662)
Net Social Security Wealth Lagged	−0.0155 (−0.580)	−0.0170 (−0.739)	−0.0051 (−0.094)	−0.0779 (−1.137)	−0.0059 (−1.786)	−0.0200 (−1.511)
$\bar{R}^2$	0.8572	0.9470	0.7238	0.4246	0.2898	0.5882
SEE	18.7039	15.4668	38.1352	48.7902	2.2846	9.6257
DW	1.7390	1.8877	2.4599	2.1110	2.2928	1.9470
γ	−0.0356	−0.0020	−0.0013	−0.0922	−0.0004	0.0091
ϕ	−0.0813	−0.0450	−0.0167	−0.1207	−0.0091	−0.0169

Table 3–7. Estimation Using Social Security Contributions

	Panel A					
	Entire Period, 1952 III–1974 II					
Independent Variable \ *Dependent Variable*	*Personal Savings (NIPA)*	*Net Savings (FOF)*	*Net Increase in Liabilities*	*Net Financial Investment*	*Life Insurance Reserves*	*Pension Fund Reserves*
Constant	−35.1821 (−0.442)	−182.7665 (−2.545)	−155.7314 (−1.34)	−230.1844 (−1.311)	0.7180 (0.087)	−54.67 (−1.700)
Dependent Variable Lagged	0.7835 (9.574)	0.6957 (11.515)	0.7204 (10.505)	0.3504 (3.349)	0.6406 (7.650)	−0.0926 (−0.774)
Change in Disposable Personal Income	0.5188 (6.206)	0.7674 (11.948)	0.3512 (2.329)	0.3467 (1.685)	0.0284 (2.673)	0.0846 (2.103)
Disposable Personal Income Lagged	0.0397 (1.135)	0.1266 (3.397)	0.0066 (0.139)	0.1537 (2.095)	0.0049 (1.365)	0.0348 (2.572)
Change in Consumer Prices	19.0152 (3.138)	28.0071 (5.612)	−13.0513 (−1.212)	31.2548 (2.046)	0.0693 (0.090)	−0.0120 (−0.004)
Consumer Prices Lagged	−0.5328 (−0.756)	−0.8439 (−1.471)	3.5989 (2.798)	−1.8226 (−1.026)	−0.0242 (−0.266)	0.3940 (1.140)

Change in Social Security Contributions	−0.6143 (−2.657)	−0.1832 (−0.986)	0.1143 (0.277)	−1.048 (−1.825)	−0.0234 (−0.808)	0.0509 (0.442)
Social Security Contributions Lagged	−0.1295 (−0.617)	−0.4246 (−2.547)	−0.4458 (−1.404)	−0.1664 (−0.369)	−0.0224 (−0.976)	0.0023 (0.026)
$\bar{R}^2$	0.9034	0.9802	0.7960	0.7340	0.5432	0.8502
SEE	16.5495	13.3452	30.3192	42.6976	2.1571	8.3077
DW	1.9040	2.2847	2.3048	2.1120	1.8677	1.9437
γ	−0.6163	0.0343	0.3922	−1.4289	−0.0149	0.1096
ϕ	−0.5982	−1.3953	−1.5944	−0.2562	−0.0623	0.0021

(Table 3–7. continued overleaf)

Table 3–7. continued

Independent Variable \ Dependent Variable	*Panel B* — *First Subperiod, 1952 III–1963 II*					
	Personal Savings (NIPA)	*Net Savings (FOF)*	*Net Increase in Liabilities*	*Net Financial Investment*	*Life Insurance Reserves*	*Pension Fund Reserves*
Constant	−312.3276 (−1.394)	−338.2180 (−1.684)	−55.2239 (−0.155)	−453.3151 (−0.803)	−20.6008 (−0.708)	23.8044 (0.275)
Dependent Variable Lagged	0.5934 (4.266)	0.5726 (4.494)	0.6683 (4.895)	0.3267 (2.107)	0.6687 (5.548)	−0.3299 (−2.056)
Change in Disposable Personal Income	0.4650 (3.614)	0.6728 (6.474)	0.5572 (2.446)	0.1311 (0.399)	0.0470 (2.653)	0.0252 (0.487)
Disposable Personal Income Lagged	0.1082 (1.132)	0.3107 (2.662)	0.0938 (0.546)	0.0658 (0.275)	0.0197 (1.386)	−0.0441 (−1.177)
Change in Consumer Prices	7.6815 (0.659)	12.3726 (1.368)	−21.0692 (−1.119)	39.3031 (1.357)	−0.3314 (−0.216)	6.6820 (1.468)
Consumer Prices Lagged	2.8545 (1.173)	−5.7874 (−2.471)	−2.6898 (−0.598)	6.7479 (1.099)	−0.3429 (−0.928)	2.7053 (2.684)

Change in Social Security Contributions	−0.7397 (−1.296)	0.3178 (0.674)	1.3825 (1.528)	0.5484 (0.384)	0.0406 (0.549)	−0.0212 (−0.097)
Social Security Contributions Lagged	−0.9628 (−2.070)	−0.3860 (−1.101)	0.1839 (0.274)	−0.9643 (−0.916)	−0.0234 (−0.434)	0.0222 (0.138)
$\bar{R}^2$	0.5807	0.8494	0.6068	0.1919	0.6541	0.5385
SEE	14.1116	11.3715	23.3749	36.4005	1.9254	5.7279
DW	1.7820	2.2580	1.9732	1.9548	0.9976	1.8535
γ	−0.3242	0.6496	1.5466	1.5536	0.0627	−0.0964
ϕ	−2.3679	−0.9031	0.5544	−1.4322	−0.0706	0.0167

(Table 3–7. continued overleaf)

Table 3–7. continued

Independent Variable \ Dependent Variable	*Panel C* — *Second Subperiod, 1963 III–1974 II*					
	Personal Savings (NIPA)	*Net Savings (FOF)*	*Net Increase in Liabilities*	*Net Financial Investment*	*Life Insurance Reserves*	*Pension Fund Reserves*
Constant	−60.8965 (−0.471)	−243.7096 (−2.204)	−159.3618 (−0.759)	−369.8587 (−1.296)	13.1929 (0.947)	−69.2578 (1.295)
Dependent Variable Lagged	0.8057 (6.996)	0.6196 (5.925)	0.6931 (6.686)	0.3319 (2.203)	0.4280 (2.837)	−0.1980 (−1.123)
Change in Disposable Personal Income	0.6300 (5.043)	0.8287 (8.719)	0.2440 (1.016)	0.5473 (1.799)	0.0201 (1.325)	0.1038 (1.690)
Disposable Personal Income Lagged	0.0638 (1.040)	0.1615 (2.724)	−0.0079 (−0.081)	0.2383 (1.785)	0.0005 (0.086)	0.0466 (1.852)
Change in Consumer Prices	22.3073 (2.206)	27.3070 (3.389)	−20.468 (−1.007)	49.7550 (1.927)	−0.6723 (−0.525)	7.6697 (1.473)
Consumer Prices Lagged	−1.7084 (−1.752)	−1.3251 (−1.533)	4.4813 (2.164)	−2.2764 (−0.907)	0.0901 (0.724)	0.7378 (1.470)

Change in Social Security Contributions	−0.6364 (−2.075)	−0.2417 (−1.011)	0.0750 (0.121)	−1.8295 (−2.389)	−0.0151 (−0.394)	−0.0430 (−0.273)
Social Security Contributions Lagged	−0.0104 (−0.033)	−0.3861 (−1.679)	−0.4656 (−0.819)	−0.7104 (−0.965)	−0.0201 (−0.563)	−0.2133 (−1.474)
$\bar{R}^2$	0.8569	0.9501	0.7320	0.4408	0.2307	0.5878
SEE	18.7188	15.0080	37.5636	48.0973	2.3777	9.6303
DW	1.9570	1.9382	2.5249	2.0861	2.2650	1.9363
γ	−0.6991	−0.0601	0.3636	−2.2138	−0.0071	0.1587
ϕ	−0.0536	−1.0150	−1.5171	−1.0633	−0.0351	−0.1780

saving and borrowing are negative. This implies that net social security wealth has not only depressed various forms of saving, but it may also have reduced the willingness to incur liabilities.

Much the same general story is told by the estimations using social security contributions. For the overall period in panel A of Table 3–7, all coefficients reveal that social security contributions reduce personal saving, net financial investment, and life insurance reserves. Long-run coefficients indicate a negative long-run effect of social security contributions on all variables.

The early subperiod yields mixed and contradictory results regarding structural coefficients. With respect to long-run coefficients social security contributions lead to increases in net liabilities and private pension fund reserves.

In the latter subperiod, social security contributions have the long-run effect of reducing all categories of saving and borrowing. With respect to structural coefficients, social security contributions lead to higher liabilities and larger increases in private pension fund reserves. Throughout, the negative long-term effect of social security contributions on net saving suggests that a $1.00 decrease in net saving accompanies a $1.00 increase in social security contributions.

Using either measure for social security, there seems to be an impact on the composition of savings. For example, using the latter subperiod, increases in net social security wealth or social security contributions lead to higher private pension fund reserves in the short run. This is consistent with our tax effect hypothesis that there is an incentive to take "wages" in the form of pension fund contributions to avoid social security taxes on those wages entirely. Over the long term, however, the incentive effect of private pensions is eroded by increasingly generous social security benefits. Life insurance policy purchases are also negatively affected by the Social Security System both in the short run and in the long run. Overall net saving and personal saving decline with increases of both net social security wealth and social security contributions. However, both structural and long-term coefficients on other types of saving are not of the same general magnitude. This itself implies that the Social Security System affects the allocation of household savings among asset classes.

An important question which could not be addressed directly with available data is whether the social security program has seriously affected risk-taking behavior on the part of savers. The Social Security System may cause changes in asset allocation for two reasons. One reason is that social security benefits are close substitutes for certain types of assets, such as life insurance. Increasing social security benefits in a portfolio may lead to a decline in holdings of a substitute asset, and thus reduce the desire to accumulate those assets in a portfolio. A second version for expecting portfolio changes is related to the risk-bearing characteristics of investors. If investors have constant proportional risk aversion, as Friend and Blume [4, 1975] suggest, then their portfolios will be structured according to the riskiness of social security benefits.

If prospective social security benefits are perceived as risky in real terms, then the composition of other assets in the household's portfolio may reflect reduced tolerance for risk. Less equity and more fixed income-type financial assets may be desired. If social security benefits are considered safe—past experience shows that social security benefits have been indexed—then the composition of other assets might reflect higher tolerance for risk. The same broad conclusions can be achieved by concentrating on social security taxes other than benefits. For example, high and rising social security taxes, which, in turn, lead to reduced saving, may reduce risk-taking willingness or capacity and hence precipitate a rising price of risk.

The time-series analysis we have conducted in this study does not provide such insight into the riskiness of social security wealth. Only substantial cross-sectional work can cope with the question of the Social Security System's influence on risk-taking. But we have raised this issue nonetheless because it is potentially quite consequential.

The view that taxes control saving does not deny an operative bequest motive; at the same time it recognizes that tax payments such as these ultimately may yield some benefit and hence seem more likely to be financed by reductions in saving than through reductions in present consumption. There is a limit to how much present consumption can be reduced before it drops to unsatisfactory levels. "Saving" in the form of social security contributions should substitute for other saving if for no other reason than that one can very likely depend upon at least a nonnegative real return on these funds. With a fairly high degree of certainty, one can expect to receive from the system at least an amount roughly equal to what was put in. This view seems quite consistent with neoclassical models; individuals do not get "fooled" easily and hence do not depend to any extent on what might be recontracted.

IV. RECENT POLICIES CONFOUND THE SAVINGS ISSUE

On December 20, 1977, the Social Security Amendments of 1977 (Public Law 95–216) became law. This act "decoupled" future social security benefit increases from rising wages. Real social security benefit levels were thus fixed; real benefit levels will no longer rise automatically with both price levels *and* wage levels, but will rise only as average wages rise. In addition, the amendments raised social security payroll taxes rather sharply, thereby reducing the probability that use of general federal revenues will be necessary to sustain the system. A third major feature of this legislation was an increase in the amount that a person above the age of sixty-five may earn before social security benefits for that individual are reduced.

In addition to the Social Security Amendments of 1977, an amendment to the Age Discrimination Act of 1967 was recently enacted. It took effect in January 1979 and makes it illegal for employers to force employees to retire prior to the age of seventy. Employers who now have mandatory age sixty-five retirement policies, must now not require employees to retire before they reach the age of seventy. Both new laws influence the Social Security System and prospective retirement patterns in ways which will ultimately affect personal saving. Analysis of these recent changes from the perspective of our theoretical and empirical results may prove helpful.

Social Security Legislation

Table 3–8, derived from Social Security Administration statistics, shows expected replacement rates, the ratio between social benefits to wages in the year just prior to retirement, for representative categories of workers. The effect of the new law has been to stabilize

Table 3–8. Benefit Levels in Terms of Replacement Rates *(percent)*[a]

Retirement Year	*Low Earners*[b]		*Average Earners*[b]		*Maximum Earners*[b]	
	Old Law	*New Law*	*Old Law*	*New Law*	*Old Law*	*New Law*
1980	56	55	44	43	34	27
1990	60	56	48	43	35	25
2000	75	56	52	43	39	27
2020	91	56	60	43	44	29
2040	101	56	66	43	47	29
2050	106	56	68	43	48	29

Source: *Social Security Bulletin*, March 1978, *41*(3), p. 13.

[a]Replacement rates (annual benefits as a percent of earnings during last working year) for hypothetical low, average, and maximum earnings, 1980–2050, or a worker retiring at age sixty-two under the old and new law.

[b]In 1976, low earners had earnings of $4,600, average earners $9,200, and maximum earners $15,300.

replacement rates. Under the old law they rose rather sharply for all categories of workers. For low-income workers (essentially part-time workers employed at the federal minimum wage) social security benefits would exceed preretirement income under the old law by the year 2040. The decrease in expected replacement rates is a direct result of decoupling social security benefits from wage and price indexes.

The net effect of this change is the reduction of net social security wealth. This change reduces the expected present value of future social security benefits less taxes. If it is expected net social security wealth which depresses personal saving, then this change, considered in isolation, should lead to an increase in personal saving.

Social security tax rates and the maximum wage base were also increased under the recent legislation. Table 3–9 shows relevant data. It shows the combined (that is, Old Age, Survivors, Disability and Health) tax rates and wage bases against which these taxes are assessed under both the old and new laws. The rates reflect the employee's share, but the combined employer/employee rates are simply double the rates shown. Taxes for the self-employed were also raised roughly proportionately.

For the employee's "share," social security taxes for a maximum wage base earner are nearly $300 higher in 1979 under the new law. By 1981 taxes will be $600 higher, and by 1987 taxes will be in excess of $1,000 more than under the old law.

This rise in tax rates and maximum wage bases has the effect of reducing the short-term social security deficit. Table 3–10 shows projections of income and outgo to the system, net of the health insurance component, through 1987. If the projections are accurate, the system will be in rough balance by 1980, and by the mid-1980s will allow for trust fund growth of approximately $20 billion per year. This accumulation will be drawn down toward the beginning of the next century as a greater portion of the population collects social security benefits.

The increase in social security contributions reduces net expected social security wealth. If net social security wealth is causally linked to personal saving, personal saving may rise as a result of the tax increase. However, if personal saving is causally influenced by social security taxes, the tax increase will reduce personal saving.

The overall effect of higher social security taxes on personal saving is likely to be negative. Higher current taxes with no corresponding increase in benefits reduce the probability of future generations recontracting future social security benefits. In the results of Feldstein and Pellechio and of Kotlikoff, less than dollar-for-dollar substitu-

Table 3–9. Social Security Payroll Taxes *(percent or dollars)*

	Combined Tax Rate	OASDHI Taxes: Old Law		Combined Tax Rate	OASDHI Taxes: 1977 Amend.	
		Wage Base	*Maximum Tax*[a]		*Wage Base*	*Maximum Tax*[a]
1977	5.85%	$16,500	$ 965	5.85%	$16,500	$ 965
1978	6.05	17,700	1,071	6.05	17,700	1,071
1979	6.05	18,900[b]	1,143	6.13	22,900	1,404
1980	6.05	20,400[b]	1,234	6.13	25,900	1,588
1981	6.30	21,900[b]	1,380	6.65	29,700	1,975
1982	6.30	23,400[b]	1,474	6.70	31,800[b]	2,131
1983	6.30	24,900[b]	1,569	6.70	33,900[b]	2,271
1984	6.30	26,400[b]	1,663	6.70	36,000[b]	2,412
1985	6.30	27,900[b]	1,758	7.05	38,100[b]	2,686
1986	6.45	29,400[b]	1,896	7.15	40,200[b]	2,874
1987	6.45	31,200[b]	2,012	7.15	42,600[b]	3,046

Source: Robertson [42, 1978, pp. 21–30, various tables].
[a]These represent employee or employer contributions, not the combined amounts.
[b]Assumes 7 percent annual inflation rate.

Table 3–10. Old Age, Survivors, and Disability Insurance Expenditures, and Level of Combined OASI and DI Trust Funds after the 1977 Amendments *($ billion)*

Year	*Income*	*Expenditures*	*Difference*
1977	$ 82.1	$ 87.6	$ −5.5
1978	92.4	97.2	−4.8
1979	106.5	106.9	−0.4
1980	119.1	117.1	2.0
1981	137.1	127.4	9.7
1982	150.2	138.3	11.9
1983	161.3	149.2	12.1
1984	172.9	161.2	11.7
1985	194.2	174.0	20.2
1986	209.0	187.6	21.4
1987	223.7	202.0	21.7

Source: Robertson [42, 1978, p. 25, Table 4].

tion of net expected social security wealth for personal accumulation was observed. Assuming these observations are correct, one interpretation might be that individuals viewed future social security benefits as uncertain. Higher current taxes and greater prospective accumulations in the relevant trust funds will tend to reduce this uncertainty.

Accordingly, even under the interpretation that a reduction in social security wealth increases personal saving, the uncertainty effect could dominate. The reduction in wealth and uncertainty through a tax increase may lead to reduced levels of personal saving. In addition, there is direct evidence that higher social security taxes lead to reduced personal saving. The recent legislation tends to eliminate the short-term social security deficit, but it may also lead to lower personal saving.

Though the Social Security Amendments were only recently adopted, there already is much agitation to reduce the enacted tax rates. Those pressing for this reduction argue that the general revenues of the federal government could be used to make up the annual deficits that would result from the Social Security System's operation. However, personal saving seems to be negatively influenced by federal government budget deficits. If general revenues are supposed to be used to finance social security deficits, but there are no tax increases or reductions in government expenditures, personal saving would still be negatively influenced because the government budget deficit would increase. If general income taxes were raised in lieu of contributions for social insurance, personal saving would still be negatively affected, but the effect would be somewhat less than with higher social security taxes. Further use of general revenues (with or without higher income taxes) in lieu of higher social security taxes would very likely have an important income redistribution effect. Different income segments of the population would be differentially affected.

Retirement Age and Earnings

The recent social security legislation increases the amount of exempt earnings for those receiving social security benefits. Individuals can earn more than before without experiencing a reduction in benefit payments. Table 3–11 shows how exempt earnings will rise over time.

This feature reduces the attractiveness of retiring at age sixty-five. Those eligible for social security benefits can continue to work at part-time jobs more hours per week without jeopardizing social security benefits. At the same time individuals who continue to work will also be subject to social security taxes. Higher exempt earnings will encourage more individuals to continue working beyond the age of sixty-five. Taxes will continue, so the net effect of this change is a reduction of net social security wealth. It also reduces the length of the period during which retirement income is needed. If the accumulation of personal savings is heavily influenced by the expected length of the retirement period, then shortening the retirement period may lead to lower personal asset accumulations.

Table 3–11. Exempt Earnings of Social Security Beneficiaries

	Exempt Amount for Beneficiaries	
Year	*Under Age 65*	*Age 65 or Older*
1977	$3,000	$3,000
1978	3,240	4,000
1979	3,480[a]	4,500[b]
1980	3,720[a]	5,000[b]
1981	3,960[a]	5,500[b]
1982	4,300[a]	6,000[b]

Source: *Social Security Bulletin*, March 1978, *41* (3), p. 14.
[a]Estimated Under Automatic Adjustment Provisions.
[b]Specified in Law.

At roughly the same time that the exempt earnings amounts were lifted, provisions for mandatory retirement at age sixty-five were banned. Except for other causes, most employees cannot now be obligated to retire until the age of seventy. An increasing portion of those over sixty-five will very probably remain in the work force. Many will earn the exempt amount or less and hence draw full social security benefits. Many, however, will earn more than the exempt amount. For them, social security benefits will be reduced. Social security taxes will, however, continue.

Both social security and the mandatory retirement legislation act to reduce net social security wealth by effectively lengthening the period over which social security taxes must be paid and shortening the period of complete retirement. Both also tend to raise expected lifetime income. Whether the shorter full retirement period or the higher lifetime income have more effect on saving cannot as yet be determined.

Increasing Personal Saving

Our findings seem to indicate only one sure way of altering the Social Security System to increase personal saving. What is needed is a reduction in benefit levels accompanied by reduction in social security taxes. Needless to say, the former may be politically difficult to achieve.

Perhaps the best that can be hoped for is stabilization of the Social Security System. The increase in social security taxes over the next several years will reduce personal saving. Corporate saving could offset this, but very likely will not. The new higher tax rates which appear roughly adequate to sustain the current social security benefit structure may be tolerable because of some offsetting corporate behavior, but more than likely will lead to reduced national saving, assuming the government deficit is unchanged.

To keep the saving effects of social security taxes in bounds there must be no further increases in real social security benefit levels. But there will always be demand for increasing benefit levels.

Recent work by James Schulz [43, 1976] suggests that, to maintain the same standard of living, retirement income need equal only about 60 percent of preretirement income. For people with average earnings, the Social Security System already approximates this goal (see Table 3–8). Moreover, with the array of private pension arrangements that many employees enjoy, the combination of social security benefits and private pensions will allow many average earners to live as comfortably after retirement as before. Accordingly, there seems to be no overwhelming "social" argument for increasing the general level of benefits beyond what they currently are.

A second argument that can be used to fend off further urgings for generally higher social security benefit levels is that the United States is roughly at par with other advanced industrial countries.

Table 3–12 shows social security replacement rates for single workers and aged couples for the United States and eleven other countries for selected years. All computations assume one wage earner. There is, for the United States, a gross disparity between the treatment of single workers and aged couples (with only one former worker), given that both units may have contributed the same amount annually to the system. This inequity should be corrected, but concern over this point should not detain us here.

The United States now provides social security benefits which, measured by replacement rates, are comparable with those of other countries. In 1965, of twelve countries, the United States ranked eighth in replacement rates for aged couples and seventh in replacement rates for single workers. By 1975, the United States ranked fourth with respect to replacement rates for aged couples. For single workers, the United States ranked eighth but still had raised the replacement rate by nearly one-third. For aged couples, the United States is now on a par with the rest of the advanced, industrial world. Retired workers in the United States presently fare roughly as well as retired workers elsewhere; in earlier years they did not. This fact should help keep the demand for further benefit increases from becoming too explosive.

The Composition of Savings

The recently enacted social security and retirement age laws will affect the composition as well as the magnitude of personal savings. The direction of effect for each saving category depends upon the way in which one believes the Social Security System affects saving. If net social security wealth is the operative influence, higher social security taxes and shorter retirement periods which reduce wealth may, in the long run, raise personal saving, lead to an increase in the rate of growth in liabilities, financial asset holdings, life insurance reserves, and private pension reserves.

V. CONCLUSION

The Social Security System adversely affects personal saving. It is not clear whether the primary cause of the adverse effect is due to the prospect of receiving benefits which have a much higher present

Table 3–12. Social Security Benefits in Various Countries; Replacement Rate of Social Security Old-Age Pensions for Men with Average Earnings in Manufacturing

		Pension as Percent of Earnings in Year before Retirement							
		Single Worker				*Aged Couple*			
Country	*Years Worked*	*1965*	*1969*	*1973*	*1975*	*1965*	*1969*	*1973*	*1975*
Austria	40	67	65	62	54	67	65	62	54
Canada	40	21	22	30	39	42	39	46	57
Denmark	40	35	29	30	29	51	42	44	43
France	37.5	49	42	47	46	65	56	62	65
Germany[a]	40	48	56	49	50	48	56	49	50
Italy[a]	40	60	67	67	67	60	67	67	67
Netherlands	50	35	36	38	38	50	51	53	54
Norway	40	25	34	39	41	38	49	53	55
Sweden	30	31	39	45	59	44	52	57	76
Switzerland	Since 1948	28	26	39	36	45	42	58	53
United Kingdom	Since 1961	23	21	22	26	36	33	33	39
United States	Since 1951	29	29	38	38	44	44	57	57

Source: Haanes-Olsen [23, 1978, p. 4, Table 1].

[a]West Germany and Italy apparently take no account of how many family members, one or two, contributed to social insurance.

value than future taxes or because of the contemporaneous social security tax burden. Previous studies in this area have primarily concentrated on the wealth effect of social security.

The wealth argument allows for trickery; it takes no account of the possibility of bequest motives. Furthermore, there is no consensus on how to estimate social security wealth figures. Final results may depend upon the robustness of wealth figures.

Tax effect, however, simply shows that the greater the tax earmarked for old-age support, the less people will currently save. Our findings regarding the tax effect of social security are consistent with neoclassical models of economic behavior. They do not rely upon a mismatch of expected benefits with expected total taxes. These findings are thus independent of wealth effects.

Our findings have important policy implications. Only by reducing real social security benefit levels, or at least by not raising them and correspondingly, reducing taxes, can one be reasonably sure that personal saving will not decline further.

We also explored the impact of federal and state and local pension programs on private saving. These programs do not appear to have any significant effect on personal saving, though it is possible that the effect is positive.

One last important question that we dealt with in this study is the possible effects of the Social Security System on the composition of personal saving. The allocation of personal saving among various assets appears to be influenced by the Social Security System. Most notably, social security taxes have a negative effect on life insurance purchases, and in the long run will have a negative influence on private pension plans. Future research in this area seems to be most promising and helpful both for public policy purposes and for business planning.

Appendix

DATA SOURCES AND DEFINITIONS

Unless the text indicates otherwise, the data used in tables and regressions were obtained from the following sources:

Table 3–3.

Variables: Personal Disposable Income, Net Saving, Private Pension Contribution, Private Pension Assets, State and Local Government Pension Assets, Total Individual Financial Assets, Total Individual Financial Liabilities.

Source: *Flow of Funds Accounts*, 1947–75, Board of Governors of the Federal Reserve System, Dec. 1976.

Variables: Population, Federal Government Surplus, Retained Earnings, Unemployment Rate, Employment, Number of Workers, Labor Force Participation, Personal Consumption Expenditures Price Deflator, State and Local Government Employees, Federal Government Employees.

Source: *Economic Report of the President*, Washington, D.C.: U.S.G.P.O., 1978. Tables: B–26, B–23, B–19, B–27, B–27, B–3, B–34, and B–34, respectively.

Variables: Personal Consumption Expenditures on Education and Research; Federal Retirement Benefits, Federal Pension Beneficiaries, State and Local Retirement Benefits, and State and Local Pension Benefits.

Source: *Historical Statistics of U.S.* (Colonial Times to Present), U.S. Department of Commerce, Bureau of the Census, Bicentennial Edition, September 1975, and Munnell and Connolly [40, 1976].

Variables: "Real" Return on Long-term Corporate Bonds.

Source: Ibbotson and Sinquefield [26, 1977].

Variable: Social Security Wealth.

Source: Feldstein [14, 1974] and Munnell [39, 1978].

Table 3–7. Panels A, B, and C; and Table 3–8, Panels A, B, and C

Variables: Net Savings, Increase in Liabilities, Net Financial Investments, Life Insurance Reserves, Pension Fund Reserves, Disposable Income.

Source: *Flow of Funds Accounts*, Quarterly Data, Household Section, Board of Governors of the Federal Reserve System, September 1977.

Variables: Personal Saving, Price Level, Social Security Contributions.

Source: National Bureau of Economic Research Time-Series Data Bank, Tymshare, Inc., W. Pertino Co.

Variable: Net Social Security Wealth.
Source: Feldstein [14, 1974] and Munnell [39, 1978].

Note: We have run quarterly regressions using different estimates of social security wealth. The techniques in estimating the quarterly social security wealth varied, from using instrumental variables such as income to estimating the quarterly growth rate of social security wealth from annual time series on Feldstein-Munnell data. The results of all techniques are quite similar to the one presented here.

REFERENCES

1. ANDO, ALBERT, and MODIGLIANI, FRANCO. "The Life Cycle Hypothesis of Saving: Aggregate Implications and Tests," *American Economic Review*, March 1963, *53* (1), pp. 55–84.

2. BARRO, ROBERT. "Are Government Bonds Net Wealth?" *Journal of Political Economy*, Nov./Dec. 1974, *82* (6), pp. 1095–1117.

3. ____. *Social Security and Private Saving—Evidence from the U.S. Time Series.* Washington, D.C.: American Enterprise Institute, 1978.

4. BLUME, MARSHALL E., and FRIEND, IRWIN. "The Asset Structure of Individual Portfolios and Some Implications for Utility Functions," *Journal of Finance*, May 1975, *30* (2), pp. 585–604.

5. BOSKIN, MICHAEL J. "Social Security and Retirement Decisions," *Economic Inquiry*, Jan. 1977, *15* (1), pp. 1–25.

6. ____. "Taxation, Saving and the Rate of Interest," *Journal of Political Economy*, April 1978, *86* (2), Part 2, pp. S3–S27.

7. BURCH, SUSAN W. "Demographic Saving Determinants as Revealed by Surveys of Consumer Expenditures." Unpublished paper presented at the American Economic Association meetings, New York, Dec. 1977.

8. CAGAN, PHILIP. *The Effect of Pension Plans on Aggregate Saving: Evidence from a Sample Survey.* National Bureau of Economic Research, Occasional Paper No. 95. New York: Columbia University Press, 1965.

9. CAMPBELL, COLIN D., and CAMPBELL, ROSEMARY. "Conflicting Views on the Effect of Old-Age and Survivors Insurance on Retirement," *Economic Inquiry*, Sept. 1976, *14* (3), pp. 369–88.

10. DARBY, MICHAEL R. "The Effects of Social Security on Income and the Capital Stock." Unpublished UCLA working paper, July 1977.

11. DAVID, PAUL A., and SCADDING, JOHN. "Private Savings Ultrarationality, Aggregation and Denison's Law," *Journal of Political Economy*, March/April 1974, *82* (2), Part I, pp. 225–49.

12. DENISON, EDWARD F. *Accounting for United States Economic Growth, 1929–1969.* Washington, D.C.: The Brookings Institution, 1974.

13. EHRBAR, A.F. "The Pension Plans Are Even Weaker Than You Think," *Fortune*, November 1977, pp. 104–14.

14. FELDSTEIN, MARTIN. "Social Security, Induced Retirement, and Aggregate Capital Accumulation," *Journal of Political Economy*, Sept./Oct. 1974, *82* (5), pp. 905–26.

15. ____. "Social Security and Saving: The Extended Life Cycle Theory," *American Economic Review*, May 1976, *66*(2), pp. 77–86.

16. ____; "National Saving in the United States," in *Capital for Productivity and Jobs.* Edited by ELI SHAPIRO and WILLIAM L. WHITE. Englewood Cliffs, N.J.: Prentice-Hall, 1977.

17. ____, and PELLECHIO, ANTHONY. "Social Security and Household Wealth Accumulation: New Microeconometric Evidence," Harvard Institute of Economic Research Discussion Paper Number 530, January 1977.

18. ____, and SUMMERS, LAWRENCE. "Is the Rate of Profit Falling?" *Brookings Papers on Economic Activity*, 1977, (1), pp. 211–27.

19. FRIEDMAN, BENJAMIN M. "Public Pension Funding and U.S. Capital Formation," in *Funding Pensions: Issues and Implications for Financial Markets.* Conference Series No. 16, Federal Reserve Bank of Boston, Oct. 1976.

20. VON FURSTENBERG, GEORGE M. "Corporate Valuation: Does Market Valuation Matter in the Aggregate?" *Brookings Papers on Economic Activity*, 1977, (2), pp. 347–97.

21. ____. "Comment on the Kotlikoff and Rosen Papers." Unpublished paper delivered at the Hoover Institution, Stanford, Oct. 1977.

22. ____, and MALKIEL, BURTON G. "The Government and Capital Formation: A Survey of Recent Issues," *Journal of Economic Literature*, Sept. 1977, *15*(3), pp. 835–78.

23. HAANES-OLSEN, LEIF. "Earnings-Replacement Rate of Old Age Benefits, 1965–75, Selected Countries," *Social Security Bulletin*, Jan. 1978, *41*(1), pp. 3–14.

24. HOLLAND, DANIEL M., and MYERS, STEWART C. "Trends in Corporate Profitability and Capital Costs." Massachusetts Institute of Technology, Alfred P. Sloan School of Management, WP 937–77, May 1977, unpublished.

25. HOUTHAKKER, HENDRIK, and TAYLOR, LESTER D. *Consumer Demand in the United States.* Cambridge, Mass.: Harvard University Press, Second Edition, 1970.

26. IBBOTSON, ROGER G., and SINQUEFIELD, REX A. *Stocks, Bonds, Bills and Inflation: The Past (1926–1976) and the Future (1977–2000).* Charlottesville, Va.: Financial Analysts Research Foundation, 1977.

27. KAPLAN, ROBERT S. *Financial Crisis in the Social Security System.* Washington, D.C.: American Enterprise Institute, 1976.

28. ____. "A Comparison of Rates of Return to Social Security Retirees under Wage and Price Indexing," in *Social Security Financing.* Edited by COLIN D. CAMPBELL. Washington, D.C.: American Enterprise Institute, 1979.

29. KATONA, GEORGE. *Private Pensions and Individual Savings.* Monograph No. 40, Survey Research Center, Institute for Social Research. Ann Arbor: University of Michigan, 1965.

30. KOTLIKOFF, LAWRENCE. "Testing the Theory of Social Security and Life Cycle Accumulation." Paper presented at the Hoover Institution, Stanford, Oct. 1977.

31. LESNOY, SELIG D., and HAMBOR, JOHN C. "Social Security, Saving, and Capital Formation," *Social Security Bulletin*, July 1975, *38*(7), pp. 3–15.

32. LINTNER, JOHN. "Savings and Investment for Future Growth: 1975–6 and Beyond." Paper presented at The Conference Board, Washington, D.C., April 1975.

33. LOGUE, DENNIS E. *Legislative Influence on Corporate Pension Plans.* Washington, D.C.: American Enterprise Institute, 1979.

34. ____, and WILLETT, THOMAS D. "A Note on the Relation between the Rate and Variability of Inflation," *Economica*, May 1976, *43*(2), pp; 151–58.

35. MILLER, MERTON H., and UPTON, CHARLES W. *Macroeconomics, A Neo-Classical Introduction.* Homewood, Ill.: Irwin, 1974.

36. MUNNELL, ALICIA H. "The Impact of Social Security on Personal Savings," *National Tax Journal*, Dec. 1974, *27*(4), pp. 553–67.

37. ____. "Private Pensions and Saving: New Evidence," *Journal of Political Economy*, Oct. 1976, *84*(5), pp. 1013–32.

38. ____. *The Future of Social Security*, Washington, D.C.: The Brookings Institution, 1977.

39. ____. "The Interaction of Social Security and Private Pensions," in *Social Security Financing.* Edited by COLIN D. CAMPBELL. Washington, D.C.: American Enterprise Institute, 1979.

40. ____, and CONNOLLY, ANN M. "Funding Government Pensions: State-Local, Civil Service, and Military," in *Funding Pensions: Issues and Implications for Financial Markets.* Conference Series No. 16, Federal Reserve Bank of Boston, Oct. 1976.

41. PHELPS, EDMUND A., and KARL, SHELL. "Public Debt, Taxation, and Capital Intensity," *Journal of Economic Theory*, Oct. 1969, *1* (3), pp. 330–46.

42. ROBERTSON, A. HAEWORTH. "Financial Status of Social Security Program after the Social Security Amendments of 1977," *Social Security Bulletin*, March 1978, *41* (3), pp. 21–30.

43. SCHULZ, JAMES H. *The Economics of Aging.* Belmont, Calif.: Wadsworth, 1976.

44. SKOLNIK, ALFRED M. "Private Pension Plans, 1950–74," *Social Security Bulletin*, June 1976, *39*(6), pp. 3–17.

45. THOMPSON, EARL A. "Debt Instruments in Both Macroeconomic Theory and Capital Theory," *American Economic Review*, Dec. 1967, *57*(5), pp. 1196–1210.

46. WACHTEL, PAUL. "Inflation, Uncertainty, and the Composition of Personal Saving," in *Understanding Financial Markets*, Vol. II. Edited by ARNOLD W. SAMETZ and PAUL WACHTEL. Lexington, Mass.: Lexington Books, 1977.

Part II

Empirical Studies: The Foreign Experiences

Chapter 4

Pensions and Saving in Canada

Michael Denny and
Samuel A. Rea, Jr.[a]

Given the similarities between Canada and the United States, an analysis of trends in Canadian saving and the role of pensions in Canada can contribute to the current debate on national saving in the United States. This debate has centered around two issues: first, the existence of trends in national saving rates, and second, the influence of social security wealth on saving. These two issues will be examined in the Canadian context.

Martin Feldstein [9, 1977] has argued that the U.S. national saving rate has fallen since the nineteenth century. The Canadian evidence differs from this. Using the Canadian national accounts, the saving rate has been stable in the past thirty years and has generally been higher than in the 1901–30 period. Adjusting the Canadian data to the methodology of the U.S. national accounts does not change these results greatly. The Canadian evidence tends to support the hypothesis of a constant private saving rate, at least descriptively.

The mere fact that the saving rate has not declined in Canada during the period when government provision for social security was expanded greatly, does not, of course, prove that this provision has not reduced saving, *ceteris paribus.* In the second half of this chapter this question is therefore addressed in a model framework. However, it does not appear that the saving rate would have been higher in the absence of the social security programs, though such an outcome

[a]The authors are both Associate Professors of Economics at the University of Toronto. The authors would like to thank George von Furstenberg and Grant Reuber for their helpful comments and David Ross for his assistance with the calculations.

may still materialize once the retirement age has stabilized at a lower level.

Specifically, prior to 1966 public pensions in Canada consisted largely of a demogrant for those over seventy. In 1966, a contributory program, the Canada Pension Plan (CPP), was introduced. Since the plan was only partially funded, introduction of the program (along with the Quebec Pension Plan) created an estimated 37.2 billion dollars in social security wealth. One would expect that this wealth would affect the personal saving rate. However, a review of the available evidence indicates that it is unlikely that there has been a significant decline in personal saving in response to the new program. A study by Ontario [13, 1977] suggests that the public benefit structure did not have a statistically significant negative impact on private saving, and that earlier retirement has had a strong positive impact on the saving rate. An equally important (unanswered) question is whether the provinces have increased their current expenditures in response to the purchase of provincial securities by the CPP fund.

This chapter consists of three main sections. In Section I the development of saving rates in Canada is evaluated and compared to the U.S. experience. In Section II Canada's public pension programs and the tax treatment of private pensions are explained for those unfamiliar with Canada's policies. In Section III an estimate of Canada's social security wealth is presented, and the possible link between saving and social security wealth is examined.

I. NATIONAL SAVING AND INVESTMENT IN CANADA

The recent debate in the United States about capital shortages has increased economists' interest in trends in the rates of national saving and investment. There are two competing hypotheses about these rates in the United States. Feldstein [9, 1977] has argued that *the rates of capital accumulation and saving have fallen in the United States since the nineteenth century.* This decline, he states, has continued in the post–World War II period. Paul David and John Scadding [4, 1974] have suggested that the gross private saving rate has been constant. As Feldstein notes, these are competing claims and the historical data will have to be investigated further before either hypothesis is validated.

Can either claim be supported by Canadian evidence? Our results are not beyond dispute, but they tend to support a modified form of the David and Scadding hypothesis. Alternatively, there is no direct evidence for the Feldstein hypothesis. The years 1946–75 will be most intensively investigated, but, as a historical reference point, we will also examine the years 1901–30. For the postwar period, the changes in the rates and sources of saving will be compared with Feldstein's analysis of the United States. The earlier period will be used to judge long-term trends in Canada's saving rates.

Feldstein [9, 1977] used simple trends in the national accounts data to support his hypothesis that the U.S. saving and investment rates were falling. No estimation of an economic model was involved. The simple use of trends in aggregate data does not permit one to know what would have occurred if policies in either country had been different. In order to compare Canada's experience with that of the United States, we will also consider only time trends. This will be supplemented with a brief analysis of David and Scadding's model.

The U.S. and Canadian national accounts are restrictive in their definitions of saving and investment. For example, Kendrick [11, 1976] shows a steadily rising saving and investment rate in the United States when saving and investment are more broadly defined.[1] The Canadian and American accounts are related but their presentations of gross saving and investment differ. In the next section, the major conceptual differences in the two accounting systems are explained. This will be followed by an analysis of the Canadian experience for 1946–75. Initially, the analysis will be done using the Canadian concepts and methodology.[2] Two reasons may be given for this choice. First, we would argue that Canadian activity can be more usefully viewed as Canada currently measures that activity. Second, the U.S. national accounting methodology is not necessarily the most desirable method of measuring any country's economic activity. For comparison we will also present the Canadian experience as it would be seen using the U.S. methodology. The contrasting methodologies may assist in showing how conceptual differences affect broad conclusions about trends in either country.

Saving and Investment in the Canadian and American National Accounts

This description of the two accounting systems is limited to an outline of the major conceptual differences that are important for comparing saving and investment in the two countries.[3] In the comparison of the two systems it is assumed that the reader is more familiar with the U.S. accounts.

Both the gross and the net national saving and investment rates are used in cross-country comparisons. The gross national saving rate equals gross saving[4] as a percentage of GNP. The net rate relates net saving to the net national product. The four sectors of the economy are government (G), persons (P), corporate (C), and foreign (F). The U.S. accounts equate national saving (S) and national investment (I), using the following identity:

$$I_C + I_P + I_F \equiv S_P + S_C + S_G \quad . \tag{1}$$

Net foreign investment (I_F) and foreign saving (S_F) are equal in magnitude with opposite signs.

The Canadian accounts present saving and investment on a *domestic* rather than a *national* basis. The identity is

$$I_C + I_P \equiv S_P + S_C + S_G + S_F \quad . \tag{2}$$

This rearrangement of the identity reflects Canadian experience. Throughout her history Canada has made use of large quantities of foreign savings. The United States in recent decades has been a large investor in foreign countries. In relative terms, the foreign sector is far more important in Canada. It has been a large and volatile component in the history of Canada's saving.

The government sector is portrayed differently in the two countries. In the United States, government saving (S_G) equals government receipts (R_G) minus government expenditure (E_G).

$$\text{United States:} \quad S_G = R_G - E_G \quad . \tag{3}$$

In Canada gross government investment (I_G) is included in national investment. Government capital consumption allowances[5] are treated like government expenditures only for the purpose of obtaining net government saving. Thus gross saving by government is:

$$\text{Canada:} \quad S_G = R_G - (E_G - I_G) \tag{4}$$

The final Canadian saving-investment identity becomes

$$I_P + I_C + I_G \equiv S_P + S_C + S_G + S_F \, , \tag{5}$$

where S_G is defined in (4). The inclusion of government capital consumption allowances increases GNP and alters the relationship between gross and net saving and investment.

There are two other differences that must be mentioned briefly. The statistical discrepancy, called the residual error in Canada, has been excluded from saving in the United States. It is included in

Canada but has an insignificant effect on the rate.[6] Both countries have recently made relatively large changes in their measurement of capital consumption allowances. There is no way of reconciling the differences. The results for gross saving are not affected but the comparisons of net saving are made more difficult.[7]

Postwar Saving in Canada

Using the Canadian methodology the broad trends in the average gross and net national saving rates are presented in Table 4–1. Since 1950, the gross saving rate has been remarkably stable. The net saving rate has been more volatile but still relatively stable. There is no evidence in Table 4–1 that the gross or net saving rate has fallen during the postwar period. Feldstein [9, 1977] suggests that these rates have declined in the United States.

Throughout this section we will include the years 1926–30 as a reference to an earlier period. In a later section the full period 1901–30 will be considered separately.[8] The average gross and net saving rate, 23.1 and 13.5, are higher than the pre-Depression rates of 21.9 and 11.7. This contradicts Feldstein's version of the American experience. Further confirmation of this difference between the countries is given in the section evaluating 1901–30.

The Distribution of Gross and Net Saving

While the aggregate gross and net saving rates have both shown little trend within the postwar period, the relative importance of

Table 4–1. Gross and Net Saving Rate in Canada, 1926–75 *(percent)*

	Gross	*Net*
1926–30	21.9	11.7
1946–50	20.3	11.9
1951–55	23.5	14.5
1956–60	24.8	14.6
1961–65	23.0	12.2
1966–70	23.6	13.6
1971–75	23.5	14.2
1946–75	23.1	13.5

Note: gross saving rate = gross saving/gross national product; net saving rate = net saving/net national product.

Sources: Statistics Canada, *National Income and Expenditure Accounts*, Vol. I and III (13-531, 13-549E) 1975; Statistics Canada, *National Income and Expenditure Accounts*, 1961-75, (13-201), 1976; Statistics Canada, Cansim data bank revisions to 13-201 for 1970-76.

Table 4–2. Distribution of Gross Saving, Canada, 1926–75
(percentage of gross saving)

	1926–30	*1946–55*	*1956–65*	*1966–75*
Personal Saving	13.3	25.3	13.2	20.2
Government Saving	7.1	14.4	6.9	13.3
Corporation Saving	19.1	14.2	16.8	15.0
Personal CCA	24.3	17.9	17.3	14.7
Government CCA	5.1	5.1	5.4	6.1
Corporation CCA	22.6	23.0	29.4	27.2
Foreign Saving	8.5	0.0	11.1	3.6

Note: Personal Saving, Government Saving, and Corporation Saving are net of Capital Consumption allowances. Percentages do not add to 100 due to rounding and omission of the residual error (note 6).

Source: see Table 4-1.

alternative sources of gross saving has changed greatly in postwar Canada. Table 4–2 provides a percentage distribution of the components of average gross saving for selected periods. There are relatively few trends in the sources during the postwar period. All sources show a peak or trough in the 1956–65 period relative to the preceding and following decades.

Net personal saving[9] was one-quarter of gross saving in the first decade. This share was cut in half during the second decade and rose to 20 percent of total gross saving in the third decade. While it is not possible to find a continuous trend in the share of net personal saving in total gross saving within the postwar period, the share has risen if the average for the entire postwar period is compared to that for 1926–30. On a gross basis the opposite is true because personal Capital Consumption Allowances (CCA)[10] are far less important in the postwar period than before the Depression. The gradual decline in the latter reflects the falling importance of unincorporated businesses.

Corporate net saving has declined from 19 percent in 1926–30 to 15 percent of total gross saving after the war. This decline was offset by an increase in the corporate CCA from 23 to 27 percent of gross saving. The two sources of corporate gross saving both reached a postwar peak during 1956–65, when the two other domestic components of gross saving bottomed out for reasons that are not analyzed here.

The government share of saving has been larger in the postwar period. The continual growth in government capital formation has resulted in a slow but steady increase in the share of government capital consumption allowances. The government contribution to gross saving has risen to an average of 17 percent in the postwar period from 12 percent in 1926–30.

Foreign saving is measured poorly in the national accounts. The current measure shows only the transactions that enter the balance of payments, leaving a substantial volume of foreign saving recorded as corporate saving.[11] The U.S. national accounts place net foreign saving in the gross investment account. To indicate the effects of this, Table 4–3 shows the distribution of gross saving when the foreign sector is excluded, but none of the major conclusions is altered.

The last two rows of Table 4–3 show the development of net saving and capital consumption allowances as a percent of gross saving. The share of net saving has increased from 43 percent in 1926–30 to 47 percent for 1946–75. Underlying this result are the sharp increases in the shares of government and personal net saving in gross saving, which were only partly offset by declines in the corporate sector.

The shares of net saving by sector are shown in Table 4–4 with the foreign sector included. The foreign sector absorbed 13 percent of net saving immediately after the war and then provided almost 20 percent of net saving during the next fifteen years. In the past ten years foreign saving has become less important, averaging only 6.3 percent.

Table 4–3. Distribution of Gross Saving in Canada Excluding Foreign Sector *(percentage of gross saving)*

	1926–30	*1946–55*	*1956–65*	*1966–75*
Personal Saving	14.5	25.3	14.8	21.0
Government Saving	7.8	14.4	7.8	13.8
Corporation Saving	20.9	14.2	18.9	15.6
Personal CCA	26.6	17.9	19.5	15.2
Government CCA	5.6	5.1	6.1	6.3
Corporation CCA	24.7	23.0	33.0	28.2
Persons	41.1	43.2	34.3	36.2
Corporations	45.6	37.2	51.9	43.8
Government	13.4	19.5	13.9	20.1
Net Saving	43.2	53.9	41.5	50.4
CCA	56.8	46.1	58.5	49.6

Note: see Table 4-2.
Source: see Table 4-1.

Table 4–4. Net Saving Distribution, Canada *(percentage of net saving)*

	Personal	*Government*	*Corporation*	*Foreign*
1926–30	26.0	13.7	40.3	20.0
1946–50	60.4	30.9	22.0	–13.3
1951–55	37.3	19.5	32.1	11.1
1956–60	24.5	12.5	33.0	30.3
1961–65	30.5	17.8	36.7	15.0
1966–70	31.6	31.6	32.1	4.7
1971–75	44.6	19.7	26.7	7.7
1946–75	38.2	22.0	30.4	9.3

Note: see Table 4–2.
Source: see Table 4–1.

The personal sector (Table 4–4) provided 60 percent of net saving from 1946–50. This declined to one-quarter in 1956–60. The recent inflationary period has seen the share of this sector rebound to almost one-half.

The government sector has provided over one-fifth of the net saving in the postwar period, and this is considerably larger than its pre-Depression share of 14 percent. For a brief period in the late 1960s the government provided almost one-third of the net saving in Canada. Since then this share has fallen back to 20 percent, so that there is no clear trend.

As an introduction to the reconciliation of the U.S. and Canadian accounts the behavior of personal saving during the postwar period is instructive. The *conceptual* differences between the countries do not seriously affect either personal saving or personal disposable income, but the new measure of economic depreciation used in the U.S. accounts tends to reduce the U.S. net personal saving rate. Consequently some of the differences in the net saving rates in the two countries can be attributed to differences in the methods used to measure capital consumption allowances.[12]

The average rates of saving out of disposable income for 1946–75 are almost identical in the two countries (Table 4–5). However, the steady growth in the United States contrasts with the U-shaped Canadian pattern that reached its low in 1956–65.

A summary of the Canadian experience will be useful before we turn to a direct comparison of the countries.

1. There has been no decline in the gross or net saving rate in Canada either during the postwar period or relative to 1926–30.

Table 4–5. Personal Saving as a Percent of Personal Disposable Income, Canada and United States, 1946–75

	Canada	*U.S.*
1946–55	7.4	5.8
1956–65	4.5	5.9
1966–75	7.3	7.1
1946–75	6.4	6.3

Source: for Canada see Table 4-1. For U.S.: Department of Commerce, *National Income and Product Accounts of the U.S. 1929-74*, 1976; Department of Commerce, *Survey of Current Business*, National Income issues, various years.

2. The weak trends in the saving rate are upward both within the postwar period and relative to 1926–30.
3. No continuous trends in the *sources* of gross or net saving exist for 1946–75. The one exception would be the decline in the importance of the foreign sector.
4. Limited evidence suggests that, relative to 1926–30,
   - the government sector is a more important source of gross and net saving;
   - the personal sector is a more important source of net saving but not of gross saving;
   - the corporate sector is a less important source of net but not gross saving;
   - the foreign sector is a less important source of both types of saving.

Approximate Reconciliation with the United States

The Canadian and American accounts are sufficiently different that the earlier description of the Canadian economy may change when we attempt a reconciliation. In this section we will describe the savings and investment behavior of the two economies during the postwar period *using the U.S. methodology*. Only the major conceptual differences are included in our reconciliation. Denny [7, 1977] provides more details.

There are two major sectors that are affected when we switch methodologies, the foreign sector and the government sector. In order to conform to the U.S. methodology the foreign sector must be placed on the investment side. The U.S. accounts do not recognize the existence of government capital formation or the use of the government capital stock. The Canadian government accounts have been recalculated under this alternative methodology. The elimination of government investment and foreign saving has made the gross and net saving rates in Table 4–6 more volatile, and the apparent slight increase in both of these rates shown in Table 4–1 is undercut. Using the U.S. rather than the Canadian definitions, the gross and particularly the net saving rates dropped sharply to a low in 1956–65 and have climbed sharply since then.

The comparable rates for the two countries are presented in Table 4–7. The Canadian gross saving rate is 18.8 percent versus 15.5 for the United States for 1946–75. The net saving rate is 9.4 percent versus 7.3 percent. It would appear that even under the U.S. methodology Canada's rates have been higher than the U.S. rates.

The change in the methodology has eliminated the apparent stability in the saving rates. However, the Feldstein hypotheses are not supported by the Canadian data. There is no convincing evidence of a decline in the saving rates during 1946–75.

Table 4–6. Gross and Net Saving Rate in Canada, 1926–75 *(U.S. definition)*

	Gross	*Net*
1926–30	17.8	8.0
1946–50	19.4	11.9
1951–55	19.3	10.8
1956–60	16.9	6.6
1961–65	18.6	7.1
1966–70	18.9	9.6
1970–75	18.9	10.2
1946–75	18.7	9.4

Source: see Table 4-1.

Table 4–7. Gross and Net Saving Rate in the United States and Canada, 1946–75 *(U.S. definition)*

		Gross	*Net*
1946–55	U.S.	15.8	8.3
	Canada	19.3	11.4
1956–65	U.S.	15.6	7.0
	Canada	17.8	6.8
1966–75	U.S.	15.2	6.5
	Canada	18.9	9.9
1946–75	U.S.	15.5	7.3
	Canada	18.8	9.4

Source: see Table 4-5 (U.S.), Table 4-1 (Canada).

The rollercoaster effect that we noted in the earlier discussion of the distribution of saving is now readily evident in the movement of the saving rates. It is instructive to compare the Canadian net saving rate under the two methodologies. The initial Canadian methodology showed a slowly rising trend in the net saving rate from 13.2 to 13.8 percent (Table 4–8). This is replaced by a sharp dip in the middle period under the U.S. definitions.[13]

The distribution of the revised Canadian gross saving is shown in Table 4–9. Since government and foreign saving are reduced, the importance of the remaining elements is changed. The government sector is a declining source of saving since government investment is not recognized. In the bottom sections of the table the personal sector has a falling share of gross saving and corporations have a rising share in the postwar period. This was evident under the Canadian methodology in Table 4–4. Net saving by all sectors is falling relative to capital consumption allowances.

Table 4–8. A Comparison of Net Saving Rates, Canada, 1946–75

	(1) Canadian Methodology	*(2) American Methodology*	*Difference (1–2)*
1946–55	13.2	11.4	1.8
1955–65	13.4	6.8	6.6
1966–75	13.8	9.9	3.9

Source: Tables 4-1 and 4-7.

Table 4–9. Canadian Gross Saving Distribution *(U.S. methodology, percentage of gross saving)*

	1926–30	*1946–55*	*1956–65*	*1966–75*
Personal Saving	11.4	28.0	18.3	25.6
Government Saving	–4.2	8.4	–6.8	2.6
Corporation Saving	26.1	16.7	23.3	18.9
Personal CCA	34.3	20.4	24.2	18.6
Corporation CCA	32.3	26.4	41.0	34.3
Personal	45.7	48.4	42.5	44.2
Corporations	58.4	43.2	64.3	53.2
Government	–4.2	8.4	–6.8	2.6
Net Saving	33.3	53.1	34.8	47.1
CCA	66.6	46.8	65.2	52.9

Note: see Table 4-2.
Source: see Table 4-1.

Table 4–10. Comparing Canadian and American Gross Saving Rates
(U.S. methodology, percentage of gross saving)

	1946–55	1956–65	1966–75	1946–75
Canada				
Persons	48.4	42.5	44.2	45.0
Corporations	43.2	64.3	53.2	53.6
Government	8.4	−6.8	2.6	1.4
U.S.				
Persons	50.6	51.7	56.4	52.9
Corporations	44.1	50.9	50.0	48.3
Government	5.4	−2.2	−5.9	−0.9
Canada				
Net Saving	54.1	34.8	47.1	45.0
CCA	46.8	65.2	52.9	55.0
U.S.				
Net Saving	46.9	40.2	40.9	42.3
CCA	53.1	59.8	60.1	57.7

Note: see Table 4-2.
Source: see Table 4-5 (U.S.), Table 4-1 (Canada).

An explicit comparison of the two countries can be made using Table 4–10. In the period 1946–75 the government sector has contributed almost nothing in either country to gross saving. In Canada, the corporate sector has been relatively more important than the personal sector. The reverse is true in the United States. The weak trends support the continuation of this pattern. The importance of the personal sector has fallen four percentage points during the postwar period in Canada while it has risen six percentage points in the United States. The share of the corporate sector has risen in both countries, but the increase is much larger in Canada. Finally, the importance of capital consumption allowances as a source has risen in both countries. CCA would appear to be a more important source of gross saving in the United States than in Canada.[14]

The net saving rate depends on the methods used to estimate capital consumption allowances (see Denny [7, 1977]). The U.S. estimates are now based on perpetual inventory capital stock estimates. The Canadian basis for corporations is the company book value rather than tax statistics. We have not attempted a reconciliation of these differences.

The evidence in Table 4–4 suggested that the personal sector was a declining source of net saving until a very recent upsurge. The other two sources, excluding the foreign sector, had no clear pattern. The relative sources of net saving under the U.S. methodology are shown

Table 4–11. Net Saving Distribution, Canada, 1946–75 *(U.S. methodology, percentage of net saving)*

	Personal	*Government*	*Corporations*
1946–50	54.6	24.3	21.2
1951–55	50.5	3.5	46.0
1956–60	53.7	–27.4	73.7
1961–65	54.1	–21.2	67.1
1966–70	44.1	11.3	44.6
1971–75	64.8	–1.3	36.4
1946–75	53.6	–1.8	48.2

Note: see Table 4-2.
Source: see Table 4-5 (U.S.), Table 4-1 (Canada).

Table 4–12. Sources of Net Saving, Canada and United States, 1946–75 *(U.S. methodology, percentage of net saving)*

	1946–55	*1956–65*	*1966–75*	*1946–75*
Canada				
Personal	52.6	53.9	54.4	53.6
Government	13.9	–24.3	5.0	–1.8
Corporation	33.6	70.4	40.5	48.2
U.S.				
Personal	60.0	67.4	87.0	71.4
Government	4.7	–8.6	–21.0	–8.3
Corporation	35.4	41.3	33.8	36.9

Note: see Table 4-2.
Source: see Table 4-5 (U.S.), Table 4-1 (Canada).

in Table 4–11. The personal sector's share shows the same movement. The corporation sector's share declined from a very high 74 percent to 36 percent between 1956–60 and 1971–75. Since government investment is ignored, the government sector is volatile and does not exhibit any trend.

The sources of net saving in Canada and the United States are shown in Table 4–12. The explosion of the personal sector's share in the United States and its high average share in the postwar period are not evident in Canada. The steady increase in the drain on net savings by the U.S. government sector has not occurred in Canada. The Canadian personal sector's share has remained very stable, when measured as a ten-year average, though the five-year averages in Table 4–11 show much more volatility. Changes in the government and corporate sectors have tended to be offsetting to produce a fairly constant total for these two sectors combined. The lack of any clear trends in the Canadian sectoral sources of gross and net saving remains.

The Canadian saving rates have been higher than the American throughout the postwar period. The Canadian corporate sector has been a more important source of gross and net saving than the American. The American government sector has had a larger impact on saving, and the volatility of this source in both countries is most noticeable.

A Historical View

The Canadian saving and investment experience of the last thirty years may be placed in a longer historical context to investigate changes during the present century. Feldstein [9, 1977] relies heavily on Kuznet's data for the years before the Depression to argue that the rate of capital accumulation and saving have fallen since the late nineteenth and early twentieth century in the United States. His evidence is not undisputed.[15] David and Scadding [4, 1974] argue that the gross private saving rate has been a constant over a similar period of time.

To compare the recent Canadian experience with pre-Depression Canada, Kenneth Buckley's [2, 1951] historical estimates may be used.[16] Gross investment in Canada averaged 22.0 percent of GNP from 1901–30 (Table 4–13). This compares with an average of 23.1 percent for 1946–75. There is no evidence of a sharp reduction in the gross investment rate since World War II. Buckley argues that the period 1901–30 was one of very heavy investment in Canada relative

Table 4–13. Canadian Gross Investment Rates, 1901–30 *(percentage of GNP)*

	Gross Investment	*Government Investment*	*Net Foreign Investment*	*Gross Investment (U.S. Methodology)*
1901–5	22.7	1.7	−5.3	15.7
1906–10	27.0	2.9	−9.2	14.9
1911–15	26.9	3.6	−12.4	10.9
1916–20	19.3	1.4	−1.3	16.6
1921–25	16.1	1.9	0.3	14.5
1926–30	20.3	2.1	−1.9	16.3
1946–75	23.1	3.6	−1.9	17.7

Source: Buckley [2], Table II, V and XXI for 1901-30. See Table 4-1 for 1946-75.

to earlier periods. The subperiods in 1901–30 show more variability than those in 1946–75. In order to understand this behavior the importance of government and net foreign investment must be considered. Government investment averaged 2.3 percent of GNP from 1901–30 and 3.6 percent from 1946–75. The government's importance has increased sharply in percentage terms but its absolute importance remains small.

The major fluctuations in the gross investment rate were created by the foreign sector. Column 3, Table 4–13, shows that net foreign investment averaged 10.8 percent of GNP during 1906–15. This very large inflow of foreign saving led to gross investment rates that have never been equaled since that time.

The Canadian gross investment rate, measured with the U.S. methodology (Table 4–13, column 4), averaged only 14.8 percent during 1901–30, which is actually lower than the postwar average rate of 17.7. We believe that there is no evidence to suggest that the Canadian rate of capital accumulation has fallen in recent decades relative to the first three decades of this century.

The behavior of the gross private saving rate merits separate discussion since this is the rate emphasized by several researchers. Buckley commented as follows on a relationship which has since become known as "Denison's Law": "Ignoring the inflated years from 1916–20—there is a remarkably stable relationship between gross saving and gross national product" [2, 1951, p. 97]. Buckley's data on gross private saving as a percentage of GNP are reproduced in column 1 of Table 4–14. Buckley's concept of gross private saving, like that of David and Scadding and Denison, excludes the government deficit. This is not the concept of gross saving that we have

Table 4–14. Canadian Gross and Net Saving Rates, 1901–30 *(percentage of GNP)*

	Gross Private Saving	*Net Saving*	*Government Deficit*
1901–5	16.4	5.7	0.7
1906–10	17.8	4.8	3.0
1911–15	17.2	0.9	6.3
1916–20	27.1	6.6	10.5
1921–25	16.8	4.5	2.3
1926–30	17.2	5.2	1.4
1946–75	17.8	7.9	–0.4

Source: Buckley [2], Tables XXI and XXII for 1901-30. See Table 4-1 for 1946-75.

used elsewhere in this chapter. The difference can be seen by comparing the last column of Table 4–13 and the first column of Table 4–14. The stability that Buckley mentions disappears when the government deficit is included. The government deficit as a percentage of GNP is given in column 3, Table 4–14. The deficit is the difference between the two concepts of gross saving.

Buckley's historical evidence is based on gross private saving. During the postwar period gross private saving has averaged 17.8 percent of GNP. Excluding the World War I period, this saving rate is slightly higher than the rate during the period before 1930. There is a slight upward trend from 1946–75. We have not investigated the changing importance of consumer durables. The evidence suggests that David and Scadding's hypothesis might be supported in Canada. If it is not, the trend is likely upward rather than downward.

Information on net saving is not readily available. The rough estimates given in Table 4–14, column 2, are derived from Buckley [2, 1951, p. 99] [17] and turn out to be volatile. Compared to the net saving rates for the postwar period given in Table 4–6, the rate for 1901–30 was much lower. There is no support for the Feldstein hypotheses in Canada. In fact, the Canadian historical evidence suggests that the saving and investment rates in Canada have increased in the postwar period relative to 1901–30.

Our description of the behavior of saving and investment rates in Canada has failed to produce any conclusive trends. However, the explanation rather than description of these trends requires models of behavior. David and Scadding report results from a behavioral model of saving behavior for the aggregate U.S. economy. Unfortunately, very little work on this problem exists in Canada. For Canada several simple models similar to David and Scadding's were estimated. For a wide range of definitions of saving the hypothesis that saving is a constant proportion of GNP cannot be rejected. These results generally support the David and Scadding hypothesis and reject the Feldstein hypothesis. The stability of the estimated parameters over different time periods is high. For some definitions of saving, the hypothesis that the same model fits over several time periods is rejected.

In the next section we will consider the role of social security programs in Canada. A description of these programs will be followed by a discussion of their impact on personal saving.

II. PENSION POLICY IN CANADA

Public policy has a significant impact on the amount of retirement income and the attractiveness of saving for retirement. Canada's policies are particularly diverse. In order to meet the requirements of various segments of the population, Canada's pension policy contains the following five components:

1. a demogrant to everyone over age sixty-five;
2. a negative income tax for those over sixty-five (supplemented by smaller means-tested provincial programs);
3. a contributory earnings-related public pension;
4. tax provisions which encourage private pensions;
5. regulation of employer pension plans.

Government sale of annuities has been suspended recently. The features of the above policies that are likely to affect saving behavior are described below. In particular we are interested in the magnitude of public pensions, the tax on earnings after "retirement," the tax on private pension income, tax treatment of pension savings, and public pension funding arrangements.[18] Ontario's programs are described as an example of provincial policies.

Demogrant—Old Age Security (OAS)

Old Age Security is a demogrant payable to everyone over age sixty-five, subject to certain residence requirements. The amount paid was $1,747 per person in 1977. A married couple would receive $3,494. The pension is adjusted quarterly as the Consumer Price Index changes. Old Age Security benefits are treated as taxable income under the Income Tax Act. This program was introduced in 1951 to replace a means-tested pension in existence since 1927.[19]

Negative Income Tax—Guaranteed Income Supplement (GIS) and Provincial Plans

The Guaranteed Income Supplement is a negative income tax with a guarantee of $1,225 in 1977 for a single individual over age sixty-five and a 50 percent tax on the recipient's own income (excluding OAS benefits and provincial pensions). This tax and guarantee imply that $2,450 can be received from the CPP and private pensions before GIS benefits are reduced to zero. The GIS benefits are not taxable under the Income Tax Act. A married couple receives a guarantee 78 percent larger than the guarantee for a single individual or pensioner with a younger spouse.[20] Benefits under GIS are indexed for inflation.

Various provinces have additional means-tested pensions. For instance, the Guaranteed Annual Income System (GAINS) program in Ontario added $467 to the federal OAS and GIS payments in 1977. The GAINS tax-back rate on income from other sources is 100 percent.

Ontario has a tax credit system which also operates like a negative income tax. Tax credits are based on property taxes (or rental payments), personal exemptions, and pensioner status. The tax-back rate is 2 percent of taxable income. Since a pensioner might have as much as $5,000 in income that is not taxable, the tax credit system is a negative income tax with a large tax exemption. It is, in effect, a lump-sum grant for those without taxable income. Assuming that $1,500 in rent is paid, a pensioner in 1977 with no taxable income would receive $210 in property tax credit, $37 in sales tax credit, and $110 in pensioner tax credit. The total tax credit in this example is $357 per annum.

Earnings-Related Public Pensions—Canada Pension Plan (CPP)

An earnings-related public program was not introduced in Canada until 1966. The Canada Pension Plan (and the separate but nearly identical Quebec Pension Plan) is a comprehensive program that provides not only retirement income but also survivor benefits, orphan benefits, disability benefits, and benefits for the children of disabled contributors. The plan is nearly universal for those earning more than $900 per year.

Contributions to the CPP are made between the ages of eighteen and sixty-five.[21] The contribution rate, split between employer and employee, totals 3.6 percent of annual earnings up to a maximum of $9,300 in 1977 (the year's maximum pensionable earnings, YMPE). There are no contributions on the first $900[22] of annual earnings. The self-employed pay both employer and employee contributions.

Retirement benefits, which are payable at age sixty-five, are based on the relationship between a worker's earnings and the Year's Maximum Pensionable Earnings. The YMPE is scheduled to increase at a 12.5 percent annual rate until it catches up with average earnings. If average earnings grow at a slower rate, the maximum pension will eventually increase at the same rate as average earnings.

In order to determine an individual's retirement pension, the ratio of his earnings to the YMPE (the ratio is set equal to 1 if earnings exceed the YMPE) is calculated for each year after the worker turned eighteen (or the year 1966, whichever is later) and averaged. The resulting fraction (or the value 1) is multiplied by the YMPE average for the year of retirement and the two previous years. The result is called the Average Pensionable Earnings (APE).[23] The retirement pension equals 25 percent of the APE. After retirement the pension increases annually with the Consumer Price Index. To illustrate the calculation in the simplest case, assume that someone earned more than the YMPE in every year between the ages of eighteen and sixty-five. His pension would be 25 percent of the average YMPE for the years in which he was sixty-three, sixty-four, and sixty-five. In 1977 the maximum yearly pension was $2,083.

A key feature of the CPP is that there is no "retirement test" or tax on retirement earnings.[24] Prior to 1975 those between sixty-five and seventy were required to retire from regular employment as a condition for receiving benefits, and earnings were taxed. As demonstrated by Feldstein [8, 1974], a retirement test increases saving if it induces a reduction in labor supply.

Table 4–15 indicates the relative importance of various programs at alternative levels of CPP and private pension income. The table illustrates two important features of the Canadian system. First, maximum CPP benefits are small in relation to the sum of other benefits available to a low-income person. In fiscal year 1976 aggregate CPP benefits were only $588 million compared to $2,976 million for OAS benefits and $1,040 million for GIS benefits. These three programs redistributed 2.7 percent of GNP in fiscal year 1976. Second, those with low retirement incomes from private sources receive little net increase in retirement income as a result of their entitlement to CPP benefits. An individual with the maximum CPP benefits in 1977 (with no other private pension) would receive only $575 more total income per year than an individual with no CPP benefits. However, the maximum CPP benefits will automatically increase in relative importance over time because maximum benefits reflect real growth in earnings as well as price changes.[25] The importance of the noncontributory programs such as OAS and GIS

Table 4–15. 1977 Retirement Income, Single Individual in Ontario
(Canadian dollars)

	Alternative Levels of CPP and Private Pension			
		GAINS Break Even	*Maximum CPP*	*GIS Break Even*
CPP	0	934	2,083	2,083
Private Pension	0	0	0	367
OAS	1,747	1,747	1,747	1,747
GIS	1,225	758	184	0
GAINS	467	0	0	0
Ont. Tax Credit	357	357	357	357
Total Income, Net of Taxes and Transfers	3,796	3,796	4,371	4,554

suggests that discussions of optimal funding of public pensions in Canada should not simply focus on the Canada Pension Plan. The funding arrangements are discussed in Section III.

Tax Provisions Which Encourage Private Pensions

The Income Tax Act offers substantial incentives to invest in private pension plans. The most straightforward incentive is an annual deduction of $1,000 in pension income in addition to an exemption for the aged of $1,420. A spouse can also claim these exemptions. An even more important tax incentive is the deductibility of pension contributions. A maximum of $3,500 can be deducted for contributions to an employer pension plan and $5,500 (or 20 percent of earnings) can be deducted for contributions to an individual plan (Registered Retirement Savings Plan—RRSP).[26] Employer pension contributions are not taxable benefits. The income tax deductions for RRSP contributions postpone taxes until income is received during the retirement years or whenever the RRSP is liquidated. The RRSP offers three types of tax advantages: (1) postponement of taxes until retirement, (2) tax-free reinvestment of RRSP income, and (3) payment of tax during retirement when marginal rates are likely to be low. Similar tax advantages apply to employer plans, although investments in these plans are not as liquid as RRSPs.

III. PENSIONS AND PRIVATE SAVING

As Feldstein [8, 1974] has pointed out, public pension programs are liable to induce a reduction in private saving if consumers treat social security wealth as a substitute for other assets. This reduction in saving may not occur if public pension programs induce earlier retirement because of retirement tests. The reduction in private saving may lead to a reduction in aggregate saving if the public pensions are not fully funded. These two issues, the funding of the public pension program and the response of private saving to public pensions, are discussed in this section.

The Canada Pension Plan is the only government pension program for which there is a fund, but the present contribution rates are insufficient to cover future liabilities. Estimates of the Canada Department of Insurance indicate that the CPP fund that has accumulated since 1966 when the plan was introduced will be exhausted sometime between the years 1995 and 2000 (Table 4–16). If the CPP reverts to a pay-as-you-go basis, contribution rates will ultimately have to be increased. However, there is now considerable debate as to

Table 4–16. Canada Pension Plan Projections

Calendar Year	*Benefits and Expenses (million $)*	*Contributions (million $)*	*Cash Flow to Provinces (million $)*	*Fund (billion $)*
1973				6.6
1974	466	1,105	639	7.7
1975	615	1,255	640	8.9
1976	814	1,385	572	10.1
1977	1,037	1,536	499	11.4
1978	1,285	1,696	411	12.6
1979	1,555	1,878	323	13.8
1980	1,844	2,039	196	15.0
1981	2,127	2,216	89	16.1
1982	2,430	2,400	–30	17.2
1983	2,753	2,592	–161	18.2
1984	3,101	2,793	–308	19.1
1985	3,476	3,003	–473	19.9
1990	5,845	4,208	–1,637	21.3
1995	9,028	5,808	–3,220	14.9
2000	13,178	8,115	–5,063	–4.1
2005	18,679	11,425	–7,254	–41.7
2010	26,678	15,899	–10,780	–109.5
2015	39,631	21,719	–17,912	–233.8
2020	58,863	29,321	–29,542	–459.3
2025	86,732	39,460	–47,272	–854.9

Note: Assumptions are an annual growth rate of earnings of 5.5 percent, an interest rate of 6.5 percent, and a rate of inflation of 3 percent.

Source: Canada Department of Insurance, *Canada Pension Plan Statutory Actuarial Report Number 3*, 1973.

whether the CPP should become fully funded on an actuarial basis. Feldstein's arguments that a fully funded pension is optimal are equally applicable in Canada (Pesando and Rea [14, 1977]), but the existing institutional arrangements complicate funding decisions. The CPP funds are now invested in provincial securities. The economic argument for full funding assumes that the fund will lead to capital formation, or at least will involve no net reduction in capital formation. If the provinces simply increase current expenditures in response to readily available funds at below-market rates of interest, increased contributions may reduce total capital formation. Casual evidence suggests that some provinces have increased their expenditures because they have treated CPP-held debt less seriously than publicly held debt. The optimality of full funding depends crucially on whether institutional arrangements can be devised that will not induce additional current government expenditure in response to increased pension contributions. Consideration is being given to the possibility of investing CPP funds in the private sector, as is now done by the Quebec Pension Plan (QPP).

The partially funded CPP created social security wealth when the plan was introduced in 1966. The extent of this wealth has been estimated using a detailed microsimulation model of lifetime income (Pesando and Rea [14, 1977]). Assuming that the real rate of interest and the real rate of growth of earnings equal 2.5 percent, the net wealth created when the plan was introduced in 1966 is estimated to equal $37.2 billion. For purposes of comparison, the value of the housing stock, excluding land, equaled $40.2 billion at the end of 1966.[27] Consumer durables equaled $20.8 billion.

Two important points must be made concerning the estimate of social security wealth. First, it assumes that contribution rates remain unchanged in the future. As noted above, contributions will have to be increased within the next twenty years. Second, it does not include the capitalized value of Old Age Security which was already in existence in 1966. Nevertheless, the estimate gives an order of magnitude for the additional wealth created in 1966. In the absence of a retirement test, Feldstein's hypothesis suggests that, *ceteris paribus*, the newly created social security wealth should lower the personal saving rate.

The magnitude of the hypothesized effect of CPP wealth on the saving rate can be indicated with some rough calculations. The permanent income equivalent of the social security wealth was $1.6 billion in 1966,[28] or 4 percent of disposable income. This figure plus current contributions equals the amount of CPP saving that individuals assume is taking place under Feldstein's hypothesis. If we add this "social security saving" to measured disposable income, income is increased by 5.8 percent. If the marginal propensity to consume equals 0.9, the *measured* saving rate should decrease by 5.2 percentage points. In fact, the saving rate (saving as a percentage of personal disposable income) is substantially higher in recent years than prior to the introduction of the CPP (Table 4–17). One possible explanation for the increase in saving is the retirement induced by the retirement test that was in existence between 1966 and 1974.[29] Those claiming retirement benefits before age seventy were required to retire from regular employment and were subject to a tax on their earnings. In addition the GIS test on earnings was introduced in 1967. These implicit and explicit taxes on earnings could reduce the labor supply of those over sixty-five and increase saving. However, the timing of the changes in saving rates is not consistent with that of the changes in earnings tests.

Table 4–17. Personal Saving as Percentage of Personal Disposable Income in Canada

1961	2.8
1962	5.6
1963	5.4
1964	4.2
1965	5.5
1966	6.7
1967	6.3
1968	5.6
1969	5.4
1970	5.3
1971	5.9
1972	7.4
1973	9.1
1974	10.3
1975	11.3
1976	11.0

Source: see Table 4–1.

A casual look at the data does not offer any support for the hypothesis that the introduction of the CPP (and QPP) reduced personal saving. However, a statistical analysis of the determinants of saving could lead to a different conclusion. Currently this issue is being examined at both the provincial and federal levels of government, but there are only two existing studies which bear on the problem. These studies are discussed in the next two sections. Unfortunately, the lack of private wealth data prevents a duplication of Feldstein's time series study [8, 1974] in Canada.

The Candide Model

The Economic Council of Canada's annual econometric model, Candide (McCracken [12, 1973]), contains an equation that measures some of the effect of government pensions on private saving. The model separately estimates private discretionary and contractual saving. Private contractual saving is defined as the sum of the saving of trusteed pension plans and life insurance companies (Schweitzer and Siedule [16, 1973]). In the model, private contractual saving is assumed to be a substitute for government contractual saving, defined as the sum of contributions to all public service pension plans, Canada and Quebec Pension Plan contributions, and provincial employer and employee contributions to industrial employees' vacations. Government contractual saving is assumed to have no effect on private discretionary saving.[30]

The coefficient of government contractual saving in the private contractual saving equation is −0.38, implying only a partial substitution of public for private saving (Figure 4–1). Schweitzer and

Figure 4–1. Regression Results

CANDIDE MODEL 1.2 M
(annual data)

$$\text{SPICC/PIPP} = \underset{(5.98)}{-6737} \quad \underset{(-5.58)}{-0.38\,(\text{SGOVCC/PIPP})}$$

$$\underset{(16.46)}{+0.108\,(\text{DISPINC/PIPP})}$$

$$\underset{(5.06)}{+10029\,(\text{LP/LT})}$$

$\bar{R}^2 = 0.9$ D.W. = 1.46. $S_e = 48.85$ Interval: 1953–73.

SPICC = Private Contractual Saving, millions of current dollars

PIPP = Implicit Price Deflator, 1961 = 1.0

SGOVCC = Government Contractual Saving, millions of current dollars

DISPINC = Personal Disposable Income, millions of current dollars
– Change in farm inventories
– Consumer expenditure on education and hospitals

LP = Primary Labor Force (Males 25–54)

LT = Total Labor Force

(*t*-statistics in parentheses)

Note: The results are from an updated version of the original Candide model.

Siedule hypothesized that this coefficient should be between 0 and −1. This is not necessarily the case. If CPP contributors take account of the fact that each dollar of contributions is worth more than one dollar in discounted future benefits (because of the lack of full funding), the effect of contributions on private contractual saving should exceed −1 in absolute value. Furthermore, the coefficient is biased in a negative direction by a shift from private to public employment.

A more basic difficulty in the Candide approach is the separation of saving into the contractual and discretionary components. First, the data may not reflect contractual saving because life insurance companies receive contributions for Registered Retirement Savings Plans. These contributions are clearly discretionary. Table 4–18 indicates the flows into life insurance companies and trusteed pension plans as a percentage of personal disposable income. The data indicate a decline in the importance of life insurance companies that ap-

Table 4–18. Private Contractual Saving and Individual Contributions
(percentage of personal disposable income)

	Net Flows			*Contributions by Individuals*	
	Insurance	*Pension Plans*	*Total*	*Employer Pension Plans*	*RRSP*
1962	2.0	1.3	3.3	1.3	0.1
1963	2.0	1.5	3.5	1.4	0.1
1964	2.1	1.5	3.6	1.4	0.2
1965	1.9	1.3	3.2	1.4	0.2
1966	1.7	1.3	3.0	1.1	0.3
1967	1.7	1.4	3.1	1.2	0.3
1968	1.7	1.9	3.6	1.2	0.3
1969	1.4	2.0	3.4	1.3	0.4
1970	1.4	2.0	3.4	1.3	0.4
1971	1.5	2.3	3.8	1.4	0.5
1972	1.9	2.3	4.2	1.4	0.9
1973	2.2	2.5	4.7	1.4	1.2
1974	2.2	2.3	4.5	1.4	1.3
1975	2.0	2.7	4.7	1.5	1.4
1976	1.9	2.7	4.6	—	—

Note: The individual contributions are gross flows.

Sources: Statistics Canada, *Financial Flow Accounts, 1962-67*, (13-530), 1969; Statistics Canada, *Financial Flow Accounts*, (13-002), quarterly 1968-76; Revenue Canada Taxation, *Taxation Statistics, Annual.*

pears to have reversed in 1972, when the RRSP contribution limits were increased. Unfortunately no data are available on the importance of RRSP contributions in the life insurance net flows, but Table 4–18 indicates the growing importance of RRSPs.

Although the contractual and discretionary saving dichotomy may be useful for short-term forecasting, the distinction is irrelevant in long-term analysis. There is no question that, in the short term, employee pension plans reduced contributions and benefits when the CPP was introduced. Most plans are, in fact, "integrated" with the government pensions in such a way that the adjustment is automatic.[31] In most cases the integration reduces the employee contributions on earnings that are also subject to CPP contributions. Private pension benefits are similarly reduced. This reduction in private contributions may only appear in the aggregate as a slowdown in the rate of growth of private pensions. The division of saving into contractual and discretionary components ignores substitution between the two components. In fact, private contractual saving fell from 65 percent of personal saving in 1962–65 to 55 percent in the 1966–76 period. The change in total saving is of greater importance from a public policy point of view.

The Ontario Study

The Government of Ontario [13, 1977] has produced the only study that directly examines the effect of social security programs on personal saving. The Ontario model attempts to separate the individual retirement effect from the saving effect. Two relationships are hypothesized. The first one is a saving function:

$$PSR = a_0 + a_1 \, YDR + a_2 \, ADR + a_3 \, RET + a_4 \, CVG + a_5 \left(\frac{B}{Y}\right) + e_1 \tag{6}$$

where

- PSR = ratio of personal saving (less farm inventories) to personal disposable income ($\times$ 100);
- YDR = ratio of population aged 0–19 to population aged 20–64 ($\times$ 100);
- ADR = ratio of population aged 65+ to population aged 20–64 ($\times$ 100);
- RET = retirement rate defined as participation rate (in percentage points) of males 65+ subtracted from 100;
- B/Y = real government public pension benefits per aged eligible individual ($\times$ 100) divided by real per capita personal disposable income;
- CVG = ratio of aged population eligible for government benefits to population aged 65+ ($\times$ 100).

Then there is the retirement function:

$$RET = b_0 + b_1 \, Y + b_2 \, CVG + b_3 \left(\frac{B}{Y}\right) + e_2 \quad . \tag{7}$$

The complete model estimates the effect of the benefit level on saving rather than directly estimating the impact of social security wealth. This approach has the advantage of permitting noncontributory programs such as OAS to be included in the analysis. The benefit levels are a rough index of gross social security wealth for the pay-as-you-go programs which predominated during the estimation period. The introduction of the CPP in 1966 complicates the estimation because CPP benefits in the initial years of the program do not reflect future levels of CPP benefits. The latter problem may not be important if GIS benefits serve as a proxy for future CPP benefits in the regression. GIS benefits were introduced along with the CPP as a supplemental program during the transition to full CPP benefits. In general the benefit variable is a poor measure of changes in net social security wealth, but a negative benefit rate coefficient suggests that public old age programs partially substitute for private pensions.

There are three sources of possible error in the retirement equation. First, expanded coverage may be a result of earlier retirement, not the cause of earlier retirement. Second, average benefits include the earnings-tested GIS and CPP/QPP benefits. These payments are not independent of the retirement rate. It would be preferable to isolate the benefit rate effect by including the lump-sum OAS benefit in a regression covering the years prior to the introduction of GIS. The earnings-tested GIS should have a much greater effect on retirement than a lump-sum increase in social security wealth. A third source of bias is the omission of welfare payments for the elderly under Old Age Assistance, which automatically fell as the GIS program was introduced.

Portions of the Ontario results are presented in Figure 4−2.[32] The first structural equation indicates that benefits had a negative but not statistically significant impact on the saving rate. The coverage variable was negative and statistically significant at the 1 percent level. Retirement is itself significantly increased by rising real income, expanded pension coverage, and increased benefit levels. The net impact of the benefit level on saving was positive because of the increase in retirement, but the coefficient is not significant at the 5 percent level.

The estimated coefficients imply that the pension programs have large effects on the saving rate, although not all of the relevant coefficients are statistically significant. The reduced-form equation predicts that the saving rate in 1975 would be 3.1 percentage points higher than observed had there been no increases in coverage and benefits between 1951 and 1975.[33] Now that coverage is nearly universal the benefit rate is the key parameter. The first two equations in Figure 4−2 suggest that the increased OAS, GIS, and CPP benefits between 1951 and 1975 *increased* the saving rate 3.6 percentage points above what it would otherwise have been. If the retirement rate had remained constant, the saving rate would have *fallen* by 3.8 percentage points as a result of the increased benefits. Future increases in benefits, without a lowering of the retirement age, are likely to reduce the personal saving rate.

IV. CONCLUSIONS

Despite the rapid increase in public pension benefits in the last ten years in Canada, there is no dramatic evidence of curtailed private

Figure 4–2. Ontario Regression Results (*annual data*)

TSLS:

$$PSR = \underset{(-0.64)}{-5.31} \quad \underset{(-4.43)}{-0.28\,(YDR)}$$

$$\underset{(3.24)}{+0.67\,(RET)} \quad \underset{(-3.01)}{-0.17\,(CVG)}$$

$$\underset{(-0.57)}{-0.08\,(B/Y)}$$

$S_e = 1.00$, $\bar{R}^2 = 0.76$, D.W. = 1.26, Interval: 1953–75

OLS:

$$RET = \underset{(11.01)}{41.17} \quad \underset{(3.63)}{+0.005\,(Y)} + \underset{(2.54)}{0.122\,(CVG)}$$

$$\underset{(3.08)}{+0.231\,(B/Y)}$$

$S_e = 0.91$, $\bar{R}^2 = 0.973$, D.W. = 1.77, Interval: 1953–75

Reduced form:

OLS:

$$PSR = \underset{(2.46)}{28.58} \underset{(-2.35)}{- 0.22\,(YDR)}$$

$$\underset{(-0.85)}{-0.96\,(ADR)} + \underset{(3.64)}{0.004\,(Y)}$$

$$\underset{(-2.24)}{-0.086\,(CVG)} + \underset{(1.79)}{0.12\,(B/Y)}$$

$S_e = 1.34$, $\bar{R}^2 = 0.63$; D.W. = 1.87; Interval: 1946–75

(*t*-statistics in parentheses)

saving. Analysis of historical saving rates indicates that, if anything, there is evidence of a weak upward trend. This is consistent with the statistical evidence on the strong impact of earlier retirement on the saving rate. If retirement is held constant, there is only weak evidence that the benefit structure influences private saving. An equally important question is the extent to which the existing CPP/QPP funding arrangement increases current government expenditure. The provincial governments' response to readily available pension funds must be investigated before any move is made toward a fully funded Canada Pension Plan.

NOTES TO CHAPTER 4

1. Investment in human capital and intangible nonhuman capital (e.g., research and development) are included in the extended definition.

2. A detailed description of the Canadian accounts can be found in Statistics Canada, National Income and Expenditure Accounts, Volume III.

3. Denny [7, 1977] provides a more detailed description of the accounting differences.

4. Gross saving is the sum of saving, including capital consumption allowances, in all sectors.

5. The abbreviation CCA is used for capital consumption allowances. This is standard practice in Canada but not in the United States. In both countries, capital consumption allowances are the depreciation measures used in the most recent National Accounts, no matter what their basis. For Canada, this is straightforward. In the United States, CCA is based on the new measures of economic depreciation, that is, depreciation used for tax purposes minus the capital consumption adjustment.

6. Using five- or ten-year averages, the Canadian residual error is less than 1 percent of gross saving and consequently alters the saving rate by less than 0.2 percent. It does not affect the Canadian trends or lack of them.

7. The new U.S. measures of economic depreciation have increased capital consumption allowances. As a percentage of GNP, the *increase* in capital consumption allowances averaged 2.24 percent for 1946–55, 0.91 percent for 1956–65, and 0.66 percent for 1966–75. Feldstein's conclusions about gross saving are not affected. The decline in net saving would have been almost eliminated under the old measurement. Unfortunately neither U.S. measure is conceptually equivalent to the Canadian measure based on company book values, not tax returns. In general, for a given asset value, the Canadian capital consumption allowances are lower than either U.S. measure. The difference between the U.S. tax-based measure and the Canadian book value measure is *not* large.

8. Prior to 1926, the data are incomplete and are not based on a firm statistical base. For these reasons, we have not attempted to integrate the total period 1901–75.

9. The term "personal saving" in Table 4–2 is net of capital consumption allowances.

10. These are the capital consumption allowances for unincorporated businesses and residential buildings.

11. Reinvested or retained earnings of foreign-owned firms in Canada are *not* measured as foreign saving if no foreign transaction is involved.

12. It is not easy to measure accurately U.S. personal saving without the capital consumption adjustment. Our rough conclusion is that the U.S. personal saving rate would be higher than the Canadian rate in the postwar period.

13. An interesting hypothesis is suggested. Ultrarationality in the David and Scadding sense or substitution effects could account for the stability in the saving rates with the more inclusive Canadian methodology. We have not investigated this hypothesis.

14. Two factors are important. The relatively higher U.S. capital consumption allowances tend to increase the importance of CCAs. This is offset by the larger role of corporations in Canadian gross saving.

15. Feldstein and David and Scadding use different sources for their U.S. data prior to 1929. Their conflict is simply a question of which historical estimates are more accurate. We cannot judge this issue.

16. Buckley's estimates are quite rough in some instances. Historical research should produce a new series within a few years. Professor Urqhart of Queen's University is currently directing a large-scale research project on improving the historical record.

17. They are equivalent to the net savings rate given in Table 4–6 with the U.S. methodology.

18. For a history of Canada's programs see Bryden [1, 1974], Schulz [15, 1974], and Simeon [17, 1972].

19. See Bryden [1, 1974], Schulz [15, 1974].

20. Spouses between the ages of sixty and sixty-four have recently been made eligible for benefits, subject to a 75 percent tax-back rate.

21. Contributions can be made up to age seventy if retirement benefits are not claimed earlier, but most contributors will find it advantageous to claim retirement benefits at age sixty-five.

22. This figure is adjusted each year to equal 10 percent of the YMPE.

23. When one has contributions from more than ten years, 15 percent of the years with low earnings can be omitted in the averaging process.

24. The Quebec Pension Plan eliminated the retirement test in 1977.

25. This assumes that inflation is less than 12.5 percent per year.

26. Those covered by an employer plan may not deduct more than $3,500 in contributions per year.

27. Data provided by the Construction Division, Statistics Canada.

28. This figure was calculated on an individual basis in the microeconomic simulation.

29. The test affected few people because relatively few retirees were eligible for CPP benefits during this period. For the earnings restrictions to have any effect, one must assume that younger workers incorrectly anticipated their continuation beyond 1974 (1977 in Quebec).

30. Discretionary saving is a function of disposable income and the unemployment rate.

31. Eighty-five percent of those with pension plans are covered by integrated plans in Canada [2, 1951, p. 19]. Regulation of integration differs between provinces, but recent legislation in several provinces prevents employees from losing accumulated private pension credits as a result of future increases in public pensions.

32. The variable ADR was omitted from the 1953–75 regressions because it had little variation.

33. This figure is calculated by multiplying the estimated coefficients by the changes in coverage and benefits between 1951 and 1975 [13, 1977, p. 23].

REFERENCES

1. BRYDEN, KENNETH. *Old Age Pensions and Policy Making in Canada.* Montreal: McGill-Queens University Press, 1974.

2. BUCKLEY, KENNETH. *Capital Formation in Canada, 1896–1930.* Toronto: University of Toronto Press, 1951.

3. CANADA, STATISTICS CANADA. *Pension Plans in Canada 1970*, 74–401. 1972.

4. DAVID, PAUL A., and SCADDING, JOHN L. "Private Savings: Ultrarationality, Aggregation and Denison's Law," *Journal of Political Economy*, March/April 1974, *82*(2), pp. 225–50.

5. DENISON, EDWARD, F. "A Note on Private Saving," *Review of Economics and Statistics*, August 1958, *40*(3), pp. 261–67.

6. DENNY, MICHAEL. "An Accounting System for a Small Scale General Equilibrium Model." Mimeo, 1973.

7. ____. "A Note on Canada-U.S. National Income Accounts." Mimeo, 1977.

8. FELDSTEIN, MARTIN S. "Social Security Induced Retirement and Aggregate Capital Accumulation," *Journal of Political Economy*, Sept./Oct. 1974, *82*(5), 905–26.

9. ____. "National Saving in the United States," in *Capital for Productivity and Jobs.* Edited by ELI SHAPIRO and WILLIAM L. WHITE. Englewood Cliffs, N.J.: Prentice-Hall, 1977.

10. ____. "Does the United States Save Too Little?" *American Economic Review*, Feb. 1977, *67*(1), 116–21.

11. KENDRICK, JOHN. *The Formation and Stocks of Total Capital.* New York: National Bureau of Economic Research; distributed by Columbia University Press, 1976.

12. MCCRACKEN, MICHAEL C. *An Overview of Candide Model 1.0.* Ottawa: Economic Council of Canada, 1973.

13. ONTARIO, MINISTRY OF TREASURY, ECONOMICS AND INTERGOVERNMENTAL AFFAIRS. "Social Security and Personal Savings: Canadian Evidence in an Extended Life Cycle Model." Mimeo, Oct. 28, 1977.

14. PESANDO, JAMES E., and REA, SAMUEL A. *Public and Private Pensions in Canada.* Toronto: University of Toronto Press, 1977.

15. SCHULZ, JAMES, et al. *Providing Adequate Retirement Income.* Hanover, N.H.: University Press of New England, 1974.

16. SCHWEITZER, THOMAS T. and SIEDULE, THOMAS. *Candide Model 1.0: Savings and Consumption.* Ottawa: Economic Council of Canada, 1973.

17. SIMEON, RICHARD. *Federal-Provincial Diplomacy: The Making of Recent Policy in Canada.* Toronto: University of Toronto Press, 1972.

Chapter 5

Social Insurance and Saving in Sweden

Aleksander Markowski and
Edward E. Palmer[a]

Beginning in 1960 the basic old-age social security pension in Sweden was supplemented with a full-fledged public pension scheme, called ATP,[1] covering all residents engaged in the labor market. This meant that, from that date on, all those who would spend sufficient time in the labor force to qualify for full pension benefits under the public plan could expect to retire with a social insurance pension of around 50–60 percent of preretirement income. This guarantee of future pension income can be expected to influence individual decisions regarding preretirement saving and perhaps even the planned disposition of time between work and retirement.

Martin Feldstein [8, 1974] has investigated the effects of social security on personal saving in the United States. He argues that the need for individuals to save on their own will decrease when the retirement age is fixed but that earlier retirement induced by public provision of retirement income brings forth an increase in the personal saving of working individuals. Feldstein's tests with U.S. data indicate that the *net* effect of these two factors is negative. Given the

[a]The views presented in this study are the authors' and do not necessarily reflect those of other staff members or the directors of the Central Bank of Sweden (Markowski) and the National Institute of Economic Research (Palmer). We are indebted to Erik Ruist and Carl-Göran Sjögren for comments and advice given during the course of the work on this study. We have greatly benefited from the comments of and discussions with Lennart Björk, Tomas Franzén, Nils Lundgren, Irma Rosenberg, Magnus Uggla and Christer Öhman. Improvements suggested by George von Furstenberg and Lars Lindberger helped us considerably in preparing the final version. The skillful assistance of Nils Gottfries and Märta Leif was an important contribution to this study.

pay-as-you-go financing of the U.S. social security system, Feldstein has given this finding a numerical interpretation in terms of the rate of growth of capital and the growth of income:

> During the 1960s, personal saving accounted for 60 percent of total private saving. By halving personal saving, social security reduced total private saving by 38 percent. In the long run, this decrease in the rate of private saving would also decrease the private capital stock by 38 percent. . . . A 38 percent decrease in the capital stock implies a substantial reduction in GNP [8, 1974, p. 922].

Given the estimate that the long-run capital stock would have been about 60 percent greater in the absence of the pay-as-you-go social security system, Feldstein estimates that GNP in the United States would have been about 11 percent higher [8, 1974, p. 923].

Even if we establish that social insurance has a negative net effect on personal saving, this does not mean that the effect on *national* saving is also negative. The effect on national saving is determined by—among other things—the question of whether the program is funded or not. Feldstein's argumentation is one—to us rather extreme—way to assess the possible effect of an unfunded program on the national product. Unlike U.S. social security, the main social pension plan in Sweden is largely funded. This provides an opportunity to examine what has happened to saving in the case of the partially funded Swedish scheme.

In this study we are going to investigate the effects of the social insurance scheme mentioned above, ATP, on saving in Sweden. Most of the discussion will be directed toward examining how this particular social income guarantee might affect personal saving and the personal saving ratio in Sweden. To put our findings into a more general context we will also look at the statistical evidence on the national saving ratio and gross fixed capital formation.

The two major components of the Swedish social insurance system are old-age and health insurance. Old-age insurance is comprised of the basic social security program and ATP. Basic old-age (and disability) social security existed prior to 1950, the starting date of our statistical analysis. This makes it impossible to compare periods with and without the program. The program was revised on a number of occasions after 1950. In addition to having been adjusted upwards to account for the rise in consumer prices, the level of basic social security benefits has also been increased at various times. In fact, *real* benefits per beneficiary (actual benefit payments deflated with an index of consumer prices) more than doubled between 1954 and 1974.

In studying the effect of public old-age pension insurance on saving we will concentrate on the saving decisions of today's working population—that is, tomorrow's pensioners. (We will neglect the long-run effects of insurance saving on income growth.) The social pension income a worker can expect upon retirement consists of basic social security along with ATP. Thus, in principle, we should study the effect of both programs together on personal saving. However, because of the magnitude of benefits promised by ATP, its potential impact on personal saving decisions can be assumed to outweigh by far the impact on expected pensions of *changes* in basic social security. Further, it is likely that most people in thinking of their future pensions think primarily in terms of ATP. Thus, due to the comparatively large weight of ATP in determining future pensions and the statistically convenient fact that it was introduced in 1960 (giving us a preprogram period to examine), we will concentrate entirely on this program.

In Sweden most medical services are provided by the public sector. Medical services obtained in hospitals and policlinics are practically free of charge for the user (provided he is a Swedish resident). Health insurance provides compensation for income lost due to sickness as well as part of the cost of private medical care and medicine. The watershed year for modern health insurance was 1955. Since the first year for which data are reasonably consistent with modern statistics is 1950, this gives us only five years preceding the health insurance reform. We should have a much longer period in order to attempt to draw conclusions from a comparison of data before and after the reform. Fortunately, the existing evidence indicates that the introduction of the general health insurance scheme was more of a qualitative than a quantitative change. In 1954 about two-thirds of the population were already covered by different voluntary health insurance schemes (see [2, 1956, p. 12]). Although income loss compensation was still comparatively limited, we believe that the increased compensation provided within the framework of the general health insurance did not affect personal saving significantly. This is corroborated by the fact that, when we reestimated the equations presented in Appendix 2 beginning in 1956, that is, after the introduction of the general health insurance, the results remained largely the same as those reported in Appendix 2. Consequently, we are going to neglect the potential effects of the health insurance on personal saving.

A large part of this chapter is devoted to a comprehensive overview of the existing statistical data. The data are presented as five-year averages so as to smooth out cyclical fluctuations. The choice of five-year averages is, of course, arbitrary. One clear advantage of this choice is, however, that, given the initial year of 1950, five-year averages allow us to provide breaks before 1955 and 1960, the two insurance reform dates. Two other points should be noted here. First, the data for 1950–54 are generally of somewhat poorer quality than for the rest of the period examined. Second, the data used for 1976 are preliminary.

The outline of the study is as follows. ATP insurance and the structure of the Swedish social insurance sector are described in Section I. In Section II aggregate data for the entire economy are examined to provide an overview of trends in public and private saving, capital formation, and consumption expenditure. The analysis starts with the largest aggregates, gross capital formation and the national saving ratio, and then concentrates on different components of naional saving, with particular emphasis being placed on the development of social insurance saving. The remaining two sections deal with the relation between personal saving and personal disposable income, that is, the personal saving rate. Possible effects on personal saving of the introduction of the ATP-insurance scheme in 1960 are assessed in Section III. The study concludes by discussing econometric evidence of the effects in Section IV. This evidence is obtained from a simple regression model of saving behavior, which is described in Appendix 1.

I. SOCIAL INSURANCE AND SOCIAL ASSISTANCE IN SWEDEN

The main types of social insurance in Sweden are (1) health insurance, which covers income loss due to sickness and job-absence due to childbirth; (2) the basic social security pension; and (3) ATP, the general supplementary pension. Basic social security and ATP provide old-age pensions, disability pensions, and survivor's pensions. In addition to these three insurance types, public insurance includes occupational injury insurance and unemployment insurance. Formally, the latter is private; however, it is heavily subsidized by the public sector. With the exception of unemployment insurance and ATP in the case of self-employed, all public insurance is compulsory. Generally, only Scandinavian citizens are entitled to basic social security benefits; the other insurance forms cover all residents.

The basic social security program in Sweden dates from 1913. In its present form, the program was established in 1946 and went into effect in 1948. Old-age pensions are by far the most important social security form. They are paid out to everyone who has reached the age of sixty-five (sixty-seven prior to July 1, 1976). Recipients need not retire to receive benefits and benefits are not reduced for persons with other income sources. Benefit payments are thus the same for all single recipients, though they are reduced for married couples receiving two social security pensions. In 1976 an old-age pension paid out through social security amounted to 9,880 Skr or $2,270 for a single person and 16,120 Skr or $3,700 for a married couple. Benefits are taxable, and thus after-tax benefits for those with other earnings are less than for those without. Benefit payments are indexed to account for increases in consumer prices.

Until 1955 the basic social security program constituted the major form of social insurance. In 1955 universal social health insurance came into being. This program provides compensation for income loss due to sickness, though only for earnings below a maximum. In 1976 this maximum, which is indexed to the price level, was about 72,750 Skr or $16,760 on an annual basis. Also, parents—originally just mothers—are compensated for up to seven months' income loss due to childbirth. Since 1974, health insurance covers 90 percent of that part of income lost due to sickness which does not exceed the maximum.[2] Since that time insurance benefits have been treated as earned income and are taxable.

ATP was introduced in 1960. It is a compulsory (for all but the self-employed), universal pension scheme that for an income earner who spends thirty years in the labor force between the ages of sixteen and sixty-five will result in a lifetime pension upon retirement amounting to 60 percent of an average of his *real* income during his fifteen highest earning years. For those who do not fulfill the thirty-year requirement for full benefits, payments are reduced by one-thirtieth for each missing year. Until July 1, 1976, the ATP old-age pension was attainable along with basic social security payments at the age of sixty-seven. On July 1, 1976, the age requirement was lowered to sixty-five. As in the case of basic social security benefits, ATP pension income is taxable.

Since it will be important for the remainder of this chapter to have a general understanding of how ATP works, we will explain in some detail how the amount of an ATP pension is determined. ATP pensions are calculated in terms of pension points, and pension points are based on annual earnings. All earned income[3] *above* a basic amount but not exceeding 7.5 times that amount gives pension points. An earner whose annual income is twice the basic amount, which we can call the base, earns one pension point for that year. An earner whose income is three times the base earns two pension points, and so forth on up to a maximum limit of 6.5 pension points (7.5 minus the unit base). Thus, people earning income in excess of the base can earn up to 6.5 points during a year. An average of an individual's fifteen best earning years is used to calculate pension benefits to be paid out upon retirement. The amount of a retirement pension is then figured according to the following formula:

$$ATP = 0.60 \times \frac{n}{30} \times \bar{P} \times B$$

where ATP = amount of annual supplementary pension;

n = number of years of gainful activity (with a minimum of 3 years and a maximum of 30 years);

$\bar{P}$ = average of pension points for 15 best earning years;

B = the basic amount for the current pension year.

The base applied in calculating pension points and retirement benefits is indexed to account for the rise in consumer prices. Further, one need not actually retire in order to begin to receive benefits upon reaching sixty-five years of age.

When ATP was introduced in 1960 it was with consideration more for the future than for the present. No one could receive full benefits initially—in principle a minimum of three years in the labor force is required to receive anything at all and thirty years are necessary for full benefits. Given the thirty-year rule, the first year in which somebody could theoretically receive full benefits, would have been 1991.[4] Had this rule been strictly adhered to, only persons who were thirty-six years old and under in 1960 could thus aspire to obtain a full pension upon retirement. A special provision was introduced, however, the effect of which was to lower this date to 1981. This extension enabled persons who were thirty-seven to forty-six years old in 1960 to obtain a full pension provided they worked continuously to their sixty-fifth birthday. Persons between forty-seven and sixty-four years of age in 1960 were to receive an ATP pension reduced by one-twentieth for every year short of twenty spent in the labor force up to their sixty-fifth birthday. Persons who were sixty-five and older in 1960 were left completely outside the ATP program.

To conclude, ATP provides a general supplementary public pension for the working population. The pension is protected against inflation. The program was designed in such a way that no one could qualify for full benefits until 1981[5]—twenty-one years after the program's introduction. Active labor-force participants achieving the age of sixty-five between 1963 and 1978 could only receive partial benefits. Thus the program started very gradually in terms of actual benefit payments. On the other hand, as each year passed after 1960 an increasing percentage of the labor force could *expect* to receive full benefits upon future retirement. Furthermore, they could expect to receive both ATP and the basic social security old-age pension.

Table 5–1 provides an overview of the relative importance of the various forms of social insurance benefits. During 1950–54, social

Table 5–1. Social Insurance Payments by Type Expressed as a Percent of Total Payments, Personal Disposable Income, and Gross National Product *(five-year averages)*

Insurance Type	*1950–1954*	*1955–1959*	*1960–1964*	*1965–1969*	*1970–1974*	*1972–1976*
	Ratio to Total Insurance Payments					
1. Social Security	79.7	67.3	69.0	62.5	56.2	54.2
2. Supplementary Pension (ATP)	—	—	0.4	4.6	12.1	15.5
3. Health[a]	13.8	26.7	26.5	29.4	27.7	26.1
4. Unemployment[b]	2.2	3.2	2.0	2.2	2.8	2.8
5. Occupational Injury	4.3	2.8	2.1	1.3	1.2	1.4
6. Total	100.0	100.0	100.0	100.0	100.0	100.0
	Ratio to Personal Disposable Income					
1. Social Security	4.1	5.1	6.0	7.5	9.0	9.6
2. Supplementary Pension (ATP)	—	—	0.1	0.6	2.0	2.8
3. Health[a]	0.7	2.0	2.3	3.6	4.4	4.6
4. Unemployment[b]	0.1	0.2	0.2	0.2	0.5	0.5
5. Occupational Injury	0.2	0.2	0.2	0.2	0.2	0.2
6. Total	5.1	7.5	8.8	12.1	16.1	17.7
	Ratio to Gross National Product					
1. Social Security	2.8	3.4	3.8	4.4	5.1	5.5
2. Supplementary Pension (ATP)	—	—	0.0	0.3	1.1	1.6
3. Health[a]	0.5	1.3	1.5	2.1	2.5	2.6
4. Unemployment[b]	0.1	0.2	0.1	0.2	0.3	0.3
5. Occupational Injury	0.1	0.1	0.1	0.1	0.1	0.1
6. Total	3.5	5.0	5.5	7.1	9.1	10.1

Source: *National Income Accounts.*

[a] Beginning in 1974 insurance benefits were increased, but also became taxable. In order to provide a figure comparable to those for 1954 and 1964 actual insurance outlays have been reduced by 40 percent, an approximate average tax rate.

[b] This entry includes only the public subsidy to unemployment insurance.

security, which consists predominantly of old-age pension payments, constituted almost 80 percent of total payments. During 1972–76 social security plus ATP accounted for about 70 percent of payments, with health insurance gaining in importance. During this period ATP pensions amounted to 15.5 percent of total payments (recall that only partial benefits were payed out). Social insurance payments have also come to comprise a significant portion of personal disposable income, due to both an improvement in benefits and an increase in the number of recipients. The development of the number of social insurance benefit recipients expressed as a percent of the total population is depicted in Figure 5–1.

Social Welfare Assistance

Social insurance benefits constitute only a part of total social welfare assistance in Sweden. It should be pointed out from the outset that the definition of social insurance is based on the organizational form rather than the substance of the assistance. This is easy to see in the case of public coverage of the costs of hospital and doctors' services, which in Sweden take two forms. One is the reimbursement of private persons for (a major part of) the costs of private medical care through social insurance. The other is the provision of payments in kind in the form of free medical care in hospitals and policlinics. Thus, exactly the same services are in the first case considered as social insurance benefits and in the second case as public consumption. Needless to say, both forms are financed by the transfer of income from taxpayers to the public sector. Since the distinction between social insurance and public consumption may be more or less arbitrary, we will now consider total social welfare assistance in Sweden.

The network of social welfare assistance in Sweden has become very extensive during the past couple of decades. In Table 5–2 total social welfare expenditure has been distributed among seven categories. Note that the first four major headings—health, occupational injuries, unemployment, and old-age and disability—all contain two types of expenditures: insurance payments and expenditures for provision of welfare services in kind. For example, public expenditures for health include social insurance payments for income lost due to sickness as well as public expenditures on health and hospital services. Similarly, public outlays for unemployment include social insurance payments to the unemployed,[6] in addition to the provison of unemployment assistance in the form of public works projects, job placement services, vocational retraining and relocation assistance. Health and unemployment insurance payments have generally been less important than expenditures on services provided directly.

Figure 5–1. Old-Age, Disability, Other, and Total Social Security Benefit Recipients Expressed as a Percent of the Total Population

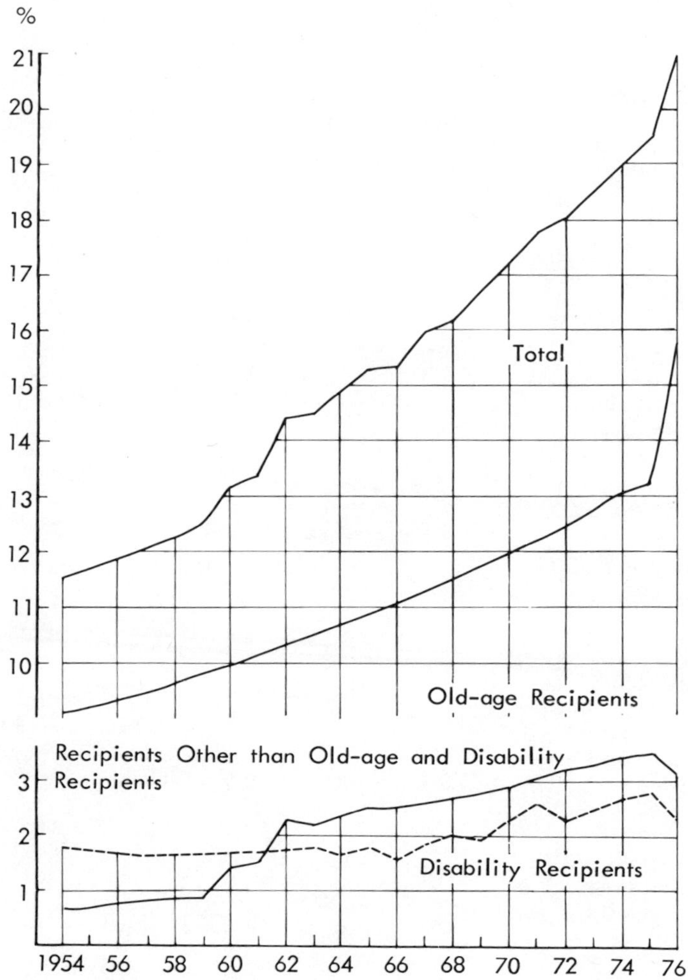

Note: Figures for disability pensioners include only persons receiving full disability pensions. Persons receiving partial pensions are included in the category "other," along with those receiving survivor pensions. The large increase in total pensions in 1976 is due entirely to the lowering of the age requirement from sixty-seven to sixty-five.

Table 5–2. Social Welfare Expenditures in Sweden[a]

	Expenditures Expressed as a Percent of GNP			*Expenditures Per Capita in U.S. Dollars[b] Expressed in Constant (1974) Prices*		
	1954	*1964*	*1974*	*1954*	*1964*	*1974*
1. *Health*	2.5	4.6	8.2	89	236	558
a. insurance and related assistance[c]	0.5	1.7	2.4	17	88	163
b. public health and hospital services	1.9	2.6	4.9	67	135	335
c. other	0.1	0.3	0.9	5	13	60
2. *Occupational Injuries[d]*	0.3	0.1	0.2	9	7	11
3. *Unemployment*	0.3	0.5	1.1	9	24	72
a. insurance	0.2	0.1	0.3	6	5	22
b. public relief works	0.0	0.2	0.4	1	9	26
c. job-placement services, retraining, etc.	0.1	0.2	0.4	2	10	24
4. *Old Age, Disability, etc.*	3.4	4.5	8.2	120	230	558
a. social security pensions[e]	3.3	4.0	5.6	116	204	377
b. supplementary pensions (ATP)	—	0.1	1.6	—	6	107
c. homes for the aged	0.0	0.3	0.5	1	13	38
d. home-help services, sheltered workshops and similar help for the aged and handicapped	0.1	0.1	0.5	3	7	36
5. *Family Welfare*	1.9	2.1	3.9	70	109	267
a. family allowances	1.1	1.1	1.6	41	56	110
b. rent subsidies to families with children	0.2	0.2	0.6	6	11	41
c. day-care centers	—	—	0.7	—	—	45
d. other[f]	0.6	0.8	1.0	23	42	71
6. *Social Assistance*	0.4	0.2	0.2	14	8	17
7. *Benefits to Military and War Casualities*	0.0	0.0	0.0	1	1	1
8. *Total* (1–7)	8.8	12.0	21.8	312	615	1,484

Notes to Table 5–2

Sources: *Social Security in the Nordic Countries* (1956 and 1964 *Statistical Reports of the Nordic Countries)* and *Statistical Abstract of Sweden*, 1976.

[a]Including most administrative costs.

[b]Data for all years have been converted with the average official exchange rate for 1974, 4,456 Skr per dollar. Note that expenditures are denominated here in terms of total population and not beneficiaries.

[c]Mainly compensation for job income lost due to sickness. Beginning in 1974 insurance benefits were increased, but also became taxable. In order to provide a figure comparable to those for 1954 and 1964 actual public insurance outlays have been reduced by 40 percent, an approximate average tax rate.

[d]Predominantly insurance benefit payments.

[e]Including rent subsidies to the elderly and disabled. (In 1974, these comprised a little less than 10 percent of what is labelled social security pensions.)

[f]Comprised of children's pensions, services for mothers and babies, home help for families with children, holiday facilities, child care and school meals.

In 1974 total welfare expenditure, as it is defined in Table 5–2, amounted to almost 22 percent of GNP. In 1954 the figure was less than 9 percent. Even in 1964 it was only 12 percent. In all three years for which figures are provided in Table 5–2 health and care of the aged accounted for over two-thirds of total welfare expenditures.

Social insurance benefits constituted approximately 50 percent of total welfare expenditure during the three years illustrated in Table 5–2. While it is probable that social insurance to some extent replaces private insurance saving, this need not be so for other forms of social welfare. Consider, for example, public medical and hospital services, which constitute an important part of total social welfare expenditure in Sweden. Had these services not been provided by the public sector, people would have covered part of their personal costs with private insurance. The remainder of the costs would have constituted a portion of normal personal consumption expenditure. Thus, to some—probably considerable—extent this sort of public consumption can be expected to replace personal consumption expenditure rather than saving.

II. SOCIAL INSURANCE, NATIONAL SAVING, AND CAPITAL FORMATION IN SWEDEN 1950–76

The determinants of national saving are many and varied. In the long run changes in the structure of the population, individual preferences and social institutions are all important. The limitations of this study preclude any attempt to identify and weigh the importance of all the factors that have influenced the pattern of Swedish saving during the past two to three decades. By ignoring a number of factors completely we will in effect be assuming them not to have been decisive in creating the picture we will examine. Though this method of examination is indeed common, it is none the safer for that. We hope that the reader will keep this in mind as we focus our attention on what has happened to national saving during a period characterized by a steady expansion of the nation's social insurance system.

Gross Capital Formation and National Saving

In the national income accounts, the sum of gross capital formation and the net of a nation's current account transactions with the rest of the world is identically equal to gross national saving. If to this we add consumption of goods and services we arrive at the country's gross national product, GNP.

If a nation's transactions with the rest of the world are in balance, gross national saving will be exactly equal to gross capital formation. Needless to say, Sweden's net transactions with the rest of the world have not been exactly zero historically. Nevertheless, on the average they have been close to zero during the period to be studied, 1950–76. This means that, on the average, Sweden has been neither a net exporter nor a net importer of capital. This is at once apparent upon examination of Table 5–3, which provides a breakdown of GNP into consumption expenditure, investment expenditure, and net foreign investment.

Table 5–3 shows that the relative share of GNP consumed decreased from an average of somewhat over 78 percent during the 1950s to around 75 to 75.5 percent during the 1960s. This decrease of 2.5 to 3 percentage points was matched closely by the increase in the share of GNP going into gross fixed capital formation. For our purposes this is by far the most important bit of information contained in the table. What it tells us is that, during the ten-year period immediately following the introduction of ATP, the portion of gross national product devoted to gross fixed capital formation was actually *higher* than before the social pension plan's existence.

During the first half of the 1970s the share of gross national product going into gross fixed capital formation sank somewhat, though it still remained above its average for the 1950s. In part, this reflects the fact that a somewhat lower share of GNP went into housing construction, due to temporary saturation of the housing market in many regions of the country. The share of GNP going into total fixed investment in buildings and machinery during the first half of the 1970s, however, remained close to the comparatively high level attained during the 1960s. Further, the share of GNP going into

Table 5–3. The Composition of GNP at Purchasers' Values *(expenditures expressed as a percent of GNP; five-year averages)*

	1950–1954	*1955–1959*	*1960–1964*	*1965–1969*	*1970–1974*	*1972–1976*
1. Total Consumption Expenditure	78.3	78.0	75.1	75.6	76.5	77.6
of which:						
Households[a]	64.4	62.3	58.6	56.1	53.4	53.1
Local Governments	6.7	7.9	8.5	11.0	14.7	16.0
Central Government	7.2	7.8	8.0	8.5	8.4	8.5
2. Gross Fixed Investment in Buildings and Machinery	14.2	15.1	17.2	17.2	16.8	17.0
of which:						
Private	8.2	8.5	10.0	9.4	9.0	9.5
Local Governments	2.7	3.2	3.7	4.8	4.8	4.3
Central Government	3.3	3.4	3.5	3.0	3.0	3.2
3. Housing Construction	5.5	5.7	6.0	6.7	5.4	4.7
4. Gross Fixed Capital Formation (2 + 3)	19.7	20.8	23.2	23.9	22.2	21.7
5. Increase in Inventory Stocks	1.2	1.4	1.5	1.1	1.1	1.6
6. Gross Capital Formation (4 + 5)	20.9	22.2	24.7	25.0	23.3	23.3
7. Exports minus Imports of Goods and Services, Including Net Factor Incomes from Abroad	0.8	–0.2	0.2	–0.6	0.2	–0.9
8. Total	100.0	100.0	100.0	100.0	100.0	100.0

Source: *National Income Accounts.*

[a]Nonprofit organizations that principally serve households, such as labor and philanthropic organizations, are included in the household sector. Churches, however, fall under the heading of local governments.

private fixed investment in buildings and machinery was higher on the average during both the 1960s and the first half of the 1970s than during the 1950s.

One of the outstanding features of the more than two-and-a-half-decade period covered by Table 5–3 is the radical change in the structure of total consumption expenditures. Comparison of the shares in GNP of household consumption expenditure and total public (local plus central government) consumption expenditure shows that the sharp, trendwise decrease in the former was counterbalanced to a considerable extent by an increase in the latter. Almost the entire increase in the share of public consumption in GNP is attributable to the relative increase in local government expenditure, around 80 percent of which consists of expenses for hospital and medical care, education and social assistance (predominantly care of the aged and provision of daycare centers and other childcare). Thus there has been a very pronounced tendency to substitute the consumption of public services for the private consumption of goods and services during the past couple of decades.

Let us sum this section up by noting that addition of lines 6 and 7 in Table 5–3 gives the share of gross national saving in GNP (see line 5 in Table 5–5). Summation of these two items, then, gives a gross national saving rate of close to 22 percent in the 1950s. During the 1960s the rate was above 24.5 percent on the average. It dropped back to 23.5 percent during 1970–74 and was almost a percentage point lower than this during 1972–76. Thus, throughout the period beginning with the introduction of ATP in 1960, the share of GNP going to gross national saving and capital formation was higher than during the ten-year period preceding its introduction. During the first half of the 1970s the gross national saving rate was still higher on the average than it was during the 1950s. However, inclusion of 1976, the worst year for business saving and gross national saving during the entire period covered (with the closest rival being 1975), pulls down considerably the average gross national saving rate for 1972–76.

The Composition of National Saving

The composition of gross national saving changed considerably during the more than two and a half decades covered by this study. The AP fund,[7] created to fund the ATP program, had a great deal to do with this.

As Table 5–4 shows, on the average 83.5 percent of gross national saving consisted of private saving during 1950–54. During 1972–76, 61.8 percent of gross national saving occurred within the private sector. If we compare just the beginning and the end of the entire period considered here, the most striking observation is that social insurance fund increases were responsible for over 20 percent of gross national saving during 1972–76 while they constituted an entirely insignificant part of gross national saving prior to the creation of the AP fund in 1960. Thus, the increase in public saving through social insurance funds (that is, the AP fund) brought about a decrease in the relative importance of private saving in gross national saving.

The share of gross national saving in GNP is derivable from Table 5–3, as was discussed above. The ratios of total gross saving and its components to GNP are given in Table 5–5. We can observe that the

Table 5–4. Gross Saving by Sector as a Percent of Gross National Saving *(five-year averages)*

	1950–1954	*1955–1959*	*1960–1964*	*1965–1969*	*1970–1974*	*1972–1976*
1. Total Private Saving	83.5	77.4	67.2	56.8	58.9	61.8
of which:						
Households[a]	34.3	32.2	27.9	19.3	21.2	27.1
Nonfinancial Businesses	44.5	41.4	36.0	33.7	31.5	28.1
Financial Businesses	4.7	3.8	3.3	3.8	6.2	6.6
2. Social Insurance Fund Increases[b]	0.0	0.4	6.9	15.0	19.4	20.3
3. Central and Local Governments	16.5	22.2	25.9	28.2	21.7	17.9
of which:						
Local Governments	11.3	13.0	12.9	19.1	16.9	15.2
Central Government	5.2	9.2	13.0	9.1	4.8	2.7
4. Total Public Saving (2 + 3)	16.5	22.6	32.8	43.2	41.1	38.2
5. Gross National Saving (1 + 4)	100.0	100.0	100.0	100.0	100.0	100.0

Source: *National Income Accounts.*

[a] See note 1 to Table 5-3.

[b] Beginning with the funding of the supplementary old-age pension scheme, ATP, in 1960, practically the entire increase in social insurance funds is attributable to the special fund—the AP fund—set up in conjunction with the ATP program. There has always been, however, a small, though steadily increasing, fund connected with other social insurance programs. Table 5-8 gives an exact distribution between the AP fund and other social insurance funds.

Table 5–5. Gross Saving by Sector as a Percent of GNP *(five-year averages)*

	1950–1954	1955–1959	1960–1964	1965–1969	1970–1974	1972–1976
1. Total Private Saving	18.1	17.0	16.7	13.9	13.8	13.9
of which:						
Households[a]	7.4	7.1	6.9	4.7	5.0	6.0
Nonfinancial Businesses	9.7	9.1	9.0	8.3	7.4	6.4
Financial Businesses	1.0	0.8	0.8	0.9	1.4	1.5
2. Social Insurance Fund Increases[b]	0.0	0.1	1.7	3.7	4.6	4.5
3. Central and Local Governments	3.6	4.9	6.4	6.9	5.1	4.0
of which:						
Local Governments	2.4	2.9	3.2	4.6	4.0	3.5
Central Government	1.2	2.0	3.2	2.3	1.1	0.6
4. Total Public Saving (2 + 3)	3.6	5.0	8.2	10.5	9.7	8.5
5. Gross National Saving (1 + 4)	21.7	22.0	24.9	24.4	23.5	22.4

Source: *National Income Accounts.*
[a, b] For notes refer to Table 5-4.

ratio of total gross *private* saving to GNP decreased from over 18 percent during 1950–54 to a little under 14 percent from 1965 on. Though it dropped slightly during the first half of the 1960s, the most substantial fall occurred during the period 1965–69. This decline was dominated by a relatively depressed rate of growth of gross personal (household) saving. Note, however, that the share of personal saving in GNP grew during the first half of the 1970s.

The gross saving rate of nonfinancial businesses declined fairly steadily throughout the entire period. During the first half of the 1970s the increase in the saving rate of financial businesses helped to hold up total business saving at a time when the gross saving of nonfinancial businesses was growing at a considerably slower rate than GNP.

In sum, the ratio of gross private saving to GNP decreased over almost the entire period mainly owing to the development of household saving through the 1960s and nonfinancial business saving over the whole period studied. At the same time the additions to social insurance funds grew from 0.0 to about 4.5 percent of GNP. We may note here that when we add total private saving and social insurance

Table 5–6. Net Saving by Sector as a Percent of GNP *(five-year averages)*

	1950–1954	*1955–1959*	*1960–1964*	*1965–1969*	*1970–1974*	*1972–1976*
1. Total Private Saving	9.1	7.8	7.4	4.9	5.1	4.7
of which:						
Households[a]	4.5	4.5	4.6	2.6	3.2	4.2
Nonfinancial Businesses	3.7	2.5	2.1	1.4	0.6	−0.9
Financial Businesses	0.9	0.8	0.7	0.9	1.3	1.4
2. Social Insurance Fund Increases[b]	0.0	0.1	1.7	3.7	4.6	4.5
3. Central and Local Governments	2.9	4.0	5.5	5.8	3.9	2.8
of which:						
Local Governments	1.8	2.1	2.4	3.8	3.0	2.5
Central Government	1.1	1.9	3.1	2.0	0.9	0.3
4. Total Public Saving (2 + 3)	2.9	4.1	7.2	9.5	8.5	7.3
5. Net National Saving (1 + 4)	12.0	11.9	14.6	14.4	13.6	12.0

Source: *National Income Accounts.*
[a, b] For notes refer to Table 5-4.

fund increases in Table 5–5 we find that together they constituted a slightly greater share of GNP during 1970–76 than during the ten-year period preceding the introduction of ATP.

Gross national saving includes capital depreciation allowances. Subtraction of these from gross national saving yields *net* national saving. Capital depreciation allowances constitute that portion of saving that households, businesses, and various government agencies would have to invest in order to maintain the capital stock at its current level. In the national income accounts, capital depreciation is calculated by applying separate depreciation rates to estimates of the stocks of different types of capital.

The ratios of net saving to GNP given in Table 5–6 indicate what was "available" for net investment, that is, after account is taken of the need to replace depreciated capital stock. The ratios of net saving to GNP provide almost the same picture as the ratios of gross saving to GNP presented in Table 5–5. The fact that the ratio of social insurance saving to GNP is the same in both Table 5–5 and Table 5–6 should be stressed, however. The social insurance funds have essentially no physical capital investments of their own. The major fund—the AP fund—is a financial intermediary that draws resources from the private sector. Thus, its growth is an important determinant of how much is left under the direct control of the private sector. The AP fund's role in accumulating net saving stands out more clearly in the presentation of net figures than in the presentation of gross figures.

For the economy as a whole Table 5–6 indicates that from 1960 the net national saving ratio remained above its level for the 1950s, though it declined considerably with the inclusion of 1975–76. These were extremely poor years for Swedish nonfinancial businesses due in large part to a sharp depression in the growth of Swedish exports of mining and manufacturing products. This held back production and, thus, impeded the profitable use of existing capacity and the employed labor force.

Table 5–7 provides an overview of the composition of net national saving. The fact that all the saving going into social insurance

Table 5–7. Net Saving by Sector as a Percent of Net National Saving *(five-year averages)*

	1950–1954	*1955–1959*	*1960–1964*	*1965–1969*	*1970–1974*	*1972–1976*
1. Total Private Saving	76.2	65.8	50.7	34.0	37.9	38.0
of which:						
Households[a]	38.0	37.9	31.5	18.1	23.8	37.0
Nonfinancial Businesses	29.9	21.3	14.1	9.9	4.0	–10.8
Financial Businesses	8.3	6.6	5.1	6.0	10.1	11.7
2. Social Insurance Fund Increases[b]	0.0	0.8	11.7	25.6	33.6	38.4
3. Central and Local Governments	23.8	33.4	37.6	40.4	28.5	23.6
of which:						
Local Governments	16.1	17.8	16.6	26.4	22.1	19.9
Central Government	7.7	15.6	21.0	14.0	6.4	3.7
4. Total Public Saving (2 + 3)	23.8	34.2	49.3	66.0	62.1	62.0
5. Net National Saving (1 + 4)	100.0	100.0	100.0	100.0	100.0	100.0

Source: *National Income Accounts.*

[a, b] For notes refer to Table 5–4.

funds is net saving stands out even more clearly in this table. Due to the relatively greater importance of capital depreciation allowances for nonfinancial businesses, the net saving of households is greater than the net saving of nonfinancial businesses throughout the whole period covered. Just the opposite was the case for gross saving.

Private and Public Insurance Saving

The component of national saving that is of special interest in this study is insurance saving. A significant part of this saving consists of pension insurance saving, which was directly affected by the ATP reform. Total insurance saving includes items from household (personal) saving, business saving, and total social insurance fund increases. Thus the separation of insurance saving entails a new division of total saving which is different from the breakdown by sector in Tables 5–4 to 5–7.

During the 1950s, additions to social insurance funds were inconsequential. Then, as now, they generally amounted to about a tenth of a percent of GNP. The creation of the AP fund in 1960 changed the picture entirely, as we have already seen. During 1960–64 the increasing flow of resources to the fund amounted to 1.5 percent of GNP, on the average. For 1965–69 the average was over 3.5 percent of GNP. During the first half of the 1970s it leveled off at about 4.5 percent of GNP, as can be seen in Table 5–8. This slower growth rate of the AP fund resulted from increased benefit payments rather than slower contribution inflow.

Private insurance saving dropped significantly during the 1960s, following the introduction of ATP, and then almost regained its pre-1960 level in the 1970s. The drop in private insurance saving was primarily due to the development of group insurance. Not surprisingly, the introduction of the ATP program in 1960 gave rise to an important institutional change in the sphere of private group insurance. It was clear that, given the comprehensive nature of ATP, the future of private collective pension schemes would lie in providing workers with benefits over and above those offered by the public scheme. In 1960 *private* pension benefits became, for the first time, the subject of collective negotiations at the national level between the National Confederation of Employers and union officials representing the organized body of white-collar workers. According to the settlement reached, employers agreed to cover all white-collar workers with benefits designed to provide a supplement to ATP. Thus a large number of white-collar workers who were previously not covered by private plans were suddenly covered. In 1973 similar benefits were negotiated for blue-collar workers.

Table 5–8. Insurance Saving in Sweden. Increases in Private and Public Insurance Funds Expressed as a Percent of GNP *(five-year averages)*

	1950–1954	*1955–1959*	*1960–1964*	*1965–1969*	*1970–1974*	*1972–1976*
1. Private Insurance[a]	2.5	2.2	1.4	1.3	2.0	2.3
of which:						
i. Private Insurance Companies	1.9	1.7	1.0	1.0	1.5	1.7
thereof:						
individual insurance	1.2	0.8	0.6	0.6	0.9	0.9
group insurance	0.7	0.9	0.4	0.4	0.6	0.8
ii. Pension Funds Retained within Businesses	0.6	0.5	0.4	0.4	0.5	0.5
2. Public Insurance	0.0	0.1	1.7	3.7	4.6	4.5
thereof:						
AP Fund	—	—	1.5	3.6	4.5	4.4
Other Social Insurance Funds	—	0.1	0.2	0.1	0.1	0.1
3. Total (1 + 2)	2.5	2.3	3.1	5.0	6.6	6.8

Sources: *National Income Accounts* and National Insurance Inspection Board.

[a]Leif Pagrotsky has pointed out to us that although the whole of private insurance saving refers to the insurance claims of households, it exceeds what is counted as personal insurance saving in the national accounts. This is due to the fact that in the national accounts changes in item ii, pension funds retained within businesses, are included in business saving rather than personal saving. Though this system is consistent as far as businesses are concerned, it results in an underestimate of the personal insurance saving claims of households.

In interpreting the picture of the development of private and public insurance funds presented in Table 5–8, it is thus important to keep in mind the fact that the introduction of ATP in 1960 forced a complete reconstruction of private pension plans. This is reflected particularly in the relative drop in the premiums going into insurance plans negotiated collectively, that is, group plans, the majority of which are pension schemes. The relative increase in group insurance occurring during the 1970s stemmed primarily from the extra private insurance obtained by blue-collar workers in 1973. The relative growth of insurance taken out directly by private persons (individual insurance) dropped considerably even before 1960. This could have been brought about by the anticipation of ATP. The relative increase in group-plan premiums might, however, also have been responsible.

As Table 5–8 illustrates, the relative growth of pension funds retained within businesses fell only slightly during the 1960s. For several decades now firms have had the choice of retaining pension funds within the business or vesting them in a separate private insurance organization designed to act as trustee for these funds. This specialized organization (called SPP) both invests funds and administers benefits to beneficiaries. Before 1960 it was not unusual for firms to contribute more to internally held pension funds than was necessitated by the capital value of future pension benefit payments. This was a convenient way to avoid profit taxes, since pension funds are nontaxable. In 1961 legislation was passed restricting pension funds of businesses to 120 percent of the estimated capital value of present and future pension obligations to employees. Beginning in 1960 firms have also been required by law to insure, at their expense, internally held pension funds with a special agency set up for this purpose (the so-called PRI/FPG system).

In sum, by the 1970s the share of GNP channeled into private insurance funds was, on the average, close to that of the 1950s. We should emphasize once again, however, that the entire spectrum of private insurance was completely changed with the introduction of ATP. What is extremely important to note is the considerable increase in the total of private and public saving that has been directed into insurance funds since 1960.

Public Insurance Saving: the Funding of the ATP Program

It was shown in the preceding section that public insurance saving gradually became by far the largest part of total insurance saving. Furthermore, we have already observed that social insurance fund increases constituted an ever more important part of national saving from the creation of the AP fund in 1960 onwards. Prior to the implementation of ATP, social insurance in Sweden was essentially unfunded. As line 2 in Table 5–8 shows, social insurance fund increases were entirely insignificant before 1960. The decision to fund the ATP program was thus crucial for society's future saving pattern. Since the saving of the AP fund has come to constitute the major part of public insurance saving, in discussing this part of insurance saving we will concentrate on the funding of ATP. It should be stressed that by funding we mean the decision to accumulate resources in a large fund rather than the introduction of a purely actuarial scheme. The ATP system is not fully funded. The contribution rate is determined by the Swedish parliament upon consideration of both political and actuarial factors.[8]

During the 1950s social security was financed almost entirely on a pay-as-you-go basis. That is, income was transferred directly from the economically active population to "inactive" pensioners. In 1958 legislation was proposed to improve the benefits provided by the then existent social security program and introduce the ATP scheme. Given the sociopolitical goal of providing substantially improved retirement benefits for pensioners, there was concern expressed over the negative effect on the private saving ratio. In addition, it was noted that the number of old-age social security beneficiaries was increasing fairly rapidly. Thus it was apparent that the combination of an increasing number of beneficiaries and improved benefits per beneficiary would take more and more of society's resources. Though the necessity was stressed for continuing to finance pensioners' retirement benefits principally on a pay-as-you-go basis during the foreseeable future, the importance of building up a fund in conjunction with the ATP scheme was heavily emphasized. One of the reasons given for creating the fund was to provide a means for "today's" labor force to accumulate funds to provide for their own retirement. To cite from the legislation proposed in 1958:

> The fund to be created in accordance with the proposed legislation of ATP would facilitate an equalization [over time] of the costs of supplementary pensions so that future contributions needed to cover the benefit payments could be less than they would otherwise be if contributions were not made to a fund [22, 1958, p. 86, authors' translation].

The other motive behind the fund's creation was to counteract the expected decline in the private saving rate and, in fact, even *increase* the national saving rate:

> The flow of income of businesses into [private] pension funds, which is often used to finance expansion, will not continue [upon the introduction of a public pension scheme]. This saving, which is used for capital investment, must be replaced by [public] saving in the form of a fund. Moreover, a rate of saving in excess [of the private rate] will permit a faster expansion of production capacity and thus an increase in the rate of growth of future production, which will benefit all [22, 1958, p. 86, authors' translation].

ATP was designed to provide mainly for the future retirement of persons with a substantial number of working years left when the program was implemented: the first year during which anyone could receive *full* benefits was set at 1981. Thus, whereas the AP fund has grown rapidly, payments of ATP pensions have been relatively small. To date, the interest income earned by the fund has sufficed to pay out ATP pensions to current pensioners.

The AP fund has grown rapidly since its inception, as we have already observed. As Table 5–9 shows, it has become increasingly

Table 5–9. The Assets of Major Financial Institutions *(stock figures and GNP in billions of Skr[a])*

	1954	1959	1964	1969	1974	1976
Type of Financial Institution						
Commercial, Savings, and Other Banks	32.5	47.6	69.5	114.3	194.3	236.9
Private Insurance Companies[b]	12.5	17.5	22.1	30.4	50.4	59.4
AP Fund	—	—	7.4	31.8	76.7	99.5
Total	45.0	65.1	99.0	176.5	321.4	395.8
GNP at Purchasers' Values	47.3	66.4	102.7	152.9	247.6	319.4
	Assets of Financial Institutions as a Percent of GNP					
Commercial, Savings, and Other Banks	68.7	71.7	67.7	74.8	78.5	74.2
Private Insurance Companies	26.4	26.4	21.5	19.9	20.3	18.6
AP Fund	—	—	7.2	20.8	31.0	31.1
Total	95.1	98.1	96.4	115.5	129.8	123.9

Sources: Bank Inspection Board, Insurance Inspection Board, AP Fund, and Central Bureau of Statistics.

[a] All values are expressed in current prices.

[b] Pension funds remaining within private businesses are not included here.

more important as a financial intermediary. By 1969 its stock of assets had surpassed the stock of assets of all private insurance companies. In 1976 it accounted for over 25 percent of the total stock of assets of all major financial institutions.

Employer Contributions for Social Insurance and the Distribution of Income between Households and Businesses

Having established the fact that the AP fund grew rapidly during the 1960s it is natural to ask who payed for it. The ATP program is financed with employer contributions (see note 8) which are transferred directly from employers to the AP fund. Even other social insurance has increasingly been financed with employer contributions.[9] Further, collectively negotiated private group insurance is also financed in this manner. As the relative share of employer contributions has increased, less of national income has remained for

Table 5–10. The Components of Domestic Factor Income Expressed as a Percent of Total Domestic Factor Income *(five-year averages)*[a]

	1955–1959	*1960–1964*	*1965–1969*	*1970–1974*	*1972–1976*
1. Income Distributed to Households	87.8	87.2	85.0	82.9	81.8
of which:					
a. Compensation of Employees, excluding employer contributions for social and private group insurance and other ends	60.7	63.8	65.9	67.3	67.0
b. Proprietors' Income and Rental Income of Persons	10.9	9.3	7.5	5.9	5.8
c. Dividends	0.9	0.7	0.5	0.5	0.5
d. Other Income[b]	15.3	13.4	11.1	9.2	8.5
2. Employer Contributions	3.9	5.9	8.8	11.5	14.6
of which:					
a. Social Insurance	0.7	2.6	5.1	7.3	9.8
b. Private Group Insurance	0.8	0.9	1.2	1.7	2.2
c. Other Contributions to the Public Sector	2.4	2.4	2.5	2.5	2.6
3. Income Retained by Businesses	8.3	6.9	6.2	5.6	3.6
4. Domestic Factor Income	100.0	100.0	100.0	100.0	100.0

Source: *National Income Accounts.*

[a]The principal difference between domestic factor income, appearing in this table, and national income, as defined and used by the U.S. Department of Commerce, is that the present table excludes net compensation of employees from abroad and net property and entrepreneurial income from abroad.

[b]The main components of this item are net interest income accruing to households, imputed income for owner-occupied homes, and an unidentified residual. A continuous decrease in the latter lies behind the relative decline in the Other Income item.

direct distribution between households and businesses. Table 5–10 provides an overview of the changes in the distribution of pretax income that have occurred while this process was taking place.

During 1955–59 employer contributions were 3.9 percent of total domestic factor income, on the average, per annum. During 1972–76 the figure was 14.6 percent. The decrease in the remainder of domestic factor income was fairly evenly borne by both households and businesses. During 1960–64 business income decreased considerably more than household income, though just the opposite occurred during 1965–69. During 1970–74 households again shouldered a large portion of the decrease. During 1975 and 1976 the balance tipped strongly against businesses.

The steep relative increase in employer contributions during 1975 and 1976 resulted from a shift from the partial financing of health insurance through taxes on the insured and through government subsidies to nearly complete financing through employer contributions.[10] As is evident in Table 5–10, businesses bore the majority of this increase, at least initially. It was mentioned earlier in the discussion of net saving that 1976, in particular, was exceptional in many ways. Industrial production declined, due to weak export markets. Employment was held high, however, and wage negotiations covering 1976 were extremely successful from the point of view of labor. All of these circumstances combined resulted in the relatively strong drop in business income indicated by the figures for 1972–76 in Table 5–10.

Table 5–10 also provides some interesting information about the changing structure of the Swedish economy during the period covered. Due largely to the decrease in the relative number of farm owners,[11] the share of proprietors' income has decreased continuously. One of the reasons for the increase in the share of compensation of employees is this gradual shift from proprietorship to a wage-earning status. Another is the relative decrease in a residual item included in "other income." Note also that dividends are a comparatively unimportant source of income—equity financing and thus shareholding are not as common as they are, for example, in the United States.

In the first and to date the only comprehensive study of the effect of ATP and the financing of the AP fund on private saving and the distribution of national income in Sweden, Börje Kragh concluded that one

> could say that the business sector had borne ATP in the sense that household income excluding ATP was able to grow at least as fast as gross domestic product [16, 1967, p. 13, authors' translation].

His conclusion was based on a comparison of the ratio of household income (excluding ATP contributions) to gross domestic product at factor prices for 1955–59 and 1960–64. There are two major differences between Table 5–10 and the data examined by Kragh. First, Kragh's denominator includes capital depreciation allowances. Second, the national accounts have been revised since Kragh's study.[12] These differences aside, comparison of the figures given in Table 5–10 for household income in 1955–59 (87.8 percent) and in

1960–64 (87.2 percent) shows why, up to the mid-1960s, it could easily have been concluded that households had not been noticeably affected by ATP's financing. The passage of time, however, has revealed a different pattern. As comparison of 1955–59 with 1970–74 indicates, households "paid" for most though by no means all of the increase in social and private group insurance contributions. Most of the large increase in employer contributions during 1975 and 1976 was, however, initially borne by businesses.

Conclusion

We will never know what might have happened to the growth and composition of national saving in the complete absence of the AP fund. Assuming the saving ratios are comparatively stable aside from the possible effects of ATP we can, however, venture to draw some tentative conclusions from the data presented above. The decision to fund the ATP program was extremely important because it affected the pattern of saving. During the seventeen-year period 1960–76, following the introduction of the ATP program and the creation of the AP fund, the national saving rate was higher, on the average, than during the ten-year period preceding 1960. Though it is not conclusive in itself, this observation provides substantial evidence indicating that the ATP program and AP fund were designed and financed in a way that not only avoided a decrease in the national saving rate but, in fact, enabled it to surpass its level during the pre-ATP decade. The fact that the sum of private and social insurance saving rates is on the average somewhat higher after 1960 than during the decade preceding this year seems to point in the same direction.

To the extent that the increase in the national saving ratio was due to ATP, it constituted forced saving. Had ATP been a perfect substitute for personal saving, we would expect—given constant preferences—the sum of private and social insurance saving to have remained unchanged. Note that ATP-saving is not affected by its rate of return, since the pension program is compulsory (see note 3) and the magnitude of the contributions is prescribed by law.

It is conceivable that the increase in the national saving ratio is only temporary and totally due to the rapid accumulation of resources in the AP fund during the 1960s. As we approach the close of the 1970s a larger and larger number of pensioners will have begun to draw on their social wealth. Further, at present there appears to be considerable (political) reluctance toward granting additional increases in the employer contribution rate. This means that we should expect the ratio of social insurance saving to GNP to decline in the near future. Consequently the national saving ratio will also decrease, unless extraneous factors cause the propensity to save of households or businesses to increase. It would seem that businesses are the least likely candidates. Thus the saving behavior of households will be instrumental in determining the future national saving ratio. There is one reason to expect that the ratio of household saving to GNP will increase somewhat as the social insurance saving ratio goes down. The decrease in social insurance saving will be due to increasing income transfers to pensioners. Since the propensity to consume of pensioners is certainly not 100 percent, part of the transferred resources will be saved in the household sector. This means that national saving will decrease by less than social insurance saving.

The main objective of this chapter is to investigate how the *personal* saving ratio is affected by ATP. We have noted that the ratio of personal (household) saving to GNP decreased through 1969. However, this decrease cannot be directly interpreted as a decrease in the personal saving ratio—defined as the ratio of personal saving to personal disposable income. This is so because the ratio of personal saving to GNP depends not only on the personal saving ratio but also on the ratio of personal disposable income to GNP. Personal disposable income is the basic determinant of personal saving. Hence, in order to investigate the effect of ATP on personal saving, the following sections will concentrate directly on the relationship between personal saving and personal disposable income.

III. POTENTIAL EFFECTS OF ATP ON PERSONAL SAVING AND THE PERSONAL SAVING RATIO

One can conceive of several ways in which the provision of old-age social pension insurance can both depress and stimulate personal saving. Numerous arguments and research findings have been presented in the literature in support of both. In Sweden, the first empirical study to investigate comprehensively the effect of ATP on personal saving was that by Börje Kragh [16, 1967] referred to above. Kragh, in examining the period 1955–64, concluded that personal saving had not been noticeably affected by the introduction of ATP.[13] Recently Franz Ettlin [6, 1976] has constructed a consumption function including a variable to measure the effect of ATP on personal consumption expenditure. His results indicate that the introduction of ATP had a negative effect on personal saving, which increased in strength up until the beginning of the 1970s and then decreased. We are skeptical about Ettlin's result due to his choice of variable to capture the ATP effect,[14] though not because we question the logic behind a negative effect or its possible occurrence.

In sum, the two attempts to determine how ATP has affected personal saving in Sweden provide essentially conflicting conclusions. In Section IV below we will thus present a new test of our own. Before we do this, in the present section we will look at some of the arguments that can be put forward for the various effects of ATP on the personal saving ratio. The section begins with a description of the relation between social insurance effects on the *level* of personal saving and the effect on the personal saving ratio.

The Relation between Social Insurance Effects on the Level of Personal Saving and the Personal Saving Ratio

Our main interest in the present and the following section is focused on the effect of the ATP reform on the personal saving ratio. Meanwhile, standard economic reasoning is formulated in terms of the effect of social insurance on the *level* of personal saving. Basically, two things can be presumed to happen when a public pension scheme is introduced. The first is that motives for saving out of personal disposable income will be influenced. This may affect the level and the form of personal saving. In addition, the financing of the public pension scheme may affect personal disposable income. Thus, the ratio between personal saving and personal disposable income will be influenced by both the effect on the propensity to save out of personal disposable income and the effect on income itself. What we can observe by studying this ratio is the net result of these effects. As we have seen in Section II, we can say very little about the actual effect of ATP on personal disposable income. Before we examine the cases for positive and negative effects on saving let us attempt to establish a general framework to encompass both the saving and income aspects of the problem.

Generally, the introduction of a social insurance scheme will lead to a *change* in the personal saving ratio if it gives rise to either a change in the level of personal saving or a change in the level of personal disposable income, or—finally—a nonproportional change in both these components. Let us assume that the social insurance program is financed with a special tax borne by households and introduced at the same time as the program. Assume further that social insurance is considered to be a perfect substitute for personal saving. This means that taxpayers keep their consumption unchanged and reduce the level of their saving by an amount (K) equal to the total value of the social insurance tax.

In the case where the social insurance program is *funded* there occurs an equal decrease in both the level of saving (S) and the level of personal disposable income (Y). At the same time, the payment of benefits (B) causes an increase in personal disposable income and—since social insurance benefits here replace the dissaving of pensioners—in the level of saving. In this simple model, B is assumed to equal the part of accumulated personal saving that pensioners would have used for consumption in the absence of a social insurance system. Under the above assumptions a fall in the personal saving ratio occurs as long as a net increase in the social insurance fund can be observed, since

$$\frac{S}{Y} > \frac{S-K+B}{Y-K+B} \qquad \text{as long as} \qquad K > B \ .$$

The ratio of national saving to GNP (the *national* saving ratio) remains unchanged, since the decrease in the level of personal saving ($K-B$) is offset by the saving of the social insurance fund. (Government decisions regarding the budget deficit in the general fund are assumed here not to be affected by social insurance fund saving.)

In the case where the social insurance system is *not funded* but financed on a pay-as-you-go basis, disposable income does not change at all, since the social insurance tax is repaid to households in the form of transfers ($B = K$). (Actually, in both the funded and unfunded case a very minor decrease in personal disposable income is conceivable to the extent that the social insurance reform cuts factor income by inducing retirement.) The level of income and saving of taxpayers diminishes by the amount taxed away, while the income of transfer recipients increases by the same amount in the form of increased pension payments. A decrease in the personal saving ratio occurs, then, as long as these pensions are not totally saved (pension benefits that replace dissaving that otherwise would have occurred are here considered as saved). The decrease in the personal saving ratio is thus due to the fact that the saving of taxpayers is redistributed to transfer recipients and is partly consumed by the latter group. This also leads to a decrease in the national saving ratio since the system lacks the built-in offsetting mechanism that a fund provides.

Let us now relax the assumption that the consumption of the taxpaying households and, in the funded case, the pensioners is unchanged. This means that the change in the level of personal saving is no longer given. In this case we can only say that the social insurance effect on the personal saving ratio will depend on the relation between the change in the level of personal saving and the change in the level of personal disposable income.[15] More specifically, the personal saving ratio will remain unchanged when the ratio between the *changes* in saving and income equals the personal saving ratio observed before the introduction of the program.

ATP and the Personal Saving Ratio

A fundamental idea common to most modern theories of consumer behavior is that the individual's economic problem is one of distributing his lifetime resources over his lifespan in a way that will avoid uncomfortable decreases in his standard of living during any phase of his life. The redistribution occurs through saving. According to the life cycle hypothesis of consumer behavior, individuals will accomplish this redistribution by saving more than usual during high-income earning years to provide a reserve for low-income earning years. For most people retirement years will be low-income years. Without a pension plan, people will have to put aside saving from their paychecks to make their own provisions for retirement. Needless to say, then, one of the important reasons for saving will be to accumulate wealth that can be used for retirement.

The age at which a person plans to retire is an important factor in determining how much he needs to save for retirement. In the complete absence of public old-age pension support, public statutes, and other arrangements establishing mandatory retirement ages and the like, people can be expected to plan to retire at different points in their lives. This might be a plan that is consistent with the individual's desires, though it might also be the result of his circumstances.

In legislating a funded pension program, such as the Swedish ATP program, in effect individuals authorize the program's managers to transfer part of their earned income to a fund against the promise that they will receive a pension when they retire in the future. If the promised public pension benefits satisfy the requirements of the contributors, they will no longer be motivated to save the equivalent amount privately. They can then reduce their saving by what they would have saved for this purpose. Alternatively they can choose to save some of the latter amount for other ends (and allow the decrease in their income to affect their consumption as well as their saving). In the first case the level of personal saving will *decrease* by the same amount as the amount of social insurance contributions paid. In the second case it will decrease by less.

In practice, the extent of the decrease in personal saving will depend on whether the public plan actually succeeds in providing a substitute for privately motivated retirement saving. Furthermore, as will be discussed below, offsetting effects may be induced by the introduction of a public insurance scheme. Nevertheless, though its strength is indeterminate on an a priori basis, it would seem indisputable that one of the potential effects of the introduction of a public pension scheme is to depress the growth of aggregate personal saving by providing a substitute for personal saving for retirement.

As was pointed out above (see note 15), it is difficult to conceive of a reasonable example in which the personal saving ratio will not decrease if the dominant effect of the pension scheme is to depress personal saving. The Swedish ATP pension scheme promises very substantial retirement benefits to the working population. Thus, if we accept the logic of the argument just presented, we would expect to find that the personal saving ratio not only dropped but dropped significantly following the introduction of ATP in 1960.

As Figure 5−2 shows, the average propensity to save, that is, the ratio of personal saving to personal disposable income, decreased in a pronounced trendlike fashion from 1965 to 1969. Though this trend might appear at first glance to provide evidence in support of the negative effect presented above, two observations lead us to question such a conclusion. First, there occurred no substantial drop in the ratio during the ATP program's first five years—1960−64. As

Figure 5−2. Total Personal Saving as a Percent of Personal Disposable Income

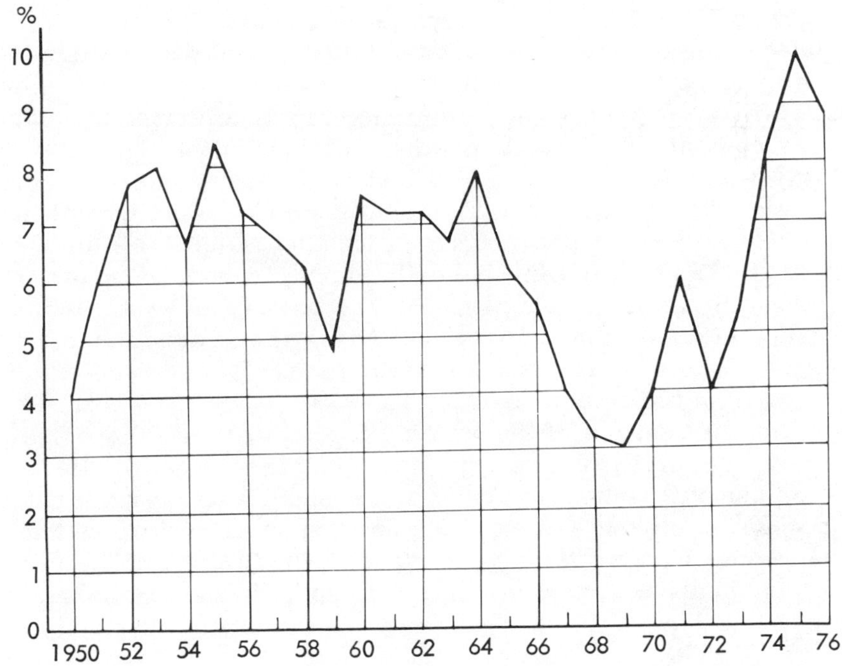

Table 5–11. Total Personal Saving as a Percent of Personal Disposable Income *(five-year averages)*

1950–1954	*1955–1959*	*1960–1964*	*1965–1969*	*1970–1974*	*1972–1976*
6.5	6.7	7.3	4.5	5.6	7.3

Table 5–11 shows, the average of annual ratios for these five years was actually *higher* than during the ten years preceding ATP. The introduction of ATP could have been anticipated at least as early as 1958. The political debate about the future role of social old-age insurance was then at its height and a national referendum that gave voters a chance to choose between alternative programs had just taken place in October 1957. Thus people were certainly conditioned to expect the emergence of a substantially improved social pension scheme and could hardly have been taken by surprise when it came in 1960. For this reason it is difficult to imagine why a negative effect should have been delayed until the middle of the 1960s and then suddenly start up and increase rapidly during a five-year period (1965–69).[16] Second, the pronounced decline in the second half of the 1960s turned in 1970. Beginning in 1970 the personal saving ratio shot up again and actually reached heights unprecedented in modern times.

As Figure 5–3 illustrates, the extreme decline in the personal saving rate during the latter half of the 1960s is wholly attributable to the drop in personal saving other than insurance saving. It is, however, difficult to weigh the importance of this observation in the present context. The fact that other personal saving fluctuates so strongly would seem to indicate that it is influenced more by short-run forces than by such enduring considerations as retirement. On the other hand, other personal saving includes acquisitions of assets such as stocks and government bonds which can serve as income reserves for retirement ends. Thus, in the absence of more definite information about the motives underlying the acquisition of the types of assets included in other saving, it is difficult to conclude anything from the development of this series.

In sum, the behavior of the personal saving rate itself does not provide clear-cut evidence of a significant, enduring negative effect of ATP on personal saving. A number of arguments have been presented by researchers in the United States in support of positive effects—which would partly offset the negative effect. Let us briefly review these arguments and then look more closely at those specific factors which could have offset the potential negative effect of the introduction of ATP.

Figure 5–3. Personal Insurance Saving and Other Personal Saving as a Percent of Personal Disposable Income

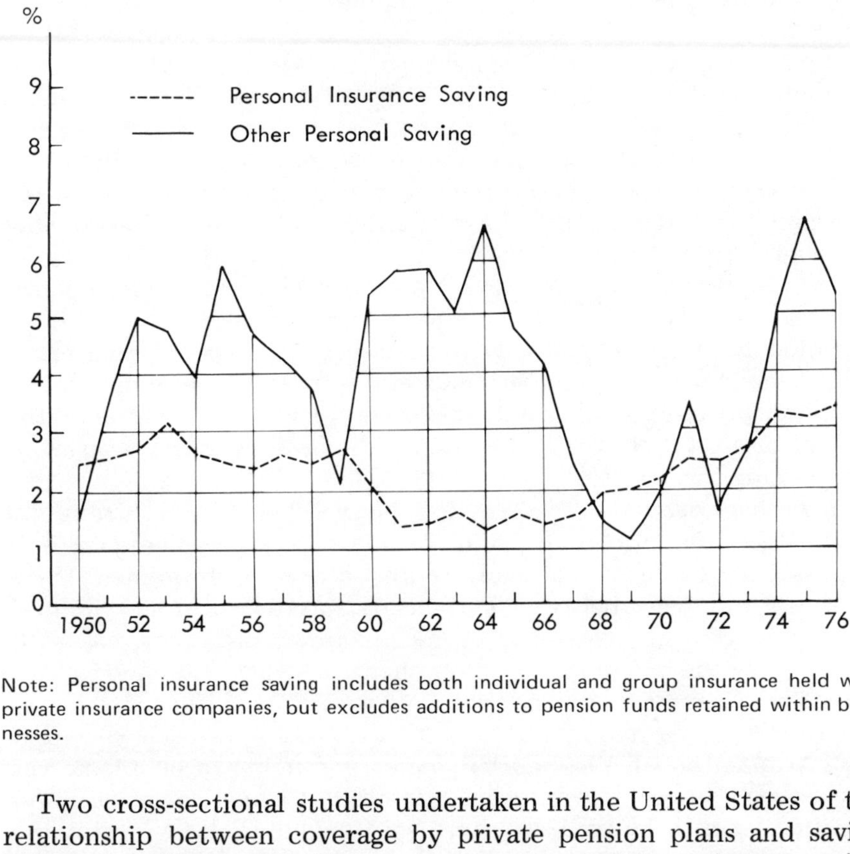

Note: Personal insurance saving includes both individual and group insurance held with private insurance companies, but excludes additions to pension funds retained within businesses.

Two cross-sectional studies undertaken in the United States of the relationship between coverage by private pension plans and saving behavior indicate that those who are covered by private pension plans save proportionally more than those who are not. Phillip Cagan [3, 1965], whose sample covered 15,000 members of the U.S. Consumers Union in 1958–59, explains his results in terms of a "recognition effect." Pension plans, according to Cagan, increase people's awareness of the need for retirement income. Alicia Munnell [20, 1976, p. 1014] has more recently reanalyzed Cagan's data base and has obtained results directly contradicting Cagan's.[17] George Katona [15, 1965], whose sample consisted of about 2,000 persons in 1962–63, also concluded that private pension plans stimulate individual saving. In the words of Katona, "The notion that people tend to reduce the amounts they voluntarily save by the amounts they are compelled to save through their own and their employer's contributions to pension plans has been contradicted" [15, 1965, p. 90].

Katona's explanation of the positive effect on saving is that the provision of some retirement income through a pension plan brings people nearer their goal and thus stimulates them to save even more for retirement.

More recently Martin Feldstein [8, 1974; 9, 1976] and Alicia Munnell [19, 1974; 20, 1976] have argued that researchers on social security have tended to overlook the fact that workers who are covered by pension schemes have an incentive to retire earlier than they otherwise would. Earlier retirement means that private assets, accumulated in order to supplement pension income and thus enhance retirement consumption, must be spread out over a larger number of years after retirement and accumulated over a shorter period before retirement. This implies a necessity to save more, which could be expected to become especially pronounced for those nearing retirement age. Thus, according to Feldstein, pension schemes have a dual effect on private saving. The first is the negative effect on the motive to save discussed above. The second is the positive effect brought on by inducing earlier retirement.

In the United States the case for the positive effect is strong due to the fact that old-age pension scheme benefit payments are only dispursed to those who actually retire. In Sweden retirement is not necessary to receive benefits. This means that the case for an induced retirement effect is weaker. Despite this, there are other reasons to believe that the existence of comprehensive social insurance to some extent might induce earlier retirement and, thus, an increase in personal saving. One reason is that, with the passing of each year since the introduction of ATP in 1960, a greater number of people nearing sixty-seven (at present sixty-five), the age at which social insurance benefits begin to be paid out, have been able to look forward to old-age social insurance benefits that come closer to full benefits.[18] At the aggregate level this means that the expected benefits for the average income earner have become better. The greater the guaranteed social insurance benefit at retirement the less the amount of extra private saving that is needed to make retirement possible and, consequently, the more people can afford to engage in this additional saving.

The second and most important reason is the labor market situation for older people. Since old-age social insurance benefits fall short of replacing preretirement income by a considerable amount, it is likely that many pension-aged persons would prefer to obtain some employment. However, given the harsh age discrimination in the job market, most will probably choose full retirement and attempt to take care of additional postretirement income needs by saving more during preretirement years. Furthermore, tax laws directly encourage this sort of behavior, the most obvious example being that private pension insurance premium payments are income-tax deductible. Even though pension benefits are taxable, this arrangement is advantageous since retirement income usually is lower than work income.

In addition to the induced retirement effect there was another important "induced" effect that was associated with the complete change in the nature of private group pension schemes. As was noted earlier, ATP practically obviated pre-ATP private group pension schemes. As a consequence they had to be redesigned to provide benefits over and above those guaranteed by ATP. Initially, however, only white-collar workers were involved since, generally, they were the only employees outside the public sector who were covered by private group pension insurance prior to ATP. Following the 1960 agreement, their extra benefits were to be of two kinds. First, a general pension age was set at sixty-five[19] with minimum benefits (comparable to old-age social insurance benefits) being extended until ATP and basic social security would take effect at age sixty-seven. Second, additional income benefits were agreed upon to provide a *supplement* to ATP from age sixty-seven throughout the remaining years of retirement. In 1971, a plan was also negotiated for the nation's blue-collar workers and this went into effect in 1973.

In 1957 8–9 percent of the work force were covered by private pension plans. As a result of the 1960 management-labor settlement for privately employed white-collar workers this number increased to 12–13 percent. In 1976 the comparable figure was 21–22 percent. In 1973 blue-collar workers were also brought into the private pension system. In 1976 the blue-collar workers covered constituted about 33 percent of the entire work force. Roughly, then, by 1976 around 55 percent of the total work force and almost 90 percent of all persons employed within the private sector (excluding the self-employed) had some form of private group pension coverage in addition to public insurance. The effect of these extensions of private group insurance was to guarantee an increasing number of private employees a pension income from public and private sources amounting on the average to at least 65 percent of preretirement income, which could be received beginning at age sixty-five. Incidentally, we can note that similar benefits were already available to public employees prior to 1960. (This means that we can expect the pure negative effect of the introduction of ATP on saving to have been somewhat smaller than it might otherwise have been.)

This development of private group insurance led to a positive effect on saving through a (comparative) increase in group insurance saving. It helped enable private insurance saving (Figure 5–3) to con-

Figure 5–4. Individual and Group Insurance Saving Expressed as a Percent of Personal Disposable Income

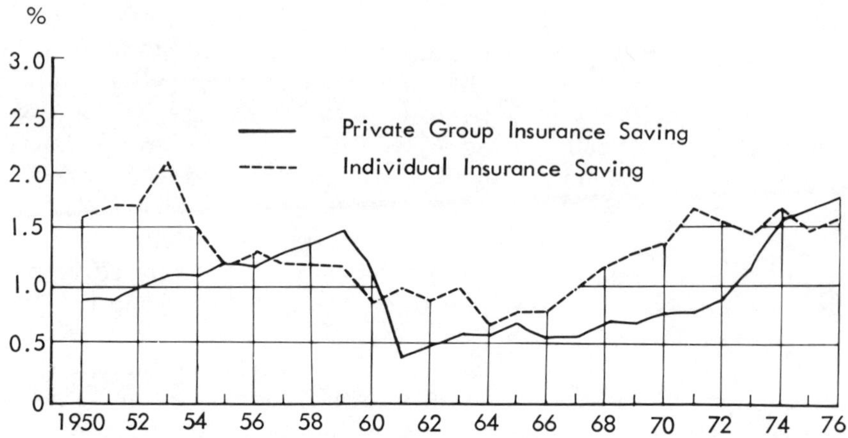

Note: In conformance with national accounts definitions private group insurance saving—as throughout in this chapter—does not include additions to pension funds retained within businesses.

tinue growing after 1960. Though the portion of disposable income going to group insurance dropped somewhat at the outset (Figure 5–4), it picked up subsequently. Private insurance in its reorganized form was extended to an increasingly larger portion of the work force. Figure 5–4 shows that the portion of personal disposable income going into individual insurance saving also increased as the 1960s progressed.

We can bring this discussion to a close by noting that our examination of the development of the personal saving ratio has thus far not revealed any unambiguous effect of the introduction of ATP. The analysis was performed under the implicit assumption that the personal saving ratio is stable over longer periods of time. The analysis indicates that there are good reasons to expect both negative and offsetting positive effects. Any conclusion about the magnitude of these effects can be drawn only upon an investigation of the effect of ATP in the context of a model of saving behavior. This will be done in the following section.

IV. AN ECONOMETRIC TEST OF THE ATP EFFECT ON PERSONAL SAVING

We shall proceed now to a formal test of the effects of the ATP reform on personal saving. In order to do this, we will specify a model for private consumption (and thus saving, since the two variables are complements) including the "invisible" income deriving from social insurance wealth. After the model has been specified, numerical values of the coefficients are estimated using multiple regression techniques. On the basis of these estimates we can attempt to assess the effect of ATP on private saving.

Feldstein [8, 1974; 11, 1977] and Feldstein and Pellechio [12, 1977] have employed the life cycle model, extended to make the individual's age of retirement endogenous, to perform various tests of the effects of social security wealth. Feldstein's time-series test [8, 1974] makes use of household net worth and social security wealth data. At present data of this kind do not exist for Sweden and any attempt to construct more than a crude approximation of these series would lie outside the scope of this chapter. We have thus chosen not to work within the framework of a formal life cycle model.

The Theoretical Framework[20]

The model to be estimated below employs the framework of the permanent income hypothesis, originally formulated by Friedman [14, 1957]. We assume that both disposable income and private consumption are comprised of a permanent and a transitory (or random) element which are not correlated with each other. Furthermore, permanent consumption is proportional to permanent income and transitory consumption is proportional to transitory income.[21] The factors of proportionality may depend on a number of characteristics of society (such as the income distribution, the demographic structure, and preferences of the population), but they are independent of the level of income. For each consumer unit permanent income is a function of its actual and expected resources as estimated at the moment.[22] In any period every consumer unit's permanent income is thus affected by its expected future income stream. Consequently, this is also true of aggregate permanent income.

The introduction of a social insurance pension program, such as ATP, will affect permanent income in two ways. First, the future income stream deriving from the pension insurance will give rise to a positive (or zero) contribution to permanent income. Thus, the latter variable will include an "invisible" part which does not derive from measured personal income. At the same time, since social insurance is—at least ultimately—financed out of personal income, the part of permanent income deriving from measured disposable income will decrease. When the two effects offset each other the pension scheme is percceived as "fair" and permanent income remains unchanged. If the pension scheme is not perceived as fair, the result will be that one of the two effects will be greater than the other.

In Section III we discussed two main effects of the introduction of a social insurance pension program: a positive (with respect to consumption) wealth substitution effect and a negative induced retirement effect. The former corresponds to the increase in permanent income described in the preceding paragraph. The induced retirement effect results in our model in a decrease in permanent income, since the lower the number of years an individual expects to be gainfully employed the lower his life resources. The "invisible" contribution of the social insurance reform to permanent income equals the net result of these two effects.

Thus, in our model, permanent income is divided into two parts: the part deriving from *future* ATP-pension benefits (equal to the net result of the wealth substitution effect and the induced retirement effect) and the remainder of permanent income. The latter part is approximated by a distributed lag over the current and past values of disposable income while the former is represented by the same distributed lag over the sum of "pensionable incomes"—which is what we will call income that yields pension points in the ATP program. Transitory income is defined as the difference between observed disposable income and that part of permanent income that derives from observed income.

The ATP Variable

The assumption behind our approximation of the part of permanent income derived from future ATP-pension benefits is twofold. First, it is assumed that this variable (denoted Y^S in Appendix 1) is determined by expected pension benefits and that its adjustment to the future pension benefits expected at the moment can be described by an adaptive expectations scheme. Second, it is assumed that in any year expected pension benefits at the aggregate level are proportional to the sum of pensionable incomes of all individuals in the same year.[23] This means that people are assumed to adapt their valuation of expected pension benefits in terms of permanent income in accordance with their experience of changes in pension points in the past.

Clearly this method of approximating the contribution of expected pension benefits to permanent income is crude. How crude it is depends on to what extent our assumptions have been violated during the relevant period 1960–75. For example, the labor-force participation rate of women has increased continuously and sharply, while that of men has decreased at roughly the same pace. Though these two trends have offset each other, this change in the composition of the labor force implies that the aggregate link between pensionable income and Y^S is not necessarily the same throughout the entire period. Further, there has been a continuous increase in the percentage of the labor force working part-time, another factor that is difficult to evaluate in the present context. Finally, the age distribution of the population has changed somewhat. The age distribution of the working population is important since, given that ATP benefits are based on an average of pension points, the nearer one is to the retirement age the less a change in real income will mean for future pension benefits. The changes in the age composition of the working population could thus have affected the stability of the aggregate relation between current pension points and expected pension benefits. However, they were small enough to be considered negligible in the present context.

One special problem occurs as a result of the design of ATP. From the moment of introduction of the ATP system it was clear for those born between 1896 and 1913 that they could only receive a reduced ATP pension. In our model the ATP variable is introduced to approximate Y^S, the part of permanent income deriving from social insurance wealth. Thus in computing the sum of pensionable incomes for all individuals the pensionable income of those who, due to the law—rather than choice—could only get a reduced old-age pension were weighted by the maximum fraction of a full pension they could expect to receive.

As was mentioned above, the ATP variable in our model has been designed to capture the contribution of future ATP-pension benefits to permanent income. To enable it to do this, it has been given zero value through 1959 and positive values beginning in 1960. Prior to 1960, however, there existed both social and private pension programs. As the reader is well aware by now these other benefit sources are still important today, though the nature of benefits offered was considerably altered with the coming of ATP. Let us briefly indicate what this means for our model.

Before 1960, people could receive old-age insurance through four channels. To begin with, practically everyone could expect to receive a basic social security old-age pension. In addition, for over three-quarters of all state and local civil servants (those not employed on a temporary basis), there existed a pension scheme providing benefits roughly equivalent to those brought by ATP. Further, a number of white-collar workers within the private sector already belonged to comprehensive group pension plans. Finally, a number of people had private arrangements with private insurance companies.

As it has zero value through 1959, the model's ATP variable will definitely not represent the influence of basic old-age social security on personal saving, since this program existed prior to 1960. This "invisible" future pension claim contributes to permanent income just as ATP does. Unfortunately we have no measure for this component, either before or after 1960. One consequence of excluding such a measure is that total permanent income is underestimated in the model and, thus, we will probably obtain an overestimate of the propensity to consume out of permanent income.

Those who had private (nongroup) pension insurance of their own do not cause any problem within the present context. After the introduction of ATP they could still collect their private insurance benefits in the future and, thus, their total future benefits really increased in relation to their pensionable income.

Before 1960 most state and local government civil servants were covered by a pension scheme providing benefits similar to ATP. The introduction of ATP meant that civil servants were from then on included in the ATP scheme and received pension points on the basis of their pensionable income. Since the civil servant pension scheme was altered in 1960 to cover the difference between the civil servant and ATP pensions, civil servants gained nothing from the introduction of ATP. Consequently, their pensionable income—which is included in our ATP variable—did not represent any change in their actual future pension benefits. This may affect our estimate of the coefficient of the ATP variable. In addition, the fact that no variable represents the contribution to permanent income of the "invisible" pension wealth of civil servants before 1960 may lead to an overestimation of the propensity to consume out of permanent income.

As we have discussed earlier, a number of white-collar workers in the private sector also belonged to private group pension plans prior to 1960. In their pre-1960 forms these pension schemes were almost entirely replaced by ATP. In the national accounts a large part of employer contributions for private group insurance (those not withheld internally by businesses) is counted both as a personal income and as personal saving (see note 1 to Table 5–8). Since contributions for that part of group pensions replaced by ATP were no longer paid within the framework of the private group pension scheme, neither were they counted as personal income. Thus, though the pensionable incomes of persons covered by schemes of this kind did not represent any increase in future pension benefits, they constituted a positive contribution to this group's permanent income. This is so because the future ATP benefits replaced the supplement to disposable income private group insurance gave rise to in its pre-1960 form. On the other hand the pensionable incomes of persons covered by pension funds retained within businesses did not contain any unmeasured contribution to the permanent income of this group.

As was discussed in a previous section, in 1960 private group insurance was completely restructured to provide supplementary benefits to ATP. The net result for those covered was an increase in expected benefits. A by-product of the negotiations that led to the change in private group insurance benefits was that a larger number of people were suddenly granted private insurance rights. As a result, employer contributions for private group insurance diminished less than they otherwise would. However, to the extent that contributions to private pension funds not held internally changed, the change affected personal disposable income and personal saving equally, owing to the way they are counted in the national accounts. Consequently, in estimated equations, the ATP variable will capture here a "nonbehavioral" ATP effect. This effect depends on the fact that the whole (national accounts) income decrease caused by the reconstruction of the private group pensions schemes was reflected in a decrease in personal saving (which meant a change in the observed personal saving ratio). In the regression equations this shift in saving will be attributed to the ATP variable.

It follows from the above discussion that not all the components of the sum of pensionable incomes (i.e., the ATP variable) implied the same increase in future pension benefits in 1960. On the other hand, beginning in 1960 all the future pension benefits derivable from pensionable income are attributable to ATP, both in reality and in our model. Hence, given our assumptions, the ATP variable is to some extent an erroneous measure of the *change* in future pension benefits that arose due to the introduction of the ATP scheme, but it is a proper measure of the *level* of benefits attributable to ATP, since these benefits will be payed by the ATP scheme.

To reiterate, the variable ATP employed to assess the ATP scheme's effect on saving equals the sum of pensionable incomes for all individuals, reduced to allow for the fact that from the outset some persons could expect only a reduced old-age pension. It is expressed in real terms by dividing it by the corresponding value of the basic amount (see Section I). The variable takes on the value zero through 1959 and is positive thereafter.

The Stability of the Propensity to Consume

A peculiarity of the Swedish ATP reform is that an overwhelming majority of people do not know how large a comparative decrease in their income this reform has caused. Since contributions are payed by employers, it is not easy for people to determine how much they actually contribute. This is further complicated by the fact that they pay only in part directly through reduced wage increases. The remainder is paid for indirectly through increased inflation and lower yields from capital. Since people have no concrete indication of how much they pay for ATP it is conceivable that they tend to believe the pension program is financed by somebody else. This lack of information about the actual cost of ATP can hardly affect permanent income as it is defined in our model. According to our assumption the part of permanent income not deriving from social insurance is determined by the observed current and past values of disposable income. Hence, if people have the wrong impression about how much ATP contributions have reduced the growth of their income, this can only affect their view of permanent income in the very short run. The evidence from current measured income will soon correct their error.

The discussion up to now was based on the implicit assumption that the aggregate marginal propensity to consume out of permanent income is constant. This parameter may, however, shift as a result of the introduction of a social insurance scheme if the pension system itself leads to a change in the social structure of the population by gradually increasing the number of pensioners. If pensioners as a group have a different average propensity to consume from the rest of the population, this will tend to affect the estimate of the aggregate propensity to consume out of permanent income. In Sweden some evidence has begun to emerge suggesting that pensioners may have a propensity to consume below that of the working population (see [21, 1974; 7, 1971]).

There is still another factor that may negatively affect the aggregate propensity to consume out of permanent income. One of the motives for saving is general precaution. Since accumulated saving is the best precautionary reserve, the propensity to save out of permanent income may be expected to depend on the fraction of permanent income derived from accumulated wealth (see [14, 1957; p. 16]). A social insurance pension scheme means that some part of household wealth (i.e., the social insurance wealth) is held by the government and is generally not available in case of emergency. (It is only available in the event the emergency leads to eligibility for a disability pension.) Then the fraction of permanent income derived from the accumulated (non-social-insurance) wealth decreases, and this can result in a decrease in the propensity to consume out of permanent income.[24] Finally, we may observe that this effect is probably somewhat reduced by the increased possibilities to obtain social help in the case of emergency.

In the least squares regressions performed below the aggregate propensity to consume out of permanent income, k, is treated as a constant. In principle, shifts in the value of k—caused by factors such as those described above—are averaged in the regression. However, if a shift in the value of k occurred in connection with the introduction of ATP—and this is a likely possibility—its effect will most probably be captured by the ATP variable. This is so because the shift in k, and thus in the intercept of the regression equation, coincides exactly with the introduction of nonzero values for the ATP variable. By the same token the ATP variable may also capture some of the effects on consumption of the expansion of other social welfare after 1960, as well as of the increase in basic social security benefits after this year.

The Results

The model is formally stated and the estimated equation is derived in Appendix 1. According to the basic equation the saving ratio is explained by a constant term, the variable ATP divided by current personal disposable income, the ratio of the preceding year's disposable income to current disposable income, and the ratio of the preceding year's consumption to current disposable income. All the variables are expressed in real terms. The equation also includes three dummy variables allowing for the buying rush preceding an announced indirect-tax increase. The model was expanded to incorporate the assumption that household saving behavior is affected by price inflation. This resulted in the inclusion of two price terms in the equation. The model was estimated using annual data for the period 1952–75.

The estimated regression equations are given in Table 5–A1 in Appendix 2. The personal saving ratio fluctuated between the values of 3 percent and 10 percent during the estimation period (see Figure 5–2). The standard error of the equations' estimates of the saving ratio is around eight-tenths of a percentage point and it shows a significant decrease when the inflation effect is accounted for (see equation A2). The general fit of the equations is thus good. In addition, the coefficients of all the variables have the sign expected on theoretical grounds. The Durbin-Watson statistic for equation A2—in our opinion the other equations are misspecified—does not indicate serial correlation. Furthermore, the absolute values of the estimated coefficients of autocorrelation of first and second order for equation A2 do not exceed 0.15. Thus serial correlation of the error term does not appear to be a problem in our model.

Values of the structural coefficients (k, a, and λ, which are defined in Appendix 1) derived from the parameter estimates in Table 5–A1 are presented in Table 5–A2 in Appendix 2. It can be seen that the estimates of k are very close to the average propensity to consume for the estimation period, which was 93.6 percent. In the computations in Table 5–A2 the expected rate of growth of income, g, was assumed to be equal to 3.1 percent, the average rate of growth of real personal disposable income for the estimation period. It can be noted that this average was fairly stable over the whole period;[25] for example, the average for 1960–75 was 3.3 percent. Furthermore, the value of g is not crucial for our results. Assuming $g = 0$ leads to different estimates of k and λ but hardly affects the estimated effect of ATP on the personal saving ratio.

Keeping in mind all the caveats mentioned earlier, the effect on consumption captured by the ATP variable is the net of a positive wealth substitution effect, a negative induced retirement effect, and a positive "nonbehavioral" effect of restructuring of the private group pension scheme. A shift in the aggregate propensity to consume out of permanent income, k, may also be reflected in the coefficient of ATP. Furthermore, the estimated coefficient for the ATP variable is affected by the fact that the emergence in 1960 of pensionable incomes for civil servants and persons covered by pension funds retained within businesses did not represent any increase in the future pension benefits of these groups. This problem is of limited importance, however, since—according to our rough estimates—the members of the two groups mentioned above constituted only 12–14 percent of the labor force in 1960.

The ATP variable can be seen to be insignificant in equation A1, where the price terms are excluded. It becomes, however, significant in equation A2, which allows for the inflation effect and thus, in our opinion, represents a more correct specification. The sign of the ATP variable is negative in both equations. This means that the wealth substitution effect, the "nonbehavioral" effect, and, possibly, an upward shift in the parameter k were dominant. Since we are estimating the net result of various positive and negative effects, nothing can be inferred about the absolute magnitude of each effect individually.

The ATP effect in the present model is derived in Appendix 1. It consists of two separate effects: (1) a change in the propensity to save out of *measured* income and (2) a change in measured income itself. The first of the two effects arises since, given measured income, ATP affects permanent income positively. The second one follows from the necessity to finance the pension scheme. As we have done throughout this chapter, we are neglecting the possibility that public insurance saving has affected the rate of inflation as well as possible long-run income effects such as (1) a decrease in income due to induced retirement and (2) an increase in income due to a larger production capacity brought about by increased public insurance saving.

As was pointed out earlier, we know very little about how ATP actually has affected personal income. Even if it seems reasonable to expect that households ultimately pay the whole bill, at present it is not clear at what pace the costs of ATP are passed on to households. Since the income change due to ATP influences the effects of ATP on both personal saving and the personal saving ratio, it was necessary to make some assumptions about its magnitude. Tables 5–12

Table 5–12. Estimated Effects of ATP Insurance on Personal Saving Ratio under the Assumption That the Whole Burden of Contribution Payments Is Passed on to Households during the Same Year *(percentage points)*

	Equation Number[a]	
Year	*A1*	*A2*
1960	−0.19	−0.78
1961	−0.39	−1.29
1962	−0.54	−1.61
1963	−0.67	−1.82
1964	−0.77	−1.97
1965	−0.92	−2.17
1966	−1.00	−2.30
1967	−1.17	−2.51
1968	−1.26	−2.59
1969	−1.32	−2.66
1970	−1.34	−2.74
1971	−1.34	−2.78
1972	−1.49	−2.92
1973	−1.47	−2.90
1974	−1.31	−2.72
1975	−1.25	−2.68
Average 1960–75	−1.03	−2.28

[a]Equation numbers refer to Table 5–A1 in Appendix 2.

and 5–13 are based on the assumption that the entire cost of ATP is passed on during the same year. The change in personal disposable income due to ATP in each year equals, then, the difference between ATP pensions paid out and contributions due in the same year. This assumption is a close approximation of a more realistic time pattern, where the costs of ATP are passed on during a period of, say, one to three years.

The estimated effects of ATP on the personal saving ratio for 1960–75 are presented in Table 5–12. The results indicate that the ATP reform led to a more than two-percentage-point *average* decrease in the ratio. The corresponding decreases in the level of personal saving are given in Table 5–13. On the average they amounted

Table 5–13. Estimated Effects of ATP Insurance on the Level of Personal Saving under the Assumption That the Whole Burden of Contribution Payments Is Passed on to Households during the Same Year and Employer Contributions Due in Each Year Minus ATP Pensions Paid Out in the Same Year *(millions of 1968 Skr)*

	Estimated ATP Effects on the Level of Saving According to Equation[a]		*Employer Contributions Due in Each Year Minus ATP Pensions Paid Out*[b]
Year	*A1*	*A2*	
1960	–192.9	–574.3	962.9
1961	–363.3	–974.5	1409.1
1962	–514.8	–1267.2	1883.7
1963	–650.1	–1491.7	2357.9
1964	–775.0	–1702.4	2287.2
1965	–891.0	–1888.4	2562.3
1966	–1015.2	–2080.2	3569.4
1967	–1124.8	–2238.8	3801.7
1968	–1218.9	–2362.4	4048.7
1969	–1322.5	–2528.0	4413.6
1970	–1437.4	–2732.0	4763.9
1971	–1530.3	–2878.4	4658.0
1972	–1588.9	–2933.9	4577.5
1973	–1646.6	–3024.3	4238.2
1974	–1728.2	–3191.8	4446.0
1975	–1825.1	–3393.4	4727.5
Average 1960–75	–1114.1	–2203.9	3419.2

[a]Equation numbers refer to Table 5-A1 in Appendix 2.

[b]The variable was deflated using the implicit deflator for consumption.

to over 2,000 million Skr in 1968 prices. This should be compared with the "theoretical" average level of saving in the case of no ATP insurance. The theoretical saving level can be obtained by adding the estimated decrease in personal saving due to ATP to observed saving. According to this method the average ATP effect constituted more than 30 percent of the average level of saving that would have occurred in the absence of ATP. At the national level, this decrease in the level of personal saving should be compared with the simultaneous increase in social insurance saving. Upon comparison of the last column in Table 5–13 with the other two it can be established that social insurance fund increases far more than offset the estimated decrease in the level of personal saving.

According to our model the ATP effect (or at least the wealth substitution effect) increases along with the real value of future pension benefits (which in turn depend on real income and labor market participation). This is illustrated in Table 5–13, where the estimated effects of ATP on the level of personal saving increase in absolute terms through 1975. On the other hand, in Table 5–12 the estimated effects of ATP on the personal saving ratio can be seen to decline in absolute terms beginning in 1973. This is a result of our assumption about how ATP has affected personal disposable income.

The importance of the assumed income effect for the estimated effect of ATP on the personal saving ratio is illustrated in Table 5–14. This table presents the ATP effects computed first under the assumption that the whole cost of ATP is passed on during the same year, then under the assumption that in each year personal income decreases by half the decrease in the first case and, finally, under the assumption that ATP does not affect personal disposable income at all. This latter assumption means that the part of employer contributions passed on to households is assumed to equal exactly the amount of ATP pensions paid out. Though the second and third cases are highly unrealistic, Table 5–14 clearly shows that both the magnitude and the time pattern of the ATP effects depend on how ATP has affected personal disposable income. The effect of ATP on the personal saving ratio becomes larger (in absolute terms) when households are assumed to have paid a smaller part of the costs of the insurance scheme.

Conclusions

The results of the analysis performed above indicate that an average decrease in the personal saving ratio of over two percentage points occurred as a result of the introduction of the ATP system. The effect increased steadily in absolute terms through 1972. Its

Table 5–14. Effects of ATP Insurance on Personal Saving Ratio Estimated Using Equation A2 under Different Assumptions about the Share of the Burden of Contribution Payments Passed on to Households *(percentage points)*

	Assumed Change in Personal Disposable Income Due to ATP[a]		
Year	*100 Percent*	*50 Percent*	*0 Percent*
1960	−0.78	−0.82	−0.86
1961	−1.29	−1.33	−1.38
1962	−1.61	−1.66	−1.72
1963	−1.82	−1.88	−1.93
1964	−1.97	−2.03	−2.08
1965	−2.17	−2.21	−2.25
1966	−2.30	−2.35	−2.41
1967	−2.51	−2.52	−2.54
1968	−2.59	−2.58	−2.58
1969	−2.66	−2.65	−2.64
1970	−2.74	−2.75	−2.76
1971	−2.78	−2.83	−2.88
1972	−2.92	−2.93	−2.93
1973	−2.90	−2.92	−2.94
1974	−2.72	−2.81	−2.90
1975	−2.68	−2.81	−2.95
Average 1960–75	−2.28	−2.32	−2.36

[a]100 percent means that 100 percent of the burden of employer contribution payments is assumed to be passed on to households during the same year. This is thus the assumption behind Table 5-12. 50 percent means that the change in personal disposable income due to ATP is assumed to amount to half of the change in the 100 percent case. 0 percent means that ATP is assumed not to have affected personal disposable income. This is tantamount to assuming that the part of employer contribution payments passed on to households in each year equals the amount of ATP pensions paid out during the same year.

magnitude depends—among other things—on the assumption about how fast the cost of ATP is passed on to households.

The estimated effects on the *level* of personal saving were smaller than the corresponding increases in the social insurance fund. Consequently, according to our results the ATP system has contributed to an increase in the level of *national* saving during the period studied. This is consistent with our findings in Section II, where it was noted that the sum of private and social insurance saving, as well as total national saving, on the average constituted a larger share of GNP after the introduction of ATP than during the decade preceding it.

Appendix 1

THE MODEL

In this appendix we are going to supplement the descriptive account of the model given in Section IV with a formal statement of the model and a derivation of the equations estimated. The model employs the framework of the permanent income hypothesis [14, 1957]. The approach followed is closer to the permanent income model developed by Stone and Rowe [23, 1962; 24, 1964] rather than to that of Friedman.

At the outset we divide private consumption, C, and disposable income, Y, into two components: a permanent component and a transitory component. The transitory components are assumed to be uncorrelated with their permanent counterparts. The introduction of a social insurance pension scheme affects the permanent part of disposable income. Future pension benefits contribute to permanent income positively through the wealth substitution effect and negatively through the induced retirement effect. Let us denote the net contribution to permanent income through these two effects by Y^S. Permanent income, Y^P, can thus be split into two parts: Y^S, derived from "invisible" future pension income, and the remainder, Y^R, derived from measured income (including pensions currently paid out). According to this division an increase in the future pension stream will involve an increase in Y^S (provided the wealth substitution effect dominates) and a decrease in Y^R, due to the necessity to finance the program. The sum of permanent and transitory income exceeds now observed disposable income by the amount of the "invisible" income Y^S. As usual we assume that, given the structure of the society, permanent consumption, C^P, is proportional to permanent income. Since our definition of consumption includes actual expenditures on durables, we assume that transitory consumption, C^T, is partly a function of transitory income, Y^T, and is partly a purely random variable with zero mean. This variable, u, which is the disturbance term, will be omitted in further derivation for the sake of simplicity. The model can then be formally written in the following way:

$$Y = Y^R + Y^T \tag{1}$$

$$C = C^P + C^T \tag{2}$$

$$C^P = kY^P \tag{3}$$

$$C^T = aY^T \tag{4}$$

$$Y^P = Y^R + Y^S \quad . \tag{5}$$

C and Y are aggregate personal consumption expenditure and personal disposable income and the superscripts P and T stand for permanent and transitory. Given the income distribution, the demographic structure and the preferences of the population, k and a, are constant. As was just mentioned Y^S is the contribution to Y^P of the future ATP pension stream and Y^R is the remaining part of Y^P.

Substituting into (2) we obtain:

$$\begin{aligned} C &= C^P + C^T \\ &= kY^P + aY^T \\ &= kY^R + kY^S + aY^T \end{aligned} \tag{6}$$

Equation (6) cannot be estimated as it is since neither the two components of permanent income nor transitory income are observable. In order to construct an operational definition of permanent income it is customary to assume that it follows an adaptive expectations scheme. This assumption implies that permanent income equals a weighted average of the current and all the past values of measured income, with geometrically declining weights:

$$Y^P = (1-\lambda)\,Y + \lambda Y^P_{-1} = (1-\lambda) \sum_{i=0}^{\infty} \lambda^i\, Y_{-i} \,, \tag{7}$$

where $-i$ means the variable is lagged by i periods.

The introduction of an old-age social insurance system, such as ATP, alters the relationship between total permanent income and measured income. For example, if the contribution of the future pension benefits to current permanent income equals what people pay as the social insurance tax, total permanent income, Y^P, will remain unchanged. Measured income, however, will be reduced by the financing of the system. Hence, if the weights in equation (7) are such that they approximate permanent income well for the years preceding the introduction of the pension scheme, then the same weights will underestimate permanent income after the introduction of the pension scheme. In fact, since it is based on the values of measured income, the right-hand side of (7) approximates Y^R rather than Y^P, as defined in (5).

Another deficiency of the adaptive expectations scheme given in (7) is that, since the sum of weights equals one, it does not account for expectations about future income growth. Since the Swedish economy expanded rapidly during the period studied and real income per capita increased steadily, it seems more plausible to assume that Y^R is affected by expected income growth. We postulate, thus,

$$Y^R = (1-\lambda)\,Y + \lambda\,(1+g)\,Y^R_{-1} = (1-\lambda)\sum_{i=0}^{\infty} \lambda^i\,(1+g)^i\,Y_{-i}\ , \qquad (8)$$

where g, the expected rate of growth of income, is assumed to be constant and $0 < \lambda < 1/(1+g)$.

Y^S is a function of aggregate expected future pension benefits, which we assume to be proportional to the sum of (real) pensionable incomes of all individuals. Pensionable income in any single year is, however, by far not the only determinant of the future pension income stream and its effect on Y^P. Thus we assume that Y^S does not adjust immediately to the sum of pensionable incomes in the current year but that it follows an "expected-growth-corrected" adaptive expectations scheme with the same adjustment coefficient as Y^R:

$$Y^S = (1-\lambda)bATP + \lambda(1+g)\,Y^S_{-1} = (1-\lambda)b\sum_{i=0}^{\infty} \lambda^i\,(1+g)^i ATP_{-i}\ . \qquad (9)$$

The variable ATP is the corrected sum of pension points, or real pensionable incomes, defined in Section IV above. Since pensionable incomes are directly related to observed income, the expected income growth rate, g, is employed again. The (constant) parameter b translates pension points into units of permanent income. It is itself the product of two other parameters: the factor of proportionality between the pension points in any year and expected future pension benefits and the factor of proportionality between expected future pension benefits and their contribution to the permanent income. Thus, for $g = 0$ b is the long-run contribution of one pension point to permanent income. The magnitude of this parameter is the ultimate object of our test, since the higher the value of b the higher the effect of the ATP insurance on permanent income and, thus, on personal saving.

Using (1), (5), (8), and (9) we can write (6) in the following way:

$$\begin{aligned} C &= kY^R + kY^S + a(Y - Y^R) \\ &= (k-a)\,Y^R + kY^S + aY \\ &= (k-a)\,(1-\lambda)Y + (k-a)\lambda\,(1+g)\,Y^R_{-1} + k\,(1-\lambda)bATP + \qquad (10) \\ &\quad k\lambda(1+g)\,Y^S_{-1} + aY\ . \end{aligned}$$

In order to eliminate the remaining unobservable variables from the equation we employ a Koyck transformation. Writing the second row of (10) for C_{-1} and multiplying by $\lambda(1+g)$ we obtain

$$\lambda(1+g)\,C_{-1} = \lambda(1+g)\,(k-a)\,Y^R_{-1} + \lambda(1+g)kY^S_{-1} + \lambda(1+g)aY_{-1}\ . \qquad (11)$$

Upon subtracting (11) from the third row of (10) we get

$$C = (k-a)(1-\lambda)Y + k(1-\lambda)bATP + aY - \lambda(1+g)aY_{-1} + \lambda(1+g)C_{-1}$$
$$= [k(1-\lambda) + a\lambda]Y + k(1-\lambda)bATP - \lambda(1+g)aY_{-1} + \lambda(1+g)C_{-1} \quad . \tag{12}$$

The equation can be directly estimated in this form. We can note that the estimation of the coefficients of Y_{-1} and C_{-1} will be subject to the collinearity problem, since the two variables are highly correlated.

Since saving, S, equals the difference between income and consumption, we can transform (12) to obtain

$$S = Y - C$$
$$= [1 - k(1-\lambda) - a\lambda]\, Y - k(1-\lambda)bATP + \lambda(1+g)aY_{-1} - \lambda(1+g)C_{-1} \quad . \tag{13}$$

Finally, in order to obtain the saving ratio as the dependent variable we divide both sides of (13) by Y:

$$\frac{S}{Y} = [1 - k(1-\lambda) - a\lambda] - k(1-\lambda)b\frac{ATP}{Y} + \lambda(1+g)a\frac{Y_{-1}}{Y} - \lambda(1+g)\frac{C_{-1}}{Y} \, , \tag{14}$$

or

$$\frac{S}{Y} = a_1 - a_2 \frac{ATP}{Y} + a_3 \frac{Y_{-1}}{Y} - a_4 \frac{C_{-1}}{Y} \, , \tag{14a}$$

where the a_i's in (14a) equal the corresponding parameter products in (14). From the theoretical assumptions about a, k, λ, and g it follows that we expect

$$a_1 \, , a_3 \, , a_4 \geqslant 0 \quad .$$

The coefficient a_2 may be either positive or negative, but the fact that the induced retirement effect is likely to be small suggests a positive sign.

The basic model can be expanded to incorporate the assumption that changes in the rate of inflation can affect the saving behavior of households. The reason for incorporating such an assumption is that there is considerable evidence that, at least from the mid-1960s, price inflation stimulates personal saving. A number of theories have been proposed that attempt to explain this relationship (see [18, 1977]). The view we favor is that inflation breeds uncertainty about the real value of future income and thus leads to precautionary saving.

The effect of inflation on the level of consumption is assumed to be proportional to the relative price change, scaled by the level of income. Consequently, (4) is replaced by

$$C^T = aY^T + d\frac{\Delta P}{P_{-1}} Y , \tag{15}$$

where $\Delta P = P - P_{-1}$, P is the consumer price level, and d is a constant coefficient. Employing the same transformations as above we obtain:

$$\begin{aligned}\frac{S}{Y} = {} & [1 - k(1-\lambda) - a\lambda] - k(1-\lambda)b\frac{ATP}{Y} + \lambda(1+g)\,a\frac{Y_{-1}}{Y} \\ & - \lambda(1+g)\frac{C_{-1}}{Y} - d\frac{\Delta P}{P_{-1}} + \lambda(1+g)\,d\,\frac{\Delta P_{-1}}{P_{-2}}\,\frac{Y_{-1}}{Y} ,\end{aligned} \tag{16}$$

or

$$\frac{S}{Y} = b_1 - b_2\frac{ATP}{Y} + b_3\frac{Y_{-1}}{Y} - b_4\frac{C_{-1}}{Y} - b_5\frac{\Delta P}{P_{-1}} + b_6\frac{\Delta P_{-1}}{P_{-2}}\,\frac{Y_{-1}}{Y} , \tag{16a}$$

where the b_i's in (16a) equal the corresponding parameter products in (16). Note that the parameter d in (16) is overidentified and can be uniquely determined only if

$$b_5 = \frac{b_6}{b_4} .$$

In accordance with our earlier results (see [18, 1977], Chapter 3) we expect the sign of d to be negative, so that

$$b_5 , \ b_6 \leqslant 0 .$$

The estimated equation is completed by including three dummy variables which account for the buying rush that precedes an increase in an indirect tax when the change is announced in advance. This buying rush and the following slack in demand are assumed to be proportional to disposable income for the years in question. This means that an indirect-tax change is assumed to affect the saving ratios for the two years equally, though in opposite directions (see [18, 1977], Section 3.13). It should be noted that a strict derivation of the model leads to additional terms, including the lagged values of the indirect-tax dummies, but the possible estimation bias arising from excluding these terms is extremely small.

Let us look, finally, at the disturbance term in equations (14) and (16). Assuming there is an additive disturbance, u, in the C^T equation—equation (4) or (15)—the transformations above imply that the error term in (14) and (16) has the form

$$z = -\frac{u - \lambda(1+g)\,u_{-1}}{Y} \quad .$$

Since u is the disturbance in the level equation and is assumed to have zero mean, it is likely to be heteroskedastic, with its variance depending on the level of Y. In that case the degree of heteroskedasticity is significantly reduced in the transformed error term, z. On the other hand, different assumptions about the kind (or lack) of serial correlation in u imply that the expression $u - \lambda(1+g)u_{-1}$ is autocorrelated. Since Y is autocorrelated itself it is difficult to say anything definite about the serial correlation in z.

The remainder of this appendix is devoted to a derivation of the ATP effect. In order to compute the effect of ATP on the level of personal saving, $\Delta^P S$, we have to go back to equation (6). This effect cannot be obtained in a straightforward way from equations (14) or (16) owing to the fact that the level of income, Y, has been affected by the existence of the ATP program. Using (1) and (6) we obtain

$$\begin{aligned} S &= Y - C \\ &= Y^R + Y^T - kY^R - kY^S - aY^T \qquad (17) \\ &= (1-k)\,Y^R - kY^S + (1-a)\,Y^T \quad . \end{aligned}$$

Assuming the ATP program has not affected transitory income[26] we have

$$\Delta^P S = (1-k)\,\Delta^P Y^R - k\Delta^P Y^S \quad , \qquad (18)$$

where Δ^P denotes the change due to the existence of ATP insurance (i.e., the ATP effect on the variable). The coefficient k is assumed to be constant in this derivation.

Since we are interested in the total effect of ATP (i.e., as compared with the theoretical situation when no ATP exists) rather than in its marginal effect we set

$$\Delta^P Y^S = Y^S ,$$

which is operationally defined in equation (9) above. From (8) we obtain

$$\Delta^P Y^R = (1-\lambda) \sum_{i=0}^{\infty} \lambda^i (1+g)^i \, \Delta^P Y_{-i} \ . \tag{19}$$

Under the assumption that the whole burden of the ATP contributions is passed on to households, $\Delta^P Y$ can be defined as (minus) the real value of the total of ATP contributions due in the year in question minus the ATP pensions paid out during the same year. Obviously, both Y^S and $\Delta^P Y$ equal zero before 1960.

The operational definitions for $\Delta^P S$ and $\Delta^P Y$ make it possible to compute the theoretical personal saving ratio, $(S/Y)^*$, that would have been observed if no ATP insurance had existed:

$$(S/Y)^* = \frac{S - \Delta^P S}{Y - \Delta^P Y} \ . \tag{20}$$

The ATP effect on the personal saving ratio, $\Delta^P (S/Y)$, is then defined as the difference between the actual saving ratio and the theoretical saving ratio:

$$\Delta^P (S/Y) = \frac{S}{Y} - (S/Y)^* \ . \tag{21}$$

The operational formula for $\Delta^P (S/Y)$ is obtained upon substitution of (20), (18), (19), and (9) into (21):

$$\Delta^P (S/Y) = \frac{S}{Y} - \frac{S - (1-k)(1-\lambda)\Sigma\lambda^i (1+g)^i \Delta^P Y_{-i} + k(1-\lambda) b \Sigma \lambda^i (1+g)^i ATP_{-i}}{Y - \Delta^P Y} \ . \tag{22}$$

Appendix 2

REGRESSION RESULTS

Table 5–A1. Coefficient Estimates[a, b]

Equation Number	*Constant*	$\frac{ATP}{Y}$	$\frac{C_{-1}}{Y}$	$\frac{Y_{-1}}{Y}$	$\frac{\Delta P}{P_{-1}}$	$\frac{\Delta P_{-1}}{P_{-2}} \frac{Y_{-1}}{Y}$
A1	0.6188 (0.1151)	−35.322 (43.214)	−0.7344 (0.1450)	0.1184 (0.1825)		
A2[c]	0.5785 (0.1033)	−111.65 (44.75)	−0.5671 (0.1201)	0.0022 (0.1493)	0.2989 (0.1118)	−0.1695 (0.0663)
A3	0.6062 (0.1130)		−0.7923 (0.1252)	0.1832 (0.1629)		
A4[c]	0.5852 (0.1130)		−0.7789 (0.1226)	0.1910 (0.1598)	0.1207 (0.1004)	−0.0940 (0.0805)

[a]Estimation was performed using annual data for the period 1952–75. Dependent variable: personal saving ratio (S/Y). The method of ordinary least squares was employed in estimating equations A1 and A3; equations A2 and A4 were estimated with the nonlinear least squares method (see note c).

[b]*C* = total personal consumption expenditure, millions of 1968 Skr.
Y = personal disposable income, millions of 1968 Skr.
ATP = corrected total sum of pension points (i.e., corrected sum of pensionable incomes divided by the basic amount), millions. The correction was performed by weighting the pension points of generations that by law only could get a reduced ATP pension by the ratio of the maximum number of years that each generation could work under the ATP scheme until retirement age to the number of years required for a full pension (twenty in this case).
P = implicit deflator for consumption.
TOT60 = dummy variable equal 1 year 1959, −1 year 1960, zero otherwise.
TOT62 = dummy variable equal 1 year 1961, −1 year 1962, zero otherwise.
VAT71 = dummy variable equal 1 year 1970, −1 year 1971, zero otherwise.
$\bar{R}^2$ = coefficient of determination corrected for degrees of freedom.
SE = standard error of estimate for the equation.
DW = Durbin-Watson statistic.

Standard errors for coefficient estimates are given in parentheses. Data sources: ATP—National Social Insurance Board. Other series—Central Bureau of Statistics and National Institute of Economic Research. Data were current as of spring 1977.

[c]Equation estimated with the nonlinear least squares method (using the *TSP* package) under the condition that the coefficient for $\frac{\Delta P_{-1}}{P_{-2}} \frac{Y_{-1}}{Y}$ equals the product of the coefficients for $\frac{\Delta P}{P_{-1}}$ and $\frac{C_{-1}}{Y}$.

Table 5–A1. continued

TOT60	*TOT62*	*VAT71*	$\bar{R}^2$	*SE*	*DW*
−0.0132 (0.0067)	−0.0054 (0.0065)	−0.0111 (0.0065)	0.7274	0.0091	1.65
−0.0090 (0.0061)	−0.0016 (0.0059)	−0.0118 (0.0058)	0.7726	0.0080	2.14
−0.0124 (0.0066)	−0.0053 (0.0064)	−0.0107 (0.0065)	0.7324	0.0090	1.64
−0.0096 (0.0068)	−0.0036 (0.0065)	−0.0110 (0.0064)	0.7224	0.0089	1.71

Table 5–A2. Structural Coefficients Derived from the Estimates in Table 5–A1 under the Assumption that g = 0.031[a]

Equation Number	*k*	*a*	λ
A1	0.9259	0.1612	0.7123
A2	0.9320	0.0039	0.5500
A3	0.9334	0.2312	0.7685
A4	0.9387	0.2452	0.7555

[a]This is the average rate of growth of real personal disposable income for 1952–75.

NOTES TO CHAPTER 5

1. ATP is the abbreviation for *Allmänna tilläggspensionsförsäkringen.*

2. In 1974 health insurance was also extended to cover a substantial portion of dental-care costs.

3. Capital income is not counted. Health and unemployment insurance payments are counted as earned income since 1974. The self-employed have the right to join or remain outside ATP according to their own discretion. However, participation must occur on an all-or-nothing basis. In 1975 about 6 percent of the income of the self-employed (which constitutes about 0.3 percent of total pensionable incomes) remained outside the system.

4. According to the rules existing in 1960 pension payments could first be received when the recipient had reached the age of sixty-seven (though pension points could only be obtained until the age of sixty-five).

5. The lowering of the pension age to sixty-five makes 1979 the first year during which a full ATP pension can be received.

6. The public sector subsidizes private unemployment insurance which is generally obtained through labor union affiliation. In 1974 the public sector paid for about half of unemployment insurance.

7. AP is the abbreviation for *Allmänna pensionsfonden.* The AP fund is described in more detail below.

8. For the self-employed, participation in ATP and, hence, contributions are voluntary. For all employers contributions are compulsory. They are determined by applying a flat rate to the part of wage income that can actually be counted by employees in determining their pension points. The initial rate in 1960 was 3 percent. The rate was gradually increased to 10 percent in 1970. During the first half of the 1970s the rate was increased much more slowly and in 1976 it reached 11 percent.

9. Today social insurance is financed almost entirely through employer contributions.

10. In 1974 employer contributions accounted for 40 percent, persons insured for 26 percent, and the central government for 34 percent of the financing of national health insurance. In 1975 business contributions financed 75 percent and in 1976 85 percent, with the central government being responsible for the rest. The flat rate for ATP payments was increased by only a quarter of a percentage point each year.

11. See [18, 1977], Chapter 2, for a more detailed discussion of the structure of the population and its potential importance for personal income and saving.

12. The last revision to affect the distribution of income in the national income accounts occurred in early autumn 1975.

13. The same conclusion dominated the rationale presented in conjunction with the official medium-term forecast of the personal saving ratio for 1970–75. See [13, 1971, p. 15].

14. Ettlin represents the income effect of ATP with the net increase in the AP-fund's assets. This would not have been a bad proxy had the ATP system been funded according to actuarial principles. As we have pointed out this was

not the case. Consequently, net changes in the assets of the AP fund do not measure future pension benefits which we believe are crucial in this context.

15. If we denote the personal saving ratio after the introduction of the social insurance program by $\frac{S + \Delta S}{Y + \Delta Y}$, then $\frac{S + \Delta S}{Y + \Delta Y} < \frac{S}{Y}$ implies $\frac{\Delta S}{\Delta Y} > \frac{S}{Y}$, assuming $\Delta S,\ \Delta Y < 0$. Furthermore, given that ΔS and ΔY are negative it is likely that the saving ratio has decreased, since $\frac{S}{Y}$ is around 5 percent while ΔS may be as large as ΔY.

16. We have shown elsewhere (see [18, 1977]) that a substantial portion of the ratio's decline in the latter half of the 1960s can be explained by the factors connected with the unexpected drop in the rate of inflation.

17. Alicia Munnell [20, 1976] has also analyzed a new sample collected during 1966–71. This sample consisted of about 5,000 American men forty-five to fifty-nine years old. She concludes:

> Contrary to earlier empirical work on the effect of pension coverage on saving, the findings of this study indicate clearly that pension coverage reduces saving efforts in other areas—at least for those older men for whom retirement is the primary saving motive [20, 1976, p. 1014].

18. The first year in which the *entire* labor force can expect full ATP benefits, at least in principle, is 1979.

19. Actually, age sixty-five for men and sixty for women with women's benefits being reduced commensurately.

20. The reader who is interested in a more rigorous presentation of the model is advised to consult Appendix 1 from the outset.

21. More precisely, transitory consumption is assumed to be proportional to transitory income only on the average. In addition to the effect of transitory income, transitory consumption is assumed to be affected by a random term with zero mean value.

22. According to Friedman [14, 1957, p. 10], given a subjective rate of discount, permanent income equals the return from the present value of lifetime resources (see also [1, 1959]).

23. This assumption seems plausible since we believe that pension expectations are largely determined by current pensionable income rather than by tedious calculations based on guesses about future income. The exact relationship between current pensionable income and future pension benefits can be illustrated in the following simple case. Assume the individual expects his earnings always to keep up with the constant rate of inflation, *r*. Assume further that he/she expects to be gainfully active for at least thirty years, that is, to obtain full pension benefits. According to the formula given in Section I (p. 172), the individual's expected pension benefits, P_T, are

$$P_T = .60 \left[\frac{1}{15} \sum_{t=1}^{15} \frac{Y_t^{PEN}}{B_t} \right] B_T \ ,$$

where Y_t^{PEN} is pensionable income in year t, B_t is the base in the same year (so that Y_t^{PEN}/B_t gives pension points) and t goes over the individual's fifteen best earning years. Since the base is adjusted for inflation we have

$$P_T = .60 \left[\frac{1}{15} \sum_{t=1}^{15} \frac{Y_1^{PEN}\,(1+r)^{t-1}}{B_1\,(1+r)^{t-1}} \right] B_T = .60\ \frac{Y_1^{PEN}}{B_1}\ B_T$$

$$= .60\ Y_1^{PEN}\,(1+r)^{T-1}\,.$$

Thus, in the simple case of expected zero real income growth the real value of expected pension benefits equals 60 percent of the current income. The example may further be complicated in an obvious way with a variable inflation rate and a variable real income growth rate. At an aggregate level our assumption holds if, for example, constant real income growth is expected. Of course, the usual requirements for a stable aggregate relation—in particular a constant age structure of the working population—must also be fulfilled.

24. "A dollar in the form of a reserve held by the government and available to the individual only under narrowly specified circumstances is worth less to him than a dollar in privately held reserves that he can dispose of at will; in consequence, each dollar increase in government held reserve would tend to produce less than a dollar decrease in private savings" [14, 1957, p. 123].

25. In a more comprehensive study of short-run fluctuations in the consumption ratio between 1965 and 1974 we present a considerably different approximation of expected income growth. The model which, due to its technical detail, cannot be presented here, is explained in [18, 1977]. We have also tested for the ATP effect in a formulation of this model designed for annual data and obtained results in line with those presented here.

26. We are thus assuming that transitory consumption is not affected by ATP. This assumption is obvious as far as equation (6) is concerned. It is more problematic in the case of the model including the inflation effect on consumption, since it leads to the exclusion of the price terms from the ATP-effect formula. It is possible that increased social insurance saving has affected the level of prices and, indirectly, saving behavior.

REFERENCES

1. ANDO, ALBERT, and MODIGLIANI, FRANCO, "The 'Permanent Income' and 'Life-Cycle' Hypothesis of Saving Behavior: Comparison and Tests," in *Proceedings of the Conference on Consumption and Saving*, Vol. II. Edited by IRWIN FRIEND and ROBERT JONES. Philadelphia: University of Pennsylvania Press, 1959.

2. BROBERG, ROLF; LINDELL, INGVAR; and SAMUELSSON, YNGVE. *Den Allmänna Sjukförsäkringen.* Stockholm: P.A. Norstedt & Söners Förlag, 1956.

3. CAGAN, PHILLIP. *The Effect of Pension Plans on Aggregate Saving: Evidence from a Sample Survey.* New York: National Bureau of Economic Research; distributed by Columbia University Press, 1965.

4. EISNER, ROBERT. "Capital Shortage: Myth and Reality," *American Economic Review*, Feb. 1977, *67*(1), pp. 110–15.

5. ERIKSEN, TOR E. *En Prognosmodell för den Allmänna Tilläggspensioneringen, ATP.* Stockholm: National Social Insurance Board, 1973.

6. ETTLIN, FRANZ. "Hushållens konsumtion och sparande i Sverige under två decennier—ett försök att bestämma orsakerna till deras förändringar," *Skandinaviska Enskilda Banken Quarterly Review*, Sept. 1976, (3)–(4), pp. 94–104.

7. *Family Expenditure Survey 1969: Preliminary Results.* Stockholm: Central Bureau of Statistics, 1971.

8. FELDSTEIN, MARTIN. "Social Security, Induced Retirement, and Aggregate Capital Formation," *Journal of Political Economy*, Sept.-Oct. 1974, *82*(5), pp. 905–26.

9. ____. "Social Security and Saving: The Extended Life Cycle Theory," *American Economic Review*, May 1976, *66*(2), pp. 77–86.

10. ____. "Does the United States Save Too Little?" *American Economic Review*, Feb. 1977, *67*(1), pp. 116–21.

11. ____. "Social Security and Private Savings: International Evidence in an Extended Life-Cycle Model," in *The Economics of Public Services.* Edited by MARTIN FELDSTEIN and ROBERT INMAN. London: Macmillan Press, 1977.

12. ____, and PELLECHIO, ANTHONY. "Social Security and Household Wealth Accumulation: New Microeconometric Evidence." Harvard Institute of Economic Research, Discussion Paper No. 530, Mimeographed, Jan. 1977.

13. *Finansiella tillväxtaspekter 1960–1975: 1970 års långtidsutredning, Bilaga 4.* Stockholm: The Swedish Government's Official Investigations, Report No. 1971:7; distributed by Esselte AB, 1971.

14. FRIEDMAN, MILTON. *A Theory of the Consumption Function.* Princeton: Princeton University Press, 1957.

15. KATONA, GEORGE. *Private Pensions and Individual Saving.* Ann Arbor: Survey Research Center, ISR, Monograph No. 40; University of Michigan, 1965.

16. KRAGH, BÖRJE. *Finansiella långtidsperspektiv.* Stockholm: The Swedish Government's Official Investigations, Report No. 1967:6; distributed by Esselte AB, 1967.

17. KRUSE, AGNETA, and STÅHLBERG, ANN-CHARLOTTE. *Effekter av ATP: En samhällsekonomisk studie.* Doctoral dissertation presented at the University of Lund, Sept. 1977.

18. MARKOWSKI, ALEKSANDER, and PALMER, EDWARD E. *Fluctuations in the Consumption Ratio in Sweden: A Study of the Period 1965–1974.* Stockholm: National Institute of Economic Research; distributed by Liber Förlag, 1977.

19. MUNNELL, ALICIA. "The Impact of Social Security on Personal Savings," *National Tax Journal*, Dec. 1974, *27*(4), pp. 553–67.

20. ____. "Private Pensions and Saving: New Evidence," *Journal of Political Economy*, Oct. 1976, *84* (5), pp. 1013–32.

21. PUURA, EVA. "A Study of Household Consumption Using Cross-section Data" (in Swedish). National Institute of Economic Research Working Paper, Mimeographed, 1974.

22. Riksdagsproposition 1958:55. Stockholm: 1958.

23. STONE, RICHARD, and ROWE, DERYCK A. "A Post-War Expenditure Function," *Manchester School of Economic and Social Studies*, May 1962, *30* (2), pp. 187–98.

24. STONE, RICHARD. "Private Saving in Britain, Past, Present and Future," *Manchester School of Economic and Social Studies*, May 1964, *32* (2), pp. 79–112.

Chapter 6

Private Saving and the Provision of Social Security in Britain 1946–75

David Barros[a]

The United Kingdom's decision, after the war, to follow a general economic strategy with strong emphasis on welfare and redistribution aspects marked the beginning of a process that has reshaped the British economy and society over the last thirty years. A major factor in the economic strategy has been the social security system. Throughout the last three decades several reforms have taken place to conform to the objectives outlined during and immediately after the war. It is important, however, to bear in mind that these reforms have not worked alone.

A score of economic policies implemented by different governments (e.g., nationalization of private companies, tax and subsidy policies, interest rate management and credit controls) have been intended to work toward the same welfare objectives. Whether or not they have succeeded is another matter. Nevertheless it is clear that, along with the growth of social security, these measures have shaped the pattern of private consumption and saving and ultimately the accumulation of wealth. In this chapter one aspect of this problem will be examined: the pattern and behavior of personal saving and its links, if any, with the provision of state welfare benefits.

A short study like this can have only a limited scope. This means that, inevitably, the effect of all economic variables on saving can not be analyzed. It may seem appropriate to warn the American reader about this because the degree of influence and control of the government and of government policies over the economy is much

[a]The author is greatly indebted to Professor Jack Revell for his constructive comment on an earlier draft of this chapter.

greater and more widespread in the United Kingdom than in the United States.

The study is divided into four main sections. The first is a description of the basic welfare system, its development and basic operations. The second section analyzes the evolution and importance of occupational pensions and state pension schemes, and the relationship between the two. The third section analyzes the postwar trends in personal and corporate saving, and the provision of welfare benefits (and their cost) through the main branches of the welfare system. The fourth and last section examines the determinants of personal saving and the links between personal saving and state provision of retirement benefits.

I. THE BASIC WELFARE SYSTEM

The provision of state welfare benefits in the U.K. can be traced back to at least 1598, with the promulgation of the "Acte for the Reliefe of the Poore," commonly known as the Poor Law Act. The rudimentary provisions established in that law, modified and expanded throughout the centuries, can be said to have been the core of the British welfare system right up to the 1900s. In 1908 and 1911 two acts created means-tested old-age pensions and unemployment benefits, respectively. Postwar British social security, however, has a very definitive starting point in the famous Beveridge Report of 1942 [1, 1942], from which the present system largely stems.

Lord Beveridge proposed the establishment of a comprehensive welfare system based on three major concepts:

1. A National Insurance Fund;
2. A National Minimum Income;
3. A National 'free' Health Service.

Even though Beveridge's detailed recommendations were not implemented in full, these three basic elements have constituted the conceptual framework of the British social security system since the late 1940s.

The National Insurance Fund (NIF)

Established by the National Insurance Act of 1946, the NIF is financed by contributions from employers and employees (including self-employed), by interest on securities, and by large grants from the Exchequer which, during the last twenty years of the survey, averaged 18 percent of the contributions received annually by the fund. It is not, therefore, self-financing, but neither does it operate on a strictly pay-as-you-go basis since, after considering government grants, a small surplus is registered which is invested in government bonds in order to accumulate a proper fund.

From its inception the fund has provided, in addition to retirement pensions, a score of ancillary benefits (detailed in the Glossary, item 12) which in this chapter are treated together under one single heading. The scheme covers all the working population, irrespective of income or personal risk, and benefits are provided as of right, without means tests.

Up to 1960 contributions and benefits were both collected and paid out on a flat-rate basis. The introduction of a graduated pension scheme in 1961 allowed for income-related contributions and benefits in addition to the flat-rate ones. At the same time it opened doors to the growth of private pension plans by allowing contracting out where comparable benefits were provided. This situation has persisted more or less till the present time, but it will change if and when the new pensions scheme starts to operate in 1978 (see Section II).

In 1966 the earnings-related concept was extended to unemployment, sickness, industrial injuries, and widows' benefits, but no contracting out has been allowed in these cases.

Noncontributory Social Security

As stated earlier, the concept of a national minimum level of income has played a fundamental role in the design of British social security policy. In the Beveridge Report the belief was that national insurance alone would provide every citizen with "an income sufficient to meet his responsibilities" [1, 1942, para. 444]. For those with inadequate coverage, especially those already retired at the time of introduction of the National Insurance Fund, it was recommended that for a transitional period of approximately twenty years social assistance would have to operate, on a means-tested basis, as a complement to National Insurance Benefits.

The evidence over the last thirty years [2, 1970], however, indicates that, contrary to the report's belief, National Insurance benefits have consistently fallen below the subsistence standard set for National Assistance (a program which was replaced by the Supplementary Benefit Program in 1966). The national minimum level of income has been met, therefore, not by social insurance alone but by complementary, means-tested National Assistance benefits. Far from dying away over a transitional period, households receiving Supplementary Benefit (National Assistance) have, in fact, increased in number during the postwar years.

The National Health Service (NHS)

The same acts that started social security in Britain provided for some of the care for the sick. Two main acts, in 1848 and 1875, established a comprehensive public health system. In 1912 medical care was established in voluntary hospitals for those paying a contribution, and this service was again expanded in 1929. The present comprehensive National Health Service was created in 1946, however, and started operations in 1948. Its creation is also derived from proposals in the Beveridge Report, and its objective has been to improve the health of the population and to prevent, diagnose, and treat illness.

Medical care is provided for all U.K. residents irrespective of insurance qualifications. NHS contributions are paid by the insured population, and nominal amounts are charged for some of the services and medicines. These, however, cover a small part of the overall cost of the service, which falls largely on the Exchequer.

The NHS underwent a major reorganization in 1974 which centralized its administration. Some criticisms have already been made to the effect that the reform has slowed and lowered patient service and has accelerated the shift of resources from medical care into administrative activity.

Between 1954 and 1974 the share of the gross national product spent on the NHS increased from 3.5 percent to 5.3 percent, and today the service is the tenth-largest employer in the world [3, 1977].

II. PENSIONS

Occupational Pensions

The first survey of occupational pension schemes was undertaken by the Government Actuary in 1956 [4, 1957]. It covered independently funded insurance schemes in both the private and the public sector. The survey showed that there were at the time approximately 37,500 pension schemes in the private sector, with approximately 4.5 million members. At the same time another 4 million belonged to schemes in the public sector (including the armed forces and nationalized industries).

Successive surveys in 1963 and 1967 [5, 1964; 6, 1968], found that the number of schemes had increased to 60,000 and 65,000 respectively, and that there were approximately 7 million members in the private sector in 1963 and 8 million in 1967. In both years the number of persons covered in the public sector remained at 4 million. A fourth survey undertaken in 1971 [7, 1972] showed that, although the number of schemes had stabilized at approximately

65,000, the number of members had declined from a combined total of 12 million (private and public sectors) to about 11 million, with all the decline taking place in the private sector. In other words, the combined membership of pension schemes was back to the 1963 level.

The survey was reluctant to relate the decline to any one single cause, although it pointed out that it was strongly related to the reduction in the labor force from 23.6 million in 1967 to 22.7 million in 1971. A fifth survey, the results of which have been only partially released [8, 1977], shows that between 1971 and 1975 a further decline in the membership of private pension schemes took place. Private membership stood, at the end of 1975, at only 6 million, with another 5.5 million persons covered by public schemes.

Table 6–1 shows the changes in membership of pension schemes between 1936 and 1975. As can be seen, membership of private schemes has shown a large decline since the mid-1960s. The combined membership of private and public schemes, however, increased during the early 1970s, thereby partially offsetting the decline experienced in the late 1960s.

Pension schemes are of two main kinds. Most large organizations in both private and public sectors set up an independent pension fund (or superannuation fund, as it is called in the official statistics) which has its own assets and is under the control of trustees. Smaller organizations arrange to pay annual premiums to an insurance company to secure the benefits promised to their employees in the pension scheme; these are known as insured schemes, and the premiums and payments appear in the statistics of life assurance. In addition, there are some schemes, of which the largest are the pension schemes for the civil service and the armed forces, which operate on a pay-as-you-go basis.

Table 6–1. Membership of Pension Schemes *(millions)*

Year	*Private Sector*	*Public Sector*	*Total*
1936	1.6	1.0	2.6
1954	3.1	3.1	6.2
1956	4.3	3.7	8.0
1963	7.2	3.9	11.1
1967	8.1	4.1	12.2
1971	6.8	4.3	11.1
1975	6.1	5.4	11.5

Source: Government Actuary, *Fifth Survey on Occupational Pensions* (unpublished).

The reduction in the membership of pension schemes did not have an appreciable effect on the aggregate amount of contributions to, or pensions paid by, life assurance and superannuation funds between 1967 and 1971, when both items increased in nominal as well as real terms. Between 1973 and 1975, however, both total contributions and total pensions declined in real value. This was aggravated by the performance of rent, dividends, and interest received by the funds, which were also eroded in real terms. A result of this was that funding became inadequate in most pension schemes, and special lump-sum contributions had to be made to the funds by employers. In spite of these extra contributions, the degree of funding today varies considerably among pension funds, and it is recognized that few of them are fully funded. The net increase in the funds of life assurance and superannuation, that is, private pension funds, is shown in Table 6–2.

Another reason for the underfunding of the schemes was that, since most pensions are calculated on a final salary basis, the rapid increase in nominal salaries made contributions paid on previous (lower) salaries insufficient to cover the cost of the new increased pensions.

Only a few schemes in the public sector offer indexed pensions. Over 70 percent of members of pension funds are, however, covered

Table 6–2. Revenue Account of Life Assurance and Superannuation Funds *(£ million)*

	1971	*1972*	*1973*	*1974*	*1975*
Current Prices					
Contributions from employers and employees	3,585	4,469	5,161	6,013	7,158
Rent, dividends & interest receipts	1,499	1,636	1,967	2,192	2,523
Pensions and benefits paid	−2,540	−2,839	−3,249	−3,799	−4,300
Administrative costs	−614	−663	−786	−916	−1,050
Net increase in funds	1,930	2,603	3,093	3,490	4,331
Constant 1975 Prices[a]					
Contributions from employers and employees	5,937	6,939	7,381	7,406	7,158
Rent, dividends & interest receipts	2,483	2,540	2,813	2,700	2,523
Pensions and benefits paid	−4,207	−4,408	−4,647	−4,679	−4,300
Administrative costs	−1,017	−1,029	−1,123	−1,129	−1,050
Net increase in funds	3,196	4,042	4,423	4,298	4,331

Source: *National Income and Expenditure 1965–1975*, HMSO, 1976, Table 4.6.
[a]Deflated by the consumers' expenditure deflator, base 1975 = 100.

by some form of augmentation after retirement. In most schemes augmentation is ad hoc and has not prevented the reduction of individual pensions in real terms in the great majority of schemes.

Evolution of State Pension Schemes

The first state pension scheme was introduced in Britain in 1908, and it remained operative until the creation of the National Insurance Fund in 1946. As mentioned earlier, the NIF provided a flat-rate pension at retirement age (sixty-five for men, sixty for women). With the introduction of graduated pensions in 1961 contracting out was allowed when occupational pensions offered equal or superior benefits. The boost to private pension schemes that this policy implied can be immediately appreciated by looking at the figures for membership of pension funds and the number of schemes, as detailed in the previous section.

The graduated state pension severely restricted benefits and imposed rather low ceilings on the maximum pensionable earnings. At a time of increasing real incomes this provided an added incentive for contracting out.

Since the introduction of graduated pensions in 1961 three different plans for improving the public pension system have been proposed. The last one became law as the Social Security Pensions Act of 1975 and became operative in April 1978.

Each of the proposed state schemes has differed drastically from its predecessors, and their implications have been widely discussed. Moreover, the last but one proposed scheme was passed by Parliament in 1973, only to be scrapped a few months later by a new government. The present scheme could well end up being modified, if not totally abandoned, by a new government. All this means that members of private schemes, firms operating schemes, and the pension funds themselves have lived in a constant state of uncertainty over the past ten years, and this could well be an important element in the decline in pension-fund membership observed by the fourth survey.

The 1978 State Pension Scheme

The new state pension scheme that started to operate in 1978 offers an index-linked, two-tier pension structure. There is a flat-rate basic pension and on top of it an earnings-related pension. The earnings-related pensions have a maximum equivalent to 25 percent of the "upper-band earnings," which are those earnings between the basic pension (the amount of which is determined regularly and automatically) and a ceiling of seven times the basic pension.

When the system is in complete operation, the second-tier pensions will be paid on the average of the best twenty years of earnings, and afterwards the pension will be increased regularly and automatically in line with movements in prices. The system is not going to be fully operative, however, until twenty years hence. This means that those already retired and those retiring during the next twenty years cannot expect to receive more than a fraction of their total corresponding earnings-related pensions.

Contributions from employers and employees will be considerably higher under the new scheme than those being paid at the present and those paid in the past, even though there has been a substantial increase in the rates in recent years. Employers may, however, contract their employees out of the earnings-related part of the state pension scheme on the strict condition that their own pension schemes provide benefits no less generous than those provided by the second tier of the state scheme. Contributions to the state scheme are much reduced for both employers and employees when a private scheme is contracted out. It has been estimated that, for employees in the upper-band earnings, the employees' contributions would be reduced from 6.75 percent in the full state scheme to 4.25 percent on contracting out; the employers' contributions would be reduced from 12.25 percent to 7.75 percent [see 9, 1976].

One major characteristic of the 1978 scheme is that it is financed largely from current income; that is, on a pay-as-you-go basis. This involves a further step away from the insurance principle of social security, in favor of the tax-transfer principle. The Exchequer contributions are expected to be maintained at 18 percent of private contributions. This feature differentiates this scheme conceptually from the one abandoned in 1973, which was an attempt to bring state pensions into line with private pension funds. This would have been done by plowing additional contributions into an investment reserve fund out of which a second tier of pensions would have been paid in excess of the basic old-age pension.

Finally an additional element has complicated not only the transition to the present pension system but also arrangements under the previous system. In recent years the government has succeeded in imposing an incomes policy in which the pay ceilings have been extended to include pension benefits that go beyond the minimum standards set for contracting out. This has meant the freezing of virtually all improvements in private pensions, especially those for a number of manual workers who were going to be raised to white-collar standards.

III. ANALYSIS OF POSTWAR TRENDS IN PRIVATE SAVINGS AND THE PROVISION OF STATE WELFARE BENEFITS

Personal Saving

Personal disposable income more than doubled in real terms between 1946 and 1975, increasing by 115 percent, as shown in Table 6–3. With the exception of 1948, 1958, and 1975, it rose every year. Consumers' expenditure increased by only 93 percent in real terms. As a consequence real personal saving showed a seven-fold increase, from £1,500 million in 1946 to £10,400 million in 1975.

The most widely watched indicator of personal savings trends is the personal saving ratio (personal saving as a proportion of personal disposable income). From the mid-1940s, this ratio first fell and then rose in several stages. During the late 1940s, and as a consequence of the disruption caused by the war, personal saving was severely reduced to less than 1 percent of disposable income in 1948. From that low point it started to increase moderately above 1 percent until 1952, when it jumped to more than 3 percent. Between 1952 and 1959 the rates behaved rather erratically, fluctuating between 3 and 5 percent. In 1960 the rate took another jump and then fluctuated between 7 and 9 percent until 1971. Thereafter it increased steadily to 14 percent in 1975.

The rapid increase in the saving ratio during the 1970s has been the subject of some studies which have advanced various hypotheses to explain it. These are analyzed later in this chapter.

Uses of Personal Saving

The main form in which personal saving has been used in Britain has been the acquisition of nonfinancial assets. As shown in Table 6–4, gross personal capital formation increased four-fold in real terms since the late 1940s. In 1974 and 1975, however, net acquisition of financial assets was greater than personal capital formation.

Net acquisition of financial assets was largely negative (borrowing offsetting acquisitions of financial assets) right up to the mid-1950s, but has been positive ever since. Between 1960 and 1972, net acquisition of financial assets behaved erratically, fluctuating between £1.2 and £2.5 billion annually in real terms. In the last three years of the survey, however, net financial investment trebled, reaching £6.3 billion in 1975.

One of the main channels of financial saving by the personal sector in Britain has been life assurance funds and, more recently, super-

Table 6–3. Personal Saving[a] *(£ million at constant [1975] prices[b])*

Year	*Personal Disposable Income*	*Consumers' Expenditure*	*Personal Saving*	*Personal Saving Ratio*	*Implicit Deflator*
	(1)	(2)	(3)	(4)	(5)
1946	34255	32747	1508	4.4	22.21
1947	34385	33547	838	2.4	23.77
1948	33719	33461	258	0.8	25.56
1949	34758	34178	580	1.7	26.06
1950	35223	34732	491	1.4	27.06
1951	35267	34844	423	1.2	29.13
1952	35863	34644	1219	3.4	30.86
1953	37673	36228	1445	3.9	31.47
1954	38940	37748	1192	3.1	32.03
1955	40794	39334	1460	3.6	33.15
1956	41842	39661	2181	5.2	34.65
1957	43758	41667	2091	4.8	34.82
1958	43274	41531	1743	4.0	36.83
1959	45526	43366	2160	4.7	37.17
1960	48541	45088	3453	7.1	37.56
1961	50489	46119	4370	8.7	38.68
1962	50868	47097	3771	7.4	40.18
1963	53086	49116	3970	7.5	40.96
1964	55181	50774	4407	8.0	42.30
1965	56448	51430	5018	8.9	44.41
1966	57688	52399	5289	9.2	46.21
1967	58536	53545	4991	8.5	47.49
1968	59602	54860	4742	8.0	49.83
1969	60106	55244	4862	8.1	52.68
1970	62301	56706	5595	9.0	55.80
1971	63687	58240	5447	8.6	60.38
1972	68681	61673	7008	10.2	64.40
1973	72873	64420	8453	11.6	69.92
1974	74260	63837	10423	14.0	81.19
1975	73727	63373	10354	14.0	100.00

Source: *National Income and Expenditure*, Annual Series.

[a]See glossary to Chapter 6 for definition of terms.

[b]Series deflated by the consumers' expenditure deflator converted to base 1975 = 100.

annuation funds. This item of saving shows a very steady growth over the period up to 1973, increasing nearly five times in real terms since the late 1940s. Between 1973 and 1975 the real value of the funds fell slightly, in spite of the substantial increase in contributions. In 1975 (and 1976), however, the real value of the funds started to increase again.

Table 6–4. Uses of Personal Saving[a] *(£ million at constant [1975] prices[b])*

Year	*Gross Personal Capital Formation*	*Net Personal Acquisition of Financial Assets*	*Growth of Life Assurance and Superannuation Funds[c]*	*Net Household Credit[c]*	*Other Financial Assets[c]*
	(1)	(2)	(3)	(4)	(5)
1946	1175	333	950	−477	−140
1947	1098	−260	888	−446	−702
1948	1021	−763	826	−415	−1174
1949	1021	−441	883	−464	−860
1950	1072	−581	968	−440	−1109
1951	1164	−741	1033	−409	−1365
1952	937	282	1108	−421	−405
1953	1284	161	1211	−502	−548
1954	1583	−391	1333	−668	−1056
1955	1732	−272	1406	−715	−963
1956	1602	579	1457	−352	−526
1957	1646	445	1620	−781	−394
1958	1599	144	1702	−815	−743
1959	1862	298	1897	−1370	−229
1960	2242	1211	2173	−1014	52
1961	2405	1965	2247	−928	646
1962	2272	1499	2325	−926	100
1963	2756	1214	2622	−1826	418
1964	3007	1400	2735	−2497	1162
1965	2834	2184	2618	−1830	1396
1966	2805	2484	2686	−1355	1153
1967	3026	1965	2889	−2411	1487
1968	3442	1300	3026	−2298	572
1969	3371	1491	2861	−1634	264
1970	3324	2271	3109	−2518	1680
1971	4122	1325	3196	−4410	2539
1972	4918	2090	4042	−7826	5874
1973	4891	3562	4424	−5998	5136
1974	4021	6402	4298	−2905	5009
1975	4078	6276	4331	−3463	5408

Source: *National Income and Expenditure*, Annual Series.
[a]See glossary to Chapter 6 for definition of terms. Personal saving equals the sum of the entries in columns (1) and (2).
[b]Series deflated by the consumers' expenditure deflator, base 1975 = 100.
[c]Detail of column (2).

On average, during the last ten years of the survey, half of the increase corresponds to life assurance and insured pension business and half to noninsured superannuation funds. In 1975, however, superannuation funds' growth exceeded that of life assurance (including insured pensions) by 50 percent.

The behavior of household borrowing has been very erratic over the period, although it has grown along a trend. During the 1970s it increased substantially, especially in 1972 at the height of the property boom. Up to the early 1970s identified borrowing for house purchase constituted just over 50 percent of total household credit advanced. In 1974 and 1975 (the last two years of the survey), however, identified loans for house purchase rose to two-thirds and three-quarters, respectively, of total credit advanced to the personal sector.

The rest of the financial assets acquired by the personal sector (other financial assets) are dominated by four items: national savings (saving certificates, National Savings Bank and trustee savings banks deposits, government savings bonds, and save-as-you-earn schemes), marketable securities, deposits with building societies (saving and loan associations), and currency and bank deposits. Over the last ten years of the survey two trends are clearly identifiable: (1) a switch away from national savings and into building society deposits (the latter were half as large as national savings in 1965 but twice as large as national savings in 1975); (2) a massive and persistent shift out of corporate securities.

The first phenomenon can be partly attributed to interest rate differentials which until very recently made national savings relatively unattractive when compared with other forms of private saving. The second reflects the trend toward the "institutionalization" of the securities market where, over the years, institutional investors like pension funds and life assurance companies have acquired stock from individual investors.

The increase in holdings of liquid assets in the form of currency and demand and time deposits remained relatively stable until 1969. Between 1969 and 1974 it rose seven-fold in real terms, the greatest increases taking place in 1972, 1973, and 1974. In 1975, however, the increase in these items declined in nominal terms to only 10 percent of the 1974 amount.

Gross Corporate Saving

Gross corporate profit more than trebled in real terms in the period up to 1974, as shown in Table 6–5. In 1975, however, it showed a substantial decrease of more than £6 billion in real terms. This decrease was reflected in lower dividends and taxes as well as in undistributed earnings (corporate saving). Undistributed earnings grew moderately and erratically in real terms during the 1950s and 1960s, in line with the performance of profits during the same period. Corporate saving as a percentage of gross corporate profit fluctuated accordingly over the postwar years, being on average just about 43 percent. Both corporate saving and corporate profit are, however, considerably reduced after allowing for replacement-cost depreciation and stock appreciation (inventory profits). In fact, net corporate saving declined considerably in real terms, from £4.2 billion in 1965 to £1.4 billion in 1975, as shown in the last column of Table 6–5.

Up to 1960 the corporate sector as a whole was in a net creditor position, providing the economy with an important amount of funds, reflected in a positive net acquisition of financial assets. Thereafter the sector was frequently a net debtor. Of course, the financial position varied among the institutions that are aggregated into the corporate sector.

With the exception of 1969, banks were in a surplus position during the last ten years of the survey. Industrial and commercial companies as a group had some large annual financial deficits, but more often surpluses, over the same period. The group that contributed most to the overall deficit position (net borrowing) of the corporate sector is "financial institutions other than banks," which includes, among others, building societies, insurance companies, and superannuation funds.

The amounts borrowed by the corporate sector moved in an erratic fashion, reaching a peak in 1974. In that same year the corporate sector's real gross capital formation also reached a peak, only to decline substantially in 1975.

National Insurance Fund Total Current Account Receipts and Expenditures

The National Insurance Fund has three main sources of current income, shown in Table 6–6: employer and employee contributions, interest on government securities, and government grants. Grants from the Exchequer amounted to about 15 percent of total receipts during the last twenty years of the survey, compared with a high of 35 percent in 1947. Other components became more important. Thus contributions and interest increased in real terms between seven and eight times since 1946, but Exchequer grants increased by only about four times over the same period.

As already explained, the NIF provides, besides pensions, a number of ancillary benefits. Pensions, however, constituted on average nearly two-thirds of total benefits paid during the last fifteen years of the survey.

Pensions paid increased substantially and steadily over the period in real terms (about 13 times). Other benefits also increased considerably (about 5 times) in real terms, but the trend was not so steady.

Table 6–5. Gross Corporate Saving[a] *(£ million at constant [1975] prices[b])*

Year	*Gross Corporate Profit*	*Dividends, Taxes, and Other Distributions*	*Corporate Saving: Undistributed Earnings*	*Gross Corporate Capital Formation[c]*	*Net Corporate Acquisition of Financial Assets[c]*	*Corporate Saving after Providing for Replacement of Fixed Capital and Inventories at Current Prices[d]*
	(1)	(2)	(3)	(4)	(5)	(6)
1946	8492	6087	2405	3751	−1346	n.a.
1947	9196	5271	3925	3504	421	n.a.
1948	9120	5090	4030	3259	771	2090
1949	9033	5618	3415	2751	664	1612
1950	11594	6148	5446	4127	1319	2601
1951	12111	5966	6145	5809	336	3282
1952	10600	6701	3899	2612	1287	2586
1953	10768	6459	4309	2132	2177	2984
1954	11533	6253	5280	3216	2064	3545
1955	12348	6893	5455	4215	1240	3374
1956	12443	6796	5647	4438	1209	3511
1957	13173	7340	5833	4825	1008	3599
1958	12522	7230	5292	3972	1320	3495
1959	13338	7531	5807	4571	1236	3730
1960	14530	7282	7248	6542	706	5025
1961	14054	7789	6265	6271	−6	3869
1962	13766	8181	5585	5493	92	3178
1963	15059	8362	6697	5659	1038	4072
1964	16256	8698	7558	7946	−388	4593
1965	16445	9176	7269	7596	−327	4222

1966	15619	9040	6579	7045	−466	3149
1967	15770	9674	6096	5945	151	2974
1968	17489	10467	7022	7013	9	3183
1969	17641	10875	6766	7800	−1034	2671
1970	18235	11454	6781	8844	−2063	1986
1971	19391	11709	7682	7327	355	2909
1972	21523	12044	9479	8070	1409	4228
1973	27448	14307	13141	13218	−77	5646
1974	28333	16174	12159	16101	−3942	1981
1975	22178	12184	9994	10583	−589	1416

Source: *National Income and Expenditure*, Annual Series. The inventory valuation adjustments and capital consumption adjustments made to column (3) to derive column (6) are from *National Income and Expenditure*, 1959, 1967, and 1966–76, respectively.

[a] See glossary to Chapter 6 for definition of terms.

[b] Series deflated by the consumers' expenditure deflator, base 1975 = 100.

[c] Detail of column 3.

[d] This concept is analogous to undistributed corporate profits including the IVA and CCA in the U.S. National Income Accounts.

Table 6–6. National Insurance Fund: Total Current Account Receipts and Expenditures[a] *(£ million at constant [1975] prices[b])*

Year	NIF Contributions and Interest	NIF Government Grants	NIF Total Receipts[c]	NIF Retirement Pensions	NIF, Other Benefits, etc.	NIF Total Benefits[d]
	(1)	(2)	(3)	(4)	(5)	(6)
1946	855	270	1125	338	413	751
1947	1068	572	1640	896	407	1303
1948	1409	579	1988	1021	505	1526
1949	1780	576	2356	955	772	1727
1950	1748	565	2313	935	754	1689
1951	1689	474	2163	927	707	1634
1952	1688	246	1934	1011	758	1769
1953	1821	264	2085	1090	820	1910
1954	1814	247	2061	1093	793	1886
1955	1946	293	2239	1255	824	2079
1956	2011	306	2317	1299	851	2150
1957	1976	313	2289	1344	870	2214
1958	2226	405	2631	1643	945	2588
1959	2276	568	2844	1779	1006	2785
1960	2287	506	2793	1808	961	2769
1961	2578	484	3062	1989	1050	3039
1962	2743	500	3243	2031	1122	3153
1963	2944	552	3496	2271	1330	3601
1964	3180	556	3736	2416	1277	3693
1965	3582	657	4239	2711	1445	4156

1966	3671	662	4333	2772	1487	4259
1967	3765	653	4418	2845	1712	4557
1968	4050	734	4784	3112	1806	4918
1969	3937	699	4636	3047	1752	4799
1970	4407	763	5170	3217	1847	5064
1971	4334	818	5152	3226	1830	5056
1972	4845	885	5730	3637	2000	5637
1973	5322	897	6219	3954	1902	5856
1974	5943	947	6890	4297	2009	6306
1975	6462	1140	7602	4479	2220	6699

Source: *National Income and Expenditure*, Annual Series.

[a] See glossary to Chapter 6 for definition of terms.

[b] Series deflated by the consumers' expenditure deflator, base 1975 = 100.

[c] Column (3) = (1) + (2).

[d] Column (6) = (4) + (5).

Table 6–7. Total Current Welfare Expenditures Financed by the Exchequer[a]
(£ million at constant [1975] prices[b])

Year	NIF Current Account Surplus (−) or Deficit (+) before Government Grants[c]	NHS Current Account Deficit (+)	Total Non-contributory Social Security Benefits	Total Current Welfare Expenditures Financed by the Exchequer[d]
	(1)	(2)	(3)	(4)
1946	−104	0	1040	936
1947	235	0	867	1102
1948	117	712	778	1607
1949	−53	1416	837	2200
1950	−59	1692	917	2550
1951	−55	1634	896	2475
1952	81	1585	995	2661
1953	89	1605	1035	2729
1954	72	1608	1033	2713
1955	133	1674	1026	2833
1956	139	1757	1013	2909
1957	238	1809	1057	3104
1958	362	1618	1043	3023
1959	509	1717	1092	3318
1960	482	1869	1166	3517
1961	461	1914	1146	3521
1962	410	1862	1159	3431
1963	657	1968	1223	3848
1964	513	2083	1241	3837
1965	574	2283	1230	4087
1966	588	2441	1242	4271
1967	792	2649	1436	4877
1968	868	2733	1656	5257
1969	862	2732	1833	5427
1970	657	2964	1827	5448
1971	722	3092	1949	5763
1972	792	3387	2185	6364
1973	534	3523	1929	5986
1974	363	4148	1994	6505
1975	237	4725	2069	7031

Source: *National Income and Expenditure*, Annual Series.
[a]See glossary to Chapter 6 for definition of terms.
[b]Series deflated by the consumers' expenditure deflator, base 1975 = 100.
[c]NIF deficit obtained by subtracting column (6) from column (1) in Table 6–6.
[d]Column (4) = (1) + (2) + (3).

The total value of accrued rights to state pensions, including widows' benefits, can be taken as proxy for the net national insurance pension "wealth." This wealth was estimated to be £154 billion in April 1975 [10, 1975]. It represented more than twice the GNP of 1974. Of this figure only a minute £1.8 billion was derived from graduated pensions. All the rest were flat-rate pension rights.

The fact that, on an annual basis, pensions paid have tended to increase in real terms means that in the long run the total amount of state pensions was not eroded by inflation. This has been confirmed for the period 1948–72 [11, 1973]. The level of individual pensions, however, is a different matter. In many instances individual pensions have been the victims of short-term deteriorations in real terms between two statutory raises, particularly in recent years. This has led to provisions to increase the frequency of adjustments and to raise the average level of pensions in the new state scheme.

Total Current Welfare Expenditure Financed by the Exchequer

The proportion of the Exchequer annual contributions toward the financing of what we have called the basic welfare system grew considerably in the period under study (see Table 6–7). In 1975 these contributions were approximately £7 billion, which represented 7.5 percent of the GNP. The biggest share of the cost of welfare expenditure was, of course, that of the National Health Service (NHS), which represented about two-thirds of the total in 1975. On the whole contributions and interest covered less than half of the total cost of the welfare system. As a consequence the Exchequer had to finance between 51 and 61 percent of the total current expenditure during the period.

IV. DETERMINANTS OF PERSONAL SAVING

The gradual long-term growth of personal saving, both in absolute and relative terms, up to the late 1960s was—following traditional Keynesian theory—largely attributed to the growth in real income [12, 1966; 13, 1977]. Two additional elements may have helped raise the personal saving rate: (1) the spread of owner-occupation of housing and the associated increase in building society deposits and (2) the promotion of private pension funds, especially after the introduction of state graduated pensions and contracting out in 1961.

During the 1970s a sharp increase in personal saving has been noted in the presence of high rates of inflation and unemployment.

These developments have changed the view that personal saving is determined almost exclusively by real income toward an acceptance of the idea that, under special circumstances, people may react more to certain financial phenomena, such as the erosion by inflation of the real value of their financial assets.

Up to 1973 the personal sector stock of liquid assets as a proportion of personal disposable income (liquid assets ratio), remained fairly stable. In 1974 and 1975, however, in spite of considerable additions to liquid asset holdings, the sector's liquidity ratio fell sharply in the presence of high rates of inflation (19.1 and 24.9 percent respectively). The observation of these phenomena led to the postulation of new alternative hypotheses of the determinants of personal saving.

Saving for Transactions and Precautionary Motives

Current discussions stress the effects of unprecedented inflation rates and the consequent negative rates of interest in eroding the real value of the personal sector's liquid assets. This erosion has also led to a greater than desired reduction in the proportion of liquid assets held in relation to personal income for transaction and precautionary purposes. As a reaction, the personal sector has attempted to rebuild its liquid asset position by increasing the acquisition of financial assets. This action, however, has not prevented the overall decline in the sector's liquidity.

Empirical evidence [14, 1975] shows that the relationships between the saving ratio and the liquid assets ratio (liquid assets net of bank borrowing/disposable income) is a negative one. The lower the stock of liquid assets as a proportion of disposable income, the higher the associated saving ratio.

The liquidity-saving trade-off suggests that, in the presence of moderate inflation and real positive interest rates, the saving ratio will respond mainly to changes in real income. In the presence of negative interest rates and a persistent erosion in the real value of assets, however, the liquid assets ratio plays a dominant role in determining changes in the saving ratio. This hypothesis, however, only attempts to explain marginal changes under special circumstances and is not an attempt to replace the existing theories of the long-run determinants of personal saving.

There are some complementary hypotheses to explain the increase in the saving ratio, which have been tested recently with relative success [15, 1976]:

1. Liquid assets seem to be very important in the planning of consumption expenditures. It is not clear, however, whether this is

because of their absolute size (a wealth effect) or relative size (a portfolio balance effect). A reduction in the real value of these assets leads, therefore, to increased saving.

2. In the short run consumers seem to be more aware of higher prices than of their own higher nominal incomes, when the former rise faster than expected. This leads to a reduction in current expenditures and to an increase in saving.

The influence of uncertainty about future inflation rates on the building up of a larger stock of liquid assets has been more difficult to prove, and attempts to do so have been unsuccessful so far. This is believed to be caused by inadequate and insufficient data, however, and not by an inherent weakness in the hypothesis or by the lack of a relationship between uncertainty and saving.

Finally, studies have also failed to prove that individuals may have increased their current saving in order to restore part of the real value of their wealth lost through inflation. This erosion was estimated to have been approximately £40 billion, or 20 percent of all the personal sector's wealth, in 1974.

Saving for Security

We have seen so far that the rapid increase in saving during the last few years seems to have been caused by a desire to restore the personal sector's liquid assets position. A substantial part of saving, however, is made for longer-term motives, such as security in retirement. State pensions provide this security, but with a limit. It may be useful, therefore, to ask whether this provision is enough to discourage saving through other channels. Perhaps an idea can be acquired as to whether people feel securely covered and satisfied with their state pensions by looking at the proportion of their former incomes which is replaced by retirement pensions. A comparison of the basic state pensions in different EEC countries in relation to their respective average net earnings [16, 1974] showed that in 1971 the U.K. state pension replaced only about 35 percent of preretirement earnings, compared with, for example, 64 percent in the Netherlands and 60 percent in West Germany. Another study [17, 1969] which measured average state pensions as a proportion of average nonagricultural wages produced even lower figures for the United Kingdom: 18 percent in 1960 and 21 percent in 1961, and forecast replacements for 1970, 1975, and 1980 of 23, 25, and 30 percent, respectively. These figures were the lowest for EEC countries and should be compared with 60 to 70 percent earnings replacement in other Western European countries. The same study, however, showed that the two countries with the lowest proportion of state-replaced earnings, Italy and the United Kingdom, had the highest proportion of earnings replaced by complementary private schemes in the EEC. In this case complementary pensions replaced about 30 percent of average wages in the United Kingdom between 1960 and 1970 (and 35 percent in Italy), whereas they replaced only 11 percent and 12 percent in the Netherlands and West Germany, respectively.

In spite of all the shortcomings of the data and the difficulty in making valid comparisons because of the differences in coverage and terms of the different pension schemes, there is an obvious relationship between private and state provision for retirement. This relationship has a counterpart in the saving necessary to acquire the retirement pensions. The evidence from these studies seems to suggest that, in those countries where state provision for retirement is inadequate or unsatisfactory (e.g., the United Kingdom), people will continue to save through private institutions, and that increases in the coverage or the level of state pensions will not significantly reduce private savings for retirement as long as average individual state pensions remain below certain desired levels.

Given the recent introduction in Britain of an earnings-related state pension scheme in 1978, the question arises as to whether the new scheme will have an appreciable effect on private savings. An idea of what may happen in Britain can be gained by looking at the case of Sweden after the introduction of earnings-related and inflation-proof pensions in 1960. (Details are provided in the study of the Swedish experience with pensions and saving elsewhere in this volume.) The introduction of the Supplementary Pensions Scheme in Sweden had an appreciable effect on occupational pensions (which are a monopoly), whose premiums dropped in 1961 to less than 20 percent of the value they had in 1959. Life assurance premiums continued to increase normally. From the 1961 low, however, occupational pension premiums started to increase again, regaining in approximately ten years the presupplementary scheme level.

Revell [18, 1976] has pointed out that the Swedish experience and the evidence as far as the United Kingdom is concerned indicate that a high compulsory and collective provision for pensions does not necessarily lead to a lower individual use of private provision. On the contrary, the evidence indicates that, in spite of increased state provision, private provision has paradoxically also increased in the United Kingdom. This phenomenon was also detected by El-Mokadem [19, 1973], who tested econometrically the impact of the present value of national insurance retirement benefits (national insurance pension "wealth") on the amount of premiums paid by individuals to life assurance in the United Kingdom between 1952–66.

This testing obtained small but *positive* regression coefficients for the national insurance variable, indicating that an increase in the national insurance pension wealth had the effect of increasing premiums paid to life assurance.

Although the inadequacies of the data and of the explanatory variables constructed leave the substitution between private and state provision still an open question, the results of this testing are consistent with the findings of the other studies mentioned above. They also fall in line with the persistent rise in the personal saving rate since the late 1940s. This result is particularly significant in the case of the United Kingdom, where life assurance is an important vehicle for personal saving mainly as a result of tax concessions. In fact, saving by buying life policies has, under present tax circumstances, more to do with providing lump sums at retirement or annuities for the policyholder than with insuring people's lives. As such, life assurance is a good substitute for other forms of saving for retirement.

A popular explanation for the increase in personal saving in the presence of compulsory state provision has been the so-called "recognition" effect, where state provision makes people more aware of the need to save for retirement and, therefore, prevents reductions in personal saving and in many cases induces more private provision. Although Feldstein [20, 1977] implicitly rejects this effect as applicable to the United States, it seems to have operated in the United Kingdom in the past, induced in part by public and private programs to promote saving.

We do not know, of course, whether the actual level of personal saving is higher—or lower—than that which would have been achieved in the absence of state pensions, but it appears to be the case in Britain that the provision of state pensions, ancillary social security benefits, and free health care have not appreciably depressed the long-term trend of growth of personal saving. A more definitive conclusion can only be arrived at, however, by a more rigorous econometric examination of the substitution problem.

V. CONCLUSIONS

Personal saving increased substantially in real terms between 1946 and 1975. Saving as a proportion of disposable income also increased considerably, from a low of 1 percent in 1948 to 14 percent in 1975. The increase was particularly steep in the last four years of the survey.

Personal savings were channeled mainly into nonfinancial assets until 1973. Of the financial assets acquired up to the early 1970s, the main item was life assurance and superannuation funds. Between

1972 and 1975, in the presence of high rates of inflation, the growth of saving was mainly in the form of liquid assets such as building society and bank deposits and currency.

The rapid and considerable erosion, by inflation, of the personal sector's financial savings brought about a significant increase in liquid asset acquisitions during the last four years of the survey. As a consequence of this, new hypotheses about the determinants of personal saving are being explored. These hypotheses tend to explain personal saving mainly in terms of the maintenance of a desired proportion of liquid assets to personal income.

The aggregate amount of state pensions increased substantially in real terms during the years covered by the survey. The level of individual pensions was eroded in real terms, however, particularly during the 1970s. The same phenomenon occurred with regard to occupational pensions.

During the last ten years of the survey several proposals for an indexed earnings-related state pension were made. The political treatment of these proposals created a degree of uncertainty which may have inhibited both membership in and improvements of private pension schemes. During the same period an appreciable decline in the labor force and in private pension membership was observed.

The provision of ancillary social security benefits and free medical care has grown considerably in real terms during the postwar years. Of these benefits, means-tested national assistance continues to be an important element, reflecting the inadequacies of national insurance for a large section of the population.

Analyses of saving for retirement purposes in the EEC show that there is an inverse correlation between the "low" level of income replacement provided by the state pension scheme and the "high" level of replacement provided by private schemes in the United Kingdom. This phenomenon suggests that, as long as people consider state pensions insufficient or below certain desired levels, private saving for retirement will continue to grow.

Econometric tests of the effect of national insurance wealth on premiums paid to life assurance in the United Kingdom show that increases in national insurance wealth led, paradoxically, to more premiums being paid. Other experiences and the rest of the evidence in the United Kingdom suggest that the total of personal saving has not been significantly affected by the provision of state welfare benefits.

GLOSSARY

1. **Total Personal Income:** Includes wages and salaries of civilian labor force and income in cash and kind of armed forces; employers' national insurance contribution and other related contributions; income from self-employed professionals and farmers, private nonprofitmaking bodies and nonincorporated businesses before depreciation, stock appreciation, and additions to tax reserves; rent, dividend, and net interest; national insurance and other social security benefits, and other transfers and grants.

2. **Personal Disposable Income:** Equals Total Personal Income, less: paid United Kingdom taxes on income, national insurance and other social security contributions, and taxes and transfers paid abroad.

3. **Personal Sector Saving:** Is the difference between Personal Disposable Income and Consumers' expenditure. These two items are arrived at separately, and, therefore, the difference between them (saving) is subject to an important degree of error (items 5 and 7 in this glossary). For practical purposes we have broken down saving into two major categories only: Gross Personal Capital Formation and Net Personal Acquisition of Financial Assets.

4. **Gross Personal Capital Formation:** Includes gross domestic fixed capital formation, mainly in the form of dwellings and net purchases of land and existing buildings; increase in the value of inventory stocks and work in progress and net capital transfers (capital transfers paid and received less taxes on capital).

5. **Net Personal Acquisition of Financial Assets:** Is the net balance of all the recorded transactions in financial assets, including net investment abroad. It includes changes in financial saving instruments and household borrowing and also a special adjustment, "unidentified items," which represents errors and omissions in the calculation of saving (see items 3 and 7).

6. **Growth of Life Assurance and Superannuation Funds:** Shows the growth of life assurance and pension schemes managed by life assurance companies and pension schemes managed by private, noninsured pension funds. It includes receipts from employers and employees and rent, dividends, and interest, less: pensions and other benefits paid and administrative costs.

7. **Household Credit:** Includes borrowing for house purchase, for consumption, and for other purposes incurred by the personal sector. Because of inadequate information a substantial part of retailers' credit is excluded, as well as employers' loans and other minor items. These omissions have been advanced as partial explanation for the relatively large "unidentified items" in the financial accounts of the personal sector (see items 3 and 5).

8. **Gross Corporate Profit (Industrial, Commercial, and Financial Corporations):** Includes trading profit and nontrading income before providing for depreciation, stock appreciation, and additions to reserves; income from abroad after depreciation but before providing for stock appreciation. Before 1950 only actual remittances from abroad were included. From 1950 onwards this item includes all income earned by United Kingdom-owned subsidiaries abroad (on a proportional basis where minority interests are held).

9. **Gross Corporate Saving: Undistributed Income:** Is obtained as Gross Corporate Profit, less: payments of dividends and interest; paid United Kingdom

taxes on income; current transfers to charities and taxes and earnings due abroad. From 1950 onwards earnings due abroad includes all income from foreign-owned subsidiaries or a proportion thereof where minority interests are held.

10. **Gross Corporate Capital Formation:** Is Gross Corporate Saving, less: Net Corporate Acquisition of Financial Assets.

11. **National Insurance Fund Contributions and Interest:** Includes contributions from employers and employees from civilian labor force and armed forces, and interest accrued on government securities held by the fund.

12. **National Insurance Fund: Other Benefits and Current Expenditures:** Includes the following benefits paid in the United Kingdom: widows' benefits and guardians' allowances; unemployment benefits; sickness benefits; maternity benefits; death grants; injury benefits; disablement benefits and industrial death benefits. It also includes current expenditures on goods and services incurred by the fund.

13. **National Health Service Current Account Deficit:** Is arrived at by subtracting from contributions made by individuals the NHS current expenditures on goods and services and grants made to persons.

14. **Noncontributory Social Security:** Includes Supplementary Benefit (before 1966 called National Assistance) and war pensions paid in the United Kingdom, family allowances, other samll noncontributory benefits (net of redundancy fund contributions), and current expenditures on goods and services attributable to these benefits.

REFERENCES

1. BEVERIDGE, LORD. *Social Insurance and Allied Services.* London: HMSO, 1942.

2. ATKINSON, A.B. *Poverty in Britain and the Reform of Social Security.* London: Cambridge University Press, 1970.

3. TAYLOR, DAVID. *The Reorganized NHS.* Office of Health Economics. London: HMSO, March 1977.

4. GOVERNMENT ACTUARY. *Occupational Pension Schemes 1956: A Survey by the Government Actuary.* London: HMSO, 1957.

5. ____. *Occupational Pension Schemes 1963: A New Survey by the Government Actuary.* London: HMSO, 1964.

6. ____. *Occupational Pension Schemes 1967: Third Survey by the Government Actuary.* London: HMSO, 1968.

7. ____. *Occupational Pension Schemes 1971: Fourth Survey by the Government Actuary.* London: HMSO, 1972.

8. *Department of Employment Gazette.* London: HMSO, May 1977.

9. NATIONAL ASSOCIATION OF PENSION FUNDS. *The New Pension Scheme* (pamphlet). London: National Association of Pension Funds, 1976, pp. 8–9.

10. ROYAL COMMISSION ON THE DISTRIBUTION OF INCOME AND WEALTH. Report No. 1: *Initial Report on the Standing Reference.* London: HMSO, 1975, table 37, p. 91.

11. WILSON, THOMAS. "Pensions, Inflation and Growth," *Lloyds Bank Review*, April 1973, (108), pp. 1–17.

12. BANK OF ENGLAND. "Personal Saving and Financial Investment 1951–1965," *Bank of England Quarterly Bulletin*, Sept. 1966, *6*(3), pp. 246–56.

13. ____. "The Personal Sector 1966–1975," *Bank of England Quarterly Bulletin*, March 1977, *17*(1), pp. 27–33.

14. MORGAN GRENFELL & CO., LTD. "A New Analysis of the Savings Ratio," *Morgan Grenfell Economic Review*, Sept. 1975, pp. 1–8.

15. TOWNEND, J.C. "The Personal Saving Ratio," *Bank of England Quarterly Bulletin*, March 1976, *16*(1), pp. 53–73.

16. WILSON, THOMAS, ed. *Pensions, Inflation and Growth.* London: Heinemann Educational Books, 1974.

17. DE JASAY, A. "Report on the Contribution of Pension Funds to the Capital Markets of the EEC," *Economic and Financial Affairs*, Series No. 7. Brussels: Commission of European Communities, 1969.

18. REVELL, JACK R.S. *Saving Flows in Europe: Personal Saving and Borrowing.* London: Financial Times Publications, 1976.

19. EL-MOKADEM, A.M. *Econometric Models of Personal Saving, The United Kingdom 1948–1966.* London: Butterworths, 1973, Chapter 5.

20. FELDSTEIN, MARTIN, and PELLECHIO, ANTHONY. *Social Security and Household Wealth Accumulation: New Macroeconomic Evidence.* Harvard Institute of Economic Research, Discussion Paper No. 530, Jan. 1977.

Chapter 7

Data and Studies on Saving in France: A Survey

Bruno A. Oudet[a]

The amount of private saving in France is not known with a great degree of accuracy. The saving data of the national accounts are certainly the least accurate item in the accounts. The second source of information on saving, the household saving surveys, is too recent to permit time series analysis of saving behavior. The first large survey was conducted in 1967, and only three large surveys have been conducted since, in 1969, 1973, and 1975.

The sectoral composition of net private saving in France differs markedly from that in the United States. French households save a larger part of their disposable income than their U.S. counterparts, but they also use a much larger part of their savings for housing investments. Life insurance is much more developed in the United States than in France. Lastly, unfunded social insurance benefits account for a much larger percentage of disposable income in France.

This chapter reviews data and studies on saving in France before attempting some cross-country comparisons. It shows that there is no firm evidence that expansion of social insurance programs has lowered the net private saving rate out of GNP.

[a]Professor, Université Scientifique et Médicale de Grenoble and Laboratoire IMAG. I am grateful to André Babeau, General Secretary of C.R.E.P., Antoine Coutière of Direction de la Prevision, and Philippe L'Hardy for helpful comments on an earlier version of this chapter. George von Furstenberg provided very detailed comments for which I am grateful. Pierre Marie Larnac and Thierry Chauveau helped me with useful suggestions in the early part of the study. I am, of course, responsible for any remaining errors.

In the first section the existing data on private saving (both corporate and personal) are presented. In the second section studies explaining personal saving behavior are reviewed.

I. FRENCH DATA ON PRIVATE SAVING

Two types of data are available on French saving: time series from the national income accounts and results from surveys. Surveys exist only for personal savings. Series on total private saving are not published and must be computed from the national accounts. There are two ways to obtain total private saving. The first is to add the corporate and personal saving components which may lead to compounding of measurement errors in the two components. The second gives more reliable results; it starts from the saving investment identity. Gross private saving is equal to investment plus inventory change plus net foreign investment and minus public saving. Such series were computed jointly by Jean-Jacques Carré, Paul Dubois, and Edmond Malinvaud [6, 1972, p. 365] for the period 1896–1969. The authors observed that the evolution of the gross saving rate (expressed in percent of the gross national product) is surprisingly smooth. It goes from 17 percent at the beginning of the century to 20 percent in 1938. It then rises from 20 percent in the 1950s to 22 percent in the 1960s. However, the authors indicate that if we subtract capital transfers, such as war damage compensation and equipment subsidies obtained by corporations and households, from this saving, a rather constant saving rate is obtained since 1950. This adjusted rate was abnormally low in 1950 and reached its original level of 17 percent in 1960. In this section time series and survey data on personal and corporate saving are analyzed in succession.

Data on Personal Saving

Time Series Data on Personal Saving. Time series data on personal saving can be obtained from either flow data or stock data. The flow data can be obtained from the sources or the uses of saving. Flow data on the source of saving are reported in the French national accounts. In order to be able to appreciate these data both their contents and their derivation are reviewed briefly.

The measure of the personal saving flow is the difference between gross disposable income (revenu disponible brut) and end consumption (consommation finale) in the household accounts (comptes des ménages). To appreciate the content of this saving data one needs to know the definition of the three concepts involved: households, gross disposable income, and end consumption. Households are defined as "institutional units located in France whose main function is consumption, possibly production if this last one is organized within a personal business" ([23, 1976, p. 275], author's translations throughout). In other words, household saving includes saving from unincorporated enterprise. The role of personal business is very important in France: 32 percent of the national value added was produced by this sector in 1975. Personal saving thus includes a large part of personal business saving. In order to obtain a measure of nonbusiness personal saving, investment in personal business, the item that gets closest to the measure of personal business saving, has to be subtracted. The consumption concept in the accounts includes purchases of most durable goods. Only the purchase of new buildings and major home improvements are considered investment in the accounts. Gross disposable income in the income account (compte de revenu) is equal to personal income minus personal taxes. To obtain gross disposable income, social security taxes are subtracted from personal income along with other personal taxes. Household saving can thus be considered a voluntary form of saving, whereas social security taxes are forced saving.

Some information about the source of the data in the accounts previously described can be found in Jean-Etienne Chapron and Michel Séruzier [9, 1976]. Consumption is computed in the accounts essentially on the basis of statistical series on sales obtained from tax authorities. Data on income are obtained from the accounting statements of public administrations and public enterprises and from statistics of tax authorities. While the sum total of employee compensation is probably reported rather accurately, private business income can only be approximated (see [9, 1976, p. 90]).

The measure of personal saving flow can also be obtained by the addition of the various uses of saving. Three broad uses of saving can be distinguished: they each account for about one-third of the total.

1. Household Investment (Formation brute de capital fixe): As indicated above, this item includes only purchases of new homes and home improvements and major repairs. Information on this component comes from survey data and administrative data on building licences.

2. Investment of Personal Businesses (Formation brute de capital fixe des entrepreneurs individuels): This item aggregates very different data (changes in inventory stocks, farm investment, and so on). Available statistical sources permit only a very rough estimate of this investment.

3. Financial Investment: Data on financial investment are obtained from the various financial institutions. The problem is to allocate the total financial investment between households and business firms. While changes in household deposits are known fairly accurately, the estimates of the net bond and stock purchases of households are probably poor.

The inaccuracy of the saving data obtained from either the sources side or the uses side becomes evident when the two measures of saving (gross saving, and gross investment, including net financial investment) are compared. These two series are in theory identically equal. In practice they differ for a number of reasons (see [23, 1976, pp. 171–72]). Thus in 1976 the statistical discrepancy, called Adjustment (Adjustement) was F. −18,876 billion (gross investment exceeded gross saving by 18,876 billion) compared to net financial investment of 85,942 billion (change in assets minus change in liabilities outstanding). In the same year the adjustment is equal to −9.1 percent of reported gross saving.

To conclude this review of the national accounts data on saving, Louis Fortran and Gérard Klein [21, 1970] can be cited. According to these authors, the saving data have two shortcomings. The first is the consequence of errors and lack of statistical precision. Saving is treated as a residual; it is measured after better-known items have been filled in. The second is the result of aggregation and the absence of any reference to household wealth or stock statistics.

Besides flow data, personal saving can be measured from stock data. Saving is then equal to the change in real net wealth. Such a measure of saving will be available in the near future in the new system of national accounts. The new accounting system (see [23, 1976]) received the attribute "enlarged" in part because of the intention to include wealth accounts. The first wealth accounts are due to be published in 1978. One can reasonably expect that the need to reconcile the flow and stock accounts will result in the publication of more accurate data.

Some stock data are already available. They concern mainly financial stock data. Wealth data for the period 1959–67 can be found in Nicole Campion [7, 1971]. More recently data were constructed at the Direction de la Prévision of the Ministry of Finance and at the Caisse de Dépôts. The series of housing wealth comes from Antoine Coutière [15, 1974]. The series was computed from an approximation of an initial stock to which annual investment flows were added. The value of the stock is corrected each period for inflation. The financial data were computed from the raw data of the financial institutions by various authors: Jacques Boullé (liquid assets), Thierry Chauveau (bonds), Michel Séruzier and François Nicolas (household liabilities). These data are reproduced in the report of the financial planning commission [11, 1976, p. 287]. They are considered the most reliable presently available for these items.

Other wealth data have been computed by the Research Center on Saving and Wealth (CREP). For explaining the household saving behavior, CREP computed annual rates of growth of the various wealth items using the model Ephèbe (see Babeau, Masson, and Strauss-Khan [1, 1973] and Fanton, Masson, and Strauss-Khan [19, 1977]). Starting from an initial point (1949) inferred from tax information, the model is designed to generate missing data on wealth on the basis of hypotheses about saving behavior. The realism of this stock flow model can be appreciated by comparing its estimates with figures computed from the 1967 survey data. The results are fairly good since the wealth-age distribution of the 1967 survey is approximated within a 5 percent error range.

Is the quality of the stock data superior to that of the flow data of the national accounts? Although there is no proof, it is generally recognized by the specialists that the stock data are more accurate than the flow data of the financial accounts. The national income accountants massage some raw flow data to make the accounts balance while data on financial stocks are less exposed to manipulation.

Survey Data on Personal Saving. Surveys on household wealth are the second source of data on saving. The change in net worth computed from these surveys cannot be taken as a measure of the flow of saving. Changes in net worth result not only from saving but also from price changes of existing assets and from differences in the household sample from survey to survey. They provide, however, the best source of information on the structural determinants of private saving (see Section II). The first surveys were conducted in 1962–63 by CREP. During the period 1962–68 CREP conducted various surveys for different population groups such as farmers and retailers. Descriptions of these surveys can be found in Fortran and Klein [21, 1970] and Lisle [36, 1967]. These studies were conducted on a fairly small scale.

The first large-scale study was conducted in 1967 by the National Institute of Statistics and Economic Studies (INSEE), starting the era of systematic surveys. Other surveys were taken in 1969 and in 1973 by INSEE and in 1975 by CREP. The 1967 and 1969 surveys used a sample of 3,000 households and 6,200 households, respectively. Only the latter includes households of "independent" workers, that is, the self-employed. Questions in the survey relate to income and wealth items, including both assets and debts. The 1975 CREP survey employed a sample of 3,000 households.

Other surveys are conducted by both INSEE and CREP on more specific components of wealth such as housing, life insurance policy reserves, and deposits in savings institutions. The results of the INSEE survey are published in *Economie et Statistiques* and *Collection de l'I.N.S.E.E.*, Série M. Surveys from the CREP are generally unpublished (for the 1975 results see Babeau and Strauss-Khan [4, 1977]).

What is the quality of the data obtained from these surveys? The best indicators are found in L'Hardy and Hoffman [30, 1970] and L'Hardy and Turc [35, 1976]. The results of the surveys are compared to data obtained from financial institutions. The authors note that the survey data account for only between 20 and 60 percent of the totals depending on the item. The most reliable data are deposits at the savings institutions; the least reliable pertain to stocks and bonds. Comparing their results to the national accounts data, the authors conclude that the results are fairly good for physical wealth, fairly bad for financial wealth. A comparison of results from housing surveys with national accounts data has been carried out by Olivier Marchand [38, 1977].

The gap between the survey data and the other data should, however, be appraised in terms of all possible uses. L'Hardy and Turc [35, 1976] found that the survey reflected accurately the relations and rates of change of the variables. Thus, despite their shortcomings, survey data are probably the best source to study personal saving behavior.

Inflation and Personal Saving. If saving is measured as the change in real net wealth, additional issues arise. To the extent households are net lenders, inflation reduces the real value of their net financial assets; it has the effect of a decrease in income. What is the importance of this income reduction? François Callignon [5, 1975] measured this reduction on the basis of the financial assets and liabilities series. For measuring the capital loss the author used the consumption price index in the case of short financial assets and liabilities, and the investment price index for long-term assets and liabilities. His results show that households lost between 0.5 and 11 percent of their net financial assets annually because of inflation over the period 1956–75, the highest losses occurring in 1958 (9 percent) and 1975 (11 percent). After deducting these losses from both disposable income and saving, Callignon computed a "corrected" saving rate: This corrected personal rate fluctuated generally between 9 and 16 percent of disposable income whereas the usual uncorrected rate was between 13 and 18 percent. For a similar study see Goldet, Nicolas, and Séruzier [22, 1975].

Another study of the loss due to inflation has been carried out by Alain Cotta [13, 1976]. Whereas Callignon measures the losses only for the real values of financial assets and liabilities, Cotta attempts to deal with all nonhuman wealth items (housing, inventories) as well. Cotta distinguishes the effect on two types of households. Those who had been able to accumulate residential capital experienced an annual gain of 3 percent of their total net worth on average over the period 1963–74, while the other category had a capital loss of 11 percent [13, 1976, p. 163]. The results of this study are not to be taken at face value. There are doubts as to the quality of the stock data used by the author; the evolution of the unit value of each wealth item can be debated. Nevertheless, it shows that capital losses are important only for households owning a large fraction of their wealth in liquid assets, thus indirectly confirming Callignon's conclusion. For a study of the same nature see Babeau, Masson, and Strauss-Kahn [2, 1975].

Data on Corporate Saving

Data on corporate saving are available from the national accounts and the various balance sheet data banks. The new enlarged national accounts system contains data on saving in the central accounts (cadre central) and in the new business intermediary accounts (comptes intermédiaires des entreprises). Data on corporate saving in the central system are found in the accounts of three sectors: nonfinancial corporations and quasi-corporations, (sociétés et quasi sociétés non financières), credit institutions (institutions de crédit), insurance corporations (entreprises d'assurances). The attribute "quasi" denotes production entities that have a separate accounting system but are not separate judicial entities (for example, branches of foreign firms; see [23, 1976, pp. 65–66]).

As in the household sector, the saving of corporations can be measured from the sources side. There is reason to believe that the measure of corporate saving is more accurate than that of personal saving since personal business income, which is the largest source of error in the case of households, is absent. A study carried out by Marc Jaudouin confirms this conclusion [24, 1976]. Jaudouin computed an aggregate balance sheet for all nonfinancial corporations. He estimated retained earnings by the sum of past saving. This estimated retained earnings came close to retained earnings computed as the residual required to balance assets and liabilities.

Saving can also be obtained by adding the total uses of savings. One nonfinancial item, however, needs special mention: the change in inventories is known only very roughly. It is the largest source of error in the measurement of corporate saving from the uses side. As in the case of households, an adjustment item is introduced to equate the sources and uses of saving. This adjustment amounted to +12.6 percent of gross corporate saving in 1976.

Data on corporate saving can also be found in the intermediary accounts of the enlarged national accounting system. These accounts are based on the financial reports of corporations to the tax authorities. There are three intermediary accounts: the production account (compte de production), the cost account (compte d'exploitation), and the profit-loss account (compte de résultat). Data on saving are found in this last account. Two items can measure saving: capacity for self-financing (capacité d'autofinancement) and actual self-financing (autofinancement). Actual self-financing is equal to capacity for self-financing minus dividends and distributions to wage earners under profit-sharing plans.

The data of the intermediary accounts are probably the most reliable source of information on corporate saving. These data have, however, two limitations. The first results from the coverage of the data since there are excluded firms which give only partial accounting information at present (firms showing agricultural profits, for example). The second results from the publication delays. The accounts for the year 1973 were published only in June 1977. Because of this delay, INSEE now publishes intermediary accounts computed from a sample of firms. Such accounts were published, for example, in March 1977 for the year 1975. It is to be noted that the after-tax profits and retained earnings or self-financing items are not computed at this level because of lack of data. Here, the item closest to saving is gross current profit before tax (profit brut courant avant impôt).

Besides the national accounts, saving data can be obtained from the balance sheet data banks. Such data banks are kept by Caisse de Dépôts–Sedes, Crédit National, Banque de France, and INSEE–BIC. Information on these data banks is contained in the report of the financing planning commission [11, 1976, p. 180].

Of these data banks only INSEE–BIC provide regular publications. How do these data compare with those of the national accounts? An impression can be gained in another study in the above report [11, 1976, pp. 145–55], where return on investment indexes, computed from the data banks and the national accounts, are compared. Peaks in the two indexes are attained in different years. The divergence is explained mainly by differences in the valuation (historical or replacement cost) of fixed capital and inventories owned and used up.

Inflation and the Level of Corporate Saving. Inflation has a favorable effect not recognized in the official accounting for corporate profits because it reduces the real value of corporate debt. This advantage is important in France because external financing is higher than in the United States. Studies based on the balance sheet data banks [11, 1976, pp. 161–80] have shown a decrease of rates of return on sales during the period 1965–73. On the other hand, debt financing has been rising and now represents 40 percent of the total book liabilities, compared to 30 percent in the 1960s.

Cotta [13, 1976] has attempted to evaluate the effect of inflation on corporate wealth. The approach is the same as in his study of household wealth mentioned above. The author concludes that, for the year 1974, the reduction in real indebtedness was equal to 10 percent of the gross income of corporations. Because of the quality of the data used, this figure is again to be taken as a very rough approximation of the inflation effect.

Goldet, Nicolas, and Séruzier [22, 1975] also provide measures of the effect of inflation. While Cotta evaluates the effect of inflation on all balance sheet items, these authors limit their computation to the effect on corporate debts. They found that, despite the rising debt ratio, the cost of the debt has remained, because of inflation, a constant fraction of actual self-financing.

In this section a survey of the existing data on private savings has been presented. It has been indicated that the computation of saving as a residual between income and consumption results in the inclusion of the errors in these two items. This problem is especially important at the level of the household because of the inaccuracy of the data on personal business income. The measurement of saving by the sum of its uses is more direct. It is probably from this side that progress will come in the future because of the growing interest in measuring household wealth and because of the development of balance sheet data banks.

II. DETERMINANTS OF PERSONAL SAVING

The long-term evolution of saving in France since the Second World War has been analyzed in Carré, Dubois, and Malinvaud [6, 1973, pp. 370–78]. The authors analyze the immediate postwar period (up to 1953) where particular factors were in play. The saving rate is low during this period and rises progressively. The low rate of saving is explained by the reconstitution of the stock of durable goods treated as consumption, the difficulties of obtaining consumer credit, and the development of the social security system which rendered the accumulation of financial reserves less pressing. The authors note the importance of forced saving due to inflation during this period. Such saving accounted for approximately 2.5 percent of household income. To explain the evolution of saving during the period 1953–69, the authors examine the role of changes in the distribution of income, of home financing, and of forced saving. They conclude their analysis by stating that "during the postwar period household saving has not been stimulated mainly by the anticipation of interesting financial investment, but much more by the need for home financing and the need for restoring their cash balances" [6, 1973, p. 379].

In this section reviewing the studies conducted on the survey and time series data on saving, the roles of these various factors are examined more closely. In the first part of this section studies based on survey data are reviewed; they permit one to isolate the characteristics and structural determinants of savings. In the second part results from regressions are presented; they show the determinants of short-run variations of aggregate saving.

Characteristics and Structural Determinants of Private Saving

Studies of the survey data have been conducted by two institutions, INSEE and CREP, which own the data. Results from CREP are mentioned only briefly here since most of their research is unpublished. Because of the small number of observations (four general surveys have been conducted starting in 1967) much of what follows is descriptive.

Descriptions of the saving pattern found in the surveys are reproduced in the various L'Hardy publications and in Babeau and Daloz [3, 1975]. There are three salient characteristics of nonhuman wealth accumulation and thus of saving: the paramount role of real estate, and above all the principal residence, the growing role of liquid assets in recent years, and the high inequality of wealth. Table 7–1 provides the main characteristics of the structure and the evolution of household assets.

In this table one observes the large share of principal residences. The comparisons of the 1967 and 1972 data seem to indicate that a ceiling has been reached. Also, they show an inclination of households toward liquid saving at the expense of saving for housing and the purchase of stocks. The tendency of the share of liquid saving to grow is confirmed by the time series data.

A third structural characteristic is a high degree of inequality in the distribution of wealth. This inequality is expressed in L'Hardy [31, 1973] by indexes of central spread (fractile ratios) and concentration (Gini coefficients) for both total wealth and the principal wealth items. In L'Hardy [31, 1973] and L'Hardy and Turc [35, 1976] inequalities of distribution among various population groups, classified by age and professional categories, are shown. L'Hardy and Turc show that the degree of inequality has not changed between the 1969 and 1973 surveys.

On the basis of his analysis of the 1967 and 1969 surveys, L'Hardy [31, 1973; 32, 1973] proposed a classification of wealth into four groups: (1) young household's saving: associated with the couple setting up house, they correspond with life insurance premium payments and housing, (2) high yield assets: mainly stocks held principally by executives, (3) liquid assets: distributed relatively evenly throughout the population, (4) saving for retirement: bonds, government securities. Several determinants of saving are mentioned. Income is of course the main determinant of saving. But other explanatory variables influence saving behavior of households. They are in order of importance: housing investment and the large contractual

Table 7–1. Distribution of Main Household Assets *(percent)*

	Sample of Total Household Population		*Sample of Wage Earners and Nonactive Households*	
	1967	*1972*	*1967*	*1972*
Principal residence[a]	61	55	55	56
Liquid assets	19	26	23	26
Government securities, bonds, stocks	20	19	22	18
Total	100	100	100	100

Source: L'Hardy and Turc [35, 1976].
[a]Gross value.

saving it entails, life cycle considerations, changes in income and wealth concentration, and social security programs. These explanations are reviewed here.

Contractual Saving Resulting from Housing Investment. As shown in Table 7–1, real estate, mostly principal residences, represents the largest component of nonhuman wealth. Households must make a considerable financial effort to acquire a residence. L'Hardy [28, 1970] stresses that their investment in real property and the indebtedness, which normally accompanies it, are out of all proportion with other investments and debt. The cross tabulations constructed in L'Hardy's article show that the highest rate of home buying occurs around age thirty and to a lesser extent around age sixty (the retirement age). Income plays the largest role in explaining differences in home ownership rates at any age.

Past investment in a home entails large contractual saving for repaying the debts. Statistical series on debt contracted for housing investment can be found in Goldet, Nicolas, and Séruzier [22, 1975]. The authors observe that its share of total debt has tripled from 1964 to 1973.

Evaluation of the Life Cycle Hypothesis. Cross tabulations of the distribution of wealth by age groups are contained in L'Hardy [31, 1973] and Strauss-Khan [40, 1975]. L'Hardy stresses that the observed age influence can be due to a generation effect and an age effect. The generation (or cohort) effect results from differences in the saving habits of the various generations. The age effect can result from a direct age influence (the true age effect) or the influence of other variables related to age. Because of the small number of observations, it is impossible to isolate the true age effect. Aware of this limitation, L'Hardy [31, 1973] and L'Hardy and Turc [35, 1976] try to evaluate the life cycle hypothesis. L'Hardy [31, 1973] compares the actual change in financial assets of the different age groups between 1967 and 1969 to the change that could be expected from the life cycle hypothesis (Figure 7–1). L'Hardy concludes that observed variations of the main financial assets have the overall shape of Figure 7–1. Financial dissaving, however, is not observed. A reduction in assets is observed only for checking accounts. But this decline is compensated for by the increase in other financial assets during retirement. In other words, there is no financial dissaving but merely a change in the composition of assets.

L'Hardy and Turc [35, 1976] also study the wealth of active and nonactive groups separately. The nonactive group is composed of families whose heads declare that they are not in the labor force.

Figure 7–1. Age Distribution of Changes in Assets According to the Life Cycle Hypothesis

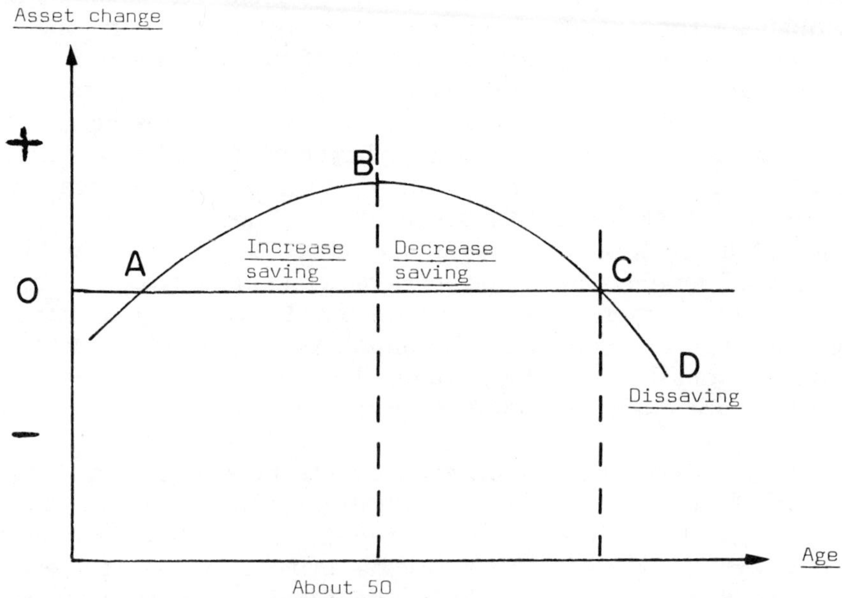

Persons of sixty-five and more years of age constitute 75.2 percent of this group. To isolate differences in saving behavior between active and nonactive persons they further divide the two groups according to the actual or former (in the case of nonactives) profession of the family head. They observe that the two groups differ little in regard to the size of their total wealth but significantly in the structure of that wealth. The proportion of housing wealth for nonactive persons is smaller, but it is compensated by larger holdings of government securities and deposits at saving institutions. The study by Strauss-Khan [40, 1975] points in the same direction. From a factor analysis of the 1967–69 survey data he concluded that differences in age and in income do not explain wealth concentration. The cause of the inequality must be looked for in other factors, among which inter-generational wealth transmission ranks first.

Inequalities as a Determinant of Saving Rates. A study of the change in the saving rate that could result from a reduction in income inequality has been carried out by CREP [11, 1976, pp. 299–306]. The study is based on the simulation of a model fitted on the 1967 and 1972 survey data. Housing investment, loans for housing, and income are exogenous in the model. Debt repayment and personal housing investment are endogenous. The model is used to measure the effect of various hypothetical reductions in income inequality. The authors found that the cost of reducing income inequality within five years to the level of the Netherlands or Denmark is only 1.5 percent of the annual saving rate after the transition has been completed. Other results of the simulation are worth mentioning. The fall in the saving rate is larger for financial saving. The structure of financial saving is modified; it is characterized by a lower fraction of stocks, a growth of the share of bonds, and a constant share of liquid assets. The results of these simulations should be interpreted in their proper perspective. The model describes only a partial process: there is no feedback from the reduction of saving to variables such as income and economic growth. It can be concluded, however, from this study that a reduction of income inequality is not likely to have a pronounced effect on the saving rate.

Effect of the Social Security System on the Saving Rate. Social security refers to the set of administrations whose main objective is the payment of social security benefits. Beside the three funds (caisses) of the general system (régime general) of the wage earner (family, illness, aged), it includes the following institutions: agriculture system (régime salarié, exploitants agricoles), nonwage worker systems (régimes autonomes), special systems (régimes speciaux), complementary systems of retirement (régimes complémentaires), mutual associations (sociétés mutualistes), and diverse funds.

A more detailed list can be found in Martel, Launay, and Perdriau [37, 1972]. For a detailed study of the very complex retirement systems see Chadelat and Hossard [8, 1976]. The reciprocal way by which short-term economic policy and the social security system react upon each other has been studied by Jeanjean [25, 1977, pp. 206–30].

The social security system was created in 1945. Its benefits were at first restricted to wage earners but now extend to the entire population. Five categories of benefits are distinguished: benefits for the aged (retraites), family benefits (prestations familiales), illness benefits (assurance maladie, maternité, décès), unemployment benefits (assurance chômage), and miscellaneous.

The respective shares of these different benefits are given in Table 7–2. The sources of financing of the social security system are shown in Table 7–3.

According to Table 7–3, 11.4 percent of the total receipts of the social security system in 1976 were paid from the general budget and

Table 7–2. The Share of Social Security Benefits in Disposable Income, 1970–76 *(percent)*

	1970	*1971*	*1972*	*1973*	*1974*	*1975*	*1976*
Illness[a]	6.5	6.8	6.8	6.9	7.1	7.6	8.2
Family benefits[a]	4.1	3.8	4.2	4.3	4.1	4.2	3.6
Benefits for the aged[b]	9.4	9.5	9.5	9.7	8.9	9.7	11.5
Unemployment[b]	0.2	0.2	0.3	0.3	0.4	0.8	1.0
Other[c]	4.5	4.3	4.1	4.1	5.4	5.9	4.9
Total	24.7	24.6	24.9	25.3	25.9	28.9	29.2

Source: Direction de la Prévision, Division des Etudes Sociales.
[a]Nontaxable.
[b]Taxable.
[c]Generally nontaxable.

Table 7–3. Evolution of the Financing Structure of the Social Security System, 1962–76 *(percent)*

	1962	*1965*	*1970*	*1975*	*1976*
Social security tax	88.2	88.7	88.4	84.6	86.6
Subventions	6.2	6.0	7.2	9.2	6.8
Tax financing[a]	4.0	3.7	3.4	4.2	4.6
Other	1.6	1.7	2.0	2.0	2.0

Source: Direction de la Prévision, Division des Etudes Sociales.
[a]Specific earmarked taxes other than social security.

special taxes to balance the account. This represents thee pay-as-you-go deficit of the unfunded system. This deficit is likely to grow in the future. Unpublished results from the simulation of the social security model indicate that France will go from the actual artificial surplus (because of tax financing, total resource inflows exceeded the benefits paid by F. 6.6 billion in 1976) to a large deficit by 1982.

Since unfunded social security benefits account for a much larger percentage of disposable income in France than in the United States, one could argue that the question raised by Martin Feldstein about the substitution of social security wealth for private wealth is even more pressing in France. However, this question has received little or no attention at all among French researchers. Comunetti et al. [12, 1976] have evaluated the net wealth equivalent of retirement benefits following Feldstein's procedure [20, 1974]. They evaluate this capital as around F. 3,070 billion for 1974. This figure can be compared with F. 3,950 billion of total household net worth estimated by CREP and with a 1974 GNP of F. 1,272 billion.

No other study similar to that of Feldstein has been conducted in France. However, arguments which appear to be adverse to Feldstein's hypothesis can be found in various studies. Turc [41, 1973] conducted a survey to study life insurance coverage. He observed that only 36.5 percent of the households in his sample had subscribed to insurance at least once in their life (as opposed to 80 percent in the United States). Turc computed a theoretical life insurance participation rate using only the income and the age of household heads as explanatory variables. He found that the observed participation rate is higher than the theoretical rate for households covered by an additional retirement fund and households affiliated with a mutual pension plan in addition to social security. He concluded that additional protection seems to favor life insurance subscription. In other words, people are more aware of the risks and they search for more protection when they are protected. This type of argument is confirmed by a CREP survey on the motivation of saving. Despite a well-developed social security system, 50 percent of the households surveyed gave protection of their living standards in case of emergency and in old age as their principal motive for saving.

Another argument can be found in the preeminence of saving for housing investment. This important type of saving is accumulated despite the existence of the social security system. Lastly one should mention the intergenerational wealth transmission that plays an important role in France. According to a CREP survey, 40 percent of the population receive inheritances at one time or another in their lives. CREP estimated that roughly 40 percent of net worth is the result of inheritance. The importance of inheritance is indirectly confirmed by Strauss-Khan [40, 1975] and the study by L'Hardy and Turc [35, 1976]. These last two authors found that, when grouped by their former and actual profession, wealth of the active and nonactive groups differs in structure but not in total. They concluded that the 1967 and 1973 surveys accord with the hypothesis that the origin of the wealth inequality is linked to intergenerational transmission (education and wealth transmission).

In another study L'Hardy et al. [29, 1971] show the significant effect of risk on saving behavior despite the protection afforded by the social security system. From the 1967–69 survey data the authors compute an index of income dispersion. This index was taken as a proxy of household uncertainty about future income. They run regressions on household saving with income and the risk index as explanatory variables. Both coefficients were found to be statistically significant with the expected sign.

Explanation of Short-Run Fluctuations of Saving from Time Series Data

Time series analysis can show the effect of variables such as inflation, rates of interest, and government taxes and subsidies on the supply of saving. Two directions of research can be distinguished. The first explains total saving and does not distinguish among its various uses. The second studies the different components of saving. This last direction appears more promising to study saving motivation, through it has been undertaken only recently.

To explain variations in the aggregate personal saving rate, income, interest rates, inflation, liquid assets, and government measures to stimulate saving have been used. The last variable is not included in the regressions since it has been quantified only for the years 1960, 1970, and 1975 (for 1975, see [11, 1976, pp. 360–61]). Rates of return variables are also not included in most studies since they are supposed to affect certain financial investments but not the total.

The various regressions can be distinguished according to their hypotheses about household behavior during inflation.

L'Hardy [33, 1975] and Coutière and Teyssier [16, 1977] estimate simple Keynesian saving functions. Coutière and Teyssier explain real consumption as a linear function of real disposable income. L'Hardy writes the nominal saving rate as a linear function of the rate of growth of real disposable income. In these regressions inflation has no direct effect on the saving rate.

Vallet [42, 1975] and Nasse [39, 1977] hypothesize that inflation has a direct effect on saving. In Valley, the logarithm of per capita saving is a decreasing function of the logarithm of the price level. In Nasse, inflation has two opposing effects. On the one hand, acceleration of inflation stimulates consumption. On the other hand, inflation tends to stimulate saving because households seek to rebuild their real cash balances.

Studies have also begun to appear which analyze particular components of saving. The demand for liquid assets has been studied by David [18, 1970] and Coutière [14, 1975], the demand for bonds by Chauveau [10, 1975].

A first attempt to provide a detailed explanation of saving with a simultaneous equation model has recently been made by Lapierre-Donzel [26, 1977]. Five behavioral equations are estimated; they explain consumption, housing investment, demands for investment assets, liquid assets other than money, and the demand for money. Simulations of these models provide interesting information on saving behavior. For example, a higher exogenous rate of inflation does not affect the saving rate. On the other hand, the authors notice a substitution in favor of money from the investment assets.

Upon review of the various regressions it appears that one still has to be very cautious in explaining fluctuations of the saving rate, especially with respect to inflation. Our lack of knowledge is well illustrated by the work of Coutière and Teyssier [16, 1977]. The authors estimate five different models of household behavior during inflation. The models range from a "naive" Keynesian model to a pure monetarist model. In the former, real income determines consumption while saving is a residual. In the latter, a change in real income leads to an equiproportional change in real cash balances, and real consumption is computed as a residual. Coutière and Teyssier concluded that one is unable to select the best model empirically since the five models fit the data equally well.

III. CONCLUSION

In this study, various bodies of data have been described and analyzed in hopes of identifying a negative effect of unfunded social insurance wealth on private saving. Some arguments but no solid evidence have been advanced against this hypothesis. Despite the large social security program in France, the protection motive is the most frequently mentioned reason for saving. Furthermore, the saving ratio has been high in the recent past because housing investment and intergenerational wealth transmission continue to be important motives for saving.

As yet, the poor quality of the available data precludes any thorough analysis of the determinants of saving. Business saving may be measured fairly accurately, but this is not the case for personal saving. Only some components of household assets are reported with an acceptable degree of accuracy over successive periods. The quality of the data, however, is likely to improve in the future with the publication of wealth accounts in the national accounts system. One can thus expect that a better understanding of the determinants of saving will be reached in coming years.

REFERENCES

1. BABEAU, A.; MASSON, A.; and STRAUSS-KHAN, D. "Les Patrimoines des Ménages Salariés et Inactifs de 1949 à 1967," *Revue Economique*, July 1974, *25*(3), pp. 611–34.

2. ____. *Inflation et Partage des Surplus: le Cas des Ménages.* Paris: Cujas, 1975.

3. BABEAU, A., and DALOZ, J.P. *Le Livre Blanc de l'Epargne.* Paris: Confédération Générale de l'Epargne, 1975.

4. BABEAU, A., and STRAUSS-KHAN, D. *La Richesse des Francais: Epargne, Plus-values, Héritage.* Paris: PUF, 1977.

5. CALLIGNON, F. "Epargne et Consommation des Ménages. Une Esquisse de Comportement du Patrimoine," Direction de la Prévision Research Report, No. DOF 325–079, Oct. 1975.

6. CARRÉ, J.J.; DUBOIS, P.; and MALINVAUD, E. *La Croissance Francaise.* Paris: Seuil, 1972.

7. CAMPION, N. "Nouvelle Evaluation de la Fortune des Ménages (1959–67)," *Consommation*, Jan. 1971, *17*(1), pp. 35–72.

8. CHADELAT, J-F., and HOSSARD, D. "Le Système des Retraites en France," *Notes et Etudes Documentaires*, Feb. 1976, (4260–61), pp. 7–78.

9. CHAPRON, J.E., and SÉRUZIER, M. *Initiation Pratique à la Comptabilité National selon le Nouveau Système.* Paris: Masson, 1976.

10. CHAUVEAU, T. "La Demande d'Obligations Emanant des Ménages 1953–1972," *Revue Economique*, Sept. 1975, *26*(5), pp. 806–33.

11. COMMISSARIAT GENERAL DU PLAN. *Rapport du Comité Financement, Annexes.* Paris: Documentation Francaise, 1976.

12. COMUNETTI, G., et al. "Inegalités et Patrimoine." Rapport des Elèves de l'Ecole Nationale d'Administration, Dec. 1976.

13. COTTA, A. *Taux d'Intérêt, Plus Values et Epargne en France.* Paris: PUF, 1976.

14. COUTIÈRE, A. "Un Modèle du Système Monétaire Francaise," *Statistiques et Etudes Financières*, Série Orange, Jan. 1975, (17), pp. 33–80.

15. ____. "Une Mesure Possible du Patrimoine Immobilier des Mènages." Direction de la Prévision Research Report, No. GRM 424, Dec. 1974.

16. ____, and TEYSSIER, R. "Un Comportement des Ménages Intégrant leurs Opérations Financières," *Statistiques et Etudes Financières*, Série Orange, (29), pp. 27–54.

17. CREP *Rapport D'activité 1975 et Programme 1976.* CREP, Paris: 1976.

18. DAVID, J.H. "Moyens de Réglement et Epargne Liquide des Ménages," *Annales de L'I.N.S.E.E.*, Jan. 1970, (3), pp. 49–80.

19. FANTON, M.; MASSON, A.; and STRAUSS-KHAN, D. *Patrimoine et Inégalité 1949–75.* CORDES Report, June 1977.

20. FELDSTEIN, M. "Social Security, Induced Retirements and Aggregate Capital Accumulation," *Journal of Political Economy*, Sept./Oct. 1974, *82*(5), pp. 905–26.

21. FORTRAN, L., and KLEIN, G. *L'Epargne des Ménages.* Paris: PUF, 1970.

22. GOLDET, H.; NICOLAS, F.; and SÉRUZIER, M. "L'endettement des Entreprises et des Ménages de 1954 à 1974," *Economie et Statistiques*, Dec. 1975, (73), pp. 21–38.

23. INSEE. "Système élargi de Comptabilité Nationale," *Collections de l'I.N.S.E.E.*, Série C, May 1976, (44–45), pp. 1–368.

24. JAUDOUIN, M. "Les Séries Patrimoniales des Entreprises." Direction de la Prévision Research Report, No. DRM 501, June 1976.

25. JEANJEAN, P. "A Social Security System and Short-Term Economic Policy," in *The Economics of Public Services.* Edited by M. FELDSTEIN and R.P. INMAN. London: Macmillan Press, 1977.

26. LAPIERRE-DONZEL, C. "Un Modèle de Comportement des Ménages," *Statistiques et Etudes Financières*, Série Orange, 1977, (30), pp. 3–21.

27. LE MOIGNE, J., and STRAUSS-KHAN, D. "Epargne et Inégalité des Revenus," *Revue Economique*, Jan. 1977, *28*(1), pp. 71–108.

28. L'HARDY, PH. "Epargne et Patrimoine Immobilier des Ménages," *Economie et Statistiques*, June 1970, (13), pp. 3–12.

29. ____ ; HERICOURT, F.; MARCHAND, O.; and TURC, A. "Théorie de l'Aversion pour le Risque," *Annales de l'I.N.S.E.E.*, Sept. 1971, (8), pp. 25–82.

30. ____ , and HOFFMAN, G. "Epargne des Ménages et Gestion du Patrimoine," *Collections de l'I.N.S.E.E.*, Série M, Nov. 1970, (6), pp. 3–104.

31. L'HARDY PH. "Les Disparités du Patrimoine," *Economie et Statistiques*, Feb. 1973, (42), pp. 3–24.

32. ____ . "La Dispersion du Patrimoine des Salariés et Inactifs," *Economie et Statistiques*, March 1973, (43), pp. 29–46.

33. ____ . "L'Epargne dans l'Inflation," *Economie et Statistiques*, March 1975, (66), pp. 39–43.

34. ____ , and TURC A. "Enquête Epargne 1973: Premiers Résultats." Documents I.N.S.E.E., 1976.

35. ____ . "Patrimoine des Ménages: Permanences et Transformations," *Economie et Statistiques*, March 1976, (76), pp. 3–25.

36. LISLE, E.D. *L'Epargne et l'Epargnant.* Paris: Dunod, 1967.

37. MARTEL, P.; LAUNAY, G.P.; and PERDRIAU, H. "Le Modèle de Projection des Opérations de la Sécurité Sociale," *Statistiques et Etudes Financières*, Série Orange, 1972, (6), pp. 3–23.

38. MARCHAND, O. "Le Patrimoine en Logement des Français," *Economie et Statistiques*, June 1977, (90), pp. 69–72.

39. NASSE, PH. "La Consommation des Ménages dans Metric." I.N.S.E.E. Note, Division Comptes Trimestriels, March 1977.

40. STRAUSS-KHAN, D. "Structure et Inegalités des Patrimoines," *Consommation*, Jan. 1975, *21* (1), pp. 5–32.

41. TURC, A. "La Clientèle de l'Assurance Vie en 1970," *Economie et Statistiques*, Oct. 1973, (49), pp. 46–51.

42. VALLET, D. "Epargne à Moyen Terme. Une Approche Econométrique," *Economie et Statistiques*, March 1975, (66), pp. 44–47.

Chapter 8

Old-Age Security and Saving in the Federal Republic of Germany

Martin Pfaff, Peter Hurler, and Rudolf Dennerlein[a]

In marked contrast to the United States of America (USA) only scant attention has been accorded in the Federal Republic of Germany (FRG) to the presumed connection between social security and personal saving. This holds for the scientific discourse in German-language journals and also for the public dialogue relating to the problems and prospects of the social security system as a whole.

This situation can be explained as follows:

1. In the Federal Republic personal saving has been increasing steadily and strikingly ever since the 1950s.
2. Furthermore, since the beginning of the recession of 1974, economic stabilization policy was particularly concerned about the excessive level and rate of personal saving.
3. There exists a further and rather significant difference when compared with the USA: In the organization of the German old-age security system private pension funds (including corporate pension plans) play a relatively minor role as compared with the social insurance system laid down by law on a compulsory basis for all employees. Thus corporate pension plans may be viewed more as a part of the pattern of rewards granted by private enterprise and less as an instrument of social policy. Thus they represent additional and voluntary transfers. And—most importantly—

[a]The authors are Director, Research Assistant, and Research Associate, respectively, in the order shown, at the International Institute for Empirical Social Economics (INIFES), Augsburg-Leitershofen. The first author is also Professor of Economics at the University of Augsburg.

these funds play hardly any role in the internal mobilization of financial resources by corporations.

Entirely different cause-effect relationships and transmission mechanisms appear to pertain to the formation of personal saving versus the formation of real capital in the overall economy. Not surprisingly, therefore, we do not find as yet a similar concern in the FRG as in the USA about the impact of public pension plans on the development of private pension plans which would lead to a retardation in the rate of real capital formation.

Among the few studies undertaken to explore the relationship between social security and personal saving most are concerned with an empirical test of the behavioral hypotheses advanced by George Katona [15, 1965] and Phillip Cagan [5, 1965]. Thus they focus less on the purely economic aspects of saving than on the psychological and social-psychological determinants of saving behavior. There have been a few attempts at an estimation of the effects of social security on private saving. But all of these have led to rather unsatisfactory results, partly due also to the unsatisfactory nature of the data base.

Not surprisingly, therefore, our own macroeconomic investigation of this phenomenon leads to the following conclusion: In the FRG an expansion of old-age insurance (which is reflected in an increased social security tax burden to be borne by private households) has not affected adversely the level and rate of personal saving. In any case, there is no evidence which would lend strong empirical support to the Friedman-Feldstein hypothesis [12, Friedman, 1957; 9, Feldstein, 1974; 10, 1976] about the negative effect of social security on personal saving.

I. INTRODUCTION

Economists, particularly in the United States, have been concerned in the last few years with the antecedents and determinants of the rate of saving and real capital formation. This concern was motivated in part by the fear that real capital formation was less than what would be required for purposes of economic growth (see [11, von Furstenberg and Malkiel, 1977]).

If this phenomenon were to be found also in other countries it would surely merit increased attention. Its effects would or could endanger the goals of economic growth and of long-run economic stabilization. Furthermore, political and social strife could result from such developments. To these we may add fears of a secularly stagnating or even declining economy.

Among the major explanatory variables which are held to account for the reduced rate of real capital formation we find the expansion of the social security system, which would eliminate or reduce the necessity for individual provision against calamities relating to old age, ill-health, unemployment, and so on. This would lead to reduced personal saving insofar as it is determined by the precautionary and security motive (see [2, Bohn, 1969]).

In this vein, Milton Friedman assumes that "the availability of assistance from the state would clearly tend to reduce the need for private reserves and so to reduce saving" [12, 1957, p. 123]. Friedman's hypothesis has been accorded widespread attention and it has spurred further empirical research in this field [21, Munnell, 1975; 15, Katona, 1965; 9, Feldstein, 1974].

Within the German-language area, however, economists have paid little attention to this hypothesis, and generally the problem has not been discussed in economic literature. This is partly due to the unsatisfactory state of the data which would be required for a more thorough empirical investigation. The few German papers pertaining to this problem are generally based on the extensive theoretical work done in the United States (see [23, Schmähl, 1973, p. 82]).

This chapter is addressed to the investigation of the impact of old-age security on personal saving in the post–World War II period within the FRG. The following specific questions are posed in this context:

1. Does social security discourage personal saving in the FRG? Or does empirical evidence indicate that the reverse may hold?
2. Which prior investigations have been addressed to the question posed under (1)? Which methods were employed and what were the results?
3. Turning to our own empirical work: Which patterns can be noted in the time series pertaining to macroeconomic capital formation, especially to the development of personal saving? What are the patterns noticeable in the development of expenditures for old-age security [1] and for promoting personal saving?
4. Which role does corporate and government saving play in the FRG when compared with personal saving?
5. What do our own estimates indicate as regards the relationship between personal saving and
   - gross or net pension income?
   - changes in the tax provisions of the public old-age pension system, especially in the upper income limit beyond which

the compulsory social security payment does not increase in absolute terms, as well as in the social security (tax) rate?

- the structure of the population (especially an increase in the share of pensioners)?

II. SOME EARLIER WORK ON OLD-AGE SECURITY AND PERSONAL SAVING IN THE FRG

Interdependencies exist between the system of old-age security and personal saving both at the micro- and macro-level. Any attempt at an explanation of these interdependencies must make reference to both levels of aggregation. On the other hand, the quality of these interdependencies differs between these two levels.

At the *micro-level* we may start with two different models: (1) The behavioral approaches of Katona [15, 1965] and Cagan [5, 1965] are based on the assumption of rising aspiration levels and the "goal-gradient hypothesis" and lead them to the conclusion that "collective retirement plans promote individual saving." (2) Alternatively, and in juxtaposition to these conclusions, we may refer to the partly modified life cycle models (see [9, Feldstein, 1974; 21, Munnell, 1975]). In these models, micro-units behave according to a criterion of rationality which is based on the precautionary and security motive; these, then, serve as central determinants of saving. If social security shields individuals against certain risks (in this case the risk of old age) then the precautionary and security motive for saving will cease to exist. Thus a decrease in saving of private households must necessarily follow. On the other hand, the relevance of these models is limited since expectations, learning processes, and changes in preferences are not being considered.

When we turn to the *macro-level*, the adaptive responses of micro-units and their effects on the circular flow of economic life are being included in the model. Thus macroeconomic interdependencies result and are passed on above all through the circular flow of economic life. Among these we find the effects of saving on investment and of investment on the extent of social security contributions which result from the income effects yielded by investment.

In the German-language area, Konrad Littmann [19, 1957] has been concerned with these interdependencies, and also with the effects of increasing transfer payments by the government and by parafiscal institutions on long-run macroeconomic development. This approach goes beyond the short-run perspective implicit in Keynesian models: Social transfers have not only an anticyclical function which is reflected in their role as automatic stabilizers; rather, the expansion of transfer payments occurring in the area of social security represents also a long-run phenomenon [19, 1957, p. 133]. The rate of saving is viewed as a determinant of growth. Thus a relatively high rate of saving would be a prerequisite for a significant future increase in real income. But, under certain circumstances, "the overall level of growth can be restrained by the dominant tendency that increasing social transfers will influence the private saving rate negatively and thus will tend to hinder the forces of development" [19, 1957, p. 138] (authors' translation throughout).

The most important results of micro-level analyses of old-age security and saving have been derived from opinion surveys [14, 1968; 3, 1972; 17, 1970]. These results generally tend to support the hypotheses of Katona and Cagan.

1. When interviewed by the *Institut für Demoskopie Allensbach* [14, 1968, p. 21], 65 percent of the insured, and 75 percent of the recipients of old-age pension incomes, declared that their claims toward old-age social security payments are more important to them than private saving and private reserves. However, one cannot conclude from these statements that private saving has in fact become less important since subsidiary saving is of particular import for those who have acquired adequate claims against the public old-age security system. Thus the authors of the study arrive at the conclusion that "a good old-age security system [encourages] the ability to save" [14, 1968, p. 21].

   If the demographic changes currently observable continue into the future, ever more individuals will reach a pension age while being physically fit. Thus, as an addition to old-age security, private saving will be more significant the more individuals view the time after retirement as an active phase in their life cycle which they can shape according to their own desires.

   Among various explanatory hypotheses we find the notion that with an adequate old-age security system (which is linked dynamically to an expanding economy) more subtle and differentiated motives for saving will tend to replace the relatively more primitive motives which were and are based on the elementary need for security. Thus the public old-age security system has brought about in the FRG a change in motivations which on the whole has tended to affect saving behavior rather favorably: "With hope one tends to save more than with fear" [14, 1968, p. 23].

2. Another opinion survey by Brandt and others arrives at a similar conclusion for the year 1970: The precautionary motive for saving is still the most important among all motives for saving. But "the further expansion of social security systems obviously does not reduce the impulse toward saving; rather it makes it possible for workers to realize new saving goals" [3, 1972, p. 146].

3. In order to assess the effects of an expanded old-age security system on personal saving, evidently we must focus not only on quantitative indexes of its economic performance but also on the subjective evaluations of the quality of social security. Franz-Xaver Kaufmann [17, 1970, p. 341 ff.], for example, found that most individuals who have acquired claims against the old-age security system do not have excessive hopes as regards the old-age income to be derived therefrom. On the contrary, they would judge the development of these incomes in a rather pessimistic fashion. The discussion about old-age pensions currently taking place in the Federal Republic would lend support to these conclusions. Thus it is possible that, quite independently of the objective factors relating to old-age security, purely subjective evaluations of the quality of social security would tend to influence the motivation toward additional and voluntary provision for old age in the form of saving.

   These results would lend support to the behavioral theory focusing on changes and aspiration levels—in any case, as far as the Federal Republic is concerned. The German old-age security system obviously leaves ample scope for the development of motives toward saving other than the precautionary and security motives. However, the expansion of old-age security systems does not necessarily have to be accompanied by a substitution of motives. Many individuals hold the view that old-age security is not adequate, so that the precautionary motive is not influenced in a negative fashion. A case in point: By no stretch of the imagination can the German system of providing old-age security for women be viewed as being adequate. In 1969, 25 percent of all single women under the age of sixty and about 60 percent of all single women above the age of sixty who received old-age pensions, survivors pensions, or accident pensions would have to be counted among the poor.

4. Another study by Schmähl [23, 1973] attempts to bridge the void of empirical evidence pertaining to the problem under investigation by posing the following questions:

- Is the level of social security contributions negatively correlated with the rate of saving of employees' households? (Similarly, is saving correlated with the monetary transfers made by institutions responsible for social security, especially for old-age security?)
- Has there been a structural change in the maturity distribution of the assets acquired from saving in the post–World War II period?

With regard to the first question Schmähl states "that at least a reduction of saving of employee households through the payment of social security contributions cannot be proven" [23, 1973, p. 103]. However, an ultimate conclusion about these interdependencies cannot be arrived at on the basis of the methods used and on the basis of the definitions and the sources employed [23, 1973, p. 92]. In attempting to answer the second question he reviews a hypothesis advanced earlier by Schmölders: "The whole development of the welfare state, in which the public old-age and sickness-insurance largely replaces private provision and private saving, will tend to make the dispositions over own monetary income more and more short-run in nature" [24, Schmölders, 1966, p. 92].

According to Schmähl, however, individuals used their savings to acquire fixed-interest assets "as an expression of long-run dispositions" [23, 1973, p. 112]. In his view, the Schmölders hypothesis cannot be falsified as long as the influence exerted by the social security system on private saving cannot be isolated as a determining factor [23, 1973, p. 114]. On the other hand he argues that, on the basis of the maturity of the assets, one cannot conclude anything about the presence or absence of saving motives; other determinants influence the way in which individuals use their savings, such as yield and liquidity as a function of interest rates, the deterioration in the value of money, expectations, and so on. Finally, Schmähl concludes that his results would contradict the conclusions of traditional saving theory and that they would provide empirical support to the behavioral theory of saving sketched out above [23, 1973, p. 117 ff.].

Given the inconclusive nature of the micro-level evidence marshaled thus far, we shall turn to our own macro-level investigation of the phenomenon under study.

First, the development of saving and old-age security is reported to gain insights into the processes likely at work. Thereafter, some macro-level hypotheses are tested more rigorously with the help of single-equation methods.

III. DEVELOPMENT OF PERSONAL SAVING AND OF AGGREGATE SAVING

Our major interest centers on personal saving, that is, on saving by private households (S_{prHh})[2]: Given a household's *ability to save*, we postulate that the burdens imposed on households through social security (tax) contributions, together with the subjective evaluation of the probability of receiving transfer incomes in the future, are major determinants of the household's microeconomic expenditure decisions, particularly of its *willingness to save*. This leads to a concern with the rate of personal saving taking place in households in relation to disposable income.

These magnitudes are reflected in Table 8–1. They indicate that personal saving has continuously increased since 1950 (with a few exceptions resulting from cyclical determinants), with a peak in 1975 when saving represented 15.4 percent of disposable income of German households.

Table 8–1. Personal Saving as a Percent of Disposable Income, 1950–77[a]

Year	$(S_{prHh}/Y^D_{Hh})^d$
1950–1954[b]	4.9
1955–1959[b]	7.8
1960–1964	9.4
1965–1969	12.2
1970–1974	14.2
1975	15.4
1976[c]	13.4
1977[c]	12.5
1950–1977	10.1

Legend: S_{prHh} = saving by private households (= personal saving).

Y^D_{Hh} = disposable income of households.

Source: National Accounts of the FRG.

[a]Including private nonprofit organizations.

[b]Without the Saarland and West Berlin.

[c]Preliminary results.

[d]Without retained corporate earnings (incorporated firms).

This high propensity to save can be explained by security and precautionary motives which seemingly are particularly strong in recessionary periods—exactly at a point in time when individual motives conflict with the aims of overall economic stabilization policy. Thus far all appeals by the government to the population to save less and to consume more during recessions, in order to make their contribution to economic revival, have not had any success.

The rapid increase in personal saving is of little surprise when additional determinants of personal saving are taken into account, since, obviously, economic variables (such as income) explain only a fraction of the variance in saving behavior. Some cultural and institutional determinants have to be taken into account as well [26, Strümpel, 1971]. Thus, in a comparative study pertaining to saving behavior of private households in five Western countries, Strümpel arrives at the following conclusion: "Both total saving and net financial saving have been consistently much higher in Germany than in the United States. This is so in spite of considerably more 'forced saving' through the German Social Security system resulting in considerably more continuity extending beyond the working years" [26, 1971, p. 212].

Strümpel explains the high German saving rate (when compared to that of the USA), by "a greater felt need for financial reserves providing protection for contingencies and rainy days, brought about by characteristically pessimistic expectations for the future"; "a perceptible trend toward satiation with consumer goods making it easier for a saving motive of given strength to be translated into behavior"; "a policy of subsidizing mass saving, thus strengthening the instrumentality of saving for medium and long-term accumulation"; "the ingrained practice of saving in advance of purchasing real estate and consumer durables rather than incurring installment debt, thus making saving highly instrumental for acquiring consumer investment goods" [26, 1971, p. 212].

In our view, the third set of explanations warrants particular attention: The extensive system for promoting personal saving and corporate saving was developed in the wake of the currency reform of 1948. Explicit or implicit transfers, taking the form of subsidies or tax deductions, are made for time deposits, acquisition of certain stocks and bonds, life insurance premiums, and contractual saving channeled through building and loan associations.

The absolute and relative significance of public expenditures for promoting personal saving becomes evident from Table 8–2, which indicates the development of public expenditure for promoting private savings in the Federal Republic for the period 1965–78.

The effects of the system of promoting saving are also reflected in the development of private insurance saving, particularly in the expansion of German life insurance institutions in the period 1950–78 (as shown in Table 8–3).

Finally, the government provided strong incentives for employees to devote part of their wages and salaries to asset formation. The effective interest rate of such premiums (often as high as 10 to 15 percent!) often exceeded market rates of interest.

Thus contractual saving led to a stabilization of saving behavior. Similar to the effect of habitualization, contractualization tends to exert long-term effects [13, 1972, p. 284 ff.].

Personal saving thus has increased in absolute and relative terms, where the latter is of greater import than the former for the connection between saving and social security. At first sight, this development, again, lends little general support to the hypothesis that "social security discourages saving" [21, 1975, p. 28]. This would help explain why this topic has received little attention from German economists.

Perhaps a widening of the vista appears in order. Instead of focusing solely on personal saving we may extend the investigation to encompass aggregate saving—private and public.

When S_{prHh} denotes personal saving, S_U corporate saving, and S_{St} government saving, then aggregate saving (S_A) can be expressed as $S_A = S_{prHh} + S_U + S_{St}$.

As Table 8–4 indicates, aggregate saving has declined in the past five years, mainly due to the reduction of corporate saving (S_U) and saving by the government (S_{St}).

How can these developments in the FRG be explained?

The sudden decrease in S_{St} reflects budgetary restrictions resulting from the need to finance increased public expenditures at a time when tax incomes were reduced by the impact of recession.

Another explanation is found in the legal requirement that the federal budget should make grants-in-aid to the parafiscal institutions (such as old-age and unemployment insurance) in order to assure their liquidity. Budget deficits which result from this obligation are financed through taxes and an increase in public debt.

It is generally more attractive for the individual saver to purchase government loan certificates due to the comparatively low risk and high yield. (The real yield from private stocks and bonds may be less than the interest on public loans, because the government is able to fix loan conditions irrespective of market conditions.) Thus it appears conceivable that real capital formation may stagnate in the corporate sector.

Table 8–2. The Development of Public Expenditures for Promoting Private Saving in the FRG, 1965–78

Year	*In Absolute Terms (millions DM)*	*As a Percent of the Social Budget*	*As a Percent of GNP*
1965	2,743	2.4	0.60
1966	3,200	2.6	0.65
1967	3,424	2.6	0.69
1968	3,737	2.6	0.69
1969	4,161	2.7	0.69
1970	6,063	3.5	0.88
1971	9,738	4.9	1.28
1972	11,524	5.1	1.38
1973	13,066	5.2	1.41
1974	15,182	5.3	1.52
1975	16,276	4.9	1.58
1976	16,839	4.7	1.50
1977	18,826	5.0	1.58
1978	17,008	4.2	1.33

Sources: Federal Ministry of Labor and Social Affairs [7, 1976, p. 104 ff., p. 471 ff., 1978, p. 167 ff.].

Note: The first social budget was published in the beginning of 1969; the figures for the earlier years represent ex-post calculations.

Table 8–3. Development of German Life Insurance Institutions, 1950–77

Year	*Number of Contracts (in 1,000's)*	*Insured Value (DM, in Billions)*	*Average Insurance Value per Contract —Stock— (in DM)*	*Average Insurance Value per Contract —New Addit.— (in DM)*
1950	24,025	15.005	625	1,023
1955	33,531	32.422	967	1,713
1960	40,517	65.616	1,619	3,136
1965	47,992	130.854	2,727	5,997
1970	53,375	235.234	4,407	8,150
1975	60,469	447.589	7,402	14,050
1976	61,377	494.793	8,062	15,635
1977	62,552	554.799	8,869	17,885

Source: [1, Association of Life Insurance Companies, several years].

Table 8–4. The Structure of Aggregate Saving, 1960–77

	Aggregate Saving $S_{prHh} + S_{St} + S_U$		Share of Personal Saving	Share of Government Saving	Share of Corporate Saving
Year	DM, in Billions)	(as a Percent of NNP)	(as a Percent of Aggregate Saving)		
1960	63.60	22.8	25.2	33.6	41.2
1961	66.00	21.7	28.0	38.9	33.1
1962	66.82	20.3	28.7	38.7	32.6
1963	65.81	19.0	35.9	37.0	27.1
1964	79.44	20.9	37.3	35.3	27.4
1965	80.94	19.5	44.2	27.8	28.4
1966	82.32	18.7	44.0	29.1	26.9
1967	73.47	16.6	49.0	21.5	29.5
1968	89.95	18.7	47.7	22.1	30.2
1969	105.41	19.5	48.5	34.7	16.9
1970	124.60	20.4	47.7	31.9	20.4
1971	127.93	18.9	50.4	32.3	17.3
1972	134.16	18.1	58.2	29.1	12.7
1973	149.01	18.1	54.8	37.6	7.6
1974	140.62	16.0	66.1	27.9	6.0
1975	105.25	11.5	99.4	–7.0	7.6
1976	131.23	13.1	73.9	10.9	15.3
1977	135.05	12.7	70.1	19.2	10.7

Source: National Accounts of the FRG.

Additionally, the ability of corporations to provide for their own capital formation may decrease due to declining corporate saving (S_U).

If this rerouting of (monetary) capital flows into the social budget would continue to be ever more significant, a long-term decrease or stagnation in real capital formation may in fact result through a decrease in corporate saving. Such a development would not only be of import for economic growth but also for social policy simply because social incomes of a particular reference period always have to be financed out of the national product of that particular period [20, Mackenroth, 1952]. Thus the circular flow of economic life imposes severe limits to the production of immaterial goods, such as social security.

IV. THE SYSTEM OF OLD-AGE SECURITY IN THE FRG: PUBLIC OLD-AGE INSURANCE AND PRIVATE PENSION FUNDS

Whereas in the USA a public old-age security system exists only since 1935, the German system of old-age security can be traced back to 1884 ("Das Gesetz über die Invalidität und Alterssicherung der Arbeitnehmer," or: The Law Pertaining to the Worker's Security in Case of Invalidity and Old Age). This law is part of the presently valid "Reichsversicherungsordnung" (RVO) which, however, has been changed in the form of more than 200 additional laws and adjusted to the needs of the present period. (Among these changes we find the Old Age Reform Laws of 1957 and 1972).

The German old-age security system can be characterized as follows:

1. Coverage under the public old-age insurance system is mandatory under the law for all employed workers whose employment yields an income or who are presently undergoing training. Compulsory coverage is independent of the level of income earned by these individuals.
2. Additionally, self-employed individuals are not obliged to participate in this system but are offered an opportunity to participate voluntarily in the legal old-age insurance system ("Gesetzliche Rentenversicherung" [GRV]).
3. Compulsory old-age insurance does not apply to civil servants who are entitled to receive public pensions upon retirement out of systems specifically catering to civil servants.

In 1976 the total number of those who were insured in the public old-age insurance system amounted to about 21.6 million individuals [4, Deutscher Bundestag, 1978, p. 72] (out of a total population of about 26.9 million economically active individuals).

The development of expenditures for old-age security, as reflected in the social budget of the FRG, is shown in Table 8–5 for the years 1965–78. Evidently there has been a striking absolute and a noticeable relative increase (when compared to the total social budget and also to GNP) of old-age security benefits in the FRG.

In the same span of time, total social security expenditures increased from 24.6 percent of GNP in 1965 to 31.5 percent of GNP in 1978 (see Table 8–6). Clearly, the expansion of old-age security accounts for a good part of this expansion.

Table 8–5. Expenditures for Old-Age Security, 1965–78

Year[a]	*In Absolute Value (DM, in Millions)*	*As a Percent of the Social Budget*	*As a Percent of GNP*
1965	37,654	33.4	8.18
1966	41,431	33.2	8.44
1967	45,971	34.5	9.28
1968	50,295	35.5	9.31
1969	55,721	36.3	9.21
1970	61,462	35.2	8.97
1971	68,018	34.2	8.93
1972	77,043	34.4	9.24
1973	87,214	34.5	9.41
1974	100,407	34.9	10.08
1975	114,128	34.6	11.08
1976	127,065	35.8	11.31
1977	138,602	36.5	11.61
1978	146,548	36.4	11.47

Source: [7, Federal Ministry of Labor and Social Affairs, 1976, p. 471 ff.; 1978, p. 167 ff.].

[a]The first social budget was submitted at the beginning of 1969. The data for earlier years represent estimates.

Table 8–6. Total Expenditures for Social Security, 1965–78, as a Percent of GNP

Year	*1965*	*1966*	*1967*	*1968*	*1969*	*1970*	*1971*
Social security as a percent of GNP	24.6	25.6	27.0	26.5	25.7	25.5	26.1

Table 8–6. continued

Year	*1972*	*1973*	*1974*	*1975*	*1976*	*1977*	*1978*
Social security as a percent of GNP	26.9	22.3	28.9	32.1	31.5	31.8	31.5

Source: [7, Federal Ministry of Labor and Social Affairs, 1976, p. 165].

The old-age security system of the Federal Republic is formally based on the insurance principle. It starts from the assumption that individuals should first be able to help themselves. Thus everyone obtains on the basis of contributions (within the context of the community of the insured) the entitlement for a level of protection which is commensurate with his social security contributions. The obligatory insurance system can be viewed as a form of enforced self-help. Elisabeth Liefmann-Keil [18, 1961, p. 137], however, characterizes it as a system of collective forced savings. Its aim is to facilitate an intertemporal income transfer for a particular group and financed by a particular group [18, 1961, p. 137]. Presently social security contributions amount to 18 percent of gross income.

Old-age social security contributions are financed in equal parts by the insured and by their employers. The amount of benefits to be received is determined on the basis of the so-called "pension formula." This formula is based on the work income of the insured and the duration of the insurance, which is identical with the duration of the time worked. While the latter reflects personal characteristics some additional factors are reflected in the "pension formula":

$(P \times J) \times (B \times St)$ = pension per year, where

P = the gross work income of the insured individual as a percent of the gross work income of all insured persons;

J = the number of insured years which are applicable in arriving at the total claims;

B = the general basis for apportionment ("Allgemeine Bemessungsgrundlage"); it equals the average gross income per year of all workers and employees, as reflected in a three-year average, computed prior to the start of the old-age insurance payments;

St = the incremental rate applicable for each year of insurance (this rate varies from one type of pension to another).

The old-age security system is based on a pay-as-you-go principle. This implies that the currently working population finances, from a part of its current work income, the pension incomes of individuals who are not working. In the context of this implicit contract between the generations, therefore, the social security contributions are *not* accumulated within a fund but are merely redistributed between the generations.

Reserves can arise in this system only to the extent that current receipts of the social security institutions responsible for the old-age security program exceed current expenditures. The development of these reserves is determined largely by the overall economic situation. Due to the high level of unemployment noted in the Federal Republic in the last few years social security receipts have lagged far behind the expected receipts. Thus it seems well-nigh impossible that future increases in social security contributions can be avoided which would have significant impacts on micro-level behavior and on macroeconomic processes.

Ceteris paribus, a pay-as-you-go-financed tax-transfer system does not change aggregate disposable income. Changes in personal saving result only (1) if the marginal propensities to save differ between the working and the nonworking populations (of which the retired represent the largest share); and (2) if the consumption behavior of the taxed households remains unchanged. Interestingly enough, the saving rate of the retired is higher in the FRG than that of the working population.[3] Furthermore, it is very likely that the level of consumption of the taxed household will be affected by the social security (tax) contribution. Thus one might conclude that, given these propensities to save, the pay-as-you-go mode of financing social security will not affect personal saving adversely, *ceteris paribus.* Still, this does not rule out that the stock effects of social security wealth may lower the saving of those currently working, since such wealth will not be the same with and without the program even if disposable income is.

Due to the existence of this compulsory public insurance system, private pension plans play a rather small role in the Federal Republic when compared to their role in the USA. Their importance has always been rather limited, and even though they have increased in absolute terms their relative import has decreased over time (see Table 8–7).

Private pension funds consist of contractual or voluntary benefits paid by employers. Employers are allowed to accumulate such reserves to a limited extent for the purposes of making old-age disbursements. Thus they may be viewed less as an instrument of social policy and more as a part of the reward strategies used by employers. This conclusion is warranted particularly since the level of benefits paid under such schemes is based on the number of years during which an employee has been working in a particular enterprise. Thus they may be viewed merely as an addition to the legal old-age security system. Furthermore, their purpose had been questioned from the point of view of social policy. Those who receive an above-average income from pensions under the old-age security system are also likely to be those who can expect an additional corporate old-age pension.

Table 8–7. Old-Age Benefits, 1965–78

	Old-Age Benefits from the Legal Pension System		*Employers' Contractual and Voluntary Old-Age Benefits*	
Year	*In Absolute Amounts (DM, in Millions)*	*As a Percent of Total Old-Age Benefits*	*In Absolute Amounts (DM, in Millions)*	*As a Percent of Total Old-Age Benefits*
1965	20,894	55.5	1,870	5.0
1966	23,544	56.8	2,040	4.9
1967	26,788	58.3	2,210	4.8
1968	29,857	59.4	2,380	4.7
1969	33,508	60.1	2,550	4.6
1970	36,349	59.1	2,805	4.6
1971	39,506	58.1	3,060	4.5
1972	45,761	59.4	3,315	4.3
1973	52,365	60.0	3,570	4.1
1974	61,504	61.3	3,825	3.8
1975	70,370	61.7	4,165	3.6
1976	79,745	62.7	4,505	3.5
1977	88,363	63.8	4,930	3.6
1978	93,808	64.0	5,185	3.5

Source: [7, Federal Ministry of Labor and Social Affairs, 1976, p. 270 ff., p. 350 ff.; 1978, p. 238 ff., p. 278 ff.].

A major difference can thus be found to exist between the USA and the FRG: Private pension funds have a central function in the USA also in the internal financing of enterprises. Thus they represent a major factor in the process of overall real capital formation. They tend to reduce the necessity to rely on external sources of financing which are considered to involve greater risks and expenses than internal sources of financing.

Thus a basic link between saving and social security may exist more in the case of the USA and, if at all, on an entirely different level in the FRG. In the USA an increase in public pension plans may, in fact, lead to a reduction in private pension plans. Thus it may be expected to have negative effects on real capital formation. This development appears as corporations are confronted by a reduction of a potential source of internal financing. To the extent corporate pension plans are now funded more fully, they represent a source of external finance. This offset problem evidently does not arise within the FRG. Undoubtedly social security contributions represent a form of forced saving. However, they are not accumulated but merely redistributed between the generations. Still, they do not appear to lead—at least not directly—to a retardation in the rate of real capital formation.

In order to pursue these preliminary insights with greater rigor, and with more empirical evidence, our own tests of the central hypotheses are carried out next.

V. THE INFLUENCE OF OLD-AGE INSURANCE ON PERSONAL SAVING: TESTS OF SOME MACRO-LEVEL HYPOTHESES[4]

The results presented below are based on single-equation econometric estimates applying the LS-procedure. They are based on data from the national accounts and from a national micro-census of households.[5] Private household saving as a percent of gross household income is treated as a dependent variable.

The hypotheses contained in the following questions were tested:

1. Does an increase in public pension income (when compared to net household income) tend to influence personal saving negatively? (As an indicator we employ the quotient: pension income over net income.)
2. Is saving reduced as and when social-security contributions represent a larger share of the gross income of households?

3. Does a change in the financing provisions employed by the old-age social security system (particularly the [upper] income limit beyond which the compulsory social security payment does not increase in absolute terms ["Beitragsbemessungsgrenze"] or the social security [tax] rate) affect saving?
4. Does a change in the structure of the population affect saving? Specifically, does an increase in the share of pensioners among the total population lead to a reduction in saving?

Table 8–8 shows the results of several regression analyses which were performed to test these hypotheses for the case of the FRG. Only for hypothesis 1 does the quotient "pension income over net income" exhibit the negative sign which may be expected on the basis of the U.S. evidence (see equation 2 in Table 8–8). However, this coefficient is *not* statistically significant.

The sign of the coefficient for the quotient "social security contributions over gross income" (as reflected in equations 3, 4, and 12 of Table 8–8) would quite clearly *contradict* hypothesis 2 listed above. Furthermore, this coefficient *is* statistically significant. Evidently this coefficient reflects the pattern of development of the rate of saving and the rate of social security contributions which is characteristic of the Federal Republic—a phenomenon which we have pointed out before. The sign is changed again when "household net income in real terms" is included in the regression equation (see equation 11). However, in this case the coefficient is again not statistically significant.

Unambiguous results can, however, be reported for the two aspects of the financing instruments employed by the old-age social security system: "social security tax rate" and "the [upper] income limit beyond which the obligatory social security payment does not increase in absolute terms ["Beitragsbemessungsgrenze"]." The signs and the *t*-values of the coefficients pertaining to these two variables (as reflected in equations 1, 5, 6, and 7) would allow the conclusion that an increase in social security contributions resulting from changes in these two instruments would exert no negative influence on saving.

Hypothesis 4 is contradicted by the sign and *t*-values of the coefficients for the quotients pertaining to individuals above sixty-five years of age. These values would indicate that the rate of saving tends to *increase* with the share of individuals aged sixty-five and above among the total population. This confirms a pattern reported earlier.

Table 8–8. Results of the Regression Analysis *(dependent variable: private household saving as a percent of gross household income in real terms)*

Number of the Equation	*Number of the Independent Variables*					
	0	*1*	*2*	*3*	*4*	*5*
1	0.0363 (2.470)					
2	−0.0741 (5.591)	−0.199 (1.33)				
3	0.0233 (1.306)		0.8048 (2.516)	−0.397 (0.725)		
4	0.0211 (1.221)		0.5835 (6.198)			
5	0.0343 (1.744)					
6	0.1384 (2.457)					
7	0.0475 (1.089)					
8	−0.0353 (1.344)	0.738 (4.605)				
9	−0.0759 (5.604)					
10	0.1002 (1.022)					−0.4638 (1.663)
11	0.0393 (2.809)		−0.4686 (1.73)	0.1888 (0.624)	0.0292 (5.975)	
12	0.0328 (1.444)	0.179 (0.699)	0.704 (1.974)	0.4121 (0.737)		

Table 8–8. continued

Number of the Independent Variables					
6	7	8	9	R^2	Durbin–Watson Statistic
		0.050 (6.50)	0.0004 (0.016)	0.9356	1.3447
	1.525 (7.256)			0.9213	1.6573
				0.7433	0.8837
				0.7330	0.9652
			0.0011 (6.097)	0.7265	0.6907
		0.0386 (12.90)			
0.0002 (9.201)				0.8581	0.8025
				0.6024	0.6467
	1.282 (11.93)			0.9105	1.4451
				0.1649	0.3598
				0.9354	1.6157
				0.7532	0.8364

(Table 8-8. Description of the Independent Variables . . . continued overleaf)

Table 8–8. continued

Number of the Independent Variables	*Description of the Independent Variables*
0	constant term
1	quotient: public pension income over net household income
2	quotient: total social security contributions over gross income
3	quotient: income taxes over income
4	net household income in real terms
5	share of individuals aged twenty to sixty-four among the total population
6	(upper) income limit beyond which the obligatory social security payment does not increase in absolute terms ("Beitragsbemessungsgrenze"/in nominal terms)
7	share of individuals aged sixty-five and above among the total population
8	(upper) income limit beyond which the obligatory social security payment does not increase in absolute terms ("Beitragsbemessungsgrenze"/in real terms)
9	old-age social security (tax) rate

Source: Own computations; *t*-values are shown in parentheses.

VI. CONCLUSION

The regression results reported lend support to the conclusion that an expansion of the old-age social security system has *not* led to a reduction of personal saving within the Federal Republic of Germany.

Some qualifications appear in order: (1) Single-equation estimations are not adequate to the complexity of the subject at hand. Undoubtedly, the investigation should be extended on the basis of an interdependent model which—ideally—would have to include a disaggregated household sector. (2) The investigation would have to be addressed to both the micro- and the macro-level. (3) An even more satisfactory approach would include all primary adaptive effects of the macroeconomic aggregates within an integrated micro-macro-model. As a first step one could extend and improve the existing macro-models and complement them with micro-simulation models.

These would at least permit an understanding of the primary adaptive responses taking place within the individual sectors given certain alternative assumptions about the system. Even if we could reach this partial goal it would help narrow the gap between micro- and macro-level explanations. The aggregation of group- or level-specific primary effects appears to be thus far the only possible way to arrive at an approximation of the total incidence of the system of social security.

On the other hand, expectations about the performance of more sophisticated models cannot be overly optimistic. Quite obviously they are restricted by their assumptions, for example, by the assumption that a legally regulated system of old-age security would eliminate at once the dominant saving motives. This assumption surely ignores very important noneconomic determinants of saving. Furthermore, as a rule, such models are based on static approaches which again are formulated on the basis of a rather narrowly defined concept of economic rationality; they tend to ignore expectations, processes of learning, and changes in preferences. Such an omission leads to obvious problems, particularly for time series analyses involving longer stretches of time. Thus, not surprisingly, studies based on life cycle models and using primarily economic data would tend to come to quite opposite conclusions when compared to investigations based on field surveys, focusing also on noneconomic factors of the type indicated (such as subjective time preference, psychological determinants of saving and of expectations). We would tend to conclude that the motives for saving are much more complex than those postulated within the context of life cycle models.

The explanatory value of such models is limited for the following reasons:

1. Consumer preferences will not remain constant over longer stretches of time; and, obviously, every observable change in consumer preferences is likely to affect the consumption (and saving) function significantly.
2. The very definition of "consumption" already predetermines the results of the investigation to some extent. Thus one would have to come to different conclusions if one were to include the purchase of material goods (such as durables) as a form of saving.
3. When defining saving as a residual magnitude little is said about the motives for saving nor about the changes in such motives over time [6, Farrell, 1966, p. 339].
4. The magnitude of aggregate saving, that is, the overall ability to save, is determined largely by the distribution of income and

wealth and also by the demographic structure of the population. (However, these determinants are implicitly being treated as constants in these models.)

5. These models start with a relatively constant and given ability to save. This assumption appears to be somewhat questionable, particularly as regards recipients of lower incomes. The life cycle models abstract in all possible ways from the realization of a level of consumption which would conform to the minimum standard of existence required for a particular period.
6. The assumption that individuals hold certain expectations about their own individual age of death would appear to be valid only to a limited extent. Even if such assumptions were based on some degree of rationality and if they were to be based on mortality tables, they must still be treated as probabilistic statements. Thus, at the very least, the incomes expected for the future would have to be weighted with the respective subjective probabilities of reaching particular ages [27, Tobin, 1967, pp. 231–56].

All of these caveats would tend to caution us against giving undue credence to results based on life cycle models which would indicate that an expansion of social security tends to reduce the rate of personal saving and thus of real capital formation. In any event, the empirical evidence available for the Federal Republic, however incomplete, indicates either that no such effect exists at all, or else that it would tend to be negligible.

An active public policy designed to promote private household saving could, more likely than not, serve as an incentive to personal saving also in countries where fears about the future rate of real capital formation can be based on more solid evidence.

Appendix 1

GROSS AND NET ASSET FORMATION AND AGGREGATE SAVING WITHIN THE SYSTEM OF NATIONAL ACCOUNTS

An empirical foray into the macroeconomic patterns of old-age security and saving necessarily must start with the system of national accounts [8, 1971]. Some notes on the German system of national accounts thus appear in order [25, 1972].

The component "gross saving" found in the U.S. national accounts is paralleled in the FRG component "gross asset formation":

$$S + D = I^{br} + (X - M) \qquad (1)$$

where: S = aggregate saving;

D = capital consumption allowances;

I^{br} = gross investment;

$(X-M)$ = exports minus imports ($X-M > 0$, denotes an export surplus[6]; and $X-M < 0$ an import surplus).

and:

$$S = S_U + S_{St} + S_{prHh} \qquad (2)$$

where: S_U = corporate saving;

S_{St} = government saving; and

S_{prHh} = personal saving.

The left-hand side of equation (1) represents the gross increment in national assets during a particular time period; it is composed of the increment in gross investment (i.e., the real increment in assets) and in foreign (monetary) assets.

Table 8–A1 indicates the ratio of aggregate saving (S) plus capital consumption allowances (D) over GNP in market prices (GNP^M). The time series pattern suggests a relatively constant process of development of this indicator. During the early 1960s, it amounted to about 29 percent (with a slope of the trend of + 0.015); in the period 1970–74 it decreased—relatively mildly, however—and since the recessionary phase of the 1970s it decreased relatively strongly.

Table 8–A1. Gross Increment in National Assets Relative to GNP, 1950–76

Year	$(S + D)/GNP^M$ *(as a percent)*
1950–1954[a]	23.81
1955–1959[a]	27.35
1960–1964	27.74
1965–1969	26.61
1970–1974	26.82
1975[b]	21.51
1976[b]	22.71
1950–1976	26.19

Source: Statistisches Bundesamt (Federal Statistical Office). *Volkswirtschaftliche Gesamtrechnungen*, Series 18. Stuttgart/Mainz: Kohlhammer, 1971. Revised Series starting 1950, and own computations.

[a]Without the Saarland and West Berlin.

[b]Preliminary results.

Table 8–A2. The Rate of Aggregate Saving, 1950–76

Year	S/NSP^M *(as a percent)*
1950–1954[a]	16.93
1955–1959[a]	20.89
1960–1964	20.92
1965–1969	18.60
1970–1974	18.29
1975[b]	11.46
1976[b]	12.99
1950–1976	18.70

Source: Statistisches Bundesamt (Federal Statistical Office). *Volkswirtschaftliche Gesamtrechnungen*, Series 18. Stuttgart/Mainz: Kohlhammer, 1977. Revised Series starting 1950, and own computations.

[a]Without the Saarland and West Berlin.

[b]Preliminary results.

As an alternative to gross asset formation we may focus on net asset formation as it is affected less by cyclical factors (which affect the volume of capital consumption allowances and thus gross asset formation). Furthermore, net asset formation serves as a more pertinent indicator of the net increment in assets—which is of paramount import for economic growth.

$$S = I^n + (X-M) \tag{3}$$

where I^n = net investment .

Thus aggregate saving (S) denotes the net asset formation of a period, with the increment in national assets being the sum of the net increment in real assets (I^n) and in foreign (monetary) assets ($X-M$). When related to Net National Product (NNP)—which equals $GNP^M - D$—we arrive at the aggregate saving rate or the net rate of aggregate asset formation (S/NSP^M).

As Table 8–A2 indicates, S/NSP^M on the average amounted to 18.7 percent during the period 1950–76; it shows a slightly declining trend in the rate of aggregate saving for the same period (with a slope of -0.096). However, the entire decline may be due to the depressed level of economic activity toward the end of the data period. In our judgment one cannot draw any conclusions from these cyclical fluctuations which would substantiate a long-run decline in the rate of aggregate saving.

Appendix 2

TEST OF A MICRO-LEVEL HYPOTHESIS

In order to explore the relationship between old-age security and personal saving also at the micro-level, the following hypothesis was tested: The increasingly higher burden imposed on employee households by direct taxes and/or social security contributions has *not* led to a substitution of private saving through social insurance claims (against the community of the insured individuals or against the whole of society); rather, it has increased the rate of long-term (monetary and real) capital formation.

The rate of saving (SQ_{Hhi_t}) thus represents the independent variable, while alternative rates of burdens ($BELT^{dir}_{Hhi}$, $BELSOZV_{Hhi}$) are treated as dependent variables.

The following linear regression model served as the basis of the statistical test of the above hypothesis:

$$SQ_{Hhi_t} = \alpha + \beta\ BELT^{dir}_{Hhi_t} + \gamma\ BELSOZV_{Hhi_t}$$

where

SQ_{Hhi_t} = $\dfrac{\text{Net addition (+)/Net reduction (−) of monetary and real assets}}{\text{disposable household income of the } i\text{th household in the year } t}$

$BELT^{dir}_{Hhi_t}$ = relative burden imposed on current household income through direct taxes, for the household i and for the year t.

$BELSOZV_{Hhi_t}$ = relative burden imposed on current gross household income through social security taxes, for the household i and for the year t.

i = 2, 3 to denote household types 2 and 3; household type 2 denotes a 4-person white- and blue-collar household whose head of household receives a medium-level income; and household type 3 stands for a 4-person white-collar and civil-servant household with higher-level income. These household types are found in the Current Economic Accounts as reported by the Federal Statistical Office.

α, β, γ = regression coefficients.

t = year: for type 2: 1958–75
for type 3: 1964–75.

Table 8–A3 indicates the monetary and real asset formation of employee households (types 2 and 3 of the current economic accounts), and Table 8–A4 the burdens imposed on current household income through social security (tax) contributions and direct taxes for the same two types of households, and for the identical periods of time (1958–75 for household type 2, and 1964–75 for household type 3, respectively). The results of the regression analysis, furthermore, are shown in Table 8–A5.

As the regression coefficients indicate *there has been a well-nigh proportional development of the rate of saving and of the relative burden imposed on households* through social security (tax) contributions and direct taxes. The high t-values would indicate a high level of statistical significance; but these can be explained almost exclusively by the trend present in the data. Similar caveats apply to the

Table 8–A3. Monetary and Real Asset Formation of Employee Households *(household type 2 of the current economic accounts)*, **1958–1975**

Year	Disposable Household Income	Net Real Asset Formation[a]	Net Monetary Asset Formation[b]	Total Asset Formation	Asset Formation as a Percent of Disposable Household Income
	(in DM, average monthly values)				
	1	2	3	4	5
1958	566.00	1.94	17.93	25.90	4.58
1959	607.96	8.58	28.76	41.83	6.89
1960	639.49	7.64	22.45	35.05	5.48
1961	698.71	0.45	18.57	30.45	4.41
1962	756.79	7.04	23.07	39.44	5.21
1963	810.24	1.55	20.74	39.42	4.87
1964	849.78	1.83	24.56	28.54	3.36
1965	921.90	19.16	−21.22	2.75	0.30
1966	972.34	4.13	39.01	54.81	5.64
1967	958.05	10.11	42.07	61.53	6.42
1968	972.46	8.43	36.68	48.52	5.02
1969	1056.12	18.92	54.69	61.36	5.81
1970	1165.43	14.87	69.27	97.04	8.33
1971	1305.20	39.76	95.68	135.80	10.40
1972	1433.32	52.47	202.17	243.31	16.97
1973	1602.52	81.39	163.37	201.73	12.59
1974	1766.26	74.60	177.59	232.44	13.16
1975	1980.45	68.69	233.87	290.40	14.66

Table 8–A3. continued

Monetary and Real Asset Formation of Employee Households *(households type 3 of the current economic accounts)*, **1964–1975**

Year	Disposable Household Income	Net Real Asset Formation[a]	Net Monetary Asset Formation[b]	Total Asset Formation	Asset Formation as a Percent of Disposable Household Income
			(in DM, average monthly values)		
	1	2	3	4	5
1964	1739.37	68.23	147.92	228.66	13.15
1965	1795.83	70.08	122.31	226.14	12.59
1966	1898.37	56.72	202.88	281.60	14.83
1967	1852.81	57.59	139.51	229.07	12.36
1968	1840.93	110.65	166.97	242.35	13.16
1969	1941.63	126.88	152.77	258.13	13.29
1970	2136.64	221.29	185.64	311.94	14.60
1971	2332.55	303.53	147.66	411.68	17.65
1972	2481.73	349.77	116.29	433.94	17.49
1973	2721.85	436.01	229.02	515.87	18.95
1974	2993.74	527.20	102.05	539.68	18.03
1975	3308.80	330.34	387.33	675.83	20.43

Source: own computations on the basis of the Current Economic Accounts of the Federal Statistical Office.

[a] "Real asset formation" represents expenses for the acquisition of private properties and buildings, *minus* the incomes received from the sale of private properties and buildings.

[b] "Net monetary asset formation" consists of the difference: (deposits with credit institutions, postal deposits, deposits with building associations [bank], purchase of stocks and bonds, credits granted by households, life insurance premiums, increases in cash held) minus (withdrawals from accounts with credit institutes, from the postal system, and withdrawals from building associations [banks], sale of stocks and bonds, and repayment of credits made, income from life insurance policies, and reduction in cash held).

values of R^2. The results are, therefore, not conclusive. It is safe, however, to conclude that they do not lend support to the Friedman-Feldstein hypothesis.

Table 8–A4. Burdens Imposed on Current Household Income through Social Security (Tax) Contributions and Direct Taxes *(household type 2 of the current economic accounts)*, **1958–1975**

Year	*Burden of Direct Taxes* 1	*Burden of Social Security Contributions* 2	*Total Burden (1 + 2)* 3	*Net Burden Imposed on Household Income*[a] 4
1958	1.76	10.15	11.91	8.71
1959	1.44	10.15	11.59	9.07
1960	2.04	10.00	12.04	9.31
1961	3.19	9.49	12.68	9.62
1962	4.00	8.86	12.86	9.76
1963	4.73	8.84	13.57	10.93
1964	5.41	8.91	14.32	11.14
1965	5.35	8.40	13.75	10.92
1966	5.82	8.71	14.53	11.90
1967	5.91	9.18	15.09	12.33
1968	6.43	10.04	16.48	14.01
1969	7.47	10.31	17.78	15.80
1970	8.91	10.79	19.70	18.18
1971	10.13	11.07	21.20	19.35
1972	10.67	11.33	22.00	20.38
1973	11.50	11.64	23.14	21.69
1974	12.47	11.55	24.01	22.05
1975	11.17	11.60	22.76	16.56

Table 8–A4. continued
Burdens Imposed on Current Household Income through Social Security (Tax) Contributions and Direct Taxes *(household type 3 of the current economic accounts)*, **1964–1975**

Year	*Burden of Direct Taxes* 1	*Burden of Social Security Contributions* 2	*Total Burden (1 + 2)* 3	*Net Burden Imposed on Household Income*[a] 4
1964	11.58	0.56	12.14	11.66
1965	10.80	0.86	11.66	10.98
1966	10.92	1.12	12.04	11.40
1967	11.17	1.23	12.40	11.90
1968	11.29	3.18	14.47	14.10
1969	11.97	2.95	14.92	14.52
1970	13.01	2.81	15.82	15.42
1971	14.77	2.99	17.75	17.05
1972	15.03	3.35	18.39	17.71
1973	16.17	3.62	19.79	19.17
1974	17.52	3.58	21.09	20.52
1975	16.21	3.90	20.11	16.80

Source: own computation on the basis of the Current Economic Accounts of the Federal Statistical Office.

[a]The net burden denotes the reduction in household income due to social security (tax) contributions and direct taxes, *plus* current (income) transfers made by government and by the social insurance institutions.

Table 8–A5. Results of the Regression Analysis

Household Type	*Independent Variable(s)*	*Constant Term*	*Regression Coefficient(s) (t-Value)*	*Independent Variable(s)*	R^2	*Standard Error*	*F–Values*
2	$BELT^{dir}_{Hh2}$	SQ_{Hh2} = 0.01079 +	0.96852 (4.99)	$BELT^{dir}$	0.609	0.194	24.917
	$BELSOZV_{Hh2}$	SQ_{Hh2} = −0.27488 +	3.47407 (6.95)	$BELSOZV_{Hh2}$	0.752	0.499	48.386
	$BELT^{dir}_{Hh2}$	SQ_{Hh2} = −0.20671 +	2.42180 (3.97)	$BELSOZV_{Hh2}$	0.809	0.635	15.765
	$BELSOZV_{Hh2}$	+	0.41961 (2.13)	$BELT^{dir}_{Hh2}$		0.197	4.551
3	$BELT^{dir}_{Hh3}$	SQ_{Hh3} = 0.01346 +	1.06199 (7.42)	$BELT^{dir}_{Hh3}$	0.846	0.143	55.042
	$BELSOZV_{Hh3}$	SQ_{Hh3} = 0.11230 +	1.71738 (3.48)	$BELSOZV_{Hh3}$	0.548	0.493	12.123
	$BELT^{dir}_{Hh3}$	SQ_{Hh3} = 0.01626 +	1.02170 (4.19)	$BELT^{dir}_{Hh3}$	0.847	0.244	17.590
	$BELSOZV_{Hh3}$	+	0.10296 (2.13)	$BELSOZV_{Hh3}$		0.490	0.044

Source: own computation on the basis of the Current Economic Accounts of the Federal Statistical Office.

NOTES TO CHAPTER 8

1. Of the DM 334.7 billion of the social budget for the year 1975, old-age and health insurance represent the major components (36.2 percent and 31.7 percent, respectively), followed by family allowances (16.1 percent), unemployment insurance (6.2 percent), public promotion of personal saving (4.7 percent), housing allowances (2.3 percent), payments resulting from the consequences of political factors (2.3 percent), and general aid (0.5 percent). In this chapter, considerations of health insurance are omitted in the belief that they would not materially alter the conclusions derived from a narrower focus on old-age insurance. The social budget represents an integrated summary of all social expenditures undertaken during a particular year by the government and parafiscal institutions. Some social transfers made by corporations to households are included as well (see references to the "Sozialbericht" listed below).

2. See Appendix 1 for a note on "Gross and Net Asset Formation and Aggregate Saving within the System of National Accounts."

3. There is ample micro-level evidence existing in the FRG which indicates that the retired save *more* than the working population. (See: FEDERAL MINISTRY OF LABOR AND SOCIAL AFFAIRS. "Rentner sparen mehr als Arbeitnehmer," in *Sozialpolitische Informationen.* Bonn: Federal Ministry of Labor and Social Affairs, Year XII/5, March 8, 1978, p. 1).

4. See also: "Test of a Micro-Level Hypothesis" (Appendix 2).

5. The German Micro-Census represents an annual 1 percent national cluster sample of the resident population.

6. During the entire post–World War II period an export surplus may be noted for the FRG.

REFERENCES

1. ASSOCIATION OF LIFE INSURANCE COMPANIES ("Verband der Lebensversicherungsunternehmen e.V."), ed. *Die deutsche Lebensversicherung.* Yearbook. Bonn: Verband der Lebensversicherungsunternehmen e.V. (several years).

2. BOHN, PETER. *Konsumenten- und Sparverhalten.* Stuttgart: G. Fischer-Verlag, 1969.

3. BRANDT, FRANZ; PETER, RUDI; and WERTH, MANFRED. *Das Sparverhalten der Arbeitnehmer im Rahmen des Vermögensbildungsgesetzes*, Vol. 19. Köln: Series of the Federal Ministry of Labor and Social Affairs, 1972.

4. DEUTSCHER BUNDESTAG. Bundestagsdrucksache 8/1615. Bonn: Verlag Dr. Hans Heger, 1978.

5. CAGAN, PHILLIP. *The Effect of Pension Plans on Aggregate Saving: Evidence from a Sample Survey.* New York: NBER; distributed by Columbia University Press, 1965.

6. FARRELL, MICHAEL J. "Die neuen Theorien der Konsumfunktion," in *Konsum und Nachfrage.* Edited by M. STREISSLER and E. STREISSLER. Köln: Kiepenheuer & Witsch, 1966.

7. FEDERAL MINISTRY OF LABOR AND SOCIAL AFFAIRS. *Sozialbericht.* Bonn (several years).

8. STATISTISCHES BUNDESAMT ("Federal Statistical Office"). *Volkswirtschaftliche Gesamtrechnungen*, Series 18. Stuttgart/Mainz: Kohlhammer, 1977. Revised Series starting 1950.

9. FELDSTEIN, MARTIN S. "Social Security, Induced Retirement, and Aggregate Capital Accumulation," *Journal of Political Economy*, Sept./Oct. 1974, *82*(5), pp. 905–26.

10. ____ . "Social Security and Saving: The Extended Life Cycle Theory," *American Economic Review*, May 1976, *66*(2), pp. 77–86.

11. VON FURSTENBERG, GEORGE M., and MALKIEL, BURTON G. "The Government and Capital Formation: A Survey of Recent Issues," *Journal of Economic Literature*, Sept. 1977, *15*(3), pp. 835–78.

12. FRIEDMAN, MILTON. *A Theory of the Consumption Function.* Princeton, N.J.: Princeton University Press, 1957.

13. HÖPFNER, FRIEDRICH G.; VON KNORRING, EKKEHARD; and VON ROSENSTIEL, LUTZ. "Die Bestimmungsfaktoren des privaten Konsum- und Sparverhaltens aus makroökonomischer und psychologischer Sicht: Der Versuch einer Synthese," *Zeitschrift für Wirtschafts- und Sozialwissenschaften*, 1972, *92*(3), pp. 271–88.

14. INSTITUT FÜR DEMOSKOPIE ALLENSBACH. *10 Jahre Rentenreform. Die Meinung der Versicherten 1958–1968.* Allensbach: Institut für Demoskopie Allensbach, 1968.

15. KATONA, GEORGE. *Private Pensions und Individual Saving.* Ann Arbor: Survey Research Center, ISR, Monograph No. 40, University of Michigan, 1965.

16. KATONA, GEORGE; STRÜMPEL, BURKHARD; and ZAHN, ERNEST. *Aspirations and Affluence: Comparative Studies in the United States and Western Europe.* New York: McGraw-Hill, 1971.

17. KAUFMANN, FRANZ-XAVER. "Sicherheit als soziologisches und sozialpolitisches Problem," in *Soziologische Gegenwartsfragen*, New Series, Vol. 31. Edited by K. NEUNDÖRFER, H. SCHELSKY, and F.H. TENBRUCK. Stuttgart: Enke-Verlag, 1970.

18. LIEFMANN-KEIL, ELISABETH. *Ökonomische Theorie der Sozialpolitik.* Berlin/Göttingen/Heidelberg: Springer-Verlag, 1961.

19. LITTMANN, KONRAD. *Zunehmende Staatstätigkeit und wirtschaftliche Entwicklung—Versuche über die Wirkungen staatswirtschaftlicher Prozesse in der spätkapitalistischen Periode.* Köln/Opladen: Westdeutscher Verlag, 1957.

20. MACKENROTH, GERHARD. "Die Reform der Sozialpolitik durch einen deutschen Sozialplan," in *Schriften des Vereins für Socialpolitik, Gesellschaft für Wirtschafts- und Sozialwissenschaften*, New Series, Vol. 4. Berlin: Duncker & Humblot, 1952.

21. MUNNELL, ALICIA H. "The Impact of Social Security on Personal Saving," *New England Economic Review*, January/February 1975, pp. 27–41.

22. PASCHKE, WERNER. *Bestimmungsgründe des persönlichen Sparens.* Berlin: Duncker & Humblot, 1961.

23. SCHMÄHL, WINFRIED. *Systemänderung in der Altersvorsorge.* Frankfurt: Westdeutscher Verlag, 1973.

24. SCHMÖLDERS, GÜNTER. *Psychologie des Geldes.* Reinbek: Rowohlt-Verlag, 1966.

25. STOBBE, ALFRED. *Volkswirtschaftliches Rechnungswesen.* Berlin/Heidelberg/New York: Springer Verlag, Third Edition, 1972.

26. STRÜMPEL, BURKHARD. "Saving Behavior in Western Germany and the United States," *American Economic Review*, May 1975, *65*(2), pp. 210–16.

27. TOBIN, JAMES. "Life Cycle Saving and Balanced Growth" in *Ten Economic Studies in the Tradition of Irving-Fisher.* Edited by W. FELLNER et al. New York: Wiley, 1967, pp. 231–56.

Part III

Demographic Factors, Life Cycle Saving, and Government Debt in Theoretical Models

Chapter 9

Age Structure and Personal Saving Behavior

Charles Lieberman and
Paul Wachtel

Structural changes in the economy that may affect the overall level of saving by individuals are of considerable interest because of the importance of personal saving for capital formation. Although buffeted by innumerable changes in the structure of the economy, the gross private saving rate has been remarkably stable in the United States for all of recorded history (which is about a century for aggregate saving). It is also the case, however, that the composition of saving among sectors and, within sectors, by assets is subject to change. Thus it cannot be taken for granted that the saving rate will remain stable in the future. This chapter examines one particular structural influence on saving—the age distribution of the population.

Discussions of saving behavior and capital formation often raise the specter of an aging population whose dissaving will inhibit capital formation and growth. However, the line of reasoning connecting changes in the age distribution and life cycle saving behavior for individuals to aggregate saving is often unclear. The issues are both theoretically and empirically complex, and, as we shall see below, the implications of changes in the age structure for aggregate saving are not at all obvious.

These issues are neither new nor unexplored. The literature summarized by Dorothy Brady [4, 1956] and Dorothy Projector [21, 1968] shows that the earliest survey data established that there are large differences in saving behavior among demographic groups. However, research was concentrated on saving behavior and its implications for stabilization policy, thereby ignoring the long-run implications for aggregate capital formation. Thus the recent development of interest in capital formation problems led to a reopening of these issues.

In the postwar period there have been several projects—the Survey Research Center Surveys of Consumer Finances [25], and the Survey of Changes in Family Finances [21, Projector, 1968] among others—that have documented the differences in saving behavior by age groups. However, one is hard pressed to find any conclusions about the effect of changes in age structure on aggregate saving behavior in this literature. Although survey data are potentially of great assistance in making historical generalizations about saving behavior little headway has been made. The literature remained largley descriptive and research interest declined by the 1960s. An exception is W. Eizenga's [7, 1961] analysis of the 1950 Consumer Expenditure Survey which estimates the effect of demographic change on aggregate saving between 1900 and 1950.

There are numerous reasons why it is difficult to draw aggregate conclusions from survey data (see [13, Friend, 1954]). The enormous variability of saving behavior among individuals tends to compound the serious measurement problems. Survey respondents often provide erroneous information or information that is inconsistent—generally by accident, but all too often by intention. These problems make it difficult to determine whether variability from survey to survey is due to actual changes in behavior or due to measurement difficulties. Nevertheless, existing survey and time series data can support some tentative conclusions which have not previously been drawn. In this study, we make use of the more recent survey data on saving, as well as of some time series data, and attempt to develop methodological approaches that allow ımplications to be derived for aggregate behavior.

The interest in the aggregate level of saving stems from the concern about "capital shortages" that has surfaced in the last five years (see [33, Wachtel, Sametz, and Shuford, 1976]). This is not the place to examine these broader issues, but it is worth noting that the demographic effect on personal saving is often mentioned as one of the villains in the oft-predicted capital shortage problem. Concern about levels of capital formation began with the essentially ad hoc forecasts of the demand and supply for capital prepared by the New York Stock Exchange in 1974. Those forecasts assert, without any documentation, that

> ... the ratio of personal saving to GNP will decline smoothly over the period—from 4.25% in 1973 to 3.9% in 1985 ... because [of] among other things the shifting age distribution of the U.S. population toward the low-saving 20–35 age bracket. [20, 1974, p. 14]

Unfortunately, assertions like this, though numerous, have been largely unsubstantiated. Since interest in the determinants of capital formation has increased, a look at the evidence is clearly in order.

A further difficulty in analyzing the effect of age structure is that it is virtually indistinguishable from other demographic and structural changes in the economy. For example, decreasing family size is a related phenomenon with ambiguous effects on saving. Smaller families may have reduced consumption demands for some goods, but they also have fewer savings goals to satisfy. Similarly, differences in the occupational structure and labor force participation rate can affect saving behavior in the long run in either direction. In our analysis, we will abstract from these interrelated problems and concentrate on the specific issue of the age effect.

Casual observations about the effect of age structure on saving seem to be based on the assumption that saving behavior follows some humped shape over the life cycle. That is, saving is done in midlife while the very young and the old (retired) often dissave. These nonsaving groups are growing in relative size, hence the conclusion that a changing age structure will reduce saving.

Indeed, the changes in the demographic distribution of the population have been large. The savers (families with a head aged thirty-five to sixty-five), which constituted 60 percent of all families immediately after World War II, are now just over 45 percent of all family units. If the other groups do not save at all and if all household incomes are equal, then the changing age structure could reduce saving by as much as 25 percent. However, because all age groups typically engage in some saving and households that save typically have higher incomes than those that do not, the actual reduction in saving is likely to be much smaller. Still, demographic effects on aggregates can be of major significance, as suggested by the simple example above.

The development of the life cycle theory was an important step in our understanding of aggregate consumption behavior and stabilization policy. However, the emphasis on aggregate behavior is less appropriate for studying capital formation problems. The influence of the personal sector on business capital formation depends largely on the sector's level of net financial investment, which represents resources available for capital formation by other sectors. Net financial investment depends on the size of the components of saving, and the importance of various uses of saving for business capital formation tends to be overlooked by life cycle theory. Life cycle patterns of total saving can be quite different from the life cycle pattern of the components. For example, accumulation of residential capital, durable assets, and debt and financial assets are likely to follow very different paths over the life cycle.

The chapter begins with a theoretical model of life cycle behavior. The model indicates that life cycle theory provides little information about the effects of changes in the age distribution on saving rates. Section II develops the methodology for analyzing age effects on saving from survey data and discusses the postwar demographic trends. The empirical analysis of age effects with the survey data is found in Section III and with time series data in Section IV. The consequences for aggregate capital formation are brought out in the concluding section.

I. LIFE CYCLE THEORY

The life cycle model of consumption introduced by Franco Modigliani and Richard Brumberg [19, 1954] and extended by Albert Ando and Modigliani [1, 1963] relates consumption to expected lifetime labor income and to nonhuman wealth. For any single individual, the marginal propensity to consume further depends upon the remaining expected lifespan over which the stock of assets are to be spent. As a result, the individual's propensity to consume, and by the same token the propensity to save, are functions of the age of the individual.[1] Although the importance of age in any life cycle model is obvious, the implications of age for saving rates have never been fully examined. As it turns out, life cycle theory provides no simple solution for the age profile of saving rates.

In this section we employ the life cycle utility approach to consumption to examine the effect of age structure on saving, using the following assumptions:

1. constant real labor income,
2. a constant interest rate,
3. perfect foresight as to future, lifespan, income . . . ,
4. zero initial net worth (no inheritance), zero bequest,
5. no capital gains.

These simplifying assumptions are quite restrictive, but they can be relaxed without changing the qualitative nature of the results.

Further assume that

$$C_i = \alpha_i Y \text{ for } i \leq n, \tag{1}$$

$$C_i = \beta_i W_i \text{ for } n < i \leq T, \tag{2}$$

where C_i is consumption in the ith year; Y, labor income (constant for all years); W_i, the initial net worth for year i; n, the number of work years; and T, the total number of work and retirement years.

This last pair of equations dichotomizes consumption into spending during the working life to be financed entirely out of labor income and retirement consumption which is a function only of wealth. Wealth is the accumulated sum of saving and interest income. This procedure provides information simultaneously on spending out of a stream of income flows (out of labor income) and out of a stock of assets (wealth). Generally, models employ either a stream of income flows, as in Crockett and Friend [6, 1978], or out of a fixed stock of assets, as in Samuelson [24, 1969]. As will be demonstrated, these procedures are equivalent.

The equivalence of these formulations is seen most simply by recognizing that, since capital gains and other windfalls are excluded from the model presented here, asset accumulation can only occur due to saving out of labor income during the working life.[2] If the utility function implies a smooth saving rate over time, net saving out of labor income will occur in each and every working year.[3] Thus, as long as wealth is ultimately for consumption during retirement and income is partly for saving, a model containing the suggested dichotomy will be theoretically equivalent to one in which consumption is a constant portion of the present value of future labor and nonlabor income.[4]

This dichotomy also eliminates an identification problem at the micro-level. As the problem is usually formulated, consumption during the working life is a function of income and wealth. However, an infinite number of linear combinations of income and net worth exist which will yield a given level of consumption (that level of consumption which maximizes utility for a given period). Each extra dollar not spent out of income permits one dollar of net worth, which would otherwise have been consumed, to remain a part of wealth. Similarly, each extra dollar spent out of assets permits an extra dollar of income to enter net worth. Thus, a determinate solution exists only if some relative propensity to consume out of income and wealth is specified.

The usual treatment of the problem constrains the propensities to consume out of the present value of labor and nonlabor income to be equal. Since saving is defined as occurring out of income, the dichotomy employed here is consistent with the definition of saving while it is equivalent to the standard specification.

Assume an additive log utility function,

$$U = \ell n C_1 + \lambda \ell n C_2 + \lambda^2 \ell n C_3 + \ldots \lambda^{T-1} \ell n C_T , \tag{3}$$

where λ is the rate at which households discount future consumption. Using equations (1) and (2), (3) may be rewritten as

$$U = \sum_{i=1}^{i=n} \lambda^{i-1} \ell n(\alpha_i Y) + \sum_{i=n+1}^{i=T} \lambda^{i-1} \ell n(\beta_i W_i), \tag{4}$$

where $W_0 = 0,$

and $$W_t = \sum_{i=1}^{i=t} (1-\alpha_i)\, Y(1+r)^{t-i} \qquad t \leq n,$$

$$W_t = W_n (1+r)^{t-n} \cdot \prod_{j=n+1}^{j=t} (1-\beta_{j-n}) \qquad n < t \leq T-1.$$

The last two expressions describe the wealth position of the individual household at any point in time. The first expression presents the sum of incremental savings and income generated by the stock of wealth during the work phase while the second expression describes decumulation in wealth due to expenditures made during retirement and additions to wealth due to interest earned on the unspent stock of wealth.

Substituting the expression for wealth holding during retirement into equation (4) gives

$$\begin{aligned} U = {} & \ell n(\alpha_1 Y) + \lambda\, \ell n(\alpha_2 Y) + \lambda^2 \ell n(\alpha_3 Y) + \ldots + \lambda^{n-1} \ell n(\alpha_n Y) \\ & + \lambda^n \ell n(\beta_1 W_n) + \lambda^{n+1} \ell n[\beta_2 (1-\beta_1) W_n (1+r)] \\ & + \lambda^{n+2} \ell n[\beta_3 (1-\beta_2)(1-\beta_1) W_n (1+r)^2] \\ & + \ldots + \lambda^{T-1} \ell n[(1-\beta_1)(1-\beta_2)\ldots(1-\beta_{T-n-1}) W_n (1+r)^{T-1}]. \end{aligned} \tag{5}$$

This condition also implicitly incorporates a lifetime budget constraint. Utility may be maximized with respect to the $T-1$ propensities to consume, yielding exactly $T-1$ first-order conditions. The solutions for the α_i, obtained by mathematical induction are

$$\alpha_1 = \frac{1}{(1+r)^{n-1}} \; \frac{\sum_{j=0}^{j=n-1} (1+r)^j}{\sum_{j=0}^{j=T-1} \lambda^j}$$

and

$$\alpha_i = \alpha_1 (\lambda)^{i-1}(1+r)^{i-1} \quad .$$

The expression for α_i may also be written as

$$\alpha_i = (\lambda)^{i-1}(1+r)^{i-1} \frac{\sum_{j=1}^{j=n} \frac{1}{(1+r)^{j-1}}}{\sum_{j=1}^{j=T} \lambda^{j-1}} \quad .$$

This solution is exactly equal to the solution obtained when an additive log utility function is maximized with respect to a lifetime budget constraint without specifying an a priori consumption function.[5]

The solution for the β_i is easily obtained by maximizing the utility function with respect to the β_i and solving directly for the β_i.

In general,

$$\frac{\partial U}{\partial \beta_i} = \left[\frac{1}{\beta_i} - \sum_{t=1}^{t=T-1} \frac{\lambda^t}{1-\beta_i} \right] \qquad T > i > n$$

and the solution can be written as

$$\beta_i = \frac{1}{\sum_{t=0}^{t=T-i} \lambda^t} \quad . \tag{6}$$

This result is exactly equal to the solution obtained by Samuelson [24, 1969] for the additive log utility function when all future labor and nonlabor income is discounted into a wealth variable and a portion of wealth is consumed each period.[6]

The model as examined thus far depends only upon current income which is assumed fixed, a rather simplistic assumption. Even so, unless permitting income to vary affects the personal discount rate (λ), the propensities to spend out of assets will be unaffected. Only the propensities to spend (and save) out of income during the working life will be affected.

For example, assume, alternatively, that income grows by some constant factor (γ). The assumption that $Y_t = \gamma\, Y_{t-1}$ leads to a solution where

$$\alpha_i = \lambda^{i-1}(1+r)^{i-1} \frac{\sum_{j=1}^{j=n} \frac{\gamma^{j-1}}{(1+r)^{j-1}}}{\sum_{j=1}^{j=t} \lambda^{j-1}} \qquad i \leq n, \qquad (7)$$

and

$$\beta_i = \frac{1}{\sum_{t=0}^{t=T-i} \lambda^t} \qquad n < i \leq T\,. \qquad (8)$$

The propensity to spend out of wealth is unaffected, whereas the propensity to spend out of income is uniformly higher throughout the working life. Note that equations (5) and (7), which represent propensities to consume out of income, are also functions of the age of the individual and provide information on the age profile of saving and spending rates.

If $(1+r)\lambda > 1.0$ the MPC will tend to rise over time.

If $(1+r)\lambda < 1.0$ the MPC will tend to fall over time.

Thus the relative value of the market rate of interest to the household's rate of time preference determines whether the propensity to consume during the working life increases or decreases. The market rate of interest reflects society's rate of time preference which may differ from each individual's personal discount rate. If an individual has a higher personal discount rate than the market, that is, $(1+r)\lambda < 1.0$, the individual will tend to spend a higher portion of his income earlier in life. However, as the individual grows older and the urgency increases to meet the desired level of net worth upon retirement, the spending rate will decrease. Similarly, an individual who tends to save a higher proportion of his earlier lifetime's income will accumulate savings more rapidly and his retirement wealth will eventually exceed the targeted level unless he increases his spending rate. In this case, the spending rate will increase with age and the saving rate will decline.

The thrust of the solution may be restated in the following manner. Given the household's tastes, a certain stock of accumulated assets must be available by the end of the last day of the work life to sustain the desired consumption program planned for retirement.

What remains to be determined is the household's accumulation pattern, the savings rate profile over the working life. If the household's rate of time preference exceeds (is exceeded by) the market interest rate, early consumption will be high (low) and the saving rate will rise (fall) so as to reach the targeted level of asset accumulation by retirement. However, it ought to be noted that targeted wealth upon retirement is not independent of the household discount rate. Households with higher (lower) discount rates will also have lower (higher) targets for wealth at the end of the work phase of their lives.

For the population as a whole, personal discount rates properly weighted equal the market rate of interest. Thus, the aggregate propensity to consume could remain constant over time as long as the weighted mean discount rate of the newly born equals the mean discount rate of the dying. In this event, the aggregate propensity to save will be constant even though the propensity to save for any given household will change over its lifetime.

Upon retirement, the theory is unambiguous and indicates that dissaving rises monotonically relative to the stock of wealth. By assumption, the individual desires no end of lifetime wealth since bequests are set equal to zero. Thus the last period's consumption rate equals 100 percent to finish up without losing out on any possible additional consumption. Rewards in the next world for thrift in this world are not considered.[7]

Thus standard life cycle theory provides little information on the effects of changes in the age distribution on saving rates since saving rates depend upon individual preferences. Stated more positively, the theory indicates why little of a definitive nature emerges regarding the age profile of an individual's saving rate. The age profile of the saving rates of a household depends upon the household's discount rate compared to the market discount rate. Since the market discount rate is nothing more than a weighted average of household discount rates, weighted by saving to clear the financial market, the behavior of households with declining saving rates over time is offset by other households with increasing saving rates.

We may also wish to consider a still more general formulation in which personal discount rates may be functionally related, at least in part, to age. In this event, a shift in the age distribution of the population will clearly affect the aggregate saving rate. If older (younger) individuals have higher (lower) propensities to save and there are more older (younger) households, the aggregate saving rate will rise (fall). The nature of the relationship would be quite complex. Moreover, solving such a model would require assumptions regarding the age profile of saving, which is the presumed objective of this chapter. If saving preferences are age related, it is an empirical matter to uncover the nature of the behavior, a task to which we now turn. Since age groups may have different propensities to save in different forms, changes in the age distribution of the population may have very important implications for the distribution of saving whether or not there are also aggregate saving effects.

II. METHODOLOGY AND DATA

Survey data on saving behavior is, as noted earlier, not abundant. It is therefore not possible to construct a time series of saving data by demographic groups. However, the effect of demographic change on saving can be inferred from the available survey evidence. This may be accomplished by applying the estimates of saving behavior for demographic groups from a particular survey to the demographic structure that existed at different periods of time. In this section the methodology for these comparisons is outlined, and the surveys to be examined are briefly described.

Let R_i be the saving rate for the ith demographic group from a survey of saving behavior. Then

$$S_t = \sum_i R_i Y_{it} N_{it} ,$$

where Y_{it} is the mean income of individuals in the ith group and N_{it} is the size of the group. To estimate the effect on saving of demographic change compare S_t to $S_{t,\,t'}$ where $S_{t,\,t'}$ is the predicted level of saving at t if the demographic structure at time t' prevailed:

$$S_{t,\,t'} = \sum_i R_i Y_{it} N_{it'} \frac{N_t}{N_{t'}}$$

and $N_t = \sum_i N_{it}$. Note that $S_{t,\,t'}$ is a prediction of saving at time t using income and total population that prevailed at t, but the relative weights given to each age group are those of time t' .

We can use the ratio of S_t to $S_{t,\,t'}$ as an indication of the effect of demographic change from t' to t on saving. Results are shown with t and t' about a decade apart. If $S_t/S_{t,\,t'}$ exceeds unity, it indicates that changes in the demographic mix of the population over the decade from t' to t tended to increase aggregate saving.

Changes in the relative sizes of the demographic groups are a determinant of changes in income distribution as well. As a particular age group becomes relatively more numerous, average income within this age group may well decline relative to other age groups. In this case, changes in income distribution are caused by changes in demographic distribution. Of course, the income distribution among age groups is determined by a large variety of factors. These include secular changes in the average age of labor force entry and of retirement, and secular change in the relative productivity of persons of different ages (due to increased education and the reduced importance of physical labor). In addition, there are short-term, cyclical factors which affect the income distribution among age groups, for example, the differential incidence of unemployment.

Thus changes in income distribution can in part be attributed to changes in the demographic distribution. For example, as shown later, rapid growth in the number of young families in the 1960s led to a decline in the proportion of all family heads aged thirty-five to fifty-four from 41 percent in 1963 to 34 percent in 1974. At the same time, their mean income increased from 124 percent to 130 percent of the overall mean. That is, as prime aged family heads became relatively more scarce, their incomes increased disproportionately. This shift may indicate that older (less agile) and younger (less experienced) workers are only imperfect substitutes for the scarcer group.

If changes in the income distribution are viewed as a demographic phenomenon, another interesting calculation is the predicted level of saving at time t with both the age and income distribution that prevailed at t'. In this case, total income and total population are held to the levels which prevailed at time t while the distribution of income and population is that of period t':

$$S_{t,t'} = \sum_i R_i Y_{it'} \frac{Y_t}{Y_{t'}} N_{it'} \frac{N_t}{N_{t'}} ,$$

where Y_t is the overall mean income. Again an appropriate measure of the impact of demographic change on saving is the ratio of saving at $t(S_t)$ to what it would be if the income and age distribution of t' had prevailed ($S^*_{t,t'}$).

It is reasonable to expect that changes in the age and income distributions should be offsetting. An increase in the relative size of an age group should lead to a decline in its relative earnings. That is, when $N_{it'}/N_{t'} < N_{it}/N_t$, we expect that $Y_{it'}/Y_{t'} > Y_{it}/Y_t$. The effect on savings can be seen by writing the ratio of S_t to $S^*_{t,t'}$

$$\frac{S_t}{S^*_{t,t'}} = \frac{\sum_i R_i \frac{Y_{it}}{Y_t} Y_t \frac{N_{it}}{N_t} N_t}{\sum_i R_i \frac{Y_{it'}}{Y_{t'}} Y_t \frac{N_{it'}}{N_{t'}} N_t} .$$

Since age and income distribution effects tend to be offsetting, demographic effects on saving when taken alone tend to be larger than when age and income distribution effects are considered simultaneously.

Not only is the income distribution subject to short-run cyclical variation, but so are the saving rates themselves. This would not be a problem for the analysis suggested if the cyclical variation in the aggregate level of saving were evenly distributed across age groups. However, this is clearly not the case. For example, an increase in aggregate saving due to a housing boom could increase the saving rate of young families more than proportionately. If saving rates from a survey taken at that time are used for our demographic comparisons, too much emphasis will be given to the influence of change in the relative number of young families. The lack of any reliable panel data on saving rates by age groups makes it impossible to calculate the differential impact of cyclical variation in saving.[8]

In order to test the sensitivity of our conclusions on the effect of demographic change to the point in the cycle at which the survey of saving took place, we can make some assumptions about the potential impact of cyclical phenomena on the saving rates of age groups. That is, the R_i can be adjusted judgmentally to reflect changed cyclical conditions, and the demographic comparisons may then be reestimated. This simulation exercise provides some indication of the robustness of the results on demographic effects.

The same procedure will be used to correct the data on saving for survey response error. It is well known that saving surveys are subject to large response errors, particularly for certain saving categories.[9] Comparison of aggregate saving from survey data with flow of funds (FOF) data indicates that the survey response error is often a serious problem. For certain savings categories (e.g., savings deposits) the FOF data from institutional sources are likely to be more accurate and the frequently observed discrepancy with survey data can be attributed to response error.[10] In these cases the discrepancy is judgmentally distributed among age groups and the adjusted R_i used to reestimate the demographic effects. It should be noted that, in other cases, the survey data might well be more accurate (e.g., net investment in noncorporate investment or in equities) and discrepancies could just as well be due to the arbitrariness of sectoral allocations in the FOF data.

In recent years there has been relatively little professional interest in cross-sectional budget studies and consumption functions because of the paucity of recent survey data on saving. The reason for this is that earlier experience indicated that it is very difficult to collect reliable data. In the early postwar period the Board of Governors sponsored the surveys conducted by the Survey Research Center, but concluded that reliable information necessitated a sample size that would be prohibitively expensive since sampling and response errors were often quite large.

The only comprehensive surveys of wealth and saving in the past twenty years are the 1962–63 surveys conducted by the Board of Governors of the Federal Reserve System—the Survey of Financial Characteristics of Consumers [22, 1966] and the Survey of Changes in Family Finances (SCFF) [21, 1968]. Two additional surveys will also be analyzed: these are the 1960–61 and 1972–73 Consumer Expenditure Surveys [29, 1965; 30, 1977] conducted by the Bureau of Labor Statistics. Although these surveys provide extensive data on consumption expenditures, the data on saving flows are less comprehensive. The saving rates from these surveys are applied to the demographic and income distribution data from other years. These latter data are taken from the Current Population Survey of the Bureau of the Census [26, 1977]. Using the methodology developed above, comparisons are made in the next section for selected years approximately a decade apart.

To begin, we examine the extent to which the age and income distribution have changed and are projected to change in the postwar period. Table 9–1 shows the percentage distribution of families and unrelated individuals by age of head from 1947 to 1985. The major features to be noted are the steady increase in the relative number of older households and the large increase in young households. The proportion of families between ages thirty-five and sixty-four, the

Table 9–1. Age Distribution of Families and Unrelated Individuals

Age of Head:	*14–24*	*25–34*	*35–44*	*45–54*	*55–64*	*65 +*
1947	0.0587	0.2023	0.2188	0.2064	0.1666	0.1473
1950	0.0598	0.2050	0.2166	0.2027	0.1675	0.1485
1955	0.0545	0.1946	0.2169	0.1994	0.1666	0.1680
1960	0.0605	0.1827	0.2125	0.2035	0.1659	0.1749
1965	0.0697	0.1718	0.2017	0.1995	0.1657	0.1916
1970	0.0861	0.1849	0.1790	0.1907	0.1665	0.1929
1975	0.0973	0.2147	0.1634	0.1722	0.1561	0.1962
1985	0.1155	0.2145	0.1887	0.1393	0.1428	0.1992

Sources: U.S. Bureau of the Census [26, 1977; 27, 1967]. The 1985 forecast uses U.S. Bureau of the Census [28, 1975] series B forecast for primary families and individuals and assumes that the age distribution for secondary individuals (about 3.4 percent of the total) is the same as in 1974.

Table 9–2. Relative Mean Earnings of Families and Unrelated Individuals

Age of Head:	*14–24*	*25–34*	*35–44*	*45–54*	*55–64*	*65 +*
1947	0.54	0.81	0.97	1.00	0.89	0.60
1950	0.55	0.86	1.01	1.00	0.88	0.55
1955	0.55	0.82	0.94	1.00	0.84	0.53
1960	0.53	0.85	1.01	1.00	0.83	0.50
1965	0.55	0.83	0.96	1.00	0.80	0.47
1970	0.47	0.79	0.95	1.00	0.82	0.42
1975	0.41	0.75	0.94	1.00	0.81	0.45

Sources: Same as Table 9-1.

prime years for saving, declines from 59 percent in 1947 to 49 percent in 1975. However, by the end of the period the postwar baby boom population bulge begins to enter the saving years. These movements in population are fairly complex. For example, in the next decade, there will be no growth in the size of the oldest category, continued growth in the size of the youngest groups, and a leveling off in the decline in the middle group (as the baby boom reaches middle age). The net impact on saving is clearly not obvious.

The income distribution data are shown in Table 9–2 as ratios to mean incomes for those aged forty-five to fifty-four. The major changes—for the youngest and oldest age groups—are due primarily to shifts in the average age of labor force entry and in the average age at retirement.

The common wisdom on demographic effects is that the growth of the old and young age groups, both of which save little, should depress saving. However, lower aggregate saving may not result from the growth of groups with low saving rates if changes in the distribution of income provide a countervailing influence. For example, as the young become a relatively abundant group in the labor force, their earnings may decline relative to others. Thus their lower saving rates would receive a lesser weight in determining aggregate saving. Similarly, earlier retirement combined with longer life expectancy depresses the relative earnings of the old as their numbers have increased.

III. ANALYSIS OF SURVEY DATA

Evidence from Survey of Changes in Family Finances

The Survey of Changes in Family Finances (SCFF) [21, 1968] provides a rather complete breakdown of saving by type of asset.

Saving as a proportion of total 1963 income, for each asset type, by age group, calculated from the entire SCFF sample of 2,159 observations, is shown in Table 9–3.[11] No attempt is made to correct for systematic errors or to exclude potentially unreliable data. The analysis of these data is followed by analyses which attempt to adjust for the various data problems.

For most of the asset categories the pattern of saving rates over age groups is consistent with our expectations. Fortunately, the exceptions are usually for categories which are only a small part of total saving and often for the fifty-five to sixty-four age group.[12] There are also several categories with aggregate SCFF saving rates substantially different from the flow of funds (FOF) estimates. Categories for which FOF data from institutional sources are probably more accurate estimates of aggregate saving are insurance, installment debt, and savings accounts.[13] Another category with a substantial discrepancy between the survey and the FOF is housing expenditures. Here the survey reports substantially more saving, probably because the FOF and the income accounts underestimate additions and alterations to owner-occupied housing. For some other categories where there are discrepancies between survey and FOF savings rates, it is unclear which is in error (e.g., business assets).

In Table 9–4, the ratios of S_t to $S_{t,t'}$ and $S^*_{t,t'}$ (i.e., the ratio of saving in t to saving in t with the age or age and income distributions of t') are shown for three decade-to-decade changes. The first set of numbers reflect only the changes in the age distribution while the second set reflect both age and income distribution changes. When saving is positive, a ratio greater than one indicates that had the demographic distribution of time t' continued to prevail at time t, saving would have declined. Thus, the changed age distribution contributed to an increased level of saving. For debt categories where saving is negative, $S_t/S_{t,t'} > 1$ implies that there is more debt acquisition or dissaving.

The major implication of these numbers is that changes in the age structure, 1954 to 1985, depress total saving by about 3 percent per decade. This is seen in the last row of Table 9–4. Saving in 1963 is 2.6 percent less than it would have been with 1954 age distribution. This effect was about the same in the next decade and is projected to continue. However, this depressing effect of age structure is virtually completely offset by changes in the income distribution among age groups. If changes in the income distribution are attributed to demographic change, there is virtually no demographic effect on total saving from 1954 to 1985.

Other interesting results relate to the effects on the components of total saving. Here we emphasize the effects of changes in the age

Table 9–3. SCFF Saving as a Percent of Total Income

Age of Head:	*< 35*	*35–44*	*45–54*	*55–64*	*65 +*	*All*
Total Assets	6.56	5.84	8.04	3.51	5.98	6.17
Business assets	1.75	–0.57	1.21	–1.92	1.43	0.36
Liquid assets	–0.10	3.58	6.33	3.78	5.46	3.73
Checking deposits	0.12	0.28	0.83	0.74	0.98	0.54
Saving accounts	–0.35	3.01	4.49	2.60	4.26	2.74
Saving bonds	0.13	0.29	1.01	0.43	0.22	0.46
Investment assets	4.37	2.19	–.62	1.12	–1.01	1.41
Miscellaneous assets	0.05	–0.11	0.07	–0.50	–0.18	–0.10
Retirement assets	0.50	0.76	1.05	1.03	0.28	0.77
Total Debt	–14.84	–3.25	2.99	0.39	–4.75	–3.64
Home	–12.77	–3.49	2.42	0.38	0.62	–2.85
Investment	–1.91	1.23	–0.20	0.27	–5.07	–0.62
Personal	0.16	–0.97	0.78	–0.35	–0.42	–0.12
Installment	0.46	0.52	0.99	–0.69	0.66	0.44
Auto	–0.09	0.49	0.67	–0.29	0.10	0.24
Nonauto	0.55	0.03	0.33	–0.40	0.56	0.20
Noninstallment	–0.30	–1.49	–0.21	0.34	–1.08	–0.55
Life insurance	–0.32	–0.02	–0.02	0.09	0.12	–0.05
Housing Expenditures	19.52	6.34	2.43	3.65	–2.23	6.79
Auto Expenditures	6.24	5.25	4.83	5.90	2.28	5.16
Net Financial Investment	–8.27	2.59	11.03	3.90	1.23	2.53
Total Saving	17.49	14.19	18.29	13.45	1.28	14.47

Sources: Calculated from SCFF data tape (N = 2,159). Income is the total income received in the calendar year by all members of the consumer unit before any payroll or income tax deductions.

Table 9–4. Effect of Age and Income Distribution Changes on Saving

	Age Distribution Only $S_t/S_{t,t'}$			Age and Income Distribution $S_t/S^*_{t,t'}$		
t	*1963*	*1974*	*1985*	*1963*	*1974*	*1985*
t'	*1954*	*1963*	*1974*	*1954*	*1963*	*1974*
Assets						
Total Financial	0.984	0.972	0.975	0.998	1.001	0.986
Business and miscellaneous	0.866	2.024	0.960	0.906	1.512	0.855
Liquid assets	1.028	0.871	0.925	1.035	0.933	0.955
Checking accounts	1.039	0.909	0.923	1.030	0.974	0.953
Saving accounts	1.023	0.861	0.931	1.035	0.922	0.962
Saving bonds	1.017	0.889	0.893	1.040	0.945	0.922
Investment assets	0.900	1.153	1.106	0.922	1.108	1.089
Retirement assets	0.997	0.917	0.951	1.019	0.937	1.064
Housing Expenditure	0.921	1.147	1.050	0.941	1.113	1.038
Automobile Expenditure	0.977	0.976	0.989	0.990	1.006	1.004
Liabilities						
Total	0.897	1.333	1.127	0.895	1.230	1.088
Home	0.869	1.347	1.144	0.885	1.221	1.100
Investment	1.061	1.387	1.005	0.942	1.353	0.978
Personal	0.912	0.646	1.805	0.884	0.691	1.828
Life insurance	0.819	1.591	1.108	0.867	1.328	1.044
Net Financial Investment	1.141	0.573	0.636	1.195	0.677	0.719
Total Saving	0.974	0.970	0.973	0.996	0.998	0.988

structure alone. Total financial asset acquisitions are reduced by about 2 percent per decade by demographic change. These changes are small because acquisitions of liquid assets and of investment assets are affected in opposite directions. In the first decade, increases in liquid asset saving are offset by declines in investment assets, while in the next two decades this pattern is reversed. Over the coming decade, the results suggest that demographic changes depress liquid asset saving by about 7.5 percent and increase saving in the form of direct acquisitions of credit market instruments by more than 10 percent.

Demographic change also has a strong impact on housing expenditure. Over the 1963–74 decade housing expenditures were increased by 15 percent from the levels which would have prevailed with the 1963 age distribution, and a further 5 percent increase is projected by 1985. Thus, *ceteris paribus*, housing expenditure would be 20 percent higher than implied by the age distribution of 1963 or 10 percent higher than implied by the age distribution of 1954. These changes are mirrored by similarly large changes on the debt side. The increase in mortgate debt will in 1985 be 54 percent higher than implied by the 1973 age distribution or 34 percent higher than suggested by the 1954 age distribution, due to the shifting demographic structure.

The strongest implications are seen by looking at net financial investment, which in 1985 will be only 36 percent of the level implied by the 1963 age distribution or 42 percent with a 1954 comparison, due to shifts in the age structure. Net financial investment is probably the most significant saving concept for any discussion of the role of the personal sector in national capital formation (see [33, Wachtel, Sametz and Shuford, 1976; 32, Wachtel, 1980]). It is a measure of the saving of the household sector available to finance the external deficits of the business and government sectors. In this sense, the household sector can be viewed as a contributor to the problem of an emerging capital shortage. Although demographic shifts leave the overall level of household capital formation virtually unaffected, they severely reduce the surplus of resources made available to other sectors of the economy.

Robustness of Results with SCFF Data

As noted earlier, the reliability of these results can be questioned on several grounds. First, the aggregate SCFF saving ratios do differ from those in the FOF data, and saving surveys are generally subject to serious response errors. Second, use of the SCFF saving rates extrapolates the cyclical experience of 1962–63 into the long run. If the composition of saving varies over the business cycle, the conclusions drawn may not be broadly applicable to all phases of the cycle, nor need they be representative of the business cycle mean. In this section the robustness of the estimates of demographic effects on saving is investigated. The demographic effects are reestimated with three alternative sets of corrections of the saving rates. Corrections are made first by using estimates of survey response errors; second, by excluding potentially unreliable observations from the calculation of saving rates; and third, by adjusting the saving rates for alternative cyclical influences.

The problem of response error in the SCFF survey has been examined by Alexander Korns [18, 1973].[14] In addition, Projector [21, 1968] compared aggregate saving in 1962–63 from the FOF with the aggregates implied by the SCFF survey. In several instances underreporting of both assets and saving are indicated. Unfortunately, there is no evidence on the distribution of underreporting by age group.[15] Even if our estimates of underreporting are applied proportionately across age groups, the estimates of demographic effects could be changed, as there are enormous differences by saving component of the incidence of underreporting and the patterns of saving rates for the components differ by age group as well. Thus the corrections will alter the weights applied to the disparate components of saving, even if the pattern of saving by age group for each component is taken as reported in the SCFF.

Judgmental adjustments are made for the saving rates for demand deposits, savings accounts investment assets, home mortgages, and personal debt. Recalculations of the demographic effects are summarized in Table 9–5 and the note to the table explains each adjustment for apparent underreporting. The overall pattern of results is the same as in Table 9–4. However, with the adjusted data the depressing influence of demographic changes on saving in the 1963–74 decade is somewhat larger. Generally, the differences in demographic effects from decade to decade are larger with the adjusted data. The strongest effects are in the 1963 to 1974 decade, where demographic change had the strongest effects on both asset and liability acquisitions. In the decade ending in 1985, similar but somewhat weaker effects are expected. Thus these procedures suggest, if anything, even greater demographic effects than implied by the unadjusted saving rates.

An alternative correction for survey response error is suggested by Friend and Lieberman [15, 1975] and is also used by Clotfelter and Lieberman [5, 1978]. In their analysis of saving functions estimated with the SCFF survey data, Friend and Lieberman argue that the

Table 9–5. Effect on Saving of Changes in the Age Distribution ($S_t/S_{t,t'}$) When Saving Rates Are Corrected for Underreporting

t / t'	1963 / 1954	1974 / 1963	1985 / 1974
Total Financial Assets	1.001	0.931	0.962
Total Debt	0.931	1.190	1.077
Net Financial Investment	1.153	0.565	0.672
Total Saving	0.986	0.934	0.961

Summary of Corrections. a. Demand deposits: saving rates increased by 20 percent based on discrepancy between FOF and SCFF aggregates; b. Saving accounts: saving rates for < 25 group set to zero and others approximately doubled. Reported assets and saving flows from survey are both about one-half of Korns's and FOF's estimates; c. Bond and mortgage component of investment assets: aggregate saving flow doubled in survey as FOF saving flow is 3.5 times as large as survey and Korns reports asset underreporting of about one-third; d. Mortgage debt: increase all dissaving rates to raise total by 30 percent, to the FOF level; e. Personal debt: change saving rates for installment debt so that they are consistent with FOF totals. Survey aggregate is –$1.6 billion saving while FOF reports –$6.1 (dissaving or increase in debt); f. Physical assets: survey saving rates left unchanged, although it indicates substantially more housing expenditure than the FOF; g. Saving bonds: survey saving rates left unchanged because evidence is unclear. Korns indicates asset underreporting while comparison with the FOF indicates saving overreporting; h. Business assets: unchanged although SCFF aggregate ($3.3 billion) is much larger than FOF net investment noncorporate business (–$6.2 billion). It is not clear whether the FOF residual calculation is reliable.

respondents with suspiciously unreliable data should be eliminated from the sample. Furthermore, with their restricted samples, the discrepancy between aggregate saving from the FOF data and from the survey is reduced.[16] The calculations of demographic effect on saving should then be examined using saving rates calculated from restricted samples.

In Table 9–6 the demographic effects on some aggregate savings definitions are shown for two restricted samples. In the first case the sample is restricted to those respondents whose income in 1963 exceeds 3 percent of financial net wealth. In the second case, the sample is further reduced to exclude individuals whose mean income in 1962 and 1963 is less than $1,000 or those for whom the absolute value of saving exceeds income.[17] The aggregate levels of saving and net financial investment are not changed very much when the sample is restricted, although the level of income is increased substantially.[18]

As can be readily seen by comparison of Table 9–6 with Table 9–4, restricting the SCFF sample in order to improve the aggregate saving forecasts leaves the estimates of the influence of demographic change on saving essentially the same. Only the magnitudes of the

Table 9–6. Effect on Saving of Changes in the Age Distribution $(S_t/S_{t,t'})$ **Using Restricted Samples**

t	*1963*	*1974*	*1985*
t'	*1954*	*1963*	*1974*
	One Restriction:[a]		
Net Financial Investment	1.118	0.672	0.737
Total Saving	0.980	0.968	0.969
	Three Restrictions:[b]		
Net Financial Investment	1.287	0.524	0.598
Total Saving	0.996	0.969	0.968

[a] 1963 income exceeds 3 percent of financial net worth.

[b] Restriction in note a, or mean 1962–63 income greater than $1,000 or absolute value of saving exceeds income.

decade-to-decade changes in net financial investment are sensitive to changes in the sample. Changes in the age structure tended to increase net financial investment in the 1950s and to decrease it substantially in the ensuing decade. For total saving, the slight depressing effect of demographic change is about the same with the restricted samples as with the full sample.

The second question applied to our methodology was whether demographic effects are sensitive to the cyclical variation in saving rates. If cyclical changes in saving affected all components in the same manner, the issue would be of no importance. But just as underreporting is distributed unequally among saving components with different demographic saving patterns, the cyclical responsiveness of saving rates differs. Furthermore, we would expect that the cyclical responses of different demographic groups might differ as well. Unfortunately, no direct evidence is available on this latter issue. To test for the importance of cyclical response we can adjust the saving rates for each component to reflect differing cyclical conditions and retain the distribution among age groups indicated by the SCFF survey.

The importance of the cyclical responsiveness of saving in the period 1954–77 is shown in Table 9–7. Saving rates in recession years are compared to those in expansion years. Total saving is virtually the same in both periods, but the composition differs greatly. Recession years are characterized by about 10 percent less asset acquisitions (financial and physical) and substantially less dissaving in the form of liabilities than in the expansion years. The SCFF survey was conducted in 1962–63, when the allocation of the aggregate saving data was very much comparable to a typical expansion year. It is only necessary to compare our original results to a situation more typical of a recession year to judge the sensitivity of the conclusions about demographic change.

In Table 9–8 the age effect on saving is shown with the survey saving rate adjusted to reflect a recession situation. The specifics of the adjustment, which are based on Table 9–7, are given in the note to Table 9–8. Again, the basic conclusions about demographic effects are unchanged. However, the depressing effects of demographic change on net financial investment and total saving are substantially reduced when saving is distributed as in recessions. This is largely due to the reduction in borrowing in recessions and to the fact that much of the borrowing is done by the youngest age group whose weight in the total has been growing.

Saving and Family Structure

There are other forms of demographic change taking place in the economy which affect the saving rate as well. It is not possible to

Table 9–7. The Distribution of Saving in Recession and Expansion Years

	Recessions	*Expansions*	*1962–63*
Physical Investment	58.4%	67.6%	70.1%
Financial Assets	69.9	76.7	74.7
Liabilities	−28.3	−44.3	−44.8
Total	100.0	100.0	100.0

Source: Calculated from FOF household sector account for net acquisitions of financial assets, net increase in liabilities, and physical investment is FOF household sector residential construction expenditures plus gross auto product, personal consumption expenditures from the NIPA. Recession years are those in which real gross domestic product decreased (1954, 1958, 1970, 1974 and 1975) and expansion years are those in which it increased by more than 5.5 percent (1955, 1959, 1962, 1965, 1960, 1972 and 1976).

Table 9–8. Effect of Age Distribution Changes on Saving $(S_t/S_{t,t'})$ in "Recession" Years

t t'	*1963* *1954*	*1974* *1963*	*1985* *1974*
Net Financial Investment	1.076	0.724	0.789
Total Saving	0.971	0.983	0.978

Note: Saving rates are changed to reflect the differences between recession and expansion shown in Table 9-7. That is, dissaving in liabilities is reduced by 36 percent, saving in financial assets is reduced by 9 percent, and physical investment is reduced by 14 percent.

examine all of them, but a casual glance at saving rates indicates that differences in saving behavior by family type are important. That is, the relative numbers of families and "unrelated individuals" have changed substantially in the postwar period. These groups have very different saving rates and the increase in the proportion of unrelated individuals in the population could affect total saving.

Per dollar of income, unrelated individuals purchase more financial assets, less housing, and incur less debt than family units. Their total saving rate is about the same, but their net financial investment rate is much larger. Aggregate saving could be affected by these differences because the proportion of unrelated individuals in the population has increased steadily in the postwar period, from 18.7 percent in 1954 to 25.3 percent in 1974 and 26.6 percent in 1985. The effects of these changes on saving are summarized in Table 9–9, which uses the same methodology developed for the age comparisons. Total saving is virtually unaffected. The increased proportion of unrelated individuals increases financial asset acquisitions and reduces debt. As a result, the effect on net financial investment is substantial. Interestingly enough, the changing family structure has an effect on saving which partially offsets the effects of changes in the age composition.[19] The offset is only partial and our estimates still indicate that in the last decade demographic shifts have reduced net financial investment by at least 20 percent below what they otherwise would have been.

Evidence from Consumer Expenditures Surveys

The Consumer Expenditure Surveys (CES) conducted by the Bureau of Labor Statistics [29, 1965; 30, 1977] are another source of data on the saving patterns of households. The survey design is geared to providing detailed expenditure information, and consequently the quality of the saving data is poor. The data must be interpreted with care, as there tends to be serious underreporting of certain items.[20] Nevertheless, the data are worth examining for two

Table 9–9. Effect on Saving of Changes in Family Structure

	t / *t'*	*1963* / *1954*	*1974* / *1963*	*1985* / *1974*
Financial Assets		1.000	1.016	1.003
Total Debt		0.997	0.909	0.979
Net Financial Investment		1.005	1.150	1.027
Total Saving		1.000	1.006	1.001

reasons. First, the CES is an alternative source of saving data from a large national sample. Second, the CES is conducted periodically and therefore comparable data are obtainable from surveys at different points in time. The two most recent surveys were in 1960–61 and 1972–73. The first is about contemporaneous with the SCFF and the second will indicate whether there have been any shifts in saving patterns.[21]

The CES definitions of saving are not directly comparable with the SCFF or FOF data. However, the 1960–61 and 1972–73 CES are basically the same. The CES definition of saving is the difference between net asset change and net liability change. Assets include deposits, stocks and bonds, money owed to the unit, dwelling occupied, other dwellings and land, unincorporated business (including farms). Liabilities include all money owed to creditors. Saving as a percent of before-tax income is shown in Figure 9–1 and the data are given in Table 9–10. The patterns are broadly similar in the two surveys. The major difference is that in 1972–73 there were more asset acquisitions by all age groups and also more borrowing by the young.

The methodology developed in Section II to examine the effect of demographic change on saving can be applied to these data. In order to facilitate comparisons, the same decade-to-decade comparisons used with the SCFF data are reported here. Furthermore, the Current Population Survey (CPS) data on the age distribution and incomes of families and unrelated individuals are used.[22] Thus the primary differences between the analysis with CES and SCFF data are differences in the surveys regarding the definition and measurement of saving.

Table 9–11 presents the calculated effects on saving of changes in the age and income distributions using saving rates from the two CES surveys. The calculations shown are the same as those presented with the SCFF data. The ratio of S_t to $S_{t,t'}$ is the ratio of saving in period t to a prediction of saving in period t if the age distribution of t' had prevailed, and $S^*_{t,t'}$ is a prediction with the age and income distribution of t'. In the CES, total assets include financial assets and property, but retirement assets are excluded. The changing demographic structure depresses asset acquisitions in the first decade and leaves them unchanged in the next two decades. Over all three decade comparisons, the changing income distribution tends to increase asset acquisitions. A rough averaging of the results for total financial assets and housing with the SCFF reveals exactly the same picture. Liability increases are also decreased in the decade from 1954 to 1963, but in the subsequent decades the effect of age and income distribution changes are to substantially increase this form of dissaving. The magnitudes of these effects are not as large as they appear to be with the SCFF data.

Figure 9–1. Saving Rates from the 1960–61 and 1972–73 Consumer Expenditure Surveys

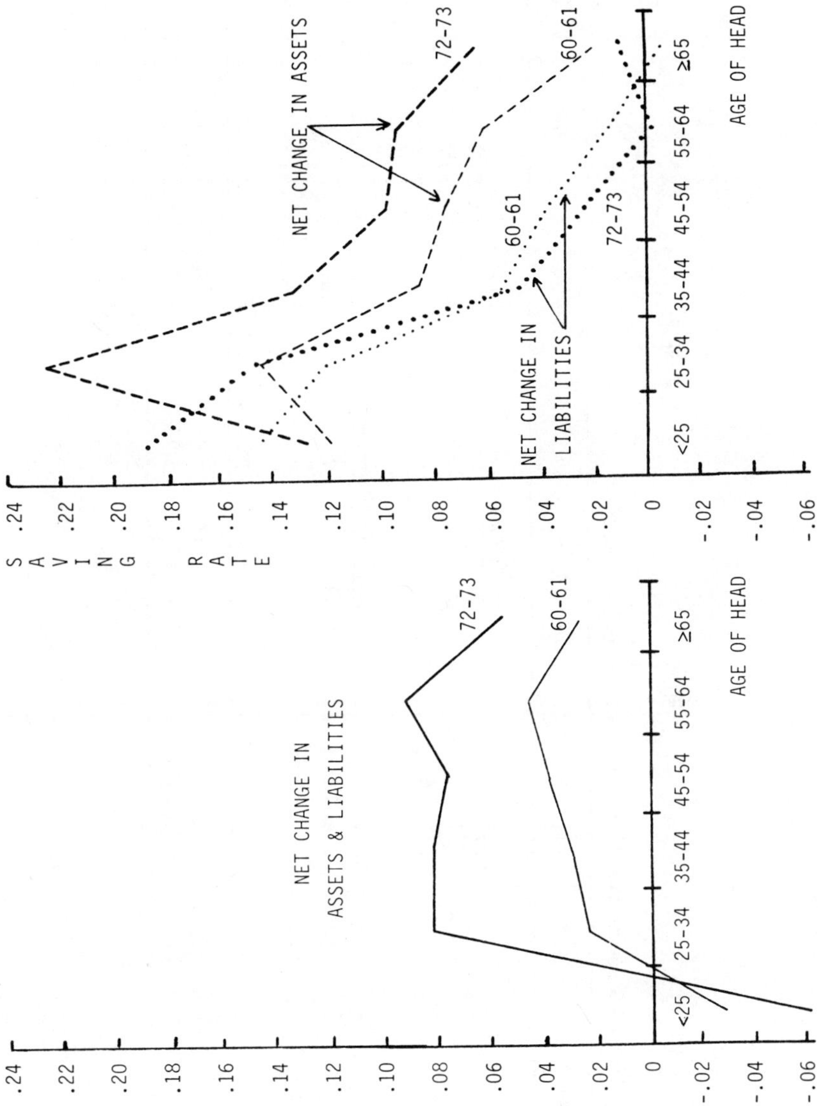

Table 9–10. CES Saving as a Percent of Before-Tax Income

Age of Head:	< 25	25–34	35–44	45–54	55–64	> 65	*Total*
Survey				*Net Changes in Assets and Liabilities*			
1960–61	–2.56%	2.50%	3.02%	3.98%	4.71%	2.72%	3.19%
1972–73	–5.92	8.36	8.18	7.75	9.37	5.62	7.22
				Net Changes in Assets			
1960–61	11.90	14.54	8.39	7.52	5.99	2.00	8.39
1972–73	12.90	22.59	13.13	9.84	9.22	6.30	12.82
				Net Changes in Liabilities			
1960–61	14.46	12.05	5.38	3.53	1.28	–0.72	5.20
1972–73	18.82	14.61	4.99	2.09	–0.15	0.68	5.60

Table 9–11. Effect of Age and Income Distribution on Saving from the CES

	$S_t/S_{t,\,t'}$ Age Distribution Only			$S_t/S^*_{t,\,t'}$ Age and Income Distribution		
t	*1963*	*1974*	*1985*	*1963*	*1974*	*1985*
t'	*1954*	*1963*	*1974*	*1954*	*1963*	*1974*
1960–61 CES						
Total Assets	0.961	1.004	0.992	0.976	1.032	1.011
Total Liabilities	0.953	1.060	1.023	0.961	1.076	1.024
Net Saving	0.974	0.918	0.939	1.001	0.961	0.988
1972–73 CES						
Total Assets	0.961	1.000	0.996	0.975	1.027	1.019
Total Liabilities	0.955	1.110	1.045	0.953	1.114	1.036
Net Saving	0.964	0.929	0.959	0.990	0.969	1.007

Table 9–12. Age Effect on Saving $(S_t/S_{t,t'})$ with 1960–61 CES

t / t'	*1963* / *1954*	*1974* / *1963*	*1985* / *1974*
Financial Assets	0.936	0.897	0.919
Deposits	1.637	0.839	1.022
Stocks and bonds	0.992	0.938	0.949
Miscellaneous[a]	0.607	0.707	0.648
Financial Liabilities	0.954	1.068	1.025
Home mortgage	0.947	1.117	1.036
Installment debt	0.971	0.991	1.007
Other debt	0.957	1.003	1.005
Home Purchase	0.961	1.035	1.009
Net Financial Investment[b]	1.053	0.865	0.934

[a] Includes net-investment in noncorporate business.
[b] See text for explanation.

Net saving as measured by the two CES surveys is reduced substantially by changes in the age distribution, by about 3 percent in the first decade, 8 percent in the next, and 5 percent in the forecast to 1985. These results are all larger than those with the SCFF (where total saving includes automobile expenditures and retirement assets). However, as in the SCFF, changes in the income distribution virtually offset the declines due to a changing age distribution.

A more detailed breakdown of the asset and liability categories is available for the 1960–61 CES. The effect of a changing age distribution on the components of saving is shown in Table 9–12, with an accounting scheme that roughly corresponds to that found in the flow of funds.

In the case of net financial investment, an ambiguity in the interpretation of the ratio $S_t/S_{t,t'}$ arises. Because of serious underreporting of some asset categories, particularly savings deposits, net financial investment is negative with the CES data. If a changing age distribution reduced net financial investment, S_t would be a larger negative number than $S_{t,t'}$ and the ratio would be greater than 1. Since aggregate household net financial investment is normally positive, the reciprocal of the ratio is shown in Table 9–12 for this category. Thus the results suggest that changes in the age structure tended to increase net financial investment in the decade ending in 1963 and to depress it in the next two decades.

A major difference between these results with the 1960–61 CES and those with the SCFF is that the age effects on financial liabilities are smaller with the CES. A changing age structure reduced borrowing in the 1954–63 decade, increased it substantially in the next decade, and is forecasted to increase it somewhat less in the next decade. Both the CES and SCFF data indicate that the effect on liabilities is almost entirely due to home mortgages.

There are also differences between the two surveys for the age distribution effect on financial asset change, although they are in substantial agreement for housing investment. The financial asset results from the CES are suspect because of substantial underreporting of asset increases.[23]

The primary inadequacy of the CES saving data is clearly the underreporting of acquisitions of cash and bank deposits, a problem which was also encountered with the SCFF data. In the SCFF data there is also underreporting of debt increases which are not apparent in the CES. For this reason, the age effects on liabilities which are more moderate with the CES data may also be considered more reliable. It is difficult to say which data set provides better information on financial asset holding. This leaves an important problem because the age effect on net financial investment is sensitive to these differences in the data. However, the direction and relative magnitude of the age effects are the same in each decade comparison for the two data sources. The CES results indicate a much more moderate depressing effect of age distribution changes on net financial investment in the 1960s and 1970s—about 10 percent per decade as opposed to 40 percent.

Before moving on to an examination of the time series data, we should make note of a study by Eizenga [7, 1961] of age effects on saving which uses the 1950 CES survey. Total saving in that survey is defined as in the more recent CES surveys. Eizenga compares saving rates in 1900 and 1950; using our methodology: $S_{1950}/S_{1950,\,1900}$ = 1.073. That is, changes in the age structure increased saving by over 7 percent in the first half of the century.[24] Eizenga also analyzes other demographic effects and concludes that saving rates would have increased substantially, primarily because of decreases in average family size. Given changes in social structure, the use of 1950 family size differences in saving with 1900 data probably distorts his results. Nevertheless, the age effect above is of interest for two reasons. First, it suggests that the age effects in postwar decades have been large relative to the size of age effects in earlier decades. Second, our findings suggest that the depressing effect of a changing age distribution on saving since the war reverses the trend of the previous half century.

IV. TIME SERIES MODEL

As noted in the previous section, there are a number of good reasons to be skeptical about time series conclusions drawn from cross-section data. Therefore it is of interest to see if the issue of demographic effects can be addressed with aggregate time series data.[25] Since most economists base their understanding of consumption behavior on time series econometric evidence, a study which examines the effects of demographic change with that data would be useful. In this section a model is developed which can be used to infer demographic effects directly from the available time series data.

Using a model developed by Blinder [3, 1975] for the study of income distribution effects, the Current Population Survey (CPS) annual data on age structure and income distribution can be used to estimate the effects of demographic structure on saving. The model is summarized briefly and then the estimates are presented. Their implications for aggregate saving behavior are then discussed, along with a comparison with our earlier results using cross-sectional data.

The model is a basic permanent income consumption function, where permanent income (Y^P) is approximated by a Koyck distributed lag on past income. The consumption function for the ith age group is

$$C_{it} = \alpha_i + \beta_i Y_{it}^P + U_{it} .$$

Permanent income for each age group is given by

$$Y_{it}^P = (1-\lambda)(Y_{it} + \lambda Y_{i,t-1} + \lambda^2 Y_{i,t-2} + \ldots).$$

It is assumed that the distributed lag coefficient, λ, is the same for each age group. The model can then be written as:

$$C_{it} = \alpha_i(1-\lambda) + \beta_i(1-\lambda)Y_{it} + \lambda C_{i,t-1} + (U_{it} - \lambda U_{i,t-1}) .$$

Summing over the age group yields

$$C_t = \alpha + (1-\lambda)\ \Sigma\beta_i Y_{it} + \lambda C_{t-1} + v_t ,$$

where $C_t = \Sigma_i C_{it}$, $\alpha = \Sigma_i(1-\lambda)\alpha_i$ and $v_t = \Sigma_i[U_{it} - \lambda U_{i,t-1}]$.

For estimation, the equation is put in ratio form:

$$\frac{C_t}{Y_t} = \alpha\frac{1}{Y_t} + (1-\lambda)\sum_i \beta_i \frac{Y_{it}}{Y_t} + \lambda\frac{C_{t-1}}{Y_t} + v_t' .$$

C_t and Y_t are aggregate consumption and income, respectively, and Y_{it}/Y_t is the share of the ith age group in aggregate income. The model is specified in this form because consumption data by age group are not available, although income data are found in the CPS. Note that the sum of the income shares is one. The ratio form is likely to remove any heteroscedasticity of the errors, v', which are, as specified, still likely to be serially correlated. The equation is therefore estimated with the Cochrane-Orcutt technique, assuming first-order serial correlation of the errors. The coefficient of serial correlation is given by ρ.

The strongest assumption imposed on this model is that the process generating the permanent income proxy is the same for each age group. For cross-section data, this assumption would clearly be indefensible. Individuals of different ages would surely have different planning horizons. However, for time series data we only assume that past income fluctuations are smoothed to generate aggregate expectations in the same way by the different groups.

The income shares data are from the Current Population Survey [26, 1977; 27, 1967]. Since 1947, the survey has, on an annual basis, collected data on the income and size of demographic groups. The data presented in the published sources are the mean income by age class for families and unrelated individuals. The income share of the ith age class is defined as $y_i / \Sigma_i y_i$, where $y_i = N_i^F \bar{y}_i^F + N_i^U \bar{y}_i^U$ and $\bar{y}_i^F$ is the mean income of the N_i^F families in the age class and N_i^U and $\bar{y}_i^U$ are defined similarly for unrelated individuals.[26]

Data for income and consumption are taken from two sources: The Federal Reserve-MIT-Pennsylvania (FMP) model databank and the National Income and Product Accounts (NIPA). The FMP data utilize a consumption services concept and a consistent definition of disposable income. The standard definitions of personal consumption expenditures and disposable income are taken from the NIPA.

Estimates of the consumption function with FMP data are found in Table 9–13 and with the NIPA data in Table 9–14. In each table equation (1) is the basic model without any demographic variables. The constant term is the short-term marginal propensity to consume (MPC). Equation (2) adds the income shares for the six age groups, denoted by $X_1, \ldots, X_6$. Their coefficients are the short-run MPC

Table 9–13. Regression Estimates of Consumption Function, FMP Data, 1949–75

Equation:	*(1)*	*(2)*	*(3)*	*(4)*[c]
Constant	0.59 (13.9)[a]			
$1/Y$	101.6 (3.1)	−23.2 (2.9)	−2.9 (1.1)	−4.1 (1.7)
C_{t-1}/Y	0.25 (3.8)	0.47 (10.2)	0.53 (11.3)	0.50 (11.5)
X_1[b]		−0.13 (0.3)	0.18 (3.2)	0.16 (3.7)
X_2		0.41 (3.2)		
X_3		0.97 (6.9)	0.52 (10.0)	0.57 (11.4)
X_4		0.05 (0.3)		
X_5		0.89 (5.0)		
X_6		0.61 (3.8)	0.62 (3.4)	0.64 (4.2)
ρ	0.94 (13.8)	0.21 (1.1)	0.16 (0.8)	0.08 (0.4)
Standard error	0.00401	0.00330	0.00399	0.00331
Durbin Watson	2.12	1.56	1.89	1.98

[a] t-statistics are shown in parentheses. The dependent variable is C/Y.

[b] The X_i are income shares for the ith age group. The ages of head for each group are 14–24, 25–34, 35–44, 45–54, 55–64, 65+. For equations (3) and (4) the groups are 14–34, 35–64 and 65+.

[c] Excludes 1953, 1965, and 1966, for which income shares data are incomplete.

Table 9–14. Regression Estimates of Consumption Function, NIPA Data, 1948–75

Equation:	*(1)*	*(2)*	*(3)*	*(4)*[c]
Constant	0.78 (8.1)[a]			
$1/Y$	19.2 (3.9)	24.0 (2.7)	12.1 (2.5)	11.2 (2.0)
C_{t-1}/Y	0.11 (1.0)	0.21 (2.2)	0.20 (1.9)	0.21 (1.7)
X_1[b]		1.36 (2.0)	0.52 (3.9)	0.49 (3.3)
X_2		0.21 (1.2)		
X_3		0.72 (2.8)	0.77 (7.5)	0.78 (6.5)
X_4		0.54 (1.5)		
X_5		1.14 (3.2)		
X_6		0.73 (2.7)	0.78 (2.4)	0.74 (2.1)
ρ	0.29 (1.6)	−0.22 (1.2)	0.06 (0.3)	0.03 (0.1)
Standard error	0.00821	0.00700	0.00763	0.00803
Durbin Watson	1.70	2.01	1.71	1.54

Notes: see Table 9–13.

for each age group. The collinearity of the X_i and the small number of degrees of freedom make these estimates impossible to interpret.[27] Consequently, the number of age groups is reduced to three in equation (3). They are: 14–34, 35–64, and 65+. Finally, equation (4) reestimates equation (3) excluding those years for which some of the demographic data were interpolated.

The average propensity to consume (APC) over the sample period is 0.91 with the FMP data and 0.92 with the NIPA data. The long-run MPC from equation (1) is somewhat smaller in both cases, 0.79 and 0.88, respectively. The addition of the six income shares variables yields rather mixed results. The individual MPCs defy interpretation, although the standard error in equation (2) is 18 percent smaller than in equation (1) with the FMP data and 15 percent smaller with the NIPA.[28]

When only three demographic groups are used, the reduction in the standard errors are much smaller. However, a pattern of increasing MPCs with age does emerge. The long-run MPCs by age groups from equation (3) are:

	FMP Data	*NIPA Data*
14–34	0.38	0.65
35–64	1.11	0.96
65+	1.32	0.98

The overall MPC, calculated by weighting the above numbers by 1975 shares of each age group, is 0.92 for the FMP data and 0.87 for the NIPA data. The small propensities to consume of the younger households could be due to their house-buying activity and their accumulation of durables (which are excluded from the FMP consumption definition).

The marginal propensities to consume for age groups should not be confused with the average propensity. The usual view of consumption patterns by age group is based on survey data on the APC. See Tables 9–3 and 9–10 for average saving rates from the SCFF and CES surveys, respectively. However, there is no necessity for the APC and MPC to be equal or to change together with age. Projector's estimates of the MPC by age groups using the Survey of Changes in Family Finances yield results that are consistent with the above estimates; that is, the MPC increases with age. Typically, her results indicate an MPC of about 0.5 for households under thirty-five, about 0.8 for middle-aged households, and about 1.3 for households over sixty-five [21, 1966, Table 17, p. 87].

Nevertheless, our interest is the effect of demographic change on the average propensity to consume. Such movements in the overall MPC are indicative of change in the overall ratio of consumption to income. Therefore, the results from equation (3) can be used to judge the effect of changes in the demographic and income distributions on consumption behavior.[29] This is done by comparing model predictions of the C/Y ratio for 1975 to the level that would be predicted if the income shares of the age groups from an earlier period had prevailed. That is, the impact of the combined influence of changes in demographic structure and in income distribution on saving will be shown with 1975 as a point of reference. Results are shown in Table 9–15.

Table 9–15 indicates that 1975 saving would have been substantially smaller if the demographic structures had remained unchanged. The predicted saving rate for 1975 is 1.4 percentage points higher (with the FMP data) and 1.1 percentage points higher (with the NIPA data) than it would have been with the 1965 age and income distribution. The difference is smaller when an earlier set of demographic variables is used. Over the whole sample period (1949 to 1975) the difference is less than one-half a percentage point.

Our major concern in this chapter is whether future changes in demographic structure will depress saving rates. The answer suggested by the time series results is no. This is shown in the last row of Table 9–15, where the 1975 consumption to income ratio is predicted using 1985 demographic data. For both data sets, the results indicate

Table 9–15. Predicted APC for 1975

Income Shares	*FMP Data*	*NIPA Data*
1949	0.9137	0.9062
1955	0.9208	0.9108
1960	0.9230	0.9127
1965	0.9227	0.9120
1970	0.9169	0.9080
1975	0.9089	0.9015
1985	0.9042	0.8978

Note: Predicted values from equation (3) of Table 9–13 (FMP) and of Table 9–14 (NIPA) using actual 1975 values for independent variables ($1/Y$ and C_{t-1}/Y), except the income shares of age groups which are as indicated. Serial correlation of residuals is ignored in making predictions since it is relatively small. For 1985, the income shares are based on the Census forecast shown in Table 9–1 and the relative income of each group is assumed to remain at the 1975 levels.

that the 1985 age structure generates a slightly higher saving rate than the 1975 age structure. The result stems from the continued growth of the less than thirty-five age group relative to the others in the next decade. The growth of the older group slows down in the next decade, although it will accelerate in later years.

These results are at variance with those discussed earlier based on the survey data. This can be seen if the three decade-by-decade comparisons used with the survey data are calculated from the time series model. In each case, the ratio of saving (in 1963, 1974, 1985) to what it would have been with the age distribution of the population as it existed about a decade earlier is shown. The calculations take into consideration only the changes in the age distribution and hold the income distribution constant at the terminal year (unlike Table 9–15, where both vary). The age effect on FMP saving gives these results: 0.949, 1.322, 1.033. The corresponding numbers from both survey data sets are always less than one.[30]

These time series results are based on a very different methodology than are the earlier cross-section results. They predict saving from the differences in the marginal propensity to consume among age groups rather than the average propensity. An appropriate dynamic model that could be applied to pooled cross section and time series data might reconcile the differences, but such data are not available. At this time, the time series results must be viewed cautiously. The uniform lag structure might be too restrictive and it may be inappropriate to use estimates of the short-run MPC to make inferences about long-run behavior.

There have been a few other discussions of these issues with time series data in the literature. Dale Heien [17, 1972] presented a life cycle model in which demographic effects enter in several ways. Although he does not explicitly calculate the effect of demographic change on the saving rate, his results can be used to provide an estimate comparable to those presented above. The Heien model combines life cycle and habit persistence approaches. The MPC out of wealth depends on the typical consumer's planning horizon (the difference between life expectancy and the median age). Wealth is lifetime income[31] which depends on the earning span of the typical consumer. Changes in demographic structure (median age, earnings span, and so on) clearly effect the model's predictions.

The major demographic shift over Heien's sample period (1948 to 1965) is the increase in the median age of the adult population of 6.39 percent. His results indicate that an increasing median age increases consumption. Heien's consumption to income ratio[32] in 1965 is 0.8 percent higher than what it would be with the 1949 median age. The corresponding estimate from our results (as in Table 9–15) is 0.9 percent with the FMP data and 0.6 percent with the NIPA data. Heien notes that decreases in the adult median age which were expected postsample would reverse the relationship. This is consistent with our comparison in Table 9–15 with the 1975 demographic structure.

A more recent study which incorporates demographic influences on consumption is the consumption function of the May 1977 version of the FMP model. The model weights the marginal propensities to consume out of income and wealth with weights that average one and vary with the age structure of the population. The motivation for the specification of the weights is not discussed. However, the implied impact of demographic change on the consumption to income ratio can be shown. Using 1974 values for all the other variables, the predicted value of C/Y is 0.9096 with the 1948 demographic structure, 0.9006 with 1960, 0.9034 with 1970, and 0.9099 with the actual 1974 demographic data. This pattern is quite different from that shown in Table 9–15. The FMP model suggests that demographic change increased saving in the early postwar period and has decreased it in the last decade. Table 9–15 indicates a period of decreases, followed by increases in the last decade. In both cases, the net result is that demographic changes have left saving rates unaffected over a thirty-year period. Clearly, a further explanation of the FMP specification would provide a useful basis for reconciling the differences.

For the present, these time-series results must be viewed as tentative. Nevertheless, the discussion lends support to the conclusion that demographic change in the next decade will have only a moderate influence on total saving rates. That is, although demographic change increased saving rates by about a percentage point in the 1960s, little further change is expected. This conclusion is the opposite of what we usually think happens when the proportion of old and young families increases; but that is based on APCs. Our earlier results using APC estimates from the survey data indicate a small depressing influence of demographic change on aggregate saving.

V. CONCLUSIONS

The empirical evidence from various cross-section and time series data presented in this chapter provides no definitive answer to the question of how changes in the age structure of the population affect personal saving behavior. Our evidence suggests that the answer depends on the time period and on the type of saving in question and might also be sensitive to the methodology and data used. In this concluding section we will briefly summarize that evidence and attempt to draw some conclusions from it.

Although total saving is defined differently in the different data sources, there is some agreement about the magnitude of the age effects. With the SCFF data, the evidence is that saving has been reduced by about 2–3 percent per decade as a result of age distribution changes during the postwar period. Our suggested corrections of the data alter the results slightly to less than 2 percent in the first decade examined and more in the later decades. This is also the pattern suggested by the results with both CES surveys. The age distribution effect on total saving from both CES surveys is for decade-by-decade decreases of 3 percent, 8 percent, and 5 percent. In both the SCFF and CES results, the depressing effect on total saving is larger in the decade just past (1963–74) than it is expected to be in the decade ending 1985 as a result of demographic shifts.

Another result common to both the CES and SCFF results is that the age effects on total saving are approximately offset by changes in the distribution of income among age groups. Relatively rapid growth in the number of households in some age groups seems to reduce their income relative to the incomes of slow-growing groups, and this has tended to mitigate the age effect on the aggregate level of saving.

The conclusion that saving is depressed by changes in the age distribution is further tempered by the results of the time-series analysis. Those results are sometimes at variance with the cross-section results. Although our confidence in the time-series methodology is limited, there is strong evidence that younger households who have low average propensity to save have a high marginal propensity to save. Consequently, as their numbers and incomes increase, the effect on aggregate saving may be unclear.

An important aspect of our results is the disaggregation of saving by asset type. The age patterns of saving rates differ widely among the components of total saving. For the broad saving components—financial assets, liabilities, and housing investment—the results from both survey sources are in basic agreement. They indicate that in the postwar period changes in the age structure have depressed financial asset acquisitions (though not by much with the SCFF data) and increased housing investment and the acquisition of liabilities since the 1960s. As noted earlier, the net effect on total saving has been small.

However, the net financial investment (NFI) of the household sector has been sharply altered by the changing age structure. In the decade ending 1963, changes in the age structure led to a sharp increase in NFI. In the subsequent decade, the age structure changes led to a sharp decline in NFI, and in the forecasts to 1985 further but smaller declines are expected. There are large differences between the SCFF (Tables 9–4 to 9–9) and CES (Table 9–11) predictions, but the patterns are in agreement. Both surveys indicate that the depressing effect of a changing age structure on NFI will be smaller in the decade beginning 1974 than in the previous decade.

The implications for overall capital formation of these changes can be judged by looking at some aggregate flow of funds saving data. (The trends in saving behavior are discussed by Sametz and Wachtel [23, 1977].) For example, the SCFF definition of total saving has averaged about 7 percent of GNP in the decade of 1965–74. We further estimated that changes in the age structure will reduce saving by about 3 percent per decade. This would reduce saving to 6.8 percent of GNP over a decade. With nominal GNP currently about $2,000 billion, the changing age structure could reduce personal sector saving from $140 billion to $136 billion in a decade's time. Since economywide capital formation is over 15 percent of GNP ($300 billion), the impact of the changing age structure is relatively small.

The differences between the CES and SCFF results make it difficult to pinpoint the effect of the age structure on NFI. NFI has been about 6.4 percent of GNP in the 1965–74 decade, or $128 billion of a $2,000 billion GNP. This can be compared to the external financing of the business sector—about 5 percent of GNP. Thus, sharp declines in household NFI could impinge upon the financing ability and capital formation of the business sector. If the more moderate age effects observed with the CES data are correct, the problem is manageable. Given the rapid responses of financial markets to business-sector financing problems and the possibility of reduced government deficits absorbing a smaller share of NFI, a 10 percent decline in household NFI is not likely to have a major impact on patterns of capital formation in the U.S. Our conclusion is that the depressing effect on saving caused by changes in the age structure of the population is not likely to be large enough to alter overall patterns of capital formation in the economy or to impinge seriously on the financing capabilities of the business sector.

NOTES TO CHAPTER 9

1. These results are analyzed in depth in Franco Modigliani and Richard Brumberg [19, 1954], Albert Ando and Modigliani [1, 1963], and Paul Samuelson [24, 1969], among others. Alan Blinder [3, 1975] examines the effects of the income distribution on spending and saving propensities. The impact of windfall income and capital gains on saving and consumption is examined in Kul Bhatia [2, 1972], Martin Feldstein and George Fane [8, 1973], and Irwin Friend and Charles Lieberman [15, 1975], among others. None of the above examines the effects of changes in the age distribution on saving rates.

2. As suggested previously, the strong restrictions can be relaxed without changing the qualitative results of the model.

3. Whether income is constant or grows smoothly, positive saving will take place each and every period. Only if income is variable (and individual spending decisions are determined by lifetime income) will there be periods during the working life when saving could be negative.

4. Even if random movements in income are permitted and saving varies (or becomes negative at some points) to smooth the consumption stream, these random movements will average out over longer periods. The basic underlying proposition, that net saving must come from income if assets are to be accumulated, remains true by definition.

5. For example see Crockett and Friend [6, 1978]. The solutions seemingly differ (except for notation) in that the numerator of equation (5) runs only through n rather than T, as in the Crockett-Friend solution. They are, nevertheless, equal since for $t > n$, the individual is retired and income is zero.

6. See Samuelson [24, 1969, p. 244]. The solutions differ only in notation:

$$\frac{a_1^i}{1 + a_1 + a_1^2 \ldots + a_1^i} = \frac{1}{1 + \lambda + \lambda^2 \ldots \lambda^i} \quad \text{since } \lambda = \frac{1}{a_1} .$$

7. Bequests may be nonzero without changing these results. The magnitude of the saving rate will be related to bequest motives while the age profile of the saving rate will be unaffected.

8. The various surveys are conceptually too dissimilar to be helpful in this regard. Savings definitions vary from survey to survey and sampling errors are often too large. Thus, it is difficult to analyze the influence of cyclical change on saving by demographic group.

9. See the papers by Robert Ferber and Ferber et al. [9, 1966; 10, 1966; 11, 1969; 12, 1969] for validation studies that estimate the magnitude of the problem.

10. Even here the FOF allocation of total deposits among sectors is subject to error.

11. The SCFF survey oversampled upper income groups to improve the reliability of the estimates. All of the results presented here employ sampling weights to obtain appropriate estimates of saving rates.

12. Projector [21, 1968, p. 15] comments on the incidence of apparent reporting errors for this group which are not explained. Other irregularities may be substantive. For example, the propensity to add to saving accounts by the over sixty-five group may reflect a desire to maintain precautionary liquid balances in the face of increased risk of extraordinary expenses (e.g., medical bills) or it could be a consequence of portfolio adjustments by these families who are net dissavers in housing.

13. For example, the SCFF indicates that saving in the form of automobile installment debt was 0.44 percent of income. Federal Reserve data indicate that in both 1962 and 1963 there were substantial net increases in automobile installment paper outstanding, or dissaving (−0.68 percent of disposable income). Also, the Flow of Funds indicates that savings account inflows were 6.67 percent of disposable income, while the SCFF saving rate is 2.74 percent.

14. Korns [18, 1973] estimates the extent of underreporting in the Survey of Financial Characteristics of Consumers, which collected asset and liability data for the SCFF respondents. He finds considerable evidence of underreporting of asset holding which suggests, though not necessarily, underreporting of saving flows as well.

15. Ferber [8, 1965] does find some weak evidence of a relationship between age and underreporting of savings account assets. The underreporting in this important category often reaches 50 percent.

16. In the full sample, as well as in the restricted samples, saving rates for each age group are calculated using weights for income classes and retirement status and moving status classes. This is necessary because the SCFF is a nonrandom sample.

17. Variations and permutations of these restrictions provided results not materially different from those reported.

18. Personal income in 1963 was $463 billion. The aggregate forecast using the unrestricted sample is $389 billion; with the net worth restriction it is $422 billion; and with all three restrictions, $409 billion. Total saving aggregates to $56.3, $63.3, and $55.9 billion for the 0, 1, and 3 restriction cases. In 1963, FOF net financial investment and housing expenditure of the household sector, plus consumption expenditures on automobiles, was $59.3 billion.

19. Note that these two aspects of demographic structure are not unrelated. The increased proportion of unrelated individuals is largely concentrated among the very old and very young.

20. The expenditure data are collected with great care and are used, among other things, to calculate the expenditure weights for the CPI. Accurate saving data would require detailed records of financial transactions that are not readily available.

21. There have been rather lengthy delays in the publication of the data from the 1972–73 survey. As of early 1978, a detailed breakdown of the saving data was not available.

22. The CES definition of consumer units does differ slightly from the CPS family and unrelated individuals. The 1960–61 CES has about 2.8 percent fewer units in the total population than the average of the CPS for 1960 and 1961. The age distributions are comparable:

	CES 1960–61	*CPS Average for 1960 and 1961*
< 25	4.8%	6.2%
25–34	18.5	18.1
35–44	22.1	21.2
45–54	19.7	20.0
55–64	15.9	16.5
> 65	19.0	18.0

The mean before-tax income was $6,246 in the 1960–61 CES; the CPS average for 1960 and 1961 is $5,793. The income concepts used in the various surveys are generally the same.

23. The 1960–61 CES indicates an increase in deposit assets of $0.4 billion. The average for the two years in the FOF Household Sector is more than $14 billion. For total financial assets the discrepancy is much smaller since FOF net investment in noncorporate business is about $8 billion less than the CES aggregate. For financial liabilities, the FOF and CES data are in basic agreement and for housing some underreporting in the FOF is indicated (see [21, Projector, 1968]).

24. The calculation uses Eizenga's data for 1950 saving by age group (Table 13) and 1900 and 1950 population (Table 21). Eizenga's results are larger because he standardizes saving rates for family size, income, and occupation.

25. This section is based on "Will a Changing Age Structure Depress Saving?" by Paul Wachtel, a paper presented at the American Economics Association meetings in New York City, December 1977.

26. For one year (1953) data for the size of each age group are missing and for two years (1965 and 1966) the mean income data for each age group are missing. In the first case, interpolations based on the movement of the total numbers of families and unrelated individuals are used, with an adjustment for a few age groups with atypical trends. The missing income means are interpolated using the medians which are available and adjusted so that they are consistent with the overall mean.

27. To reduce the collinearity, income shares were also calculated with the median incomes. The results were, however, basically unchanged.

28. The F statistics for the reduction in the sum of squared residuals is 3.37 with the FMP data and 2.95 with the NIPA data. The null hypothesis of no increase in explanatory power can be rejected at the 5 percent level in both cases.

29. Although they are relatively weak, the age effects should not be viewed as a mere consequence of multicollinearity in time series data. The income shares variables exhibit strong trends, as does the dependent variable from the NIPA data. But the dependent variables based on the FMP data are trendless.

30. These results are found in Table 9–4 (total saving, age distribution only) and Table 9–11 (net saving, age distribution only).

31. Perhaps the biggest drawback of Heien's empirical work is that it ignores all other forms of wealth.

32. Heien includes only consumption of nondurables and services. Also, there are additional demographic variables in Heien's model (e.g., retirement age) whose influence is not included here.

REFERENCES

1. ANDO, ALBERT, and MODIGLIANI, FRANCO. "The 'Life Cycle Hypothesis' of Saving," *American Economic Review*, March 1963, *51* (1), pp. 55–84.

2. BHATIA, KUL B. "Capital Gains and the Aggregate Consumption Function," *American Economic Review*, Dec. 1972, *62* (5), pp. 866–79.

3. BLINDER, ALAN. "Distribution Effects and the Aggregate Consumption Function," *Journal of Political Economy*, June 1975, *83* (3), pp. 447–75.

4. BRADY, DOROTHY. "Family Saving: 1888 to 1950," in *A Study of Saving in the U.S.*, Volume III. Special Studies by RAYMOND W. GOLDSMITH et al. Princeton: Princeton University Press, 1956.

5. CLOTFELTER, CHARLES, and LIEBERMAN, CHARLES. "On the Distributional Impact of Regulation Q," *Journal of Finance*, March 1978, *33* (1), pp. 199–213.

6. CROCKETT, JEAN, and FRIEND, IRWIN. "Consumption and Saving in Economic Development," in *Research in Finance*, Volume 1. Edited by HAIM LEVY. Greenwich, Conn.: JAI Press, 1978.

7. EIZENGA, W. *Demographic Factors and Saving.* Amsterdam: North-Holland, 1961.

8. FELDSTEIN, MARTIN S., and FANE, GEORGE. "Taxes, Corporate Dividend Policy, and Personal Savings," *Review of Economics and Statistics*, Nov. 1973, *55* (4), pp. 399–411.

9. FERBER, ROBERT. "The Reliability of Consumer Surveys of Financial Holdings: Time Deposits," *Journal of the American Statistical Association*, March 1965, *60* (1), pp. 148–63.

10. ____. "The Reliability of Consumer Surveys of Financial Holdings: Demand Deposits," *Journal of the American Statistical Association*, March 1966, *61* (1), pp. 91–103.

11. FERBER, ROBERT; FORSYTHE, JOHN; GUTHRIE, HAROLD W.; and MAYNES, E. SCOTT. "Validation of a National Survey of Consumer Financial Characteristics: Common Stock," *Journal of the American Statistical Association*, June 1969, *64* (2), pp. 415–32.

12. ____. "Validity of a National Survey of Consumer Financial Characteristics: Savings Accounts," *Review of Economics and Statistics*, Nov. 1969, *51* (4), pp. 436–44.

13. FRIEND, IRWIN. *Individuals' Saving.* New York: Wiley, 1954.

14. ____ . and JONES, ROBERT, eds. *Consumption and Saving,* Vol. 4. Philadelphia: University of Pennsylvania, 1960.

15. ____ , and LIEBERMAN, CHARLES. "Short-run Asset Effects on Household Saving and Consumption," *American Economic Review*, September 1975, *65* (4), pp. 624–33.

16. GOLDSMITH, RAYMOND. *A Study of Saving in the United States.* Princeton: Princeton University Press, 1956.

17. HEIEN, DALE. "Demographic Effects on the Multiperiod Consumption Function," *Journal of Political Economy*, Jan./Feb. 1972, *80* (1), pp. 125–38.

18. KORNS, ALEXANDER. "Debtor-Creditor Redistribution in Inflation: A Case Study in the Methodology of Policy-Oriented Research." Unpublished Ph.D. dissertation, Harvard University, 1973.

19. MODIGLIANI, FRANCO, and BRUMBERG, RICHARD. "Utility Analysis and the Consumption Function: An Interpretation of Cross-Section Data," in *Post-Keynesian Economics.* New Brunswick: Rutgers University Press, 1954.

20. NEW YORK STOCK EXCHANGE. *The Capital Needs and Savings Potential of the U.S. Economy.* New York: New York Stock Exchange, 1974.

21. PROJECTOR, DOROTHY. *Survey of Changes in Family Finances.* Washington, D.C.: Board of Governors of the Federal Reserve System, 1968.

22. ____ , and WEISS, GERTRUDE. *Survey of Financial Characteristics of Consumers.* Washington, D.C.: Board of Governors of the Federal Reserve System, 1966.

23. SAMETZ, ARNOLD W., and WACHTEL, PAUL, eds. *Understanding Capital Markets, Volume II: The Financial Environment and the Flow of Funds in the Next Decade.* Lexington, Mass.: D.C. Heath, 1977.

24. SAMUELSON, PAUL. "Lifetime Portfolio Selection by Dynamic Stochastic Programming," *Review of Economics and Statistics.* August 1969, *51* (3), pp. 239–46.

25. SURVEY RESEARCH CENTER. *Survey of Consumer Finances.* Ann Arbor: Institute for Social Research, University of Michigan, various dates.

26. UNITED STATES BUREAU OF THE CENSUS. "Money Income in 1975 of Families and Persons in the U.S.," *Current Population Reports*, Series P–60, No. 105, (June 1977).

27. ____ . "Trends in the Income of Families and Persons in the United States: 1947 to 1964." Technical Paper No. 17, 1967.

28. ____ . "Projections of the Number of Households and Families 1975 to 1990," *Current Population Reports*, Series P–25, No. 607 (August 1975).

29. UNITED STATES BUREAU OF LABOR STATISTICS. *Survey of Consumer Expenditures 1960–61.* BLS Report No. 237–93, 1965.

30. ____ . *Consumer Expenditure Survey Series: Interview Survey, 1972–73.* BLS Report No. 455–4, 1977.

31. WACHTEL, PAUL. "Inflation, Uncertainty, and Savings Behavior Since the Mid-1950s," *Explorations in Economic Research*, Fall 1977, *4* (4), pp. 538–78.

32. ____. "Financial Prerequisites for Economic Growth," in *Financial Institutions and Markets.* Edited by MURRAY POLAKOFF and THOMAS DURKIN. Boston: Houghton Mifflin, 2nd ed., 1980.

33. ____; SAMETZ, ARNOLD W.; and SHUFORD, HARRY. "Capital Shortage: Myth or Reality?" *Journal of Finance*, May 1976, *31* (2), pp. 269–86.

Chapter 10

The Life Cycle of Saving and Consumption

Robert J. Schmitz[a]

Despite much theoretical work on variations in consumption, labor supply, and saving over the life cycle, only a few empirical studies have appeared during the last decade. The paucity of studies undoubtedly results from the great demands that life cycle models place on data. But reliable estimates of life cycle consumption and saving functions are a prerequisite for assessing the influence of life cycle changes on aggregate behavior. If the consumption and saving of individual families are significantly affected by their size, age, and labor force participation and by changes in relative prices over their lifetimes then measured aggregate consumption and saving functions may drift over time if they ignore changes in the characteristics of the population.

This chapter examines the determinants of consumption and saving by families over the life cycle. Section I treats the issues and approaches that have arisen over the last half-century. Section II elaborates the life cycle model, pointing out the roles played by wealth and wages as determinants of life cycle behavior. Section III describes the empirical strategy. Alternative constructions of life cycle profiles and means of estimating consumption and saving functions are compared. Section IV discusses the data and the results. It suggests that the relation between purchased goods and leisure time in providing utility may be one of complementarity and that consumption of purchased goods is constrained to some degree by current income rather than by a broader measure of lifetime wealth.

[a]The author is indebted to James Heckman for supervision and advice.

Aggregate saving may thus be observed to be higher than predicted by current models that ignore these two features, a result consistent with recent work by Betsy B. White [34, 1978].

I. HISTORICAL PERSPECTIVE

Long before the controversy over the relation of consumption to income arose, Irving Fisher [12, 1907] had already discerned the principles that governed the size and variation of saving by families. He emphasized the profile of anticipated income and the effects of age and family size on the preference for present versus future consumption. Saving, he asserted, results from the efforts of households to redistribute consumption across the years of their lives so as to improve their welfare or lifetime utility. Demographic and other traits of the households thus influence saving through their relation to the distribution of income and desired consumption over their lifetimes. Gradual changes in the demographic composition of the population therefore can alter the supply of loanable funds to the market and lead to secular movements in the rate of interest.

Soon after the onset of the Great Depression, Keynes's *General Theory of Employment, Interest and Money* diverted attention from Fisher's life cycle theory, which emphasized the reallocative character of saving, and focused it instead on current income as the principal determinant of consumption and saving. The proportion of income saved was supposed to rise with income, and the ever-increasing rate of saving which accompanied economic growth was perceived as a potential threat to full employment. Increased government spending, reduced taxes, and redistribution of income from rich to poor were the remedies favored to counter the threat. The preoccupation with propensities to save and consume, that is with the relation between saving and income, has pervaded research on saving ever since. The postwar literature on individual saving and consumption nevertheless contains few references to the controversy over the ability of a competitive economy to maintain full employment that provided the initial impetus to such research.

In the course of empirical efforts to measure correctly the marginal propensity to save, Fisher's treatment of saving was recalled in the work of Franco Modigliani and Richard Brumberg [25, 1954] and that of Milton Friedman [15, 1957]. These contributions reiterated the Fisherian presumption of stability of personal consumption in the face of year-to-year fluctuations in income. They construed saving and dissaving as the natural mechanism for absorbing fluctuations in income to allow the family to enjoy the desired smooth path of consumption. This notion was the premise rather than the conclusion of Fisher's work some forty years earlier.

Interest in the life cycle model itself revived slowly after the publication of the work of Modigliani and Brumberg and of later articles by Robert Strotz [29, 1957] and Menahem Yaari [36, 1964]. Research has accelerated in the past decade, producing attempts to integrate the life cycle treatments of consumption, wages, and labor supply. However, little has as yet become known about the life cycle profile of assets, saving, or consumption or about their demographic determinants.

Keynes's *General Theory* [20, 1936] and most of the research on the consumption function that followed lacked a detailed account of saving behavior. While the wealthy were thought to save a disproportionate share of their incomes, the disposition of the resulting stock of wealth was not examined. The life cycle hypothesis and the permanent income hypothesis sought to remedy the omission; both hypotheses stressed Fisher's emphasis on lifetime wealth as the definition of resources appropriate to consumption and demonstrated that current income influences consumption only to the extent of its relation to discounted lifetime wealth. The empirical work stimulated by the permanent income and life cycle hypotheses has therefore attempted to free estimates of the marginal propensity to consume from the influence of variations in income that do not correspond to variations in discounted wealth.

To illustrate the sensitivity of the observed marginal propensity to save to assumptions about the nature of observed income, consider a typical consumer forming his plan for optimal consumption over his lifetime. Assume that the path of income is known and that there is no bequest motive. Under these circumstances the profile of consumption he chooses depends solely on initial assets plus discounted earnings and on the rate of time preference (a subjective rate of discount) relative to the market rate of interest. Given the present discounted value of lifetime income, the timing of its arrival has no effect on consumption. Anticipated increments to income induce no wealth effect as they arrive and, holding constant the determinants of consumption, are entirely saved. The marginal propensity of an individual to save anticipated changes in income is unity because anticipated changes in income induce no changes in planned consumption. (Hence the marginal propensity to *consume* anticipated changes in income is zero.) Friedman [15, 1957] invoked the same principle to assert that the measured propensity to consume will decline as the sample from which it is computed becomes more and more homogeneous.

Next assume that all individuals enter economic life with no assets and that all have income profiles of identical shape which differ only by a uniform percentage throughout life. Under the common assumption that the utility function is homogeneous of degree one in the consumption of different periods and is identical for all individuals, the consumption of any two individuals differs also by that uniform percentage at each age. The elasticity of consumption with respect to interpersonal differences in income is thus unity, and the corresponding elasticity of saving is zero. The relation between income and consumption is reversed because interpersonal differences in income now measure interpersonal differences in wealth. Adding a bequest motive to the example does not change the results if the wealth elasticity of bequests is unity. If the elasticity exceeds unity, however, the marginal propensity to consume lifetime wealth falls as wealth increases and high-income individuals exhibit greater propensities to save than otherwise identical individuals with lower incomes.

Although wealth has replaced income as the accepted determinant of consumption, the issue remains that of the response of consumption to resources. If increases in wealth are disproportionately consumed when they occur or if bequests rise with wealth, a Keynesian consumption relationship could still emerge. Consumption may be more variable than the life cycle model predicts and redistribution of resources from rich to poor may change the rate of national saving.

II. A SIMPLE MODEL WITH INCOME EXOGENOUS

Saving is a residual flow for the consumer measuring the excess of income over consumption at any point during life. The determinants of income and consumption, then, also determine the path of saving. Therefore it will be possible to make only the most general statements about the profile of saving and assets without imposing specific forms on the utility and wage functions. The following approach proceeds mainly from the work of Yaari [36, 1964]. The family maximizes an intertemporally separable utility function:

$$B = \int_0^T e^{-\rho t} U[X(t)]\, dt \,, \tag{1}$$

where $X(t)$ is the flow of consumption in year t and ρ is the rate at which the family discounts future utility.[1] $U[X(t)]$ is assumed to be increasing and strictly concave. At the end of life at time T the family is assumed to leave neither debt nor positive bequests, though it may enter economic life with assets of A_0. Therefore, if $h(t)$ is labor income earned in year t and r is the market rate of interest, then the family's budget constraint is

$$A_0 + \int_0^T e^{-rt}\,[h(t) - X(t)]\,dt = 0\,. \tag{2}$$

Subject to this constraint the family arranges its consumption each period so that

$$X(t) = f(\lambda e^{(\rho-r)t}) \equiv [U']^{-1}\,(\lambda e^{(\rho-r)t})\,, \tag{3}$$

where $[U']^{-1}(\cdot)$ is the inverse function of the marginal utility of consumption, guaranteed to exist since the marginal utility of consumption is monotonically decreasing; furthermore, $f'(\lambda e^{(\rho-r)t}) = 1/U''(\lambda e^{(\rho-r)t}) < 0$. The marginal utility of wealth, λ, depends on A_0, r, ρ, T, and on the path of earnings. In the absence of uncertainty, λ does not change during life since there are no surprises. Saving at any time is the difference between income (earnings plus the yield on assets) and consumption, so the path of saving is entirely determined by the paths of these variables. Current assets, $A(t)$, reflect accumulated saving plus initial assets. Hence

$$S(t) = h(t) - X(t) + rA(t) \tag{4}$$

$$\begin{aligned} A(t) &= A_0 + \int_0^t e^{r(t-v)}\,S(v)\,dv \\ &= e^{rt}A_0 + \int_0^t e^{r(t-v)}\,[h(v) - X(v)]\,dv\,. \end{aligned} \tag{5}$$

The family saves at the beginning of economic life if total income, $h(0) + rA_0$, exceeds $f(\lambda)$, the value of consumption in period 0.

Restricting the shape of the path of income permits one to plot general profiles of saving and assets. The profiles themselves involve integrals of discounted consumption and income and so are difficult to analyze and interpret in the general case. A convenient benchmark case is obtained by setting $r = \rho$. By equation (3) consumption then does not vary during life since $X(t)$ is equal to the constant $f(\lambda)$ and so may be denoted $\overline{X}$. The lifetime path of earned income may plausibly be specified as follows up to and during retirement, R:

$$\begin{array}{ll} h(t) > 0 & 0 \le t \le t_R \\ h(t) = 0 & t_R < t \le T \\ h'(t) > 0 & 0 \le t < t^* \\ h'(t) < 0 & t^* < t \le t_R \\ h''(t) < 0 & 0 < t < t_R \end{array} \tag{6}$$

Earnings rise monotonically until t^*, and then fall until retirement. Equations (4) and (5) now simplify to

$$S(t) = rA(t) + h(t) - X(t) = rA(t) + h(t) - \overline{X} \tag{4a}$$

$$A(t) = e^{rt} A_0 + \int_0^t e^{r(t-v)} h(v) dv - \overline{X}(e^{rt} - 1) / r \, . \tag{5a}$$

In this simple case, the saving function is merely a vertical translation of the (earned plus capital) income profile and so reaches a maximum at the same time in the life cycle. Extrema of the profile of assets (for $0 < t < t_R$) occur at t, satisfying $rA(t) + h(t) = f(\lambda)$. A minimum of the asset function requires that $h'(t) > 0$ and a maximum requires $h'(t) < 0$ ($r\dot{A}(t) = 0$ by the first order conditions for an extremum). Therefore, the stated assumptions on the path of earnings imply that an interior minimum of assets, if it occurs at all, must precede the maximum. If initial saving is positive, net worth remains nonnegative throughout life. After retirement, assets decline at an increasing rate until T.

The time of maximum saving occurs after the time of maximum earnings if the interest rate is positive. Saving reaches a peak when

$$\dot{S}(t) = \dot{h}(t) + r\dot{A}(t) = \dot{h}(t) + rS(t) = 0 \, , \tag{7}$$

so at the maximum

$$\dot{h}(t) = -rS(t) < 0 \, . \tag{8}$$

Saving peaks after earnings have begun to decline so long as saving is positive at its peak. Little can be said in the more complex case where $r \neq \rho$ unless the shape of the path of earnings and the form of the utility function are made more specific.

Credit Constraints and the Role of Assets

The central and most controversial feature of the life cycle theory presented above is the independence of the timing of consumption from the shape of the income stream. Because the family was constrained only by the present value of lifetime wealth, it was free to adjust the timing of consumption without any restrictions on its borrowing. Furthermore, since all loans to consumers were assumed to be repaid without fail prior to death, loans were assumed to be riskless and lending and borrowing rates were specified to be identical. Much of the criticism of the permanent income and life cycle hypotheses questions the value of these assumptions. Instead, it is maintained that current liquidity or limitations on the ability to borrow effectively constrain the family's consumption [19, Houthakker, 1958; 31, Thurow, 1968]. Alan Blinder [7, 1976] classifies households as planners, whose financial resources enable them to consume along optimal paths like those of equation (3), and reactors who are hindered in their efforts to do so by borrowing constraints of some type. Were such constraints genuinely effective, individuals with rapidly rising incomes might be classed as reactors for much of their lives. Their optimal path of consumption, coupled with the path of their income, may force their wealth to be negative early in life. Constraints on the availability of credit (due for example to the possibility of default) may prohibit families from holding negative wealth and so force them from their desired path of consumption. Increases in income, anticipated or not, will largely be consumed by reactors and saved by planners. Blinder points out that young families anticipating substantial growth in their incomes are most likely to be reactors. As Roger Bird and Ronald Bodkin [6, 1965, p. 501] point out,

> . . . households with expectations of rapid income growth are likely to find themselves constrained by a lack of immediate funds. If such a household does receive a windfall, one might expect the associated transitory income to go largely into consumption (of all the major categories), as the windfall would temporarily release the household from its funds constraint, thus allowing it to spend at levels justified by its permanent income. These considerations would lead one to expect a positive marginal propensity to consume transitory income.

The controversy surrounding tests of the life cycle and permanent income hypotheses persists largely because the hypotheses are formulated in terms of latent variables like permanent income and lifetime resources which have no obvious observable counterparts. Therefore, almost any econometric specification involving proxies for these variables is controversial and some are tautological.

Perhaps the best known test concerns the response of the consumer to windfalls (unanticipated increments to wealth). The life cycle hypothesis asserts that additional consumption induced by the windfall will be spread out over the remaining lifetime. Friedman [15, 1957, p. 215] suggested an experiment based on the National Service Life Insurance dividends paid in 1950. "This payment seems to have been largely unexpected and so to qualify as a 'windfall' or clearly transitory element." Bodkin [8, 1960] and Bird and Bodkin [6, 1965] studied the consumption of recipients and declared that the marginal propensity to consume the dividends was too high to be consistent with the hypothesized broad increase in consumption. Not surprisingly, the debate over their results centered on the extent to which the windfalls were truly unanticipated and on the magnitude of the consequent proportional increment to lifetime wealth. Bird and Bodkin withdrew somewhat from Bodkin's [8, 1960] position but failed to confirm the strict permanent income hypothesis. They supported instead a loose permanent income hypothesis in which transitory income is consumed at a lower rate than permanent income. Whether the constraints indicated by the relatively high propensity to consume windfalls seriously impair the applicability of the theory was left unresolved.

Useful evidence on the issue was provided by Michael Landsberger [22, 1970], who set out to test the proposition, implied by the life cycle hypothesis, that the marginal propensity to consume out of current wealth rises with age. Since windfalls simply augment wealth, the propensity to consume out of windfalls ought similarly to rise with age. He found that the propensity of Israeli families to consume restitution payments and other windfall income increased with age in every case for which the difference among age groups was significant. This finding supports the life cycle hypothesis even more strongly than Landsberger claimed, for precisely the opposite result would be expected if limitations on borrowing seriously interfered with the ability of families to smooth consumption over time. Young families would be particularly subject to the constraint, that is, they would predominate among the reactors and consequently would exhibit a greater marginal propensity to consume windfalls. Landsberger's results thus indicate that borrowing constraints, so often invoked to question the usefulness of the permanent income and life cycle hypotheses, may be less significant than intuition and casual empiricism suggest.

An alternative explanation which retains the spirit of explanations based on credit market restrictions is available. Landsberger [21, 1966], Doenges [9, 1966], and others have pointed out that the observed propensity to consume windfalls is inversely related to the size of the windfall. Clark Wiseman [35, 1975] rationalized this finding by noting that, under a regime of constrained borrowing, increasing numbers of individuals are entirely freed from the constraint as the size of the windfall itself increases. An ordering of propensities to spend windfalls by age similar to that recorded by Landsberger [22, 1970] could then result if younger families received systematically larger restitution payments.

III. INCOME ENDOGENOUS

The close correspondence between the consumption and income of families of different ages, displayed in survey data [10, Weitze Eizenga, 1961; 14, Janet Fisher, 1952] represents an empirical regularity unaccounted for by the Modigliani-Brumberg life cycle theory. Gary Becker's [3, 1965] treatment of the demand for time in the household provided the basis for modifying the theory in a manner that might explain the correspondence. The life cycle models of Gilbert Ghez and Gary Becker [16, 1975] and James Heckman [17, 1974] stressed that if instantaneous utility depends on consumption of both leisure and market goods ($U[L(t), X(t)]$, where $L(t)$ is leisure time) then a strong positive association between consumption of goods and wages (and hence between consumption and income) is natural if leisure and market goods are direct substitutes ($U_{12} < 0$). Therefore, they argued, the association between income and consumption of goods over life arises from the substitution of goods for leisure as the wage rate, the price of leisure time, gradually rises, with the reverse substitution occurring later in life as the wage falls.

The implications of a simple version of the new life cycle model are obtained by entering leisure as an argument of the utility function in equation (1) and by modifying the budget constraint (2) to account for the family's choice of labor and leisure. The family chooses paths for consumption and leisure to maximize utility given the discounted value of lifetime wealth which now includes the value of leisure. The path of saving is generated by the paths of earnings (via the choice of labor and leisure) and consumption. In the following, $w(t)$ is the wage available to the head at t and $z(t)$ is a vector of demographic or environmental influences on utility assumed for the time being to be exogenous. The new problem is to maximize

$$\int_0^T e^{-\rho t} U[L(t), X(t), z(t)]\, dt \tag{9}$$

subject to

$$A_0 + \int_0^T e^{-rt} [(1-L(t))w(t) - p(t)X(t)]\, dt = 0 \ . \tag{10}$$

$U[L(t), X(t), z(t)]$ is assumed to be concave in $L(t)$ and $X(t)$ and the price of goods, $p(t)$, is taken to be constant throughout life. Since total time available has been normalized to unity, $(1-L(t))$ represents the proportion of time spent working at t. Equation (10) is an elaboration of equation (2); total resources are defined as initial assets plus the discounted value of total time. These resources are consumed over the lifetime in the form of goods, $X(t)$, and leisure time, $L(t)$.

Necessary conditions for an optimum imply that demand functions can be written

$$L(t) = L(\lambda e^{(\rho-r)t}w(t),\ \lambda e^{(\rho-r)t}p(t),\ z(t)) \tag{11}$$

$$X(t) = X(\lambda e^{(\rho-r)t}w(t),\ \lambda e^{(\rho-r)t}p(t),\ z(t)), \tag{12}$$

where λ is the marginal utility of discounted human and nonhuman wealth. If future events are anticipated with certainty, λ is constant over the lifetime. Furthermore, because the utility function is separable in the utilities of distinct instants, all future wages and values of $z(t)$ influence current demand solely through λ. In general, the paths of all exogenous variables determine the value of λ. As shown subsequently, the formulation of the demand functions with λ constant provides a useful basis for econometric specifications based on equations (11) and (12).

Saving is defined as earnings less consumption plus the return on assets at t. If $N(t)$ is time spent working at t then

$$\begin{aligned} S(t) &= w(t)N(t) - p(t)X(t) + rA(t) \\ &= w(t) - [w(t)L(t) + p(t)X(t)] + rA(t)\,. \end{aligned} \tag{13}$$

The derivative of equation (13) produces the variation in saving over the lifetime. The coefficient of $\dot{w}(t)$ in equation (14) represents the response of saving to evolutionary changes in the wage over life.

$$\begin{aligned} \dot{S}(t) &= N(t)\dot{w}(t) - \left\{w(t)\dot{L}(t) + p(t)\dot{X}(t)\right\} + r\dot{A}(t) \\ &= \left\{N(t) - [w(t)L_1 + p(t)X_1]\lambda e^{(\rho-r)t}\right\}\dot{w}(t) \\ &\quad - (\rho-r)\left\{w(t)[w(t)L_1 + p(t)L_2] + p(t)[w(t)X_1 + \right. \\ &\qquad\qquad \left. p(t)X_2]\right\}\lambda e^{(\rho-r)t} \\ &\quad + r\dot{A}(t) - (w(t)L_3 + p(t)X_3)\dot{z}(t)\,. \end{aligned} \tag{14}$$

Because all changes are anticipated, their influence on λ was determined at the beginning of life, so λ remains constant. All terms in square brackets in (14) are negative if $L(t)$ and $X(t)$ have positive wealth elasticities at each instant (see [17, Heckman, 1974]).[2] Therefore, evolutionary growth of the wage during the life cycle leads to increased saving by individuals who are working. James P. Smith [28, 1975] made the same point using a utility function with constant elasticity of intertemporal substitution. Thus, while the new life cycle theory typically explains the rising path of consumption with age by assuming that goods and time are substitutes in utility ($U_{12} < 0$), the increase in current income generated by the increasing wage must dominate the rise in consumption so that saving also increases if leisure is a normal good.

The time of maximum saving occurs when $\dot{S}(t)$ in equation (14) is equal to zero. As was the case with income exogenous, if $r = \rho$, saving reaches a maximum after the wage does. While the implied paths of saving and assets generated by the foregoing model may differ in level and curvature from the corresponding paths generated by the earlier model with exogenous income, the general shape remains the same. The current formulation differs from the previous one not only in its explicit recognition of the utility provided by leisure time, but also in the introduction of $z(t)$ to represent the effect of demographic influences on utility and therefore on the demand for market goods and leisure. As equation (14) indicates, the rate of saving during life is affected by changes in the demographic character of the household.

Only Ghez [16, Ghez and Becker, 1975] and Smith [28, 1975] have estimated the type of life cycle consumption and saving functions just described. Their estimates, however, do not in any sense test that theory. Because the sign of U_{12} is unrestricted, the new life cycle theory is consistent with a variety of possible paths of consumption over life. Indeed, precisely how one might reject the theory with consumption data is difficult to say. The positive response of saving to life cycle changes in the wage is surely falsifiable, yet it too is predicted by competing theories. The hypothesis that young families are unable to borrow sufficiently to consume along consumption and leisure paths given by (11) and (12) suggests nevertheless that, for such families, anticipated increases in the wage may not elicit the increase in saving predicted above. As the rising incomes that accompany age and experience release more and more families from the constraint, the response of saving to the wage would rise. The life cycle model itself predicts no age ordering of the response of saving to the wage. This test thus follows the earlier interpretation of Landsberger's evidence on the age pattern of the marginal propensity to consume windfalls.

Demographic Influences on Consumption and Saving

The environmental and demographic variables represented by the vector $z(t)$ affect the demand for consumption and leisure time both directly as seen in (11) and (12) and also through the effect which their paths over the life cycle exert on the value of λ. Differences among households in anticipated size of family, for example, will therefore cause differences in consumption of leisure and goods at every age which correspond to differences in λ. Differences in anticipated size become differences in current family size as children are born and grow up, producing additional changes in demand through the direct effect of $z(t)$ in equations (11) and (12).

The attempt to produce a means of comparing the consumption of families differing in size and composition has generated a substantial literature on "equivalence scales," for example, Anton Barton [2, 1964] and John Muellbauer [26, 1977]. Proper tests of the life cycle model similarly require some explanation or at least some assumptions about how the consumption of families changes as their composition changes over time. This allows tests in which the influences of family size and composition do not obscure the influences of other economic variables, say income, with which they may be correlated. For example, if the positive correlation between income and consumption over the life cycle were due merely to changes in the number and age of children living at home (which in turn is perhaps spuriously correlated with changes in income), then other explanations would be superfluous.

Furthermore, the partial effects of family size and children's age are themselves of crucial importance for attempts to produce an aggregate saving or consumption function from the estimated microrelation. It would clearly be undesirable for the aggregate function to require a fixed demographic structure, particularly in light of current changes in family size and the aging of the U.S. population.

Even if expected total family size itself is taken to be exogenous, the problem of elucidating the ways in which the changing composition of the family affects consumption and saving is complicated. The complication arises because increased family size influences behavior both through the effect of current family size on current consumption and through the effect of total family size on lifetime consumption (through a "wealth effect" displayed here by the change in λ). This second (wealth) effect asserts that couples whose children have already left home will consume less and save more than otherwise identical couples. When children are present, the two effects work in opposite directions, although the first must dominate at least for a short period. But the effect of an increase or decline of the birthrate on aggregate saving is far from clear. Irving Fisher, aware of the opposing influences, conjectured that the second would dominate [13, Fisher, 1930, p. 87]:

> Not only does regard for one's offspring lower impatience, but the increase of offspring has in part the same effect. So far as it adds to future needs rather than to immediate needs, it operates like a descending income stream, to diminish impatience. Parents whose families are increasing often feel the importance of providing for future years far more than parents in similar circumstances but with smaller families. Consequently, an increase in family size, other things being equal, will reduce the rate of interest.

IV. AN EMPIRICAL APPROACH

Still assuming that $p(t)$ is constant, equations (11) and (12) may be expanded to linear terms about their means to produce a basis for estimating the determinants of consumption and saving:

$$L(t) = a_1 + a_2(\rho - r)t + a_3(\lambda - \overline{\lambda}) + a_4 w_t + a_5 z_t \tag{15}$$

$$X(t) = b_1 + b_2(\rho - r)t + b_3(\lambda - \overline{\lambda}) + b_4 w_t + b_5 z_t . \tag{16}$$

Expanding about geometric means rather than arithmetic means produces an approximation identical to (15) and (16) except that λ, w_t, and z_t are replaced by their logarithms. The influence of omitted variables and errors of optimization induces randomness in (15) and (16) which is represented by additive disturbances attached to the two equations. Assume for now that the individual perfectly anticipates future values of w_t and z_t so that λ is constant through life. The expected signs of b_3 and b_4 in (16) are of particular importance for interpreting the equations to be estimated here. Under the assumptions of the model the coefficient b_4 in (16) indicates the relationship between time and goods in utility; its sign is opposite that of U_{12} and so is not determined by utility theory. As noted previously, the explanation for the relationship between income and consumption over the life cycle advanced by Ghez and Becker [16, 1975] relies on a negative value of U_{12} and thus on a positive sign for b_4. Blinder [7, 1976], on the other hand, claims that it is reasonable to suppose that leisure and market goods are complements in utility so that, for example, households plan to consume relatively heavily during retirement.

Although λ cannot be observed, knowing the expected sign of b_3 is useful for subsequent analysis. Since $b_3 = w_t X_1 + p_t X_2$ (evaluated at means), b_3 is negative if market goods are normal in all periods (see page 368). The role of λ in the present formulation corresponds to that of permanent income or discounted wealth in other studies of consumption and saving. The common problem of the unobserved variable arises in so many studies because of their common assertion that consumption and saving at any time depend on the income and wages prevailing during other periods and not just on the values observed during the current period. A typical solution is to find a proxy or instrumental variable for permanent income, such as house value, occupation, or a weighted average of past incomes. In the present study, the availability of panel data (a short time series of cross section observations) permits the estimation of a model in which the influence of λ on consumption is fixed over time, an approach developed by Thomas Macurdy [23, 1978] and by James Heckman [18, 1978].

The initial and most restrictive formulation used here incorporates the following two assumptions which, although severe, provide for a useful comparison with other models estimated on cross-section data.

1. Additive error terms attached to (15) and (16) are uncorrelated for a given individual. That is, individual heterogeneity not captured in λ or in z_t, affects the demand for X_t and L_t independently.
2. Wages and other income are correctly anticipated three years into the future by the individual. Changes in wages and other income over time therefore reflect life cycle variation and induce no wealth effects; changes in λ that occur during the sample period (due for example to revisions in anticipated future income) are uncorrelated with current changes in wages and other income.

By definition a saving equation can be written as current income, denoted Y, minus the expression for consumption, equation (16): $S = Y - b_1 - b_2 (\rho - r)t - b_3 (\lambda - \overline{\lambda}) - b_4 w_t - b_5 z_t$. Y incorporates the influence of the explanatory variables of equation (15) on the choice of labor and leisure; the other variables affect saving through their effect on consumption only. The saving equation for family i in year t can be written in a form appropriate to linear regression as follows:

$$S_{it} = c_1 + c_6 Y_{it} + c_2 (\rho - r) AGE_{it} + c_3 (\lambda_i - \overline{\lambda}) + c_4 w_{it} + c_5 z_{it} + e_{it}, \quad (17)$$

where e_{it} is the negative of the disturbance attached to equation (16). Referring to (16), it is clear that $c_1 = -b_1$, $c_2 = -b_2$, and so on. Hence, the model of Ghez and Becker predicts a negative sign for c_4. Furthermore, the way in which (17) was derived implies that c_6 ought to be equal to unity. The implication, however, depends crucially on the assumption that the actual receipt of current income has no effect on current consumption, that is, that the marginal propensity to save anticipated changes in income is unity, as argued in Section I. Families who face limitations on their ability to smooth consumption by borrowing (Blinder's reactors) may consume some or all of any increment to income. For these families c_6 may lie between zero and one.

The term $(\lambda_i - \overline{\lambda})$ is not observed and so (17) cannot be estimated as it stands. The availability of panel data, however, and the assumption that λ is fixed over time for each family permit estimation of the coefficients of (17). The procedure, outlined by Yair Mundlak [27, 1961], is equivalent to inserting a dummy variable for each family into (17). The same result is achieved by performing the regression on first differences:

$$S_{it} - S_{it-1} = c_6 (Y_{it} - Y_{it-1}) + c_2 (\rho - r) + c_4 (w_{it} - w_{it-1})$$

$$+ c_5 (z_{it} - z_{it-1}) + u_{it};\ u_{it} = e_{it} - e_{it-1}\,. \qquad (18)$$

When equation (17) computed in year $t-1$ is subtracted from its value in year t the term $c_3(\lambda_i - \lambda)$ drops out since it was assumed not to change during the one-year interval. Assumption (2) is required to prohibit unanticipated changes in wages or income which produce revisions of λ_i.

Any attempt to estimate (17) with only one year of data would force $c_3(\lambda_i - \lambda)$ into the disturbance. Its correlation with the explanatory variables of (17), particularly with income and wages, induces a simultaneity bias analogous to the errors-in-variables problem that led Friedman and Modigliani and Brumberg to criticize simple cross-section estimates of the marginal propensity to consume. The disturbance term in a regression using (17) and cross-section data is of the form $v_{it} = u_{it} + c_3(\lambda_i - \lambda) = u_{it} - b_3(\lambda_i - \lambda)$. Using a standard result of specification analysis [30, Theil, 1971, p. 549], the vector of parameters $\underline{c}$ can be shown to be estimated with a bias composed of the coefficient of the omitted variable, $-b_3$, multiplied by the vector of coefficients $\underline{k}$ from the linear relation between the omitted and included variables:

$$E(\underline{\hat{c}}) = \underline{c} - b_3\ \underline{k}. \tag{19}$$

Since b_3 is negative, the least squares estimate of c_4, for example, is biased upward or downward as the relation between $(\lambda_i - \lambda)$ and w_{it} is positive or negative. Some association is surely expected since λ_i itself is a function of initial assets, the path of wages and the demographic traits.

Ghez and Becker [16, 1975] and Smith [28, 1975] have attempted to produce consistent estimates of the parameters of equations like (16) and (17) with cross-section data by forming a so-called synthetic cohort. Arithmetic means of all variables are formed within age cells, $b_3(\lambda_i - \lambda)$ is impounded in the disturbance, and least squares estimates are formed from the forty or so observations of the resulting artificial lifetime. Because age itself is assumed to be uncorrelated with cross-section disturbances (that is, uncorrelated with λ) the grouping by age results in consistent least squares estimates in much the same way as the straight-line methods of Abraham Wald [33, 1940] and M. Bartlett [1, 1949]. Not only are the estimates generally biased in finite samples, however, but, in the presence of secular change in the wage and other variables, λ will also change over time, resulting in a correlation between age and λ in a cross section. Even consistency, then, cannot be guaranteed using synthetic cohorts. The correlation (between age and λ) arises because at any given time, younger individuals receive the benefits of economic growth at an earlier age than do older individuals. Therefore, for example, the difference between the mean wage of thirty-five-year-olds and the mean wage of forty-year-olds understates the growth of wages rationally anticipated by individuals who are now thirty-five. At any instant, differences in age coincide with differences in year of birth, and so at that instant the observed variation of a number of descriptive magnitudes with age is composed of a pure effect of age and an effect attributable to the differences in habits, attitudes, and social and economic conditions confronting persons born in different periods. This last effect is frequently referred to as a vintage or cohort effect.

V. DATA AND RESULTS

The sample consists of some 590 households headed by males who worked sometime during each year from 1967 to 1969. It was drawn from the years 1967 to 1970 of the *Survey of Consumer Finances.* Households were reinterviewed each year to ascertain wages, hours of work, family composition, and the size of several components of assets. The following types of households were eliminated from the original sample of 1,434 families:

1. households headed by women;
2. households headed by men who did not work during one or more of the years from 1967 through 1969;
3. households that experienced a change in marital status during the period of the sample;
4. households that did not know or refused to divulge the value of some component of assets in any year;
5. households that responded inconsistently, for example, a household that acknowledged owning corporate stock but reported its value to be zero; whether these are truthful responses, memory lapses, or unspecified conventions used in coding the data has not been determined.

The net worth of each household was computed by summing the values of checking and saving accounts, stocks, bonds, real estate, and own home and subtracting mortgage and other debt. In addition, values were imputed to the families' stocks of automobiles and major durables and added to the measure of wealth. Saving was computed as the change in net worth in adjacent years.

In computing the household's total income, reported inheritances and an estimate of accrued capital gains were added to the stated figure for disposable income. Gains on corporate equity were computed as the change in the stated value of stock in adjacent years net of the value of reported purchases and sales. The value of bonds in an initial year was multiplied by the proportionate change in the Standard and Poor's Aaa bond price index to estimate the capital gains on bonds in adjacent years. Deficiencies in the data made it impossible to approximate reliably the capital gains on homes or real estate. The omission naturally leads income to be underestimated. A rough guide to the magnitude of omitted capital gains is provided by the rate of change of the ratio of the housing class of the Consumer Price Index to the overall Index. This method indicates that homeowner's incomes in 1969 are underestimated by about nine-tenths of 1 percent of the value of the home; furthermore, no error at all is made for 1968 income.

Since the hourly wage is not directly reported, total earnings were divided by reported hours worked in order to approximate the average hourly wage for both husband and wife. A consumption variable was created by subtracting the constructed saving measure from the income value just described.

Some Life Cycle Profiles

Figures 10–1 through 10–4 illustrate life cycle profiles of net worth, head's wage, head's income, and family income plotted from the data. Two approximations to the life cycle profile are shown. The synthetic cohort approximation was computed by plotting the mean value of the variable for all individuals in each age group against age itself. The points displayed on the synthetic cohort profile constitute the raw data for the least squares estimates computed by regression on synthetic cohorts. The panel approximation was computed by first constructing the mean difference in the value of the variable in adjacent years for individuals of the same age. The availability of observations for each individual in successive years makes this procedure possible when panel data are used. Taking age twenty as a starting value, successive differences are summed to form the panel approximation.

The easiest way to compare the two approximations is to suppose that the wage, for example, depends on the age, A, and year of birth, $t-A$, of an individual, where t is the current year. The simplest way to express this is

$$w = g(t-A) + h(A); \quad g' > 0,\ h' > 0\,. \tag{20}$$

Secular trends in wages as well as other historical and social circumstances unique to each generation may lead the life cycle profile of the wage to drift over time, as suggested by the hypothetical profiles in Figure 10–5. The term $g(t-A)$ in equation (20), which does not change over life, anchors the individual to a particular path in Figure 10–5; $h(A)$ indicates the growth of the wage along a given path. The upward drift in profiles of successive cohorts portrayed in Figure 10–5 resembles the shift in real income profiles documented in a recent *Economic Report* [U.S. President, 32, 1974, p. 147]. The dashed line illustrates the observed profile which results from computing a synthetic cohort approximation using cross-section data in the presence of such drift. A general growth of wages produces an observed rate of life cycle growth that is lower than the true rate and may indicate a peak in wages much earlier in life than is actually the case.

The computed change in the wage between age A and age $A+1$ using a synthetic cohort approximation (indicated by the subscript "sc") is the difference between the wage of an individual now aged $A+1$ and an individual now aged A:

$$(w_{A+1} - w_A)_{sc} = g(t-(A+1)) + h(A+1) - g(t-A) - h(A)$$

$$< h(A+1) - h(A)\,. \tag{21}$$

The final inequality holds because $g(t-(A+1)) < g(t-A)$ in the presence of secular growth of wages. Equation (21) understates the life cycle growth of the wage by measuring along the dashed line of Figure 10−5 rather than along the profile of any given generation.

The panel approximation exploits the opportunity which panel data provide to compute the difference in the wage earned by a single individual between the ages of A and $A+1$. Since $g(t-A)$ is constant for any individual, the panel approximation (indicated by the subscript "p") measures the change along a solid path in Figure 10−5:

$$(w_{A+1} - w_A)_p = g((t+1)-(A+1)) + h(A+1) - (g(t-A) + h(A))$$

$$= h(A+1) - h(A)\,. \qquad (22)$$

If the effect of age and the effect of birth year or cohort on the paths of the variables displayed in Figures 10−1 through 10−4 are additively separable, as in equation (20), then the panel approximations in the figures should provide a reasonably accurate look at the life cycle paths anticipated by a twenty-year-old male in the late 1960s. Notice that the panel approximations lie well above the synthetic cohort approximations, rise faster, and peak later. These differences are consistent with bias like that illustrated in Figure 10−5 in depressing the synthetic cohort approximations. Further interpretation of the differences is provided by the regressions of the next section.

The Empirical Results

This chapter confines itself to estimating life cycle functions like equations (15) to (18) that are linear functions of their parameters. Before proceeding to the results a brief remark on the data is in order. The sample means for variables of interest are reported in Table 10−1. Of particular concern here is the unreasonably high mean change in real income between 1968 and 1969. The discrepancy is highlighted by comparison with the magnitude of mean income change excluding computed capital gains. That figure is comparable to the change in median family income between the two years, $307 [32, U.S. President, 1974, p. 274 (deflated to 1967 dollars)]. Hence, about $1,000 of the mean change in income is accounted for by capital gains, a surprising phenomenon for a year in which the Standard and Poor's common stock price index fell some 20 percent. Evidently, then, computed capital gains are subject to substantial error and bias, perhaps due to widespread understate-

Figure 10–1. Life Cycle Profiles of Net Worth; synthetic-cohort approximation from cross-section observations (□) and panel approximation from accumulated differences (●).

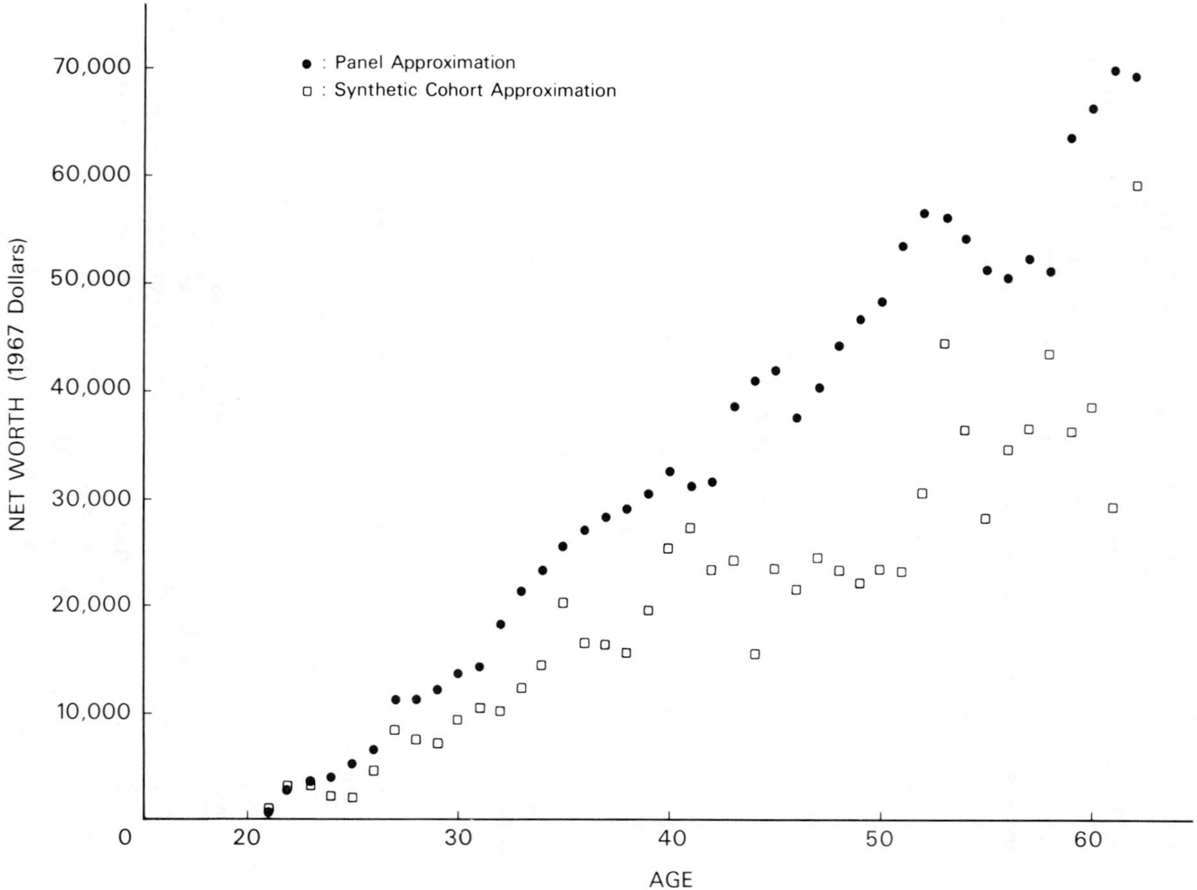

Figure 10–2. Life Cycle Profiles of the Wage of Male Household Heads; synthetic-cohort approximation from cross-section observations (□) and panel approximation from accumulated differences (●).

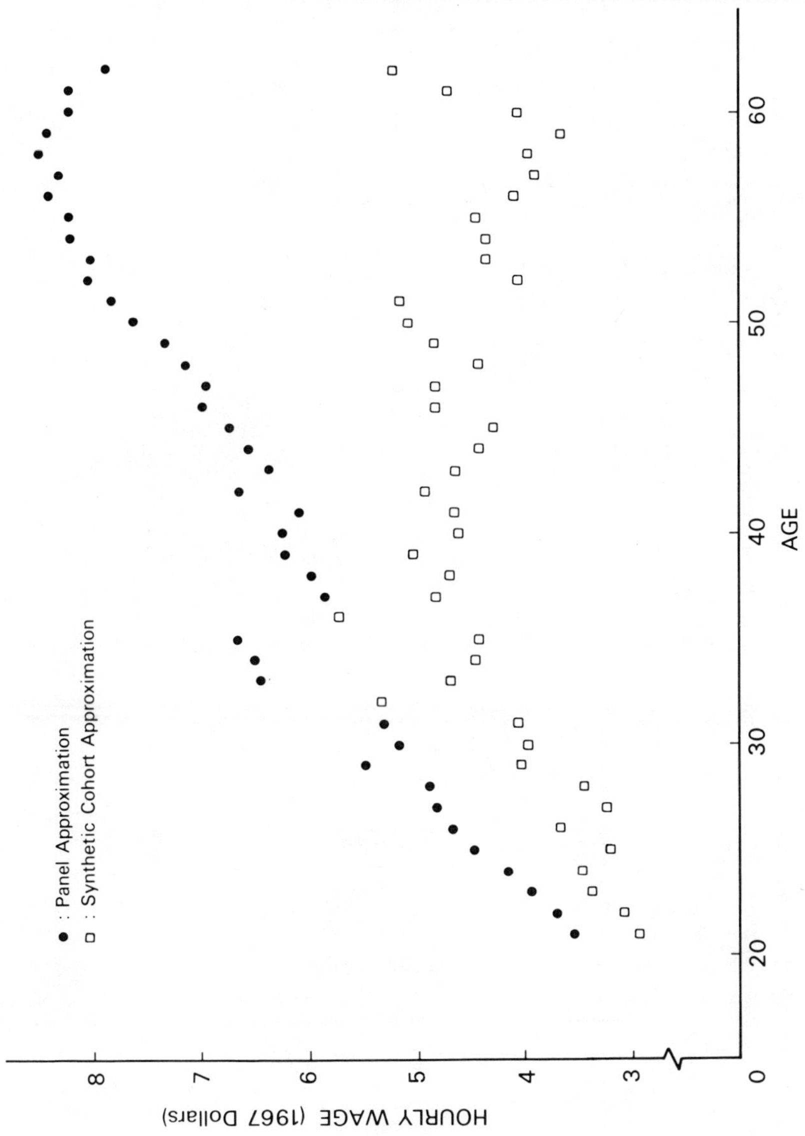

Figure 10–3. Life Cycle Profiles of Earnings of Male Household Heads; synthetic-cohort approximation from cross-section observation (□) and panel approximation from accumulated differences (●).

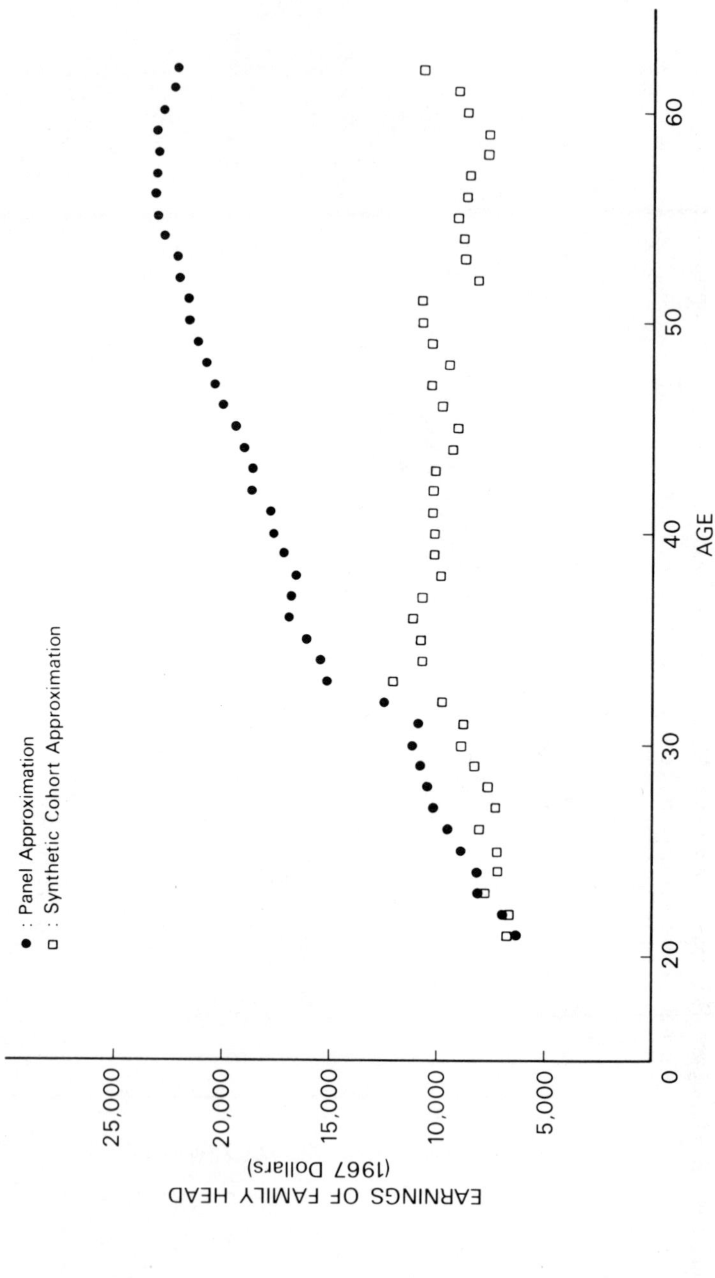

Figure 10–4. Life Cycle Profiles of Total Family Earnings; synthetic-cohort approximation from cross-section observations (□) and panel approximation from accumulated differences (●).

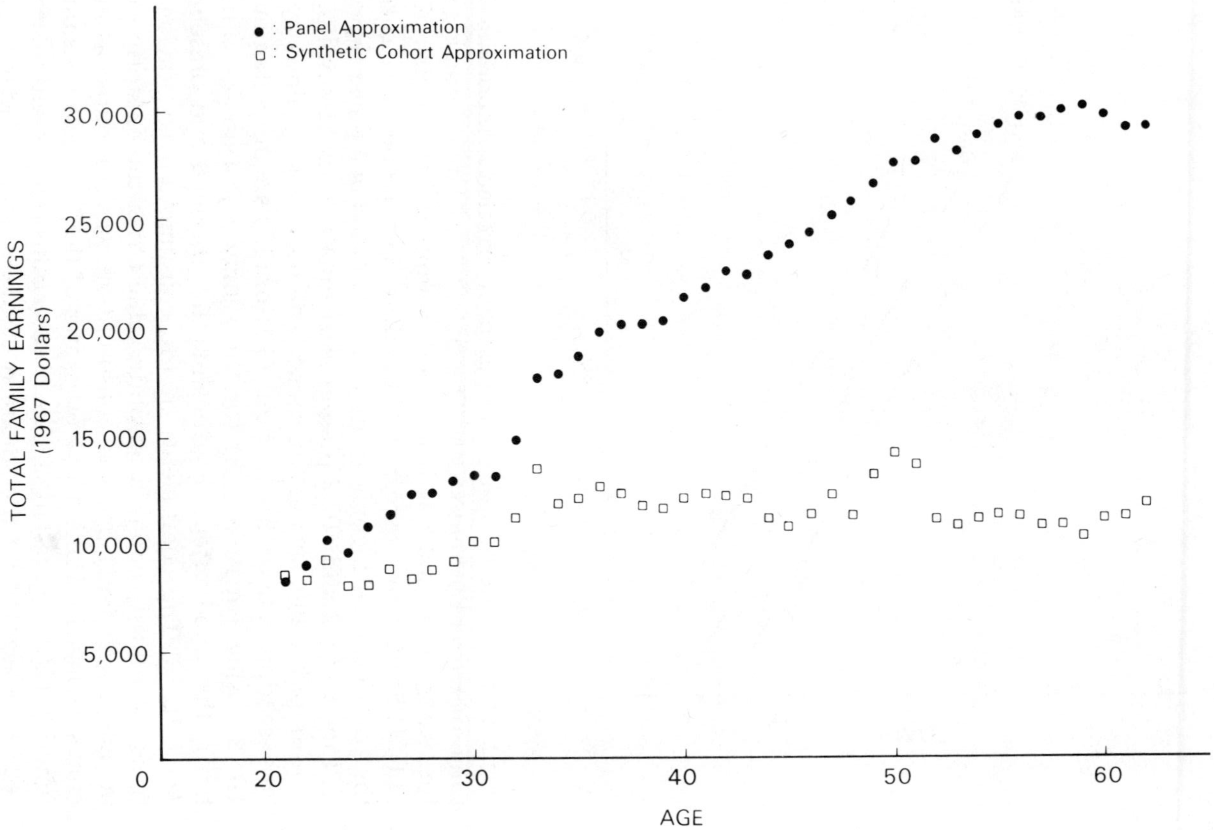

Figure 10–5. Real Wage Profiles of Successive Generations with Secular Growth of Wages (solid lines) and Observed Life Cycle Wage Profile from Cross-section Observations (dashed line)

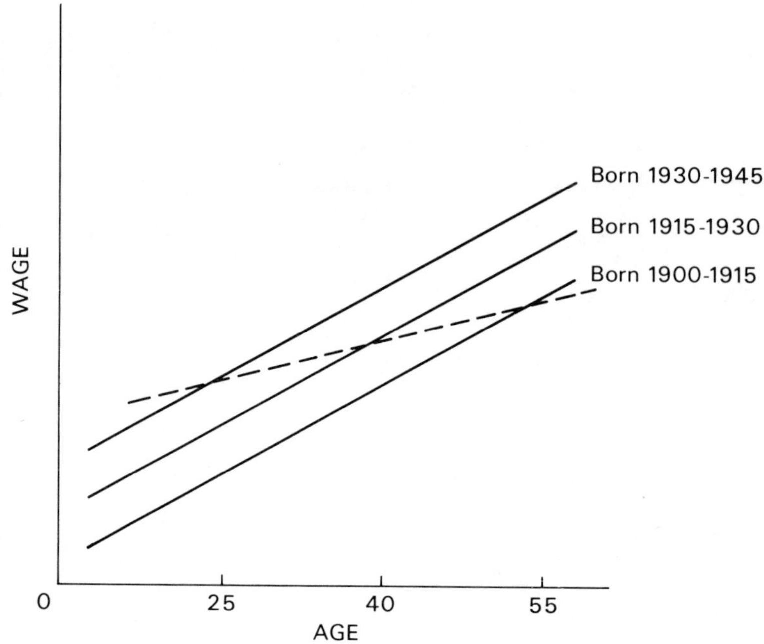

ment of the value of stock purchased or erroneous reporting of the value of currently held stock. The presence of large reporting errors for assets in general has been well documented (see Robert Ferber [11, 1968]). Some care must therefore be exercised to insure that the coefficient of income is properly estimated in a linear regression.

Tables 10–2 and 10–3 present least squares estimates of life cycle consumption and savings functions. The estimates obtained by using cross-section data with equations (16) or (17) are presented in Table 10–2. Using equation (18) (or the similar equation for consumption), the fixed effects coefficients are obtained and presented in Table 10–3. The coefficients of the consumption and saving functions are roughly equal in absolute value (with the exception of the income coefficient) because consumption was computed as income minus saving. In Table 10–4 estimates of the life cycle consumption function (16) are presented. The observations (means within each age cell) are weighted by the square root of cell size in order to correct for the heteroscedasticity of disturbances which results from aggregation.

Table 10–1. Description of the Data

	Mean	*Standard Deviation*
Age	42.30	10.32
Number of Children (NKIDS)	1.77	1.55
Head's Hourly Wage (1967 Dollars)	4.37	2.79
Proportion of Working Wives	0.48	
Wife's Hourly Wage (1967 Dollars)	2.72	3.18
Income (1967 Dollars)	10,225.06	4,667.17
Consumption (1967 Dollars)	8,671.84	9,455.04
Saving (1967 Dollars)	1,547.96	8,446.74
Change in Income between January 1969 and January 1970 (1967 Dollars)	1,404.21	15,059.99
Change in Income between January 1969 and January 1970 (net of imputed capital gains—1967 Dollars)	402.68	3,065.54

Other Abbreviations Used in Tables 10-2 through 10-8:

KAGE = number of children under eighteen multiplied by average age of children

WFWRK = 1 if wife works, 0 otherwise.

AOLD = 1 if head of family is aged forty or older in 1969.

AYNG = 1 if head of family is aged thirty-nine or under in 1969.

A striking feature that emerges from Tables 10–2 through 10–4 is the variation in sign of the coefficient of the wage. Estimates computed from a simple cross section and from a synthetic cohort yield positive implied values for b_4, the effect of the price of time on the demand for market goods. The estimates are consistent with those obtained by Ghez [16, Ghez and Becker, 1975] and Smith [28, 1975]. Such estimates, however, are likely to be contaminated with a bias arising from unobserved wealth effects, as argued earlier. The estimates of the fixed effect models presented in Table 10–3 are purged of that bias if assumptions (1) and (2) of the previous section are maintained. The wage coefficients contained there imply a negative sign for b_4 and suggest that market goods may be complementary with leisure time, as conjectured by Blinder, but contrary to the previously cited results of Ghez and of Smith. This result, if sustained, is important for two reasons. First, it means that substitution of market goods for leisure time as the wage rises cannot be invoked to explain the association of consumption and income over the life cycle and some other rationale is necessary. Second, it argues that growth of an individual's wage over the life cycle will elicit greater saving than predicted by a model that treats market goods and leisure

Table 10–2. Estimates of Life Cycle Saving: Cross Section Model *(standard errors in parentheses)*

	Consumption		*Saving*	
Dependent Variable	*1*	2	3	4
Intercept	3542.40 (1873.28)	−1238.66 (1754.84)	2525.85 (2080.29)	−594.68 (1874.29)
Income		0.62 (0.04)		0.62 (0.04)
Age	33.24 (37.76)	−24.94 (35.07)	−11.38 (41.94)	−30.56 (35.38)
Head's Wage	747.69 (112.83)	−482.51 (108.18)	−49.18 (125.30)	
Log (Head's Wage)				−1811.55 (623.82)
NKIDS	137.47 (502.24)	−207.37 (466.30)	−321.58 (557.74)	−262.87 (470.84)
KAGE	15.60 (45.63)	−2.81 (42.37)	18.08 (50.67)	0.18 (42.84)
R^2	0.08	0.30	0.00	0.29
N	597	597	597	597

time as substitutes or even by a Modigliani-Brumberg formulation that ignores interaction between the two.

Under the pure life cycle hypothesis the coefficient of current income should be zero in the consumption function and one in the saving function. While Table 10–3 displays coefficients of income closer to the values implied by the life cycle hypothesis, the associated standard error indicates that the coefficients are nevertheless significantly different from unity in the saving function and zero in the consumption function. Hence the sample may contain a number of "reactors" whose borrowing is restricted. Further evidence of these restrictions is contained in column 10 of Table 10–3, which demonstrates that young families save only about one-third of additional income while older families save nearly all of it, consistent with the expectation that young families would predominate among reactors. Consumption, then, may rise with income as borrowing restrictions ease even if market goods and leisure time are unrelated or directly complementary in utility.

The standard Chow test was applied to test the equality of corresponding columns of Tables 10–2 and 10–3 and Tables 10–3 and 10–4. The F statistics for the test are presented in Table 10–5. The

Table 10–3. Estimates of Life Cycle Saving: Fixed Effects Model *(standard errors in parentheses)*

	Consumption			*Saving*		
Dependent Variable	*5*	*6*	*7*	*8*	*9*	*10*
Age	892.35 (652.13)	500.77 (628.35)	786.22 (655.64)	−356.45 (631.86)	691.03 (775.81)	−350.69 (631.48)
Income		0.29 (0.04)		0.71 (0.04)		
AOLD · Income						0.84 (0.05)
AYNG · Income						0.34 (0.08)
Head's Wage	−1047.25 (315.21)	−1014.87 (302.58)	−1015.34 (308.87)	984.22 (296.38)	908.37 (365.49)	842.03 (296.64)
NKIDS	398.65 (1481.46)	744.87 (1422.76)	−792.63 (2153.18)	805.94 (2065.88)	838.37 (2547.84)	615.06 (2072.40)
KAGE			124.82 (180.63)	−164.81 (173.40)	−262.28 (213.74)	−129.91 (178.11)
Wife's Wage	−13.83 (168.44)	−6.06 (161.68)				−5.22 (157.75)
R^2	0.02	0.10	—	—	—	0.39
N	581	581	594	594	594	581

Table 10–4. Estimates of Life Cycle Saving: Synthetic Cohort Model *(standard errors in parentheses)*

	Consumption		*Log (Consumption)*	
Dependent Variable	*11*	*12*	*13*	*14*
Intercept	1474.40 (6530.48)	195.85 (6088.78)	10.46 (2.14)	10.47 (2.17)
Income		0.44 (0.16)		0.00003 (0.00005)
Age	90.20 (47.86)	65.73 (45.45)	0.04 (0.02)	0.04 (0.02)
Head's Wage	524.81 (634.94)	−20.93 (625.90)		
Log (Head's Wage)			2.66 (0.83)	2.51 (0.88)
NKIDS	1070.80 (631.60)	866.50 (592.15)	0.63 (0.23)	0.63 (0.23)
Wife's Wage	427.96 (721.53)	11.09 (689.24)	0.20 (0.21)	0.17 (0.23)
R^2	0.57	0.64	0.90	0.90
N	41	41	41	41

Table 10–5. *F* Statistics for Hypothesis of Equality of Specified Regressions: Tables 10–2 through 10–4

	Degrees of Freedom			
Columns	*Numerator*	*Denominator*	*F*	*Significance*
2 and 8	5	1185	6.25	0.99
1 and 7	4	1187	9.38	0.99
4 and 9	4	1187	2.84	0.95
6 and 12	5	613	0.71	<0.90
5 and 11	4	615	1.75	<0.90

hypothesis of equality of the entire coefficient vector is rejected with better than 95 percent confidence for all comparisons between the pure cross-section model of Table 10–2 and the fixed effects model of Table 10–3. The coefficients of the synthetic cohort model are not different from those of the fixed effect model at conventional levels of significance despite the obvious variation in magnitudes of corresponding coefficients.

Table 10–6. Estimates of Life Cycle Saving: Two Stage Least Squares *(standard errors in parentheses)*

	Saving		
Dependent Variable	*15*	*16*	*17*
Age	−449.54 (752.87)	−393.70 (759.28)	77.00 (820.92)
Income	0.84 (0.30)	0.81 (0.30)	0.46 (0.38)
Wage	937.42 (299.15)		905.87 (1561.15)
Log (Head's Wage)		1047.11 (2195.32)	
NKIDS	1406.27 (2093.89)	1446.77 (2109.19)	1286.78 (2159.50)
KAGE	−274.08 (174.89)	−283.83 (176.15)	−287.34 (179.65)
N	597	597	593

Col. 17: Instruments for Income Change: previous income change excluding capital gains (1966–67), age, age squared. Instruments for Wage Change: previous wage change (1966–67), age, age squared, education.

The inaccuracy in computing capital gains gives rise to errors in the measurement of income and leads naturally to the suspicion that ordinary least squares estimates are misleading. Because holdings of corporate stock appear on both the left-hand side of the saving equation (since saving is computed as the difference in assets in successive years) and on the right-hand side (in order to compute capital gains), errors in measurement of stock can, among other things, account for the disproportionately high value of the cross-section marginal propensity to save recorded in Table 10–2. Two-stage least squares estimates of the fixed effect model were computed and are displayed in Table 10–6. Instruments used for income change between 1968 and 1969 were age, age squared, education, and income change excluding capital gains between 1966 and 1967. These estimates are freed of inconsistency due to errors in measurement of income and furthermore eliminate the need to assume independence of disturbances in consumption and labor supply equations—assumption (1). The coefficients of Table 10–6 suggest that the least squares estimate of the fixed effects model is not greatly affected by errors in measurement of income nor much restricted by assumption (1). Indeed, the coefficient of income is no longer significantly different from unity in the saving function although this primarily reflects a rise in the coefficient's standard error.

The assumption of perfect anticipation of wages and income can also be relaxed either by finding instrumental variables for the wage as well as for income or by computing the least squares regression of equation (18) on a synthetic cohort (i.e., mean changes for each age cell) rather than on the individual observations. Both procedures allow the coefficients of equation (18) to be estimated consistently even if unanticipated changes in wages or income cause changes in the marginal utility of wealth, λ_i. These estimates are presented in column 17 of Table 10–6 and in Table 10–7. Complementarity of market goods and leisure time is again suggested by the sign of the wage coefficient in both formulations despite their lack of significance at usual levels. A substantial portion of income seems to be consumed rather than saved, strengthening the hypothesis that not all desires to borrow are fulfilled.

Finally, estimates of $c_4(\lambda_i - \lambda)$ were retrieved using the procedure given by Mundlak [27, 1961]. Because λ_i is a function of all demographic traits that affect instantaneous utility, initial wealth, or the path of wages, these estimates provide a clue to the role of those influences that change little from year to year. In this instance, the role of education and of labor force participation of the wife on the level rather than the slope of the family's saving is examined. The coefficients of the least squares regression of the estimated value of $c_4(\lambda_i - \lambda)$ (the constant term for family i) on education and the

Table 10–7. Estimates of Life Cycle Saving: Synthetic Cohort Version of Fixed Effects Model *(standard errors in parentheses)*

	Consumption		
Dependent Variable	*18*	*19*	*20*
Age	−1734.76 (2546.18)	1765.98 (2698.61)	2956.32 (2997.15)
Income	0.46 (0.17)	0.56 (0.16)	
Head's Wage	1577.00 (1149.41)	−1630.46 (1218.21)	−1433.41 (1355.27)
NKIDS	−5297.43 (6013.18)	5690.68 (6373.15)	−1380.60 (6655.01)
KAGE	−36.44 (421.93)	63.36 (447.19)	193.11 (496.07)
R^2	0.32	0.03	0.04
N	41	41	41

Table 10–8. Dependent Variable: Estimated Individual Constant Term *(standard errors in parentheses)*

Intercept	4516.07 (1122.65)	
SC2	−3715.69 (1543.42)	SC2 = 1: 9–11 years education
SC3	−5964.07 (1322.96)	SC3 = 1: high school or high school plus noncollege training
SC4	−7931.78 (1404.49)	SC4 = 1: college, with or without degree
SC5	−9426.79 (2248.96)	SC5 = 1: advanced or professional degree
WWRKDUM	1758.48 (913.24)	WWRKDUM = 1: wife worked in 1968 and 1969
R^2	0.06	
N	597	

employment of the wife are presented below. Estimates of $c_4 (\lambda_i - \lambda)$ were computed using the coefficients of column 15 (Table 10–6) and the means of the variables for each family in 1968 and 1969.

Not surprisingly, increases in educational attainment tend to lower the intercept of a family's saving equation. Increased education represents in part a sacrifice of earnings early in life in return for greater earnings later. A portion of the saving that accompanies wage growth finances the household's consumption during the early period of low earnings. The dissaving early in life is accentuated if differences in wages among educational groups are not truly equalizing but also reflect lower opportunity cost of education available to some (see Becker [4, 1967]).

Despite the insignificant effect of changes in the wife's wage on family saving seen in Tables 10–3 and 10–4, families with working wives do appear to save more. The two results are not inconsistent. Changes in the market wage of a working wife reflect primarily the change from zero to a positive number when she enters the labor force (or the reverse when she leaves). In any given period, however, a substantial number of women beginning work are likely to be responding to a financial setback suffered by the family, for example, unemployment of the head. Hence, changes in the market wage or earnings of the wife are generally found to be negatively correlated to changes in the husband's earnings and family income [24, Mincer, 1962]. In such cases a rise in saving is hardly expected. Women who are observed to be working over a *number* of years are presumably those whose productivity in the market (offer wage) is high or whose productivity in the home (shadow wage) is low. These women enter and leave the labor force infrequently and so the gradual change in their market wage is dominated by changes experienced by women entering and leaving the labor force. Because the earnings of a working wife are consumed during both the years in which she works and those in which she does not, saving is expected to increase during the years when she does work.

VI. CONCLUSIONS

During the past five years economists have attempted to explain the close association between income and consumption over the life cycle by hypothesizing that time and market goods are substitutes in utility so that the association reflects a natural substitution of goods for time as the wage rises during life. The results of this chapter provide little support for that explanation; instead they suggest that time and goods may actually be complements in utility. The results also provide some evidence that current income does constrain consumption, especially among young families. Constraints on the ability to borrow may account for the observed pattern of consumption after all.

Such constraints might now be mitigating the desired level of dissaving by members of the postwar baby boom cohort. Members of this group, now aged about twenty to thirty-two, are at a point in their lives in which substantial dissaving is predicted by simple versions of the life cycle model (and *a fortiori* with versions in which complementarity of goods and time is maintained). Increased educational attainment can magnify aggregate dissaving of this cohort by diminishing current earnings in return for greater future receipts for a large fraction of individuals. Furthermore, while statistically negligible, the results in Tables 10–2 through 10–7 indicate fairly consistently that consumption rises as children age. Anticipation of the additional claim on resources by older children should cause couples who expect large families to save more when young. If, as seems likely, the baby-boom generation plans to raise smaller families than its parents did, then another motive for saving by young families is removed.

Whether these factors can account for the decline in aggregate saving over the past ten years is open to question. Moderating them are of course the possible constraints on borrowing alluded to earlier as well as the current saving of individuals now at the peak of their earning power. If the hypothesis of complementarity is maintained, these individuals expect to consume more during retirement than they do currently. Hence, they may save more than the Modigliani-Brumberg model predicts. They are also, however, members of the smaller Depression-era cohort.

The secular rise in the number of working wives is a further influence tending to raise the proportion of aggregate income saved. The average span of continuous employment among labor force participants is much shorter for women than for men. Therefore, because the earnings of the wife are consumed by the family while she is employed and also while she is not, the proportion of total family income saved while she *is* employed rises when she enters the labor force. Increases in the number of years spent in the labor force by the typical *working* wife, however, diminish the fraction of income reallocated (by saving) from years in which she works to years in which she does not. Increased labor force participation of married women, then, might lead to higher saving only if the number of years of participation by women *in the labor force* is not also increasing.

Whether life cycle influences like those discussed above have substantial impact on aggregate saving or are washed out by aggregate fluctuations that overlay them awaits the integration of the life cycle model into a theory of the response of the household to fiscal and monetary events.

NOTES TO CHAPTER 10

1. The life cycle model, like most economic theories, generates conclusions based on the maximizing behavior of the individual, even though decisions about consumption and saving are made with regard to benefits received by the whole family. In order to make use of a "family utility function" I shall assume hereafter that one member makes positive net transfers to each other member during his life so that his utility function secures consistent behavior by the family (see Gary Becker [5, 1974]).

2. Heckman [17, 1974] shows that $[w(t)L_1 + p(t)L_2]$ and $[w(t)X_1 + p(t)X_2]$ are negative if $L(t)$ and $X(t)$ are normal at each instant. The symmetry property of demand functions implies that $X_1 = L_2$ and so $[w(t)L_1 + p(t)X_1]$ is negative as well. Note that the coefficient of $w(t)$ in (14) is identical to the partial derivative of equation (13), $\dfrac{\partial s(t)}{\partial w(t)}$.

REFERENCES

1. BARTLETT, M.S. "Fitting a Straight Line When Both Variables Are Subject to Error," *Biometrics*, Sept. 1949, *5* (3), pp. 207–12.

2. BARTON, ANTON. "Family Composition, Prices and Expenditure Patterns," in *Econometric Analysis for National Economic Planning.* Edited by P.E. HART, G. MILLS and J.K. WHITAKER. London: Butterworths, 1964.

3. BECKER, GARY S. "A Theory of the Allocation of Time," *Economic Journal*, Sept. 1965, *75*(299), pp. 493–517.

4. ____. *Human Capital and the Personal Distribution of Income: An Analytical Approach.* Woytinski Lecture No. 1. Ann Arbor: Institute of Public Administration, University of Michigan, 1967.

5. ____. "A Theory of Social Interactions," *Journal of Political Economy*, Nov./Dec. 1974, *82*(6), pp. 1,063–93.

6. BIRD, ROGER, and BODKIN, RONALD. "The National Service Life Insurance Dividend of 1950 and Consumption: A Further Test of the 'Strict' Permanent Income Hypothesis," *Journal of Political Economy*, Oct. 1965, *73*(5), pp. 499–515.

7. BLINDER, ALAN. "Intergenerational Transfers and Life Cycle Consumption," *American Economic Review*, May 1976, *66*(2), pp. 87–93.

8. BODKIN, RONALD. "Windfall Income and Consumption," *American Economic Review*, Sept. 1959, *49*(4), pp. 602–14.

9. DOENGES, RUDOLPH C. "Transitory Income Size and Savings," *Southern Economic Journal*, Oct. 1966, *33*(2), pp. 258–63.

10. EIZENGA, WEITZE. *Demographic Factors and Savings.* Amsterdam: North Holland, 1961.

11. FERBER, ROBERT. *The Reliability of Consumer Reports of Financial Assets and Debts.* Urbana: Bureau of Economic and Business Research, University of Illinois, 1966.

12. FISHER, IRVING. *The Rate of Interest.* New York: Macmillan, 1907.

13. ____. *The Theory of Interest.* New York: Macmillan, 1930.

14. FISHER, JANET. "Income, Spending and Saving Patterns of Consumer Units in Different Age Groups," in *Studies in Income and Wealth*, vol. 15. New York: National Bureau of Economic Research, 1952.

15. FRIEDMAN, MILTON. *A Theory of the Consumption Function.* New York: National Bureau of Economic Research; distributed by Princeton University Press, 1957.

16. GHEZ, GILBERT, and BECKER, GARY. *The Allocation of Time and Goods over the Life Cycle.* New York: National Bureau of Economic Research; distributed by Columbia University Press, 1975.

17. HECKMAN, JAMES. "Life Cycle Consumption and Labor Supply: An Explanation of the Relationship between Income and Consumption over the Life Cycle," *American Economic Review*, March 1974, *64*(1), pp. 188–94.

18. ____. "A Partial Survey of Recent Research on the Labor Supply of Women," *American Economic Review*, May 1978, *68*(2), pp. 200–207.

19. HOUTHAKKER, HENDRIK. "The Permanent Income Hypothesis," *American Economic Review*, June 1958, *48*(3), pp. 396–404.

20. KEYNES, JOHN MAYNARD. *The General Theory of Employment, Interest and Money.* New York: Harcourt, Brace and World, 1935.

21. LANDSBERGER, MICHAEL. "Windfall Income and Consumption: Comment," *American Economic Review*, June 1966, *56*(3), pp. 534–39.

22. ____ . "The Life-Cycle Hypothesis: A Reinterpretation and Empirical Test," *American Economic Review*, March 1970, *60*(1), pp. 175–83.

23. MACURDY, THOMAS. Labor Supply Decisions over the Life Cycle. Unpublished Ph.D. dissertation, University of Chicago, 1978.

24. MINCER, JACOB. "Labor Force Participation of Married Women: A Study of Labor Supply," in *Aspects of Labor Economics*. New York: National Bureau of Economic Research; distributed by Princeton University Press, 1962.

25. MODIGLIANI, FRANCO, and BRUMBERG, RICHARD. "Utility Analysis and the Consumption Function: An Interpretation of Cross-Section Data," in *Post Keynesian Economics*. Edited by KENNETH KURIHARA. New Brunswick: Rutgers University Press, 1954.

26. MUELLBAUER, JOHN. "Household Composition, Engel Curves and Welfare Comparisons between Households," *European Economic Review*, August 1974, *5*(2), pp. 103–22.

27. MUNDLAK, YAIR. "Empirical Production Functions Free of Management Bias," *Journal of Farm Economics*, Feb. 1961, *43*(1), pp. 44–56.

28. SMITH, JAMES P. *Assets and Labor Supply*. Santa Monica: Rand Report R. 1728, May 1975.

29. STROTZ, ROBERT. "Myopia and Inconsistency in Dynamic Utility Maximization," *Review of Economic Studies*, 1955–56, *23*(3), pp. 165–80.

30. THEIL, HENRI. *Principles of Econometrics*. New York: Wiley & Sons, 1971.

31. THUROW, LESTER. "The Optimum Lifetime Distribution of Consumption Expenditure," *American Economic Review*, June 1969, *59*(3), pp. 324–30.

32. U.S. PRESIDENT. *Economic Report*. Washington, D.C.: U.S.G.P.O., 1974.

33. WALD, ABRAHAM. "The Fitting of Straight Lines If Both Variables Are Subject to Error," *Annals of Mathematical Statistics*, Sept. 1940, *11*(3), pp. 284–300.

34. WHITE, BETSY B. "Empirical Tests of the Life Cycle Hypothesis," *American Economic Review*, Sept. 1978, *68*(4), pp. 547–60.

35. WISEMAN, CLARK. "Windfalls and Consumption under a Borrowing Constraint," *Review of Economics and Statistics*, May 1975, *57*(2), pp. 180–84.

36. YAARI, MENAHEM. "On the Consumer's Lifetime Allocation Process," *International Economic Review*, Sept. 1964, *5*(3), pp. 304–17.

Chapter 11

Government Finance in an Overlapping Generations Model with Gifts and Bequests

Willem H. Buiter[a]

The overlapping generations model has been a popular and powerful tool for the analysis of the longer-run consequences of alternative government financial policies. Paul Samuelson's [11, 1958] seminal contribution contained many important insights but was limited to the special case of exogenous production and perishable or nondurable commodities. David Cass and Menahem Yaari [5, 1966] considered storable output but still modeled production as exogenous. Peter Diamond [7, 1965] superimposed the overlapping generations model on a neoclassical production function with durable capital and labor as its arguments. This model was further developed in Cass and Yaari [6, 1967].

An important addition to this literature is found in a recent contribution by Robert Barro [1, 1974] titled "Are Government Bonds Net Wealth?" Introduction of a bequest motive into a Diamond-type overlapping generations growth model leads to the proposition that substitution of government borrowing for lump-sum taxation has no effect. His argument for neutrality is simple. Consider an economic agent whose utility depends on the consumption or utility level achieved by his immediate descendant, whose utility is similarly determined. Directly or indirectly, any agent's utility function allows for the consumption of all future generations of his line. If no generation is at a zero bequest "corner," the effective budget constraint

[a]I would like to thank Jonathan Eaton, Roger Gordon, Ed Green, Alan Blinder, and Mark Gersovitz for helpful comments on earlier drafts. Detailed and wide-ranging editorial comments from George von Furstenberg were most useful. I owe a special debt to James Tobin, first for stimulating my interest in this subject and second for many constructive suggestions.

includes the expected discounted future earnings of later generations. Households with finite lives are effectively transformed into households with infinite lives. Government attempts to redistribute income from the young to the old (e.g., through an unfunded social security scheme) are neutralized by increased voluntary transfers or bequests from the old to the young. The trajectories of capital stock and of consumption remain unchanged.

This chapter extends and qualifies Barro's contribution in a number of ways. It includes *gifts*, transfers from young to old as well as *bequests*, transfers from old to young, and it incorporates labor force growth. The long-run consumption possibility locus, with and without gifts and bequests, is shown to be amenable to very simple algebraic and diagrammatic representation. As in Barro's paper, only lump-sum taxes are considered.

I show that if households are dynastic savers (i.e., their utility functions incorporate bequest or gift motives) problems of convergence occur unless these motives are weak. If these motives are weak, however, it is more likely that a change in the government's tax-transfer-borrowing mix will be nonneutral. If there is either a bequest motive or a gift motive, but not both, there always exists a change in financial policy that is nonneutral; even the steady states can differ for different policies. If both motives are present and no convergence problems arise, government financial policy will have no effect on the steady-state capital-labor ratio and consumption pattern. Even then, however, non-steady-state behavior may be influenced by changes in public sector financial policy.

Leading up to the discussion of voluntary intergenerational gifts is a review and extension of some earlier work on the effect of public sector financing in overlapping generations models with life cycle savers—economic agents without bequest or gift motives. Throughout, the analysis borrows freely from papers by Samuelson [11, 1958], Cass and Yaari [5, 1966; 6, 1967], Diamond [7, 1965], Barro [1, 1974; 2, 1976], and Feldstein [8, 1974; 9, 1976].

I. GOVERNMENT FINANCING IN OVERLAPPING GENERATIONS MODELS WITH LIFE CYCLE SAVERS

A generation lives for two periods. Population grows at a constant one-period proportional rate n. People are identical, within and across generations. Generations are indexed by the time at which they are born. c_t^i denotes consumption in period i by a member of generation $t (i = 1, 2)$. A_t^1 denotes the value of the noninherited wealth owned by a member of generation t at the beginning of the second period of his life, r_t denotes the one-period interest rate paid, in period t, on interest-bearing assets carried over from period $t-1$ into period t. L_t denotes the size of the tth generation. K_t is the stock of commodities in existence at the beginning of period t. With life cycle saving behavior, the common utility function of each member of every generation is given by

$$U_t = u(c_t^1, c_t^2),$$

where u is increasing, strictly quasi-concave, and smooth. The individual's rate of pure time preference, really the private rate of "age-preference," δ, is implicitly defined from the slope of an indifference curve when consumption in both periods is equal:

$$\delta(c) = \frac{u_1(c, c)}{u_2(c, c)} - 1 .$$

I briefly consider a model in which output per worker is fixed and goods can be stored.

A Model with Productive Storage

Labor is the only input in the production process. The supply of labor is inelastic and full employment prevails. Through appropriate choice of units, output per worker is scaled to 1. When stored, output grows at a one-period proportional rate, Π $(-1 \leq \Pi)$. Unproductive storage without depreciation would be represented by $\Pi = 0$, perishable output by $\Pi = -1$. As was pointed out by Samuelson [11, 1958] and Cass and Yaari [5, 1966], no mutually advantageous private trades are possible in such a model. For members of the same generation this follows from the assumption that they are all identical. For trades between members of adjacent generations, it follows from the fact that those currently retired have nothing to offer those currently working. Provision for old age will therefore be through storage, unless $\Pi = -1$, in which case storage is pointless.

If $n \geq \Pi$, the decentralized competitive solution is socially suboptimal and, except for the corner solution $c_t^1 = 1$, $c_t^2 = 0$, also technically inefficient. There is too much saving, that is, too much storage. Efficient distribution schemes, when $n \geq \Pi$, involve zero inventories. The social resource constraint is

$$K_{t+1} + c_t^1 L_t + c_{t-1}^2 L_{t-1} = L_t + K_t(1 + \Pi) .$$

Let k_t denote K_t/L_t. The stationary social resource constraint is $c^1 + \frac{c^2}{1+n} = 1 + (\Pi - n)k$. The efficient stationary social resource constraint with $n \geq \Pi$ is $c^1 + \frac{c^2}{1+n} = 1$. It would be more efficient for young workers of generation t to provide for retirement by distributing part of their current labor income to the retired members of generation $t-1$, if they could count on similar treatment, after they retire, from the young members of generation $t+1$. Since the proportional rate of population growth exceeds the return to storage, it is preferable to transfer resources over time as the "biological rate of return" n rather than at the "inventory own rate of return" Π.

Taxation and Borrowing in a Model with Productive Storage. A public borrowing scheme offering real-valued, one-period bonds paying a one-period rate of interest of n will induce private economic agents to hold the socially optimal (zero) level of inventories. (We assume that, unless their rates of return differ, government bonds and commodity inventories are perfect substitutes in private portfolios). Any interest rate greater than Π will lead private savers to substitute public sector bonds for commodity inventories. Any interest rate less than or equal to n can be offered by the government without its having to redeem this debt in the aggregate, even though each individual private investor is fully repaid. Assume $n > 0$. The government runs a successful "Ponzi game," servicing its debt obligations to those about to retire by selling bonds to those just entering the labor force. Let D_t be the value of the bonds sold in period t. Interest payment and repayment of principal take place in period $t+1$.

In the presence of a government offering debt obligations bearing an interest rate n, a member of generation t solves the following optimization problem:

$$\max_{c_t^1,\, c_t^2} \quad u(c_t^1, c_t^2)$$

$$c_t^1 + \frac{c_t^2}{1+r_{t+1}} = 1 \tag{1a}$$

$$r_{t+1} = n \tag{1b}$$

$$c_t^1, c_t^2 \geq 0 . \tag{1c}$$

In terms of single-period budget constraints, this becomes

$$(1-c_t^1)(1+r_{t+1}) = A_t^1 = (D_t/L_t)(1+r_{t+1}) \tag{2a}$$

$$A_t^1 = c_t^2 . \tag{2b}$$

The market solution with government borrowing is stationary. The private budget constraint, (1a) and (1b), is the same as the efficient stationary social resource constraint. Let $D_t/L_t = \delta_t$. With stationarity $\delta_t = \delta$ and the government sells δ in period t to every member of the new generation (t). Total bond sales are δL_t , implying a debt service requirement in period $t+1$ of $\delta L_t(1+n)$. In period $t+1$ the government sells bonds to the larger new generation $t+1$ in amount $\delta L_{t+1} = \delta L_t(1+n)$. The scheme is viable. New bond sales cover current debt service requirements. But at the end of period $t+1$ the government, having just repaid its obligation to generation t, has a net debt to generation $t+1$ of δL_{t+1}. Private financial intermediaries with (growing!) negative net worth are not viable. A nonmarket institution such as the government is required for society to realize its consumption potential.[1]

One can introduce an unfunded social security system into this model in a very simple way. Each member of generation t pays a lump-sum tax of $\frac{S}{1+n}$ when young. This tax is paid out as a lump-sum transfer payment, S, to each member of the currently retired generation. As before, any effects of such taxes and transfers on labor supply and age of retirement are ignored. The individual lifetime budget constraint, illustrated in Figure 11–1, is now

$$\left(1-c_t^1 - \frac{S}{1+n}\right)(1+\Pi) + S = c_t^2 \tag{3a}$$

$$c_t^1 \leq 1 - \frac{S}{1+n} \tag{3b}$$

$$c_t^2 , c_t^1 \geq 0 . \tag{3c}$$

For small S and for utility functions without extreme time preference, such a social security program is likely to be superior to the decentralized competitive solution (CDE lies above AB, except near the c_t^1 axis). Both schemes are dominated by the public borrowing scheme discussed earlier (BF dominates BA and, except at D, also CDE). By varying S, any point on the socially efficient consumption possibility frontier can be obtained.

Figure 11–1. Consumption Possibility Loci of the Model with Productive Storage; Intertemporal Trade-offs Between Consumption When Young (c_t^1) and Consumption When Old (c_t^2) as Functions of the Rate of Return to Storage (π), the Rate of Population Growth (n), and the Unfunded Social Security Benefit (S)

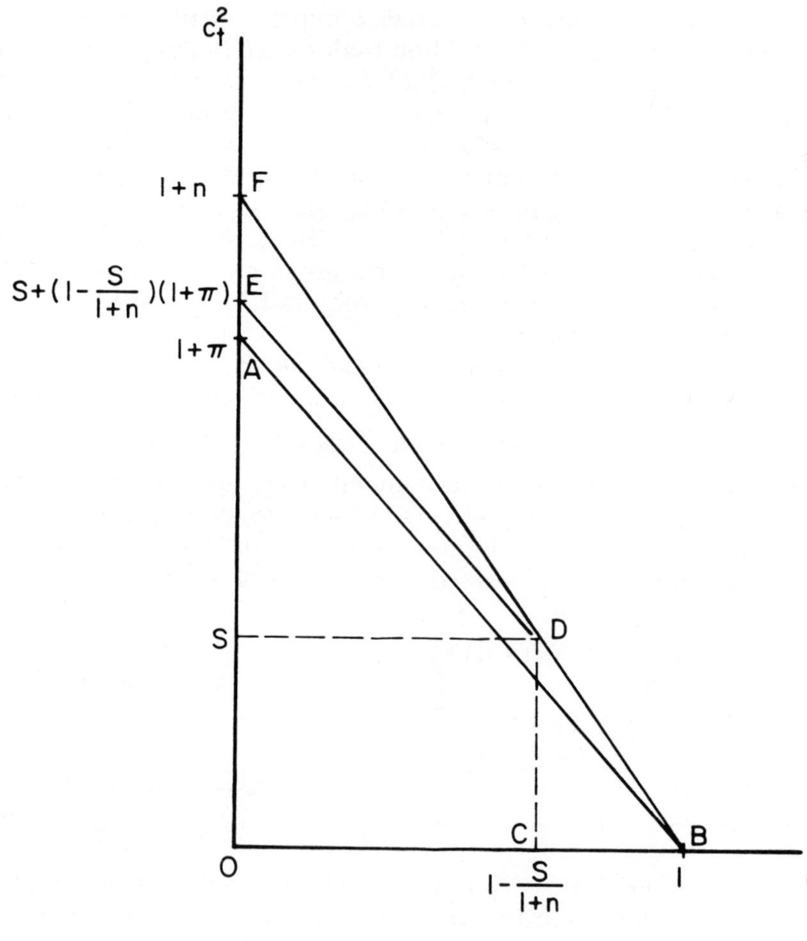

Note that private agents cannot borrow when young, using their expected future social security benefits as collateral. Potential lenders, those currently retired, will not be around to enjoy the returns on their abstinence.

A Model with a Neoclassical Production Function

We keep the same overlapping generations structure but production, Y, is now characterized by a neoclassical production function in capital and labor, $Y_t = F(K_t, L_t)$, linear homogeneous, increasing in K and L, strictly quasi-concave and smooth, with $0 = F(0, L) = F(L, 0)$. We can rewrite the production function as

$$Y_t = L_t f(k_t), \; f(0) = 0; \; f' > 0; \; f'' < 0, \; k_t \geq 0.$$

Let w_t denote the real wage in period t. In the absence of government financing operations, the individual optimization problem can now be written as

$$\max \quad u(c_t^1, c_t^2)$$

subject to

$$c_t^1, c_t^2 \geq 0$$

$$c_t^1 + \frac{c_t^2}{1 + r_{t+1}} = w_t . \tag{4}$$

Writing the individual lifetime budget constraint as two single-period constraints we can express (4) alternatively as

$$(w_t - c_t^1)(1 + r_{t+1}) = A_t^1 \tag{4a}$$

$$A_t^1 = c_t^2 . \tag{4b}$$

For the individual saving plans to be consistent, an aggregate capital market equilibrium condition needs to be satisfied. Thus, $(w_t - c_t^1) L_t = K_{t+1}$ or

$$w_t - c_t^1 = k_{t+1}(1 + n) . \tag{5}$$

From the assumption of a competitive labor market and a competitive capital rental market we have

$$w_t = f(k_t) - k_t f'(k_t) \tag{6a}$$

$$r_{t+1} = f'(k_{t+1}). \tag{6b}$$

Assuming an interior solution to the optimization problem, the first-order conditions for the individual investor are

$$\frac{u_1}{u_2} = 1 + f'(k_{t+1}).$$

The highest indifference curve is tangential to the private budget constraint. This may meet or cut the macro-feasibility frontier (5), as we shall show explicitly below for the stationary case.

If one considers only stationary solutions, the problem of an agent in a decentralized competitive setting can be summarized as

$$\max \quad u(c^1, c^2) \tag{7a}$$

subject to

$$c^1, c^2 > 0$$

$$c^1 + \frac{c^2}{1 + f'(k)} = f(k) - kf'(k) \tag{7b}$$

$$f(k) - kf'(k) - c^1 = k(1+n). \tag{7c}$$

Solving (7c) for k as a function of c^1 and substituting into (7b), one can express c^2 as a function of c^1.

$$c^2 = \psi(c^1) \tag{8a}$$

with

$$\psi' = -(1+f')\left[1 + \frac{k(n-f')}{1+f'} f''(1 + n + kf'')^{-1}\right]. \tag{8b}$$

The stationary decentralized competitive consumption possibility locus is graphed in Figure 11–2 for the Cobb-Douglas case, $Y = K^{\alpha} L^{1-\alpha}$, $0 < \alpha < 1$. At the origin its slope is $\frac{\alpha}{1-\alpha}(1+n)$.

k increases monotonically as we move from 0 to E_1 and to β. As k approaches infinity, the slope of the consumption possibility locus becomes -1. When $f'(k) = n$ (the golden rule capital-labor ratio) at E_1, $\psi' = -(1+f') = -(1+n)$. The locus is concave toward the origin. For very large k and general linear homogeneous production functions $\frac{dc^2}{dc^1}$ may become positive, denoting extreme overaccumulation. However, this is not possible in the Cobb-Douglas case. A decentralized competitive economy could settle anywhere on this locus.

A competitive equilibrium like E_2 would be dynamically inefficient because society maintains a capital-labor ratio in excess of the golden rule value of k. A competitive equilibrium like E_3, with a k below the golden rule level, is not dynamically inefficient: the stationary path of resources available for consumption per head of total

Figure 11–2. Competitive Stationary Trade-off Possibilities between Consumption When Young (c^1) and Consumption When Old (c^2) as a Function of the Steady-State Capital-Labor Ratio (k), and Socially Efficient Stationary Trade-off Possibilities as a Function of the Rate of Population Growth (n)

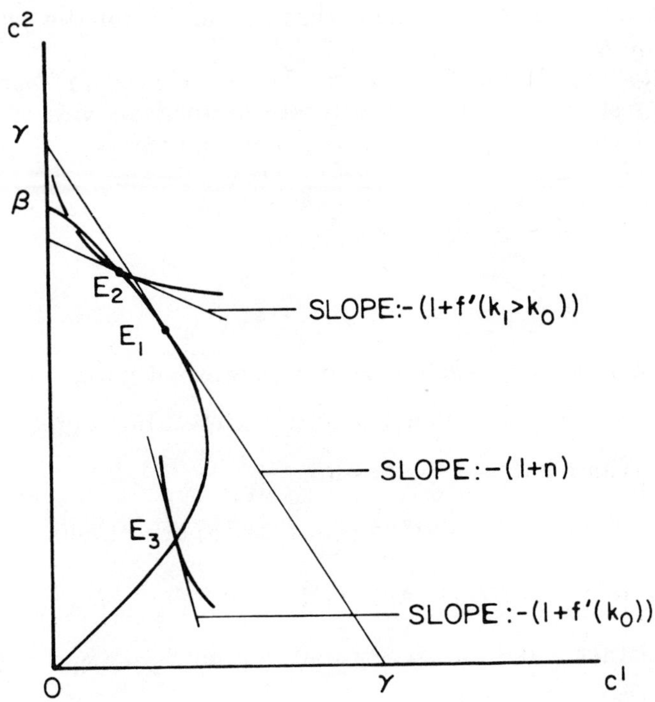

population at E_3, $c^1 + \frac{c^2}{1+n}$, is not dominated by any feasible per capita consumption path taking the economy from E_3 to any point on the efficient stationary locus $\gamma\gamma$. The efficient stationary locus will also be referred to as the social planner's consumption opportunity locus.

It should be noted, however, that in terms of utility derived from lifetime consumption an equilibrium like E_3 can be inefficient. It is shown below that by pegging the interest rate at $r = n$ the government can take the economy from any initial position to a point on the efficient boundary in one period. Consider such a one-period traverse. During the period in which the economy moves from E_3 to E_1, say, the total amount of resources available for consumption $(Y - \Delta K)$ is less than it was at E_3. Let all this reduction in consumption be at the expense of the younger generation. Once the economy achieves the golden rule capital-labor ratio, the gain in total resources available for consumption could be more than sufficient to compensate, in terms of the utility derived from *lifetime* consumption, the generation that made the initial consumption sacrifice. All subsequent generations could also be better off. This outcome is more likely the lower the pure rate of time preference and the greater the return to additional investment, that is, the greater the capital elasticity of output.

Stability conditions for this model are derived in Diamond [7, 1965]. I restate them here to facilitate comparison with the stability conditions when the public sector pursues a bond issue and taxation policy.

From the private sector life cycle utility maximization program, one obtains c_t^1 as a function of w_t and r_{t+1}:

$$c_t^1 = c^1(w_t, r_{t+1}). \tag{9}$$

If consumption in each period is a normal good, one has $0 < \frac{\partial c^1}{\partial w_t} < 1$. The effect of a change in the interest rate on period 1 consumption is ambiguous. I shall assume $\frac{\partial c^1}{\partial r_{t+1}} \leq 0$.[2]

Substituting (9), (4), (6a), and (6b) for (5) one obtains

$$f(k_t) - k_t f'(k_t) - c^1\left([f(k_t) - k_t f'(k_t)],\ f'(k_{t+1})\right) = k_{t+1}(1+n). \tag{10}$$

Assume that a unique steady-state equilibrium ($k_t = k$ for all t) exists.

It will be stable when $\left|\frac{dk_{t+1}}{dk_t}\right| < 1$, that is, when

$$\frac{\left(\frac{\partial c^1}{\partial w_t} - 1\right)kf''}{1 + n + \frac{\partial c^1}{\partial r_{t+1}} f''} < 1. \tag{11}$$

This condition is not automatically satisfied, even if $\frac{\partial c^1}{\partial r_{t+1}} \leq 0$.

The Neoclassical Model with Technical Change

The introduction of labor-augmenting technical change at a constant proportional rate γ slightly modifies the analysis. It becomes necessary to distinguish between the labor force in natural units L, and the labor force in efficiency units $\widetilde{L}$. Let Γ denote the level of labor augmentation, so that

$$\widetilde{L} = L\Gamma \text{ and } \Gamma_t = \Gamma_0 (1 + \gamma)^t .$$

Further notational changes are: $\widetilde{k}_t = K_t/\widetilde{L}_t$; $\widetilde{y}_t = Y_t/\widetilde{L}_t$, and

$$\widetilde{c}_t^1 = c_t^1/\Gamma_t$$

$$\widetilde{c}_t^2 = c_t^2/\Gamma_t .$$

However, w_t continues to denote the wage rate of a natural worker, so that:

$$w_t = \Gamma_t[f(\widetilde{k}_t) - \widetilde{k}_t f'(\widetilde{k}_t)]$$

$$r_t = f'(\widetilde{k}_t) .$$

Note that the utility function of a consumer must be specified, as before, in terms of per capita consumption $u(c_t^1, c_t^2)$ rather than in terms of consumption per unit of efficiency labor. With labor-augmenting technical change, a steady state, if it exists, will have per capita consumption in youth and old age growing at the rate of technical change; $\widetilde{c}_t^1$ and $\widetilde{c}_t^2$ will be constant. Such an outcome is possible only if the utility function is homogeneous, that is, of the general form

$$u(c_t^1, c_t^2) = (c_t^2)^i\, v(c_t^1/c_t^2),\ i \geq 0\,.$$

For this to be a sensible utility function (u increasing in c^1 and c^2) we also require: $v' > 0$ and $i(c_t^2)^{i-1} v - v' c_t^1 (c_t^2)^{i-2} > 0$. With such a homogeneous utility function the slope, curvature, and higher derivatives of an indifference curve in $(\tilde{c}^1, \tilde{c}^2)$ space are the same as those of the corresponding indifference curve in (c^1, c^2) space. In particular, they will be independent of the level of labor efficiency Γ.

The analogues of equations (7b) and (7c) with technical change are (12a) and (12b):

$$\tilde{c}^1 + \frac{\tilde{c}^2}{1 + f'(\tilde{k})} = f(\tilde{k}) - \tilde{k}f'(\tilde{k}) \tag{12a}$$

$$f(\tilde{k}) - \tilde{k}f'(\tilde{k}) - \tilde{c}^1 = \tilde{k}(1+n)(1+\gamma)\,. \tag{12b}$$

For the Cobb-Douglas production function $Y = K^\alpha\, \tilde{L}^{(1-\alpha)}$ or $\tilde{y} = \tilde{k}^\alpha$, the slope of the stationary lifetime consumption possibility locus is given by

$$\frac{\partial \tilde{c}^2}{\partial \tilde{c}^1} = \frac{(1+n)(1+\gamma)(1+\alpha^2\ \tilde{k}^{\alpha-1})}{(1-\alpha)\,\alpha\tilde{k}^{\alpha-1} - (1+n)(1+\gamma)}\,. \tag{13a}$$

At the origin, when $\tilde{k} = 0$, this slope equals $\frac{\alpha}{1-\alpha}(1+n)(1+\gamma)$. When the marginal product of capital equals the natural rate of growth, that is, when $\alpha\tilde{k}^{\alpha-1} + 1 = (1+n)(1+\gamma)$, the slope is equal to $-(1+n)(1+\gamma)$. This point may be termed the modified golden rule. As $\tilde{k}$ approaches $+\infty$ the slope goes to -1. The locus is shown in Figure 11–3, along with the stationary social planner's consumption opportunity locus, which now has a slope of $-(1+n)(1+\gamma)$.[3]

How does this locus shift when the rate of technical change or, equivalently, the rate of growth of the labor force increases? From (12a) and (12b) we obtain

$$\frac{\partial \tilde{c}^2}{\partial \gamma} = \frac{(1+n)(1-\alpha)\alpha\tilde{k}^{\alpha}[1-(1+n)(1+\gamma)] + (1+n)(1-\alpha)\alpha^2\,\tilde{k}^{(2\alpha-1)}}{(1-\alpha)\alpha\tilde{k}^{\alpha-1} - (1+n)(1+\gamma)}\,. \tag{13b}$$

Figure 11–3. Stationary Competitive Trade-off Possibilities between Consumption per Unit of Efficiency Labor When Young ($\tilde{c}^1$) and When Old (c^2) and Stationary Socially Efficient Trade-off Possibilities as a Function of the Rate of Population Growth (n) and the Rate of Labor-Augmenting Technical Change (γ)

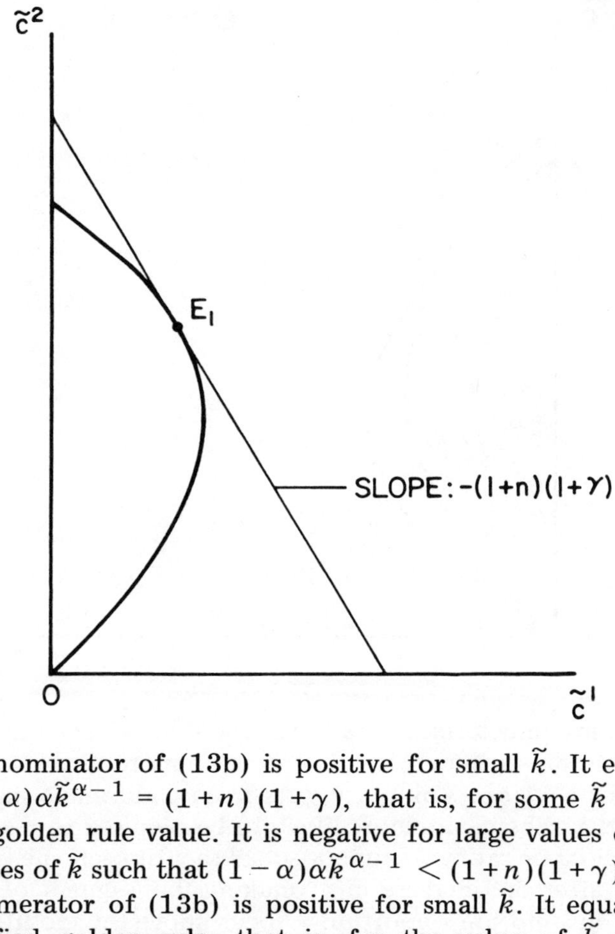

The denominator of (13b) is positive for small $\tilde{k}$. It equals zero when $(1-\alpha)\alpha\tilde{k}^{\alpha-1} = (1+n)(1+\gamma)$, that is, for some $\tilde{k}$ below the modified golden rule value. It is negative for large values of $\tilde{k}$—that is, for values of $\tilde{k}$ such that $(1-\alpha)\alpha\tilde{k}^{\alpha-1} < (1+n)(1+\gamma)$.

The numerator of (13b) is positive for small $\tilde{k}$. It equals zero at the modified golden rule—that is, for the value of $\tilde{k}$ for which $\alpha\tilde{k}^{\alpha-1} + 1 = (1+n)(1+\gamma)$. It is negative for $\tilde{k}$'s in excess of the modified golden rule value.

The solid locus in Figure 11–4 represents a lower value of γ, the dotted locus a higher value. Ω corresponds to the modified golden rule value of $\tilde{k}$.

The effect of the increase in γ on the stationary competitive solution for $\tilde{c}^2$ and $\tilde{c}^1$ is ambiguous. The following observations can be made, however. With a higher rate of technical change, the modified

Figure 11–4. The Effect of a Higher Rate of Technical Change on the Stationary Competitive Trade-off Possibilities between Consumption per Unit of Efficiency Labor When Young ($\tilde{c}^1$) and When Old ($\tilde{c}^2$)

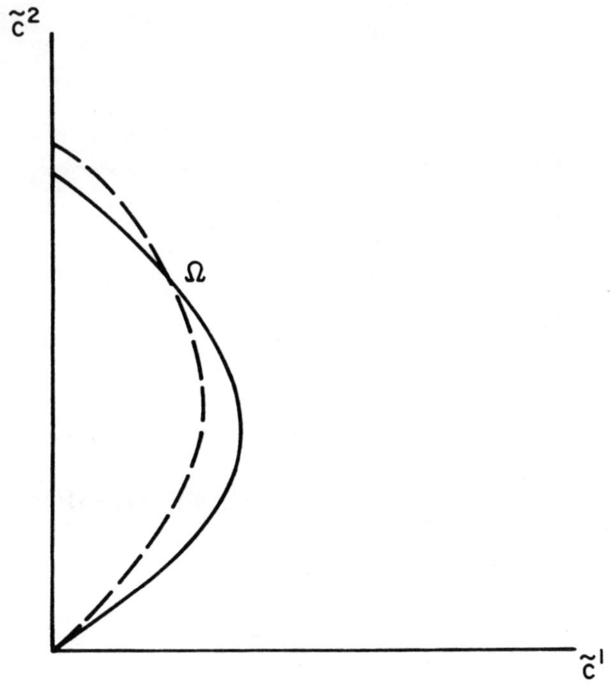

golden rule is characterized by a lower value for $\tilde{k}$. The unaided competitive economy is therefore in some sense more likely to end up in the inefficient region. Voluntary gifts from children to parents or a social security scheme are more likely to be required to reach an efficient capital-labor ratio. Assume a social security scheme exists both before and after the increase in γ, making the segment of the social planner's consumption opportunity locus above the modified golden rule value of $\tilde{k}$ available. With a reasonable utility function, the equilibrium corresponding to the higher value of γ will be characterized by a higher value of $\tilde{c}^2$. The value of $\tilde{c}^1$ could be lower. The social terms of trade between consumption when young and consumption when old are shifted in favor of the latter, and people are likely to shift consumption toward the second period of their lives. $\tilde{k}$ is lower as long as a point on the new efficient stationary consumption possibility locus is chosen.

The Effects of Taxation and Borrowing. The effect of government financing in this model is considered next. For reasons of space, I shall consider only one particular combination of public sector borrowing (lending) and taxation (transfer payments) policies. The policy in question, pegging the interest rate, is interesting both as an illustration of the important effects of alternative public sector financing policies and as an example of a policy capable of moving the economy to the golden rule path in minimal time (i.e., in one period or half a generation). The analysis reverts to the case without technical progress.

Let us briefly characterize the problem of the selection of the optimal steady state from the point of view of an omnipotent social planner. The only constraint to which this planner is subject is the aggregate resource constraint:

$$c_t^1 L_t + c_{t-1}^2 L_{t-1} = Y_t - (K_{t+1} - K_t) = L_t f(k_t) - L_t (k_{t+1}(1+n) - k_t)$$

or

$$c_t^1 + \frac{c_{t-1}^2}{1+n} = f(k_t) - k_{t+1}(1+n) + k_t . \tag{14}$$

The stationary aggregate resource constraint is therefore,

$$c^1 + \frac{c^2}{1+n} = f(k) - nk. \tag{15}$$

The planner has a stationary social welfare function $w(c^1, c^2)$, which for simplicity is taken to be the same as the stationary private utility function. There is no reason in principle for the planner's social welfare function to bear any relation to the private utility functions. Indeed, a common argument for government intervention in the saving-investment process is that the private rate of time preference exceeds the social rate of time preference.[4]

The planner selects the golden rule capital-labor ratio defined by $f'(k) = n$, in order to maximize the stationary per capita amount of resources available for consumption. The social stationary consumption possibility locus is given in Figure 11–2 by the straight line $\gamma\gamma$, with slope $-(1+n)$. This dominates the decentralized competitive consumption possibility locus without gifts or bequests, except at the point of tangency, E_1.

D_t again denotes the value of 1 period real bonds floated during period t and repaid with interest at rate r_{t+1} in period $t+1$. As government bonds and private bonds are perfect substitutes in private sector portfolios, D_t can be negative. In that case the public sector lends to the private sector. T_t denotes total lump-sum taxes paid by the young generation during period t. T_t can be negative in which case it constitutes transfer payments to the young, $\tau_t \equiv T_t / L_t$.

With government borrowing and taxes, the optimization problem faced by a representative individual in a decentralized competitive economy can be characterized as follows:

$$\max \quad u(c_t^1, c_t^2)$$

subject to

$$c_t^1, c_t^2, k_t \geq 0$$

$$(w_t - c_t^1 - \tau_t)(1 + r_{t+1}) = A_t^1$$

$$A_t^1 = c_t^2$$

$$(1 + r_t)D_{t-1} = D_t + T_t \qquad \text{(public sector budget constraint)}$$

$$(w_t - c_t^1 - \tau_t) L_t = D_t + K_{t+1} \qquad \text{(capital market equilibrium)}$$

$$w_t = f(k_t) - k_t f'(k_t)$$

$$r_{t+1} = f'(k_{t+1}).$$

From private life cycle optimizing behavior, one obtains the consumption function $c_t^1 = c^1(w_t - \tau_t, r_{t+1})$. I again assume $0 < c_1^1(\cdot) < 1$ and $c_2^1(\cdot) \leq 0$. One can now summarize the model as in equations (16a–16f):

$$c_t^1 = c^1(w_t - \tau_t, r_{t+1}) \tag{16a}$$

$$(w_t - c_t^1 - \tau_t)(1 + r_{t+1}) = c_t^2 \tag{16b}$$

$$w_t - c_t^1 - \tau_t = \delta_t + k_{t+1}(1 + n) \tag{16c}$$

$$(1 + r_t)\delta_{t-1} = \delta_t(1 + n) + \tau_t(1 + n) \tag{16d}$$

$$w_t = f(k_t) - k_t f'(k_t) \tag{16e}$$

$$r_{t+1} = f'(k_{t+1}) \tag{16f}$$

$$c_t^1,\ c_t^2,\ k_t \geq 0.$$

At each point in time, t, this system of equations determines the values of c_t^1, c_t^2, w_t, k_{t+1}, and two of the three government instruments τ_t, δ_t, and r_{t+1}, given the values assumed by the remaining government instrument and the predetermined variables, r_t, δ_{t-1}, and k_t.

I shall consider the interesting special case in which the government pegs the interest rate at some constant value each period: $r_{t+1} = r > 0$ for all t. This means that the government sells bonds to or buys bonds from the private sector in the amount required to clear the capital market at that interest rate. Any excess of debt service requirements over new bond sales is met by lump-sum taxes on those currently working. In the opposite case, lump-sum transfer payments are made.

Consider an economy that has been evolving without any government financial policy up to period t. (The system could be in a steady state equilibrium at a point like E_1, E_2, or E_3 in Figure 11–2.)

In period t the new policy of pegging the interest rate at r is introduced. Substitute (16a) and (16e) into (16c) and (16d), and replace r_{t+1} by r. The state of the economy in period t can then be described by equations (17a–17c):

$$f(k_t) - k_t f'(k_t) - c^1\left(f(k_t) - k_t f'(k_t) - \tau_t, r\right) = k_{t+1}(1+n) \tag{17a}$$

$$\delta = -\tau_t \tag{17b}$$

$$r = f'(k_{t+1}). \tag{17c}$$

k_t is predetermined and $\delta_{t-1} = 0$ by assumption.
Assume the system was initially in a steady state with

$$k_t > k_{t+1} = f'^{-1}(r) = g(r)$$

or, equivalently, $r_t < r$. The right-hand side of (17a) (the demand for capital) is smaller than in the previous period. To reduce the supply of capital we require a reduction in saving. If $c_2^1(\cdot) \leq 0$, saving will not decrease when the interest rate rises. τ_t will therefore have to be negative. In other words, the government will be selling bonds and using the proceeds from the sale to make a lump-sum transfer payment to the working population.

In period $t+1$, the state of the economy can be described by equations (18a–18b):

$$f\big(g(r)\big) - g(r)f'\big(g(r)\big) - c^1\Big([f(g(r)) - g(r)f'\big(g(r)\big) - \tau_{t+1}], r\Big) - \tau_{t+1}$$

$$= \delta_{t+1} + g(r)(1+n) \tag{18a}$$

$$(1+r)\delta_t = \delta_{t+1}(1+n) + \tau_{t+1}(1+n)\,. \tag{18b}$$

Note that the economy moves immediately (in period t) to the capital-labor ratio corresponding to r and stays there as long as the government pegs the interest rate. The only remaining dynamics comes from the public sector financing requirement. Substituting (18b) into (18a) we see that the per capita stock of public debt will converge to its steady-state value if $\left| \frac{\left(c_1^1(\cdot) - 1\right)}{c_1^1(\cdot)} \frac{(1+r)}{(1+n)} \right| < 1$. The steady-state equations are:

$$f\big(g(r)\big) - g(r)f'\big(g(r)\big) - c^1\Big([f\big(g(r)\big) - g(r)f'\big(g(r)\big)_{,} - \frac{(r-n)}{1+n}\delta], r\Big) =$$

$$\left(\frac{1+r}{1+n}\right)\delta + g(r)(1+n) \tag{19a}$$

$$\frac{(r-n)}{1+n}\delta = \tau \tag{19b}$$

$$k = g(r)\,. \tag{19c}$$

Comparing steady states,

$$\frac{\partial \delta}{\partial r} = [(c_1^1(\cdot) - 1)(k + \frac{\delta}{1+n}) - \frac{(1+n)}{f''} - c_2^1(\cdot)]\,[\frac{1+r}{1+n} - c_1^1(\cdot)\frac{(r-n)}{1+n}]^{-1}.$$

An increase in r reduces the steady-state capital-labor ration and thus the steady-state wage rate. This lowers saving (in the form of both bonds and capital) if, as we assume, $0 < c_1^1(\cdot) < 1$. An increase in

r also increases the steady-state value of taxes corresponding to any given value of δ. This too will reduce saving. (If the private sector is a net borrower vis-à-vis the public sector, this second effect will work in the opposite direction). Through its effect on the steady-state capital stock, the increase in r will, *ceteris paribus*, raise the steady-state stock of bonds $(-\frac{(1+n)}{f''} > 0)$. The intertemporal substitution effect of a higher rate of interest will also tend to increase saving $(c_2^1(\cdot) \leq 0)$. The net effect of an increase in the interest rate peg on private holdings of public debt is therefore ambiguous.

The steady state can be one with net public sector lending to the private sector ($\delta < 0$), irrespective of whether r is above or below n. During the transition to a steady state, government lending to the private sector financed initially by taxation of young households, can occur, for example, when the initial steady state has $k_t < k_{t+1} = g(r)$. It is easy to trace the steps of the argument through equations (17) and (18).

Note that by setting $r = n$ the economic system moves immediately (i.e., during the working life of one generation) to the golden rule. Steady state δ can be either positive or negative, but taxes or subsidies will be zero as debt service (loan income) is exactly matched by new debt issues (loans).

II. AN OVERLAPPING GENERATIONS MODEL WITH A BEQUEST MOTIVE

When bequests are introduced into the model, both the budget constraint and the utility function are altered. B_t denotes that part of the value of total resources available to a member of generation t in the second period of his life that he does not consume but bequeathes to generation $t+1$. The value of this bequest to a member of generation $t+1$ at the beginning of the second period of his life is $B_t(1+r_{t+2})$. When the rate of population growth is non-zero, I assume that bequests are shared equally among all descendants. A_t^1 denotes, as before, the value of noninherited wealth held by a member of generation t at the beginning of the second period of his life. An important constraint is

$$B_t \geq 0 \qquad \text{for all } t. \tag{20}$$

A bequest to a member of the next generation cannot be negative. One cannot die in debt and mortgage the next generation.

A_t^1 can be negative. People can borrow while young, for example, in anticipation of a legacy. Note that bequests are not received until the end of the first period of one's life. Equation (21) gives the lifetime budget constraint for a member of generation $t-1$, in the absence of government debt and taxation.

$$B_{t-1} = \frac{B_{t-2}(1+r_t)}{1+n} + A_{t-1} - c_{t-1}^2 \tag{21a}$$

$$A_{t-1}^1 = (w_{t-1} - c_{t-1}^1)(1+r_t). \tag{21b}$$

The utility function of a member of generation $t-1$ is

$$U_{t-1} = u(c_{t-1}^1, c_{t-1}^2, U_t^*). \tag{22a}$$

u is increasing in all three of its arguments, smooth and strictly quasi-concave. The utility of a member of generation $t-1$ depends on his own lifetime consumption, c_{t-1}^1 and c_{t-1}^2, and on U_t^*, the maximum utility level attainable by a "representative" immediate descendant,[5] that is, U_t^* is defined by

$$U_t^* = \max_{c_t^1,\, c_t^2} u(c_t^1, c_t^2, U_{t+1}^*). \tag{22b}$$

Barro [1, 1974] ignores population growth and assumes static expectations of future wages and interest rates. In view of the ample availability of correct information on future government taxation and financing policies assumed throughout his paper and this one, the static expectations assumption needs to be abandoned. Otherwise we are restricted to stationary economies.

Capital market equilibrium requires that the stock of capital in existence at the beginning of period $t+1$ be equal to the sum of the bequests made by members of generation $t-1$ at the end of their lives and the saving of members of generation t during the first period of their lives:

$$L_{t-1}B_{t-1}(1+r_{t+1}) + L_t A_t^1 = K_{t+1}(1+r_{t+1})$$

or

$$\frac{B_{t-1}}{1+n}(1+r_{t+1}) + A_t^1 = k_{t+1}(1+n)(1+r_{t+1}). \tag{23}$$

As before, we have

$$r_{t+1} = f'(k_{t+1}), \text{ and } w_t = f(k_t) - k_t f'(k_t). \tag{24}$$

The optimization problem faced by a member of generation $t-1$ can now be summarized as follows:

$$\max_{c^1_{t-1},\, c^2_{t-1}} \quad u(c^1_{t-1},\ c^2_{t-1},\ U^*_t),$$

subject to

$$c^1_{t-1},\ c^2_{t-1},\ B_{t-1} \geq 0$$

$$B_{t-1} = \frac{B_{t-2}(1+r_t)}{1+n} + (w_{t-1} - c^1_{t-1})(1+r_t) - c^2_{t-1} \tag{25a}$$

$$r_t = f'(k_t)$$

$$(1+n)k_{t+1} = \frac{B_{t-1}}{1+n} + w_t - c^1_t \tag{25b}$$

$$w_t = f(k_t) - k_t\ f'(k_t)$$

$$U^*_t = \max_{c^1_t,\, c^2_t} U_t.$$

In what follows, I shall concentrate on the stationary solutions of this problem.

The Stationary Consumption Possibility Locus with Bequests. The optimal stationary consumption possibility locus facing a social planner was found above:

$$c^1 + \frac{c^2}{1+n} = f(k^*) - nk^*; \ f'(k^*) = n.$$

The decentralized competitive stationary consumption possibility locus will coincide with the social planner's locus only when $B_t > 0$. The rest of the opportunity locus will be given by the segment of the no-bequest opportunity locus above E_1 in Figure 11–2.

We obtain the equation for the stationary opportunity locus by setting $B_t = B$, $c_t^1 = c^1$, $c_t^2 = c^2$, $k_t = k$ in equations (25a and 25b). After substituting and rearranging, we obtain

$$c^1 + \frac{c^2}{1+f'(k)} = f(k) - k\,f'(k) - \frac{B(n-f'(k))}{(1+n)\,(1+f'(k))} \tag{25a'}$$

$$f(k) - k\,f'(k) - c^1 = k(1+n) - \frac{B}{(1+n)} \tag{25b'}$$

$$c^1,\ c^2,\ B \geq 0.$$

We can solve (25a$'$ and 25b$'$) for c^2 as a function of c^1 and B

$$c^2 = \phi\,(c^1,\ B) \tag{26}$$

with

$$\phi_1 = \frac{\partial c^2}{\partial c^1} = -(1+f')\,[1 + \frac{k\,(n-f')f''}{1+f'}\ (1+n+kf'')^{-1}\,] \tag{27a}$$

and

$$\phi_2 = \frac{\partial c^2}{\partial B} = \frac{f' - n}{1+n+kf''}\ . \tag{27b}$$

The nature of the social planner's opportunity locus below E_1 as the *envelope* of the whole family of private consumption possibility loci corresponding to different positive values of B (equation 26) now becomes clear.[6] The values of c^1 and c^2, as functions of B, that characterize the envelope are found by considering equations (25a$'$, 25b$'$) and $\phi_2 = 0$. From (27b) we see that $\phi_2 = 0$ implies $n = f'(k)$. Substituting k^*, defined by $n = f'(k^*)$ into (25a$'$ and 25b$'$) we obtain

$$c^1 = f(k^*) - k^*(2n+1) + \frac{B}{(1+n)} \tag{28a}$$

$$c^2 = (1+n)^2\,k^* - B;\ \ c^1,\ c^2,\ B \geq 0;\ \ f'(k^*) = n. \tag{28b}$$

Combining (28a) and (28b), we obtain

$$c^1 + \frac{c^2}{1+n} = f(k^*) - nk^*. \tag{29}$$

Note, however, that only the segment of (29) consistent with $B \geq 0$, is available to the decentralized competitive economy. This is illustrated in Figure 11–5. To be on $\alpha\alpha$ above E_1, would require $B < 0$. The curve segment $E_1\,\beta$ is described by equation (26) with $B = 0$, that is,

$$c^2 = \phi(c^1, 0); \; f'(k) \leq n. \tag{28c}$$

I show next that a stationary decentralized competitive optimum with bequests could be achieved on the socially inefficient curve segment βE_1.

The Stationary Utility Function. The utility function $U_t = u(c_t^1, c_t^2, \max U_{t+1})$ has the recursive form familiar from dynamic pro-

Figure 11–5. The Stationary Competitive Trade-off Possibilities between Consumption When Young (c^1) and Consumption When Old (c^2) in the Presence of Bequests

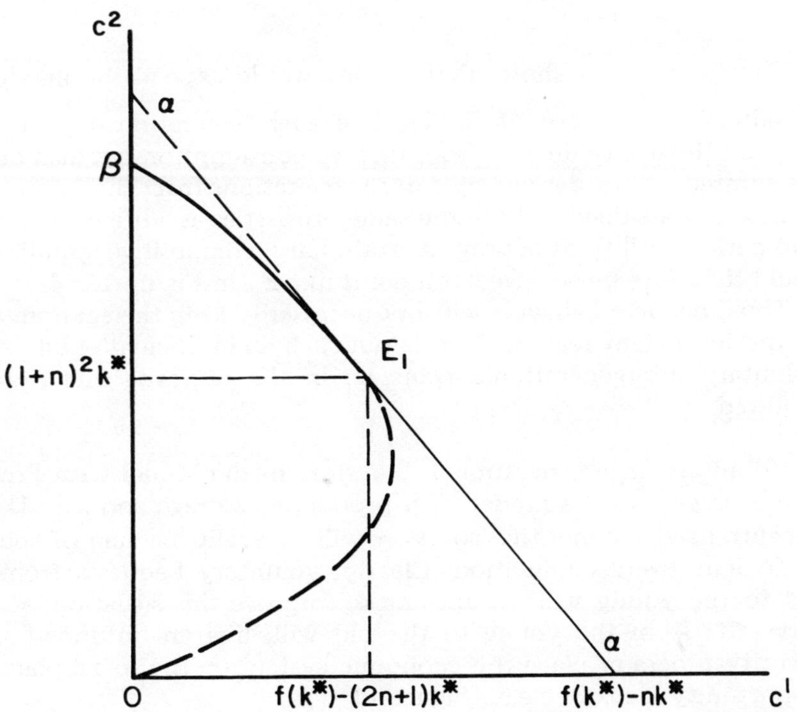

gramming. For simplicity, I shall consider an additive function $U_t = v(c_t^1, c_t^2) + (1+\rho)^{-1} \max U_{t+1}$. The v function is assumed to be the same for all generations, increasing, smooth, and strictly quasi-concave. ρ is a positive discount rate applied by a member of the current generation to the lifetime utility achieved by the next generation.[7]

One can rewrite the optimization problem of a member of generation t as

$$W_t = \max_{c_t^1,\, c_t^2} \; [v(c_t^1, c_t^2) + (1+\rho)^{-1} W_{t+1}] \,. \tag{30}$$

A stationary solution is characterized by $W_t = W_{t+1} = W^*$, $c_t^1 = c^1$ and $c_t^2 = c^2$. With $\rho > 0$, W^* will be bounded.

The optimization problem solved by each and every generation is therefore

$$W^* = \left(\frac{1+\rho}{\rho}\right) \max_{c^1,\, c^2} \; v(c^1, c^2) \,. \tag{30}$$

The factor $\dfrac{1+\rho}{\rho}$ shows that, as one would expect, the maximum sustainable stationary utility level of each generation depends not only on the utility derived from its own consumption but also on the discounted utility derived by future generations from their consumption. v was assumed to have the same properties as a life cycle saver's two-period utility function. A stationary competitive equilibrium could therefore be achieved at a point like E_2 in Figure 11–6.

Thus, bequest behavior will not necessarily keep the economy out of the inefficient region. To rule out such an inefficient equilibrium, voluntary intergenerational transfers in the opposite direction are required.

Voluntary Intergenerational Transfers in the Model with Productive Storage. In the model with productive storage and $n \geq \Pi$, the decentralized competitive solution will typically be one of socially inefficient overaccumulation. Clearly, voluntary bequests from the old to the young will do nothing to improve this situation. Voluntary gifts from the young to the old will, like an unfunded social security program, place the economic system on the social planner's opportunity locus (see e.g., Figure 11–1).

Figure 11–6. A Socially Inefficient Stationary Competitive Equilibrium in a Model with Bequests; Stationary Competitive Trade-off Possibilities between Consumption When Young (c^1) and When Old (c^2)

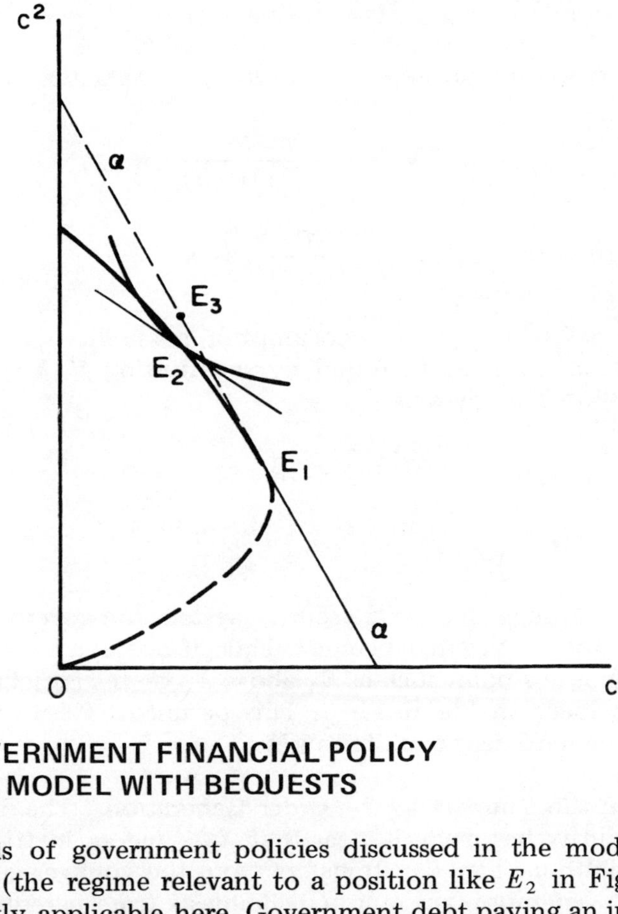

III. GOVERNMENT FINANCIAL POLICY IN A MODEL WITH BEQUESTS

The kinds of government policies discussed in the model without bequests (the regime relevant to a position like E_2 in Figure 11–6) are directly applicable here. Government debt paying an interest rate of n could be sold to the private sector with lump-sum taxes on the younger generation making up the difference between current debt service requirements and new bond sales. Through such policies the segment of $\alpha\alpha$ above E_1 will become attainable.

An unfunded social security scheme, consisting of lump-sum payments $S > 0$ to a member of the currently old generation, financed by a lump-sum tax levy $\frac{S}{1+n}$ on the currently young generation could also move the economy from a situation of overaccumulation at E_2 in Figure 11–6 to a Pareto-superior position as at E_3. To see this, note that in equation (25a) the lifetime budget-constraint of generation $t-1$ would be modified to read

$$B_{t-1} = \frac{B_{t-2}}{1+n}(1+r_t) + S + (w_{t-1} - c^1_{t-1} - \frac{S}{1+n})(1+r_t) - c^2_{t-1}. \quad (31)$$

The stationary consumption possibility loci are characterized by

$$c^1 + \frac{c^2}{1+f'(k)} = f(k) - k\,f'(k) - \frac{(n-f')}{(1+f')(1+n)}(B-S) \quad (32a)$$

$$f(k) - k\,f'(k) - c^1 = k(1+n) - \frac{1}{(1+n)}(B-S).^8 \quad (32b)$$

The "envelope" of the private consumption possibility loci for given values of B and S is again found by substituting $f'(k^*) = n$ into (32a) and (32b). This gives us

$$c^1 = f(k^*) - k^*(2n+1) + \frac{1}{(1+n)}(B-S) \quad (33a)$$

$$c^2 = k^*(1+n)^2 - (B-S). \quad (33b)$$

Note that through the social security system the government can effectively impose a negative bequest. Thus, if $B = 0$, a positive S can be used to choose a point such as E_3 above E_1 on the social planner's opportunity locus in Figure 11–6. This permits a Pareto improvement over the inefficient equilibrium E_2.

Gifts from the Younger to the Older Generation. The discussion of social security has made it clear that, to avoid an inefficient stationary equilibrium like E_2, transfers from the younger generation to the older generation are required. Bequests from parents to children cannot remedy inefficiency due to overaccumulation. Social security can be viewed as an involuntary transfer from the younger generation to the older generation (with the promise of similar treatment in the future). We can incorporate voluntary transfers from the young to the old generation by replacing the social security payment S in (31) by a voluntary transfer and setting $B_t = 0$ for all t. Let $G_t \geq 0$ denote the gift by a member of generation t to the previous generation. The lifetime budget constraint of a member of generation $t-1$ is

$$0 = G_t(1+n) + (w_{t-1} - c^1_{t-1} - G_{t-1})(1+r_t) - c^2_{t-1}. \quad (34)$$

Going through the same steps we went through for bequests, the stationary consumption possibility locus is found to be

$$c^1 = f(k^*) - k^*(2n+1) - G \tag{35a}$$

$$c^2 = k^*(1+n)^2 + G(1+n) \qquad c^1, c^2, G \geq 0;\ f'(k^*) = n \tag{35b}$$

$$c^2 = \phi(c^1, 0) \qquad G = 0;\ f'(k) > n.^9 \tag{35c}$$

Thus the stationary private opportunity locus with gifts from young to old is given by the social planner's opportunity locus *above* E_1, and by the stationary private opportunity locus without gifts or bequests below E_1 (for $f'(k) > n$). Figure 11–7 shows a decentralized private equilibrium at E_3. The capital-labor ratio at E_3, is less than at E_1 and elsewhere on the social planner's stationary opportunity locus. E_3 is therefore not inefficient in terms of per capita consumption. Still, government financial and taxation policy can move the economy from a point like E_3 to a point on the social planner's opportunity locus (or elsewhere). A policy of government lending at an interest rate of n (complemented by the appropriate amount of lump-sum taxation) or a policy of transfer payments to the young financed by lump-sum taxes on the old could bring the economy to the golden rule. This may constitute a Pareto improvement in terms of the utility derived from lifetime consumption.

The utility function of an individual with a child-to-parent gift motive is $u(c_t^1, c_t^2, U_{t-1}^*)$, where U_{t-1}^* is the maximum achievable value of the utility function of the previous generation. As with bequests—equation (30)—I shall consider the optimization problem for an additive utility function.

$$W_t = \max_{c_t^1,\, c_t^2} \left[v(c_t^1, c_t^2) + (1+\rho)^{-1} W_{t-1} \right].^{10} \tag{36}$$

The stationary utility function is the same as in the case of bequests, and there is no need to consider it.

From the discussion on the bequest and gift cases, it is clear that, when there are *both* bequests and gifts, the entire social planner's stationary consumption opportunity locus can be duplicated by stationary decentralized competitive solutions. Serious problems arise, however, with the utility function for the case when there are both bequest and gift motives. The general form of the utility function is

$$U_t = u(c_t^1, c_t^2, U_{t-1}^*, U_{t+1}^*). \tag{37}$$

Figure 11–7. The Stationary Competitive Trade-off Possibilities between Consumption When Young (c^1) and Consumption When Old (c^2) in the Presence of Gifts from Young to Old

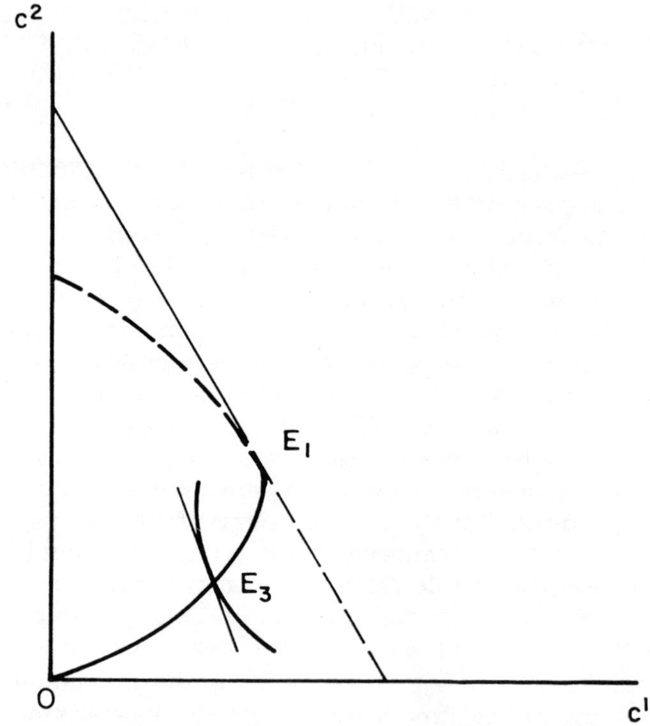

Using the simple additive specification of the utility function also used in (30) and (36), the utility maximization problem can be written in recursive form as

$$W_t = \max_{c_t^1,\, c_t^2} \left[v(c_t^1, c_t^2) + (1+\rho)^{-1} \left[W_{t-1} + W_{t+1} \right] \right] . \tag{38}$$

The stationary optimization problem now is

$$W^* = \frac{1+\rho}{\rho - 1} \max_{c^1,\, c^2} v(c^1, c^2) .$$

This makes sense only if $\rho > 1$. Thus, if one cares about both one's parents and one's children, one should not care about them too much; the consumption of parents and children is valued less than half as much as one's own consumption. This problem did not arise in Becker [3, 1974] when he discussed interdependent preferences, because he considered only finite populations. If one cares directly only for the next generation of descendants (or, equivalently, only for the previous generation), a positive generation discount rate suffices to ensure a bounded stationary utility function. If one cares directly about both the next and the previous generation, one indirectly cares for a double infinity of generations. Convergence criteria are consequently very much stricter.[11] The paradox arises because, with every generation caring "too much" about earlier and later generations, each generation tries to starve itself in order to pass on all its resources to other generations. But if every generation tries to do this, there exists no solution.[12]

IV. GOVERNMENT POLICY IN THE PRESENCE OF GIFTS AND BEQUESTS

Attempts by the government to redistribute income between generations by involuntary transfers (i.e., any combination of bond financing and lump-sum taxes or transfer payments) may fail. Voluntary private transfers may adjust in such a way as to undo the effects of the government policies. Consider an economy in competitive equilibrium, but not necessarily in a steady state. A member of generation t receives an inheritance, $B_{t-1}/(1+n)$; leaves a bequest, B_t; receives gifts from the next generation, $(1+n)G_{t+1}$; makes a gift to the preceding generation, G_t; receives social security benefits, S_{t+1}; and makes contributions to social security, $S_t/(1+n)$. The lifetime budget constraints of generation $t-1$, t, and $t+1$ are

$$B_{t-1} = \frac{B_{t-2}(1+r_t)}{1+n} + G_t(1+n) + S_t + \left(w_{t-1} - c^1_{t-1} - G_{t-1} - \frac{S_{t-1}}{1+n}\right)(1+r_t) - c^2_{t-1} \tag{39}$$

and

$$B_t = \frac{B_{t-1}(1+r_{t+1})}{1+n} + G_{t+1}(1+n) + S_{t+1} + \left(w_t - c^1_t - G_t - \frac{S_t}{1+n}\right)(1+r_{t+1}) - c^2_t \tag{40}$$

and

$$B_{t+1} = \frac{B_t(1+r_{t+2})}{1+n} + G_{t+2}(1+n) + S_{t+2}$$

$$+ (w_{t+1} - c^1_{t+1} - G_{t+1} - \frac{S_{t+1}}{1+n})(1+r_{t+2}) - c^2_{t+1} \quad . \tag{41}$$

At time t the government raises the transfer from the young generation (t) to the old generation ($t-1$), from S_t to $S'_t > S_t$. If $G_t \geq (S'_t - S_t)/(1+n)$, generation t can "undo" the effect of the increased government transfer from itself to generation $t-1$ on its own consumption, on the consumption of the preceding and following generations (and therefore on the consumption of all other generations), by reducing voluntary gifts to generation $t-1$ to $G'_t = G_t - (S'_t - S_t)/(1+n)$. If the initial situation was a competitive equilibrium, the new situation with S'_t and G'_t substituted for S_t and G_t, respectively, and with everything else unchanged will again be a competitive equilibrium. This can be verified by substituting S'_t and G'_t in (39) and (40), and noticing that all other terms in equations (39) to (41) are unaffected by the policy change.

However, if the increase in S_t exceeds the amount of the initial voluntary gift from generation t to $t-1$, the constraint $G_t \geq 0$ becomes binding. If there is no bequest motive, the redistribution will have real effects on the pattern of consumption across generations and over time. If there is a bequest motive the older generation, $t-1$, could undo the effect of the government redistribution attempt by increasing its bequest to generation t. If B_{t-1} is raised to $B'_{t-1} = B_{t-1} + S'_t - S_t$, all other terms in equations (39) to (41) remain unchanged.

Even when there is both a bequest motive and a gift motive, however, there can be situations in which both constraints ($G_t \geq 0$ and $B_{t-1} \geq 0$) are binding. Consider, for example, a situation in which the gift motive is barely operative ($G_t > 0$), and the bequest motive is inoperative ($B_{t-1} = 0$) by a considerable margin—parents would in fact leave their children a large net liability if they could. The increase in government transfer from generation t to generation $t-1$ can be so large that the gift motive becomes inoperative ($G_t = 0$), but not large enough for the bequest motive to become operative. ($B_{t-1} = 0$). Under those circumstances, the proposed compulsory intergenerational redistribution will have real effects. Similar conclusions could be reached for more complicated tax and bond finance schemes affecting any number of generations.

We can summarize the policy conclusions as follows: (a) When there is a bequest motive or a gift motive, but not both, there always exists a tax-cum-debt policy that will affect the real trajectory of the economy. $[(S_t' - S_t)/(1+n) > G_t$ or $(S_t' - S_t) > B_{t-1}$ in our simple example]; (b) When there are both bequest and gift motives, there may exist a tax-cum-debt policy that will affect the real trajectory of the economy. Lump-sum taxation and debt policy will not affect the *steady state* capital-labor ratio if there are both bequest and gift motives. However, for a decentralized competitive steady state to exist, both the bequest motive and the gift motive must be weak. Under these circumstances, tax and financial policy is likely to be able to influence the behavior of the economic system outside the steady state.

V. CONCLUSION

The preceding analysis has done much to qualify the new neutrality theorems propounded, for instance, by Barro. The simple model was nevertheless unnecessarily favorable to the neutrality proposition. Many important real-world features that would further strengthen the presumption against neutrality were abstracted from. Since these are discussed elsewhere in these volumes [12, Tobin and Buiter, forthcoming] I shall only briefly mention the most important ones here.

For the neutrality theorem to be valid, bequest and gift motives have to be operative for each and every economic agent affected by government's financial policy. If households are heterogeneous in preferences and/or endowments, that condition is unlikely to be satisfied for everyone. The observation that some households in each generation are childless increases the likelihood of nonneutrality.[13]

Real-world taxes and transfers are non-lump sum and will affect private opportunity sets in ways that will not be neutralized by offsetting changes in private behavior.

Liquidity constraints reduce the horizon relevant for consumption decisions below the lifespan of life cycle savers. They will have the same effect on dynastic savers.

Government securities are not perfect substitutes for private debt in household portfolios. The neutrality theorem assumes that government securities are a perfect hedge against tax liabilities and that households can lend and borrow on the same terms as the government. This extension of the Modigliani-Miller theorem to the level of the private sector as a whole vis-à-vis the government is extremely unrealistic. The power of the government to tax and declare its liabilities legal tender is unique.

While there are obvious risks in trying to use a theoretical model to make policy recommendations for an actual economy, some implications can be drawn with considerable confidence. In the United States, the net marginal product of capital (the social return to investment) greatly exceeds the rate of growth of labor in units of constant efficiency ($n + \gamma$). The empirical evidence (e.g., John Kendrick [10, 1976]) is unanimous that the before-tax rate of return is at least 10 percent for business capital, cycle after cycle. In the depressed stage of the business cycle the net social rate of return of additional investment will be even higher, because of the short-run real output gains associated with the operation of the Keynesian investment multiplier in a world with idle resources. Tax-financed transfers from the younger to the older generation or expansion of the unfunded social security system are likely to reduce saving and—to the extent that saving is translated into investment—real capital formation. It appears inconceivable that such policies would induce an increase in bequests sufficient to undo the negative effect on the aggregate savings rate. The possibility of exporting capital renders overaccumulation even more unlikely in an open economy.[14]

I agree with those critics of pay-as-you-go social security who contend that in the long run it results in a reduction in the capital-labor ratio, although I suspect they exaggerate the magnitude of the effect. While such a policy is not necessarily socially inefficient in the sense of being Pareto-dominated by other feasible policies, it may nevertheless be considered undesirable. By international standards, the United States saves and invests a low percentage of its national income. A reasoned concern about the adequacy of our provision for the future seems warranted.

NOTES TO CHAPTER 11

1. The institution in question would have to be immortal for people to believe in its viability. Any institution with an infinite actual and expected lifespan, and considered able and willing to honor contracts for all future time, would permit society to reach its efficient consumption boundary. The traditional lineal family is one such institution. The important point is that the institution necessarily involves nonmarket transactions.

2. From the interior first-order conditions, $u_1(c_t^1, c_t^2) = (1+r_{t+1})u_2(c_t^1, c_t^2)$, we obtain:

$$\frac{\partial c_t^1}{\partial w_t} = \frac{-[u_{12} - (1+r_{t+1})u_{22}]}{[u_{11} - (1+r_{t+1})u_{21}]\,(1+r_{t+1})^{-1} - u_{21} + (1+r_{t+1})u_{22}}$$

and

$$\frac{\partial c_t^1}{\partial r_{t+1}} = \frac{u_2 - c_t^2(1+r_{t+1})^{-1}\,[u_{21} - (1+r_{t+1})u_{22}]}{u_{11} - (1+r_{t+1})\,[2u_{21} - (1+r_{t+1})u_{22}]} .$$

3. For the general neoclassical production function $\tilde{y} = f(\tilde{k})$, the stationary consumption possibility locus is given by:

$$\tilde{c}^2 = \psi(\tilde{c}^1, \gamma) \text{ with } \psi_1 = -(1+f')\,[1 + \tilde{k}\left(\frac{(1+n)\,(1+\gamma)}{1+f'} - 1\right) f''\left((1+n)\,(1+\gamma) + \tilde{k}f''\right)^{-1}]$$

and

$$\psi_2 = -(1+n)\tilde{k}^2 f''[(1+n)\,(1+\gamma) - (1+f')]\,[(1+n)\,(1+\gamma) + \tilde{k}f'']^{-1} .$$

4. When we consider the general form of the planner's social welfare function, we must distinguish between the social rate of time preference, η_1, and the social discount rate applied to the lifetime utility of consumption achieved by successive generations, η_2. W denotes social welfare and $j(c_t^1, c_{t-1}^2)$ the planner's valuation, at t, of the per capita consumption achieved during period t by old members of generation $t-1$ and young members of generation t. η_1 is defined by:

$$W_2 = \sum_{t=0}^{\infty} j(c_t^1, c_{t-1}^2)\,(1+\eta_1)^{-t}.$$ η_2 is defined by:

$$W_2' = \sum_{t=0}^{\infty} u(c_t^1, c_t^2)\,(1+\eta_2)^{-t}.$$ The stationary social welfare function in the text is the stationary version of W_2'.

5. Each individual will have $1+n$ immediate descendants. It might therefore be plausible to specify the utility function as:

$$U_{t-1} = u(c_{t-1}^1, c_{t-1}^2, (1+n)U_t^*).$$

6. Consider a one-parameter family of curves in the xy plane. $F(x, y, \alpha) = 0$; α is the parameter. If there is a curve, C, in the plane with the following proper-

ties: (1) each curve of the family is tangent to C, and (2) C is tangent at each of its points to some curve of the family, we call C the envelope of the family. We find C by solving $F(x, y, \alpha) = 0$ and $\frac{\partial F}{\partial \alpha}(x, y, \alpha) = 0$ for x and y.

7. It should be distinguished from the private rate of pure time preference:

$$\frac{v_1(c, c)}{v_2(c, c)} - 1.$$

8. The capital market equilibrium condition when there is an unfunded social security scheme is given by: $L_{t-1} B_{t-1} + L_t(w_t - c_t^1 - \frac{S}{1+n}) = K_{t+1}$. (32b) is the stationary capital market equilibrium condition.

9. As with bequests, we can, with gifts from children to parents, solve for c^2 as a function of c^1 and G; $c^2 = \psi(c^1, G)$. It is easily shown that $\psi(c^1, 0) = \phi(c^1, 0)$.

10. Note that, as ρ is a measure of subjective private "intergenerational distance" and *not* a pure rate of time preference, the utility of earlier generations is discounted, and *not* compounded. There is, of course, no reason, in general, for a given generation to discount the utility of earlier and of later generations equally, as was assumed in the paper.

11. The convergence criteria get stricter as the number of generations one intrinsically (or directly) cares about increases. Take, for example, the case where one is interested directly in the utility levels achieved by the preceding and following two generations.

$$W_t = \max_{c_t^1,\, c_t^2} \left[v(c_t^1, c_t^2) + (1+\rho)^{-1}(W_{t+1} + W_{t-1}) + (1+\rho)^{-2}(W_{t+2} + W_{t-2})\right].$$

The stationary maximization problem is:

$$W^* = \frac{(1+\rho)^2}{\rho^2 - 2} \max v.$$

Convergence requires $\rho > \sqrt{2}$.

12. If we were to weigh earlier generations' utility more than our own, no stationary solution exists for any real value of δ

$$W_t = \max_{c_t^1,\, c_t^2} \left[V(c_t^1, c_t^2) + (1+\rho)W_{t-1} + (1+\rho)^{-1} W_{t+1}\right].$$

13. A valuable extension of the model will be to consider the effect of a non-zero probability that a member of any given generation will have no offspring. I am currently investigating the consequences of this weak link in the voluntary intergenerational chain of transfers.

14. Because of the large size of the U.S. economy relative to the rest of the world, it is probably not appropriate to treat the world rate of return as parametric to that of the United States—at any rate not in the long run. Nevertheless, the ability to export capital would seem to make significantly diminishing returns to additional saving an extremely unlikely prospect in the foreseeable future.

REFERENCES

1. BARRO, ROBERT J. "Are Government Bonds Net Wealth?" *Journal of Political Economy*, Nov./Dec. 1974, *82* (6), pp. 1095–1117.

2. ____. "Reply to Feldstein and Buchanan," *Journal of Political Economy*, April 1976, *84* (2), pp. 331–36.

3. BECKER, GARY S. "A Theory of Social Interactions," *Journal of Political Economy*, Nov./Dec. 1974, *82* (6), pp. 1063–93.

4. BUITER, WILLEM H., and TOBIN, JAMES. "Debt Neutrality: A Brief Review of Doctrine and Evidence," this volume.

5. CASS, DAVID, and YAARI, MENAHEM E. "A Reexamination of the Pure Consumption Loans Model," *Journal of Political Economy*, Aug. 1966, *74* (4), pp. 353–67.

6. ____. "Individual Saving, Aggregate Capital Accumulation and Efficient Growth," in *Essays on the Theory of Optimal Economic Growth.* Edited by KARL SHELL. New York: Maple Press, 1967.

7. DIAMOND, PETER A. "National Debt in a Neoclassical Growth Model," *American Economic Review*, Dec. 1965, *55* (5), pp. 1126–50.

8. FELDSTEIN, MARTIN S. "Social Security, Induced Retirement and Aggregate Capital Accumulation," *Journal of Political Economy*, Sept./Oct. 1974, *82* (5), pp. 905–26.

9. ____. "Perceived Wealth in Bonds and Social Security: A Comment," *Journal of Political Economy*, April 1976, *84* (2), pp. 331–36.

10. KENDRICK, JOHN W. *The Formation and Stocks of Total Capital.* New York: National Bureau of Economic Research; distributed by Columbia University Press, 1976.

11. SAMUELSON, PAUL A. "An Exact Consumption Loan Model of Interest with or without the Social Contrivance of Money," *Journal of Political Economy*, Dec. 1958, *66* (6), pp. 467–82.

12. TOBIN, JAMES, and BUITER, WILLEM H. "Fiscal and Monetary Policies, Capital Formation and Economic Activity," in *The Government and Capital Formation.* Edited by GEORGE M. VON FURSTENBERG. Forthcoming.

Index

About the Editor

George M. von Furstenberg is a Professor of Economics at Indiana University, Bloomington, from where this study was directed. He is currently serving as Chief of Financial Studies in the Research Department of the International Monetary Fund. During previous tours of duty in Washington he served as Senior Staff Economist at the President's Council of Economic Advisers and was associated with both the Brookings Institution and the American Enterprise Institute at various times.

While his chief interest is macroeconomics and public finance, he has contributed to the professional literature also in the fields of income redistribution, mortgage financing, and capital formation. In recent years he has been concerned mainly with the study of saving and investment.